Literary Criticism from Plato to the Present

Also available:

The Blackwell Guide to Literary Theory
Gregory Castle

Literary Theory: An Introduction, 25th Anniversary Edition
Terry Eagleton

A History of Literary Criticism: From Plato to the Present
M. A. R. Habib

Modern Literary Criticism and Theory: A History
M. A. R. Habib

Literary Theory: An Anthology, Second Edition
Edited by Julie Rivkin and Michael Ryan

Literary Theory: A Practical Introduction, Second Edition
Edited by Michael Ryan

The Encyclopedia of Literary and Cultural Theory
Edited Michael Ryan, Gregory Castle, Robert Eaglestone and
M. Keith Booker

LITERARY CRITICISM
from Plato to the Present

AN INTRODUCTION

M. A. R. HABIB

WILEY-BLACKWELL

A JOHN WILEY & SONS, INC., PUBLICATION

This edition first published 2011
© 2011 M. A. R. Habib

Blackwell Publishing was acquired by John Wiley & Sons in February 2007. Blackwell's publishing program has been merged with Wiley's global Scientific, Technical, and Medical business to form Wiley-Blackwell.

Registered Office
John Wiley & Sons Ltd, The Atrium, Southern Gate, Chichester, West Sussex, PO19 8SQ, United Kingdom

Editorial Offices
350 Main Street, Malden, MA 02148-5020, USA
9600 Garsington Road, Oxford, OX4 2DQ, UK
The Atrium, Southern Gate, Chichester, West Sussex, PO19 8SQ, UK

For details of our global editorial offices, for customer services, and for information about how to apply for permission to reuse the copyright material in this book please see our website at www.wiley.com/wiley-blackwell.

The right of M. A. R. Habib to be identified as the author of this work has been asserted in accordance with the UK Copyright, Designs, and Patents Act 1988.

Library of Congress Cataloging-in-Publication Data

Habib, Rafey.
   Literary criticism from Plato to the present : an introduction / M.A.R. Habib.
     p. cm.
   Revised ed. of: A history of literary criticism : from Plato to the present. Malden, Mass. : Blackwell Pub., 2005.
   Includes bibliographical references and index.
   ISBN 978-1-4051-6034-6 (hardcover : alk. paper) – ISBN 978-1-4051-6035-3 (pbk. : alk. paper)
   1. Criticism–History. I. Habib, Rafey. History of literary criticism. II. Title.
   PN86.H23 2011
   801'.9509–dc22
                              2010021915

A catalogue record for this book is available from the British Library.

Set in Sabon 10/12pt by Thomson Digital, Noida, India.
Printed in Singapore by Ho Printing Singapore Pte Ltd

1   2011

For Mughni Tabassum

Contents

Acknowledgments

I would like to thank the following people for their encouragement, inspiration, and support or endorsement: Michael Payne, John Carey, Mughni Tabassum, Joe Barbarese, Robert Grant, Ron Bush, Peter Widdowson, Frank Kermode, Emma Bennett, and Yasmeen.

Introduction

Our English word "criticism" comes from the ancient Greek noun *krites*, meaning "judge." But what does it mean to be a "judge" of literature? We might break this down into several basic questions: what is the purpose of literary criticism? How broad is this field of inquiry, and who gets to define it? What are its connections with other disciplines such as philosophy and religion? How does it relate to the realms of morality, of knowledge, and of learning? Does it have any political implications? How does it impinge on our practices of reading and writing? Above all, what significance does it have, or could it possibly have, in our own lives? Why should we even bother to study literary criticism? Is it not enough for us to read the great works of literature, of poetry, fiction, and drama? Why should we trouble ourselves to read what people say *about* literature? And surely, after all the obscure "theory" of the last 50 years or so, what we need to get back to is the texts themselves. We need to appreciate literature for its beauty and its technical artistry. In short, we need to read literature *as* literature – without the interference of some "judge" telling us what to look for or how to read.

How can we answer such skepticism? We might begin by recalling that "theory" and critical reflection on literature began at least 2500 years ago, and have been conducted by some of the greatest Western thinkers and writers, ranging from Plato and Aristotle, through Augustine and St Thomas Aquinas, Johnson, Pope, and the great Romantics to the great modern figures such as Locke, Hume, Kant, Hegel, Freud, W. B. Yeats, and Sartre. Until 200 years ago, most great thinkers, critics, and literary artists would not have understood what was meant by reading literature *as* literature. They knew that literature had integral connections with philosophy, religion, politics, and morality; they knew, in other words, that literature was richly related to all aspects of people's lives.

If we had no tradition of critical interpretation, if we were left with the "texts" themselves, we would be completely bewildered. We would not

Literary Criticism from Plato to the Present: An Introduction   M. A. R. Habib
© 2011 M. A. R. Habib

know how to classify a given writer as Romantic, classical, or modern. We would not know that a given poem was epic or lyric, mock-heroic, or even that it was a poem. We would be largely unaware of which tradition a given writer was working in and how she was trying to subvert it in certain ways. We would not be able to arrive at any comparative assessment of writers in terms of literary merit. We would not even be able to interpret the meanings of individual lines or words in any appropriate context. It has been the long tradition of literary interpretation – refined and evolved over many centuries – which has addressed these questions. It is surely naive to think that we are all endowed with some superior sensibility which can automatically discern which writers are great and which are mediocre. We do not even know for certain how the ancient Greek of Homer was pronounced; most of us cannot read the Greek of Plato or the Latin of Aquinas or the Italian of Dante or the Arabic of al-Ghazzali. How would we ever, independently, arrive at any estimation of these writers or their backgrounds or their contributions without a body of critical apparatus, without a tradition of critical exper-tise and interpretation, to help us? Shakespeare "is" a great writer because that has been the enduring consensus of influential critics. The reputations of writers can vary quite dramatically. At the beginning of the twentieth century, T. S. Eliot was a powerful critical voice, denigrating the Romantics, extolling the metaphysical poets and revaluating the very idea of tradition. Nowadays, Eliot commands far less critical authority, though his high status as a poet endures.

We can try to illustrate our actual reliance on the traditions of criticism and theory by using a particular example, Matthew Arnold's famous poem "Dover Beach":

> The sea is calm to-night.
> The tide is full, the moon lies fair
> Upon the straits; on the French coast the light
> Gleams and is gone; the cliffs of England stand;
> Glimmering and vast, out in the tranquil bay.
> Come to the window, sweet is the night-air!
> Only, from the long line of spray
> Where the sea meets the moon-blanched land,
> Listen! you hear the grating roar
> Of pebbles which the waves draw back, and fling,
> At their return, up the high strand,
> Begin, and cease, and then again begin,
> With tremulous cadence slow, and bring
> The eternal note of sadness in.
>
> Sophocles long ago
> Heard it on the Aegean, and it brought

Into his mind the turbid ebb and flow
Of human misery; we
Find also in the sound a thought,
Hearing it by this distant northern sea.

The Sea of Faith
Was once, too, at the full, and round earth's shore
Lay like the folds of a bright girdle furled.
But now I only hear
Its melancholy, long, withdrawing roar,
Retreating, to the breath
Of the night-wind, down the vast edges drear
And naked shingles of the world.

Ah, love, let us be true
To one another! for the world, which seems
To lie before us like a land of dreams,
So various, so beautiful, so new,
Hath really neither joy, nor love, nor light,
Nor certitude, nor peace, nor help for pain;
And we are here as on a darkling plain
Swept with confused alarms of struggle and flight,
Where ignorant armies clash by night.

A conventional reading of this poem based on the immediate "text" might go like this: "Dover Beach" is a lyric poem which expresses the painful doubt and disorientation of the Victorian age. The poem is unified by the image and symbolism of the sea, which is used to express the decline of religious faith. In the first section the calm of the sea is complemented by the "grating roar," and the motion of the waves, which the poem's language imitates, symbolizes the cyclical movement of human history, an idea which Arnold may have derived from his father, Thomas Arnold. This symbolism is intensified as the sea meets the "moon-blanched" land, the moon also symbolizing change, in which case "moon-blanched land" might refer to a civilization bleached or made colorless by change or progress. The picturesque opening presents a visual scene of the moonlit ocean whose calm is interrupted only when it is *heard*, as a "grating roar" which prepares the transition from the sea as physical image to symbol, infused with "The eternal note of sadness." The second section makes more precise the sea's significance: the "hearing" of the sea, and the "finding" of "a thought" in its sound, has a classical precedent, not only inscribing Arnold within a literary tradition going back to Sophocles but also stressing the universality of the human predicament. The third section uses the sea as a powerful symbol of both religious faith, which once clothed the world, and the process of secularization, which leaves the world "naked";

the symbolic "long, withdrawing roar" echoes the literal "roar" of the first section, once again creating a fusion of general and particular. The last section warns of the deceptive nature of the world's apparent beauty and variety (as presented in the poem's opening): beneath these "glimmering" surfaces are other, more threatening sounds, foreboding chaos, war, and destruction.

On a technical level, we might observe that the poem is written as a dramatic monologue, melancholy in tone, in four sections. It has no regular rhythm or rhyme scheme but traces of a sonnet form may be discernible in the first two sections; we might discern the ghost of an eroded blank verse in the gesture of many lines toward iambic pentameter, with the preceding and subsequent lines cut short to achieve various effects, as in "The Sea of Faith" which, in its present eroded state, stands alone as merely four syllables, while its comforting fullness in the past is evoked in two full pentameters beginning "Was once, too, at the full, and round earth's shore." We might also point out that the already irregular rhyme scheme *abacdbdc* breaks down in the middle of the first section: there is no word to rhyme with "roar," which might also mimic the fragmentation of the Victorian world. The poem employs numerous literary devices, most notably the metaphors (inherited from Romanticism) ascribing intelligence or sentience to elements of nature such as the sea and the night wind, the simile comparing the sea of faith to a protective "girdle," and various obvious devices such as anaphora, as in the repetition of "so" and "nor" in the final section.

It is simply not possible to ascribe any meaning to the poem without referring its words to broader trends in Victorian society. We might say that the poem represents the anxiety of a world where religious faith was called into question by numerous developments in science, scholarship, and technology: the various theories and philosophies of evolution, the German Higher Criticism which discredited much of the Bible, and the Industrial Revolution which caused a mass migration of people from the country to the towns, displacing a village life centered around the parish with a life revolving around the factory or office. Arnold was reacting against a mechanical, industrial society which prided itself on progress. The only security left is that of personal relationships. But the feelings expressed in the poem are universal: we have the theme of man's alienation and isolation, and his inability to change the world. Arnold's poem still applies today, just as it applied in the ancient Greek world of Sophocles; that is why it is a great poem. It represents its age as well as being timeless.

Already, even at this most basic level of interpretation, we have gone far beyond the "words on the page." Our reading already presupposes a knowledge of the Victorian era, its intellectual and religious currents, a knowledge of literary tradition going back to classical times, a knowledge of Arnold's biography, and an awareness of theories of poetic form, genre, and rhetorical theories of literary figures. And much literary and rhetorical theory – both ancient and modern – would challenge the view that Arnold is expressing a universal human predicament, as well as any sharp distinction between literal and figurative language. In fact the poem is very much conditioned by its historical context, a context governed by the French Revolution of 1789 and the rise to power of the middle classes through much of Europe. In England, the Reform Bill of 1832 established the power of the middle classes over the landed aristocracy. The Liberal Party, representing the middle classes, came to power in 1830. In 1867, the year in which Arnold's poem was published, the vote was extended to urban industrial workers, and in 1884 to most agricultural laborers. What Arnold expresses is perhaps his despair over the rise of middle-class society, whose narrowness and mechanical ideals he criticizes eloquently in his prose writings. Who are the "ignorant armies" that Arnold has in mind? The poem gives the impression that all such struggle is futile and ignorant but it was written in 1851, after violent revolutions in 1830 and 1848 had convulsed Europe: the main aim of these revolutions was to establish constitutional monarchies or governments where the people had some say in how they were ruled. Also, there is a contradiction between the form and content of the poem: the poet urges sentimentally that his relationship with his beloved must be one of mutuality and truth; yet there is no interaction with the woman addressed, who remains without character or voice. The very form of the dramatic monologue enacts the alienation expressed in the poem's content. Arnold was at Dover with his wife in June of 1851 and again in October, after a continental honeymoon. In the poem, which is presumably addressed to his wife, she is given no personality or individuality at all. She is reduced to a mere occasion for his grandiose reflection from his privileged vantage point on the cliffs of Dover. The poem thus invites consideration from many other perspectives, including those of feminism, Marxism, psychoanalysis and various branches of rhetoric.

None of this is to deny that "Dover Beach" is a fine poem; it is, rather, intended to show that the process of "reading" – even at the most basic level – involves vast presuppositions and ever-broadening contexts. It is the task of criticism and theory to articulate these presuppositions and to furnish the contexts in which literary "judgments" can be appropriately made. Hence the *practice* of literary criticism as applied to given texts is underlain by complex assumptions and principles. *Theory* is devoted to examining these principles. As such, theory is a systematic explanation of practice or a situation of practice in a broader framework; theory brings to light the motives behind our practice; it shows us the connection of practice to ideology, power structures, our own unconscious, our political and religious attitudes, our economic structures; above all, theory shows us that practice is not something natural or neutral but is a specific historical construct, resting on specific assumptions and motives, even if these are unacknowledged.

This book aims to offer a concise introduction to the major tendencies and figures of literary criticism and theory from ancient Greek times until the present. An endeavor of such broad scope is bound to be incomplete: there is not enough room to include, or even to do justice to, all of the important figures. I do hope, however, that the following account will have the virtues of clarity, close reading, and appropriate contextualization, in making accessible to a general reader these sometimes difficult theories, their philosophical premises and their historical contexts. We will see, in the chapters that follow, that the questions raised at the beginning of this introduction have been addressed in a rich variety of ways by great thinkers and great literary artists and critics for more than 2000 years.

Part I

Classical Literary Criticism and Rhetoric

Chapter 1
Classical Literary Criticism

Introduction to the Classical Period

The story of Western literary criticism begins shortly after 800 BC in ancient Greece, the era of the great Homeric epics, the *Iliad* and the *Odyssey*, as well as the poets Hesiod and Sappho. The so-called "classical" period, starting around 500 BC, witnessed the great tragedies of Euripides, Aeschylus, and Sophocles, and the comedies of Aristophanes. It was around this time that the foundations of Western philosophy were laid by Socrates, Plato, and Aristotle; the discipline of rhetoric and the political system of democracy were established in Athens. The classical period is usually said to end in 323 BC with the death of Alexander the Great. After this is the "Hellenistic" period, witnessing the diffusion of Greek culture through much of the Mediterranean and Middle East, a diffusion vastly accelerated by Alexander's conquests, and the various dynasties established by his generals after his death. The city of Alexandria in Egypt, founded by Alexander in 331 BC, became a center of scholarship and letters, housing an enormous library and museum, and hosting such renowned poets and grammarians as Callimachus, Apollonius Rhodius, Aristarchus, and Zenodotus. We know of these figures partly through the work of Suetonius (ca. 69–140 AD) who wrote the first histories of literature and criticism.

The Hellenistic period is usually said to end with the battle of Actium in 31 BC in which the last portion of Alexander's empire, Egypt, was annexed by the increasingly powerful and expanding Roman republic. After his victory at Actium, the entire Roman world fell under the sole rulership of Julius Caesar's nephew, Octavian, soon to become revered as the first Roman emperor, Augustus. During this span of almost a thousand years, poets, philosophers, rhetoricians, grammarians, and critics laid down many of the basic terms, concepts, and questions that were to shape the future of literary criticism as it evolved all the way through to our own century. These include the concept of "mimesis" or imitation; the concept of beauty and its connection with truth and goodness; the ideal of the organic unity of a literary work; the social,

Literary Criticism from Plato to the Present: An Introduction   M. A. R. Habib
© 2011 M. A. R. Habib

political, and moral functions of literature; the connection between literature, philosophy, and rhetoric; the nature and status of language; the impact of literary performance on an audience; the definition of figures of speech such as metaphor, metonymy, and symbol; the notion of a "canon" of the most important literary works; and the development of various genres such as epic, tragedy, comedy, lyric poetry, and song.

The first recorded instances of criticism go back to dramatic festivals in ancient Athens. A particularly striking literary critical discussion occurs in Aristophanes' play *The Frogs*, first performed in 405 BC. This comedy stages a contest between two literary theories, representing older and younger generations; it is also a contest in poetic art.[1] The two competing poets are presented as Aeschylus and Euripides. Aeschylus represents the more traditional virtues of a bygone generation, such as martial prowess, heroism, and respect for social hierarchy – all embodied in a lofty, decorous, and sublime style of speech – while Euripides is the voice of a more recent, democratic, secular, and plain-speaking generation (*Frogs*, l. 1055). Aristophanes' play reveals that for the ancient Greeks poetry was an important element in the educational process; its ramifications extended over morality, religion, and the entire sphere of civic responsibility. By the time of Plato and Aristotle, poetry had achieved considerable authority and status. Plato rejected poetry's vision of the world as unpredictable, ruled by chance, and always prone to the whims of the gods. Much of Plato's philosophy is generated by a desire to view the gods as wholly good, to impose order on chaos, to enclose change and temporality within a scheme of permanence, and to ground our thinking about morality, politics, and religion on timeless and universal truths. So Greek philosophy begins as a challenge to the monopoly of poetry and the extension of its vision in more recent trends such as sophistic and rhetoric which offered a secular, humanistic, and relativistic view of the world. Plato's opposition of philosophy to poetry effectively sets the stage for more than 2000 years of literary theory and criticism.

Plato (428–ca. 347 BC)

It is widely acknowledged that the Greek philosopher Plato laid the foundations of Western philosophy. The mathematician and philosopher A. N. Whitehead stated that Western philosophy is "a series of footnotes" to Plato, who indeed gave initial formulation to the most fundamental questions: how can we define goodness and virtue? How do we arrive at truth and knowledge? What is the connection between soul and body? What is the ideal political state? Of what use are literature and the arts? What is the nature of language? Plato's answers to these questions are still disputed; yet the questions themselves have endured.

At the age of 20, like many other young men in Athens, Plato fell under the spell of the controversial thinker and teacher Socrates. In a story later to be recounted in Plato's *Apology*, Socrates had been hailed by the Oracle at Delphi as "the wisest man alive." He devoted his life to the pursuit of knowledge, wisdom, and virtue. Using a dialectical method of question and answer, he would often arouse hostility by deflating the pretensions of those who claimed to be wise and who professed to teach. A wide range of people, including rhetoricians, poets, politicians, and artisans, felt the razor edge of his intellect, which undermined conventional views of goodness and truth. Eventually he was tried on a charge of impiety and condemned to death in 399 BC. After the death of his revered master, Plato eventually founded an Academy in Athens.

Most of Plato's philosophy is expounded in dialogue form, using a dialectical method of pursuing truth by a systematic questioning of received ideas and opinions ("dialectic" derives from the Greek *dialegomai*, "to converse"). Socrates is usually cast as the main speaker. The canon attributed to Plato includes 35 dialogues and 13 letters. The early dialogues are devoted to exploring and defining concepts such as virtue, temperance, courage, piety, and justice. The major dialogues of Plato's middle period – *Gorgias*, *Apology*, *Phaedo*, *Symposium*, *Republic* – move into the realms of epistemology (theory of knowledge), metaphysics, political theory, and art. What unifies these various concerns is Plato's renowned theory of Forms, which sees the familiar world of objects which surrounds us, and which we perceive through our senses, as not independent or real but as dependent upon another world, the realm of pure Forms or ideas, which can be known only by reason and not by our bodily sense-perceptions. Plato says that the qualities of any object in the physical world are derived from the ideal Forms. For example, an object in the physical world is beautiful because it partakes of the ideal Form of Beauty which exists in the higher realm. And so with Tallness, Equality, or Goodness, which Plato sees as the highest of the Forms. The connection between the two realms can best be illustrated using examples from geometry: any triangle or square that we construct using physical instruments is bound to be imperfect. At most it can merely approximate the ideal triangle which is perfect and which is perceived not by the senses but by reason: the ideal triangle is not a physical object but a *concept*, an idea, a Form.

According to Plato, the world of Forms, being changeless and eternal, alone constitutes reality. It is the world of essences, unity, and universality, whereas the physical world is characterized by perpetual change and decay, mere existence (as opposed to essence), multiplicity, and particularity. A central function of the theory of Forms is to unify groups of objects or concepts in the world by treating them as belonging to a class, by referring them back to a common essence, and thereby making sense of our innumerably diverse experiences. A renowned expression of Plato's theory occurs in the seventh book of the *Republic* where he recounts the "myth of the cave" where people have lived all their lives watching shadows of reality cast by a fire, with their backs to the true light of the sun.[2] Plato makes it clear that the cave in which men are imprisoned represents the physical world, and that the journey toward the light is the "soul's ascension" to the world of Forms (*Republic*, 517b–c). In his later dialogues, Plato himself severely questioned the theory of Forms.

Plato on poetry: the *Ion*

Plato's most systematic comments on poetry occur in two texts, separated by several years. The first is *Ion*, where Socrates cross-examines a rhapsode (a singer and interpreter) called Ion on the nature of his art. The second, more sustained, commentary occurs in the *Republic*. In the *Ion*, Socrates points out that the rhapsode, like the poet himself, is in a state of "divine possession," and speaks not with his own voice which is merely a medium through which a god speaks. The Muse inspires the poet, who in turn passes on this inspiration to the rhapsode, who produces an inspired emotional effect on the spectators (*Ion*, 534c–e). Socrates likens this process to a magnet, which transmits its attractive power to a series of iron rings, which in turn pass on the attraction to other rings, suspended from the first set. The Muse is the magnet or loadstone, the poet is the first ring, the rhapsode is the middle ring, and the audience the last one (*Ion*, 533a, 536a–b). In this way, the poet conveys and interprets the utterances of the gods, and the rhapsode interprets the poets. Hence, the rhapsodes are "interpreters of interpreters" (*Ion*, 535a).

The poet, insists Socrates, is "a light and winged thing, and holy, and never able to compose until he has become inspired, and is beside himself, and reason is no longer in him" (*Ion*, 534b). Not only poetry, according to Socrates, but even criticism is irrational and inspired. Hence, in this early dialogue, Plato has already sharply separated the provinces of poetry and philosophy; the former has its very basis in a divorce from reason, which is the realm of philosophy; poetry in its very nature is steeped in emotional transport and lack of self-possession.

Poetry in Plato's *Republic*

Plato's theory of poetry in the *Republic* is much less flattering. His main concern in this text is to define justice and the ideal nature of a political state. Interestingly, his entire conception of justice arises explicitly in opposition to poetic authority and tradition. Socrates mentions "an ancient quarrel" between philosophy and poetry (*Republic*, 607b). Plato views poetry as a powerful force in molding public opinion, and sees it as a danger to his ideal city, ordered as this is in a strict hierarchy whereby the guardians (philosophers) and their helpers (soldiers) comprise an elect minority which rules over a large majority of farmers, craftsmen, and "money-makers" (415a–b; 434c). The program of education that he lays out for the rulers or guardians of the city consists of gymnastics and music. The Greek word *mousike*, as its form suggests, refers broadly to any art over which the Muses preside, including poetry, letters, and music (401d–e).

Just how seriously Plato takes the threat of poetry is signaled by the fact that it is music which primarily defines the function of guardianship: "It is here . . . in music . . . that our guardians must build their guardhouse and post of watch" (IV, 424b–e). Plato advocates an open and strict censorship of poetry on the grounds of: (1) the falsity of its claims and representations regarding both gods and men; (2) its corruptive effect on character; and (3) its "disorderly" complexity and encouragement of individualism in the sphere of sensibility and feeling. Socrates stresses that poets must not present the gods as deceitful since "there is no lying poet in God" (II, 382d). This phrase suggests that poetry by its very nature is a falsifying rhetorical activity. What also emerges here is a conflict between philosophy and poetry in the right to name the divine, to authorize a particular vision of the divine world: for poetry, that world is presented as an anthropomorphic projection of human values centered on self-interest, a world of dark chance, irrational, in flux, and devoid of a unifying structure. The project of philosophy, in Plato's hands, is to stabilize that world, drawing all of its scattered elements into the form of order and unity under which alone they can be posited as absolute and transcendent.

Plato draws a powerful analogy between the individual and the state. In book X, it will emerge explicitly that poetry appeals to the "inferior" part of the soul, the appetitive portion (X, 603b–c). It is, in other words, an encouragement toward variety and multiplicity, toward valuing the particular for its own sake, thereby distracting from contemplation of the universal. In projecting this model onto the state as a whole, Plato aligns the mass of people with the unruly "multitude" of desires in the soul, and the guardians considered collectively with the "unity" of reason. The individuality of the guardians is to be all but erased, not merely through ideological conditioning but through their compulsory existence as a community: they are to possess no private property or wealth; they must live together, nourished on a simple diet, and receiving a stipend from the other citizens (III, 416d–417b). Collectively, then, the guardians' function in the city is a projection of the unifying function of reason in the individual soul.

We now approach the heart of Plato's overall argument concerning justice and poetry. The definition of justice in the state is reached in book IV: justice is a condition where "each one man must perform one social service in the state for which his nature was best adapted" (IV, 433a–b). Predictably, justice in an individual is defined as a condition of the soul where "the several parts . . .

perform each their own task," and where reason rules. In political terms, poetry's greatest crime is its refusal or inability to confine itself to one kind of task. Plato urges that the same man ought not to imitate "many things": any poetic imitation involving "manifold forms" will, says Socrates, "be ill suited to our polity, because there is no twofold or manifold man among us, since every man does one thing" (III, 397b–e). Plato then arrives at the renowned passage urging banishment of the "manifold" poet:

> If a man . . . who was capable by his cunning of assuming every kind of shape and imitating all things should arrive in our city, bringing with himself the poems which he wished to exhibit, we should fall down and worship him as a holy and wondrous and delightful creature, but should say to him that there is no man of that kind among us in our city, nor is it lawful for such a man to arise among us, and we should send him away to another city, after pouring myrrh down over his head and crowning him with fillets of wool. (III, 398a)

This general charge against poetry is elucidated in book X, where Plato presents the poet as a "most marvelous Sophist" and a "truly clever and wondrous man" who "makes all the things that all handicraftsmen severally produce" (X, 596c–d). The political implication here is that poetry can have no *definable* (and therefore limited) function in a state ordered according to a strict hierarchy of inexchangeable function. Poetry literally does not know its place: it spreads its influence limitlessly, dissolving social relations as it pleases and recreating them from its own store of inspired wisdom whose opacity to reason renders it resistant to classification and definition. In this sense, poetry is the incarnation of indefinability and the limits of reason. It is in its nature a rebel, a usurper, which desires to rule; and as such it is the most potent threat to the throne of philosophy, which is also the throne of polity in the state of the philosopher-king.

In political terms, Plato sees poetry as pandering primarily to a democratic constitution (VIII, 568a–d). Like democracy, poetry fosters genuine individuals, "manifold" men who are "stuffed" with differences and resist the reduction of their social function, or indeed their natural potential, into one exclusive dimension. Also, like democracy, poetry nurtures all parts of the soul, refusing obeisance to the law of reason. By implication, then, poetry itself is spurred by the "greed" for liberty which is the hallmark of a democratic society (X, 604e–605c).

All in all, Plato's indictment of poetry has been based on (1) its *intrinsic* expression of falsehood, (2) its intrinsic operation in the realm of imitation, (3) its combination of a variety of functions, (4) its appeal to the lower aspects of the soul such as emotion and appetite, and (5) its expression of irreducible particularity and multiplicity rather than unity. The notion of imitation, in fact, complements truth as the basis of Plato's opposition of philosophy and

poetry. In book X the poet is held up as a Sophist, a "marvelous" handicrafts-
man who can "make" anything (X, 596c–d). And what the poet imitates is of
course the appearance, not the reality, of things, since he merely imitates what
others actually produce (X, 596e, 597e). Plato elaborates his famous triad: we
find three beds, one existing in nature, which is made by God; another which is
the work of the carpenter; and a third, the work of the painter or poet. Hence,
the carpenter imitates the real bed and the painter or poet imitates the physical
bed. The poet's work, then, like that of the rhapsode, is the "imitation of an
imitation." It is thrice removed from truth (X, 597e).

The influence and legacy of Plato

The influence of Plato on many fundamental areas of Western thought,
including literary theory, continues to the present day. First and foremost
has been the impact of the theory of Forms: discredited though this may have
been since the time of Aristotle, it nonetheless exerted a powerful attraction
through its implications that the world was a unity, that our experience of
manifold qualities in the world could be brought under certain unifying
concepts, that the physical world itself is only a small part of, or manifestation
of, a higher reality, and that there exists a higher, ideal pattern for earthly
endeavors. Some of these elements have been integral in both Judeo-Christian
and Islamic theology and philosophy. The distinctions between reason and
sense, reason and emotion, soul and body, while not original to Plato,
continued through his influence to provide some of the basic terminology
of philosophical and religious thinking. Plato's impact on literary critics and
theorists has embraced many issues: the doctrine of imitation; the educational
and didactic functions of poetry; the place of poetry in the political state and
the question of censorship; the treatment of poetry as a species of rhetoric; the
nature of poetic inspiration; and the opposition of poetry to various other
disciplines and dispositions, such as philosophy, science, reason, and
mechanism. We are still grappling with the problems laid down by Plato.

Aristotle (384–322 BC)

The most brilliant student at Plato's Academy was Aristotle, whose enormous
contribution to the history of thought spans several areas: metaphysics, logic,
ethics, politics, literary criticism, and various branches of natural science. In
343 BC King Philip of Macedon invited Aristotle to serve as tutor to his son
Alexander at his court in Pella. Later, Aristotle opened his own school of
rhetoric and philosophy, the Lyceum, in Athens. Plato's Academy placed
emphasis on mathematics, metaphysics, and politics, while at the Lyceum
natural science predominated.

At the heart of Aristotle's metaphysics and logic is the concept of "substance," which he views as the primary reality, underlying everything else. Aristotle basically holds that there are 10 categories through which we can view the world: whatness (substance), quantity, quality, relation, place, time, position, state, action, and affection.[3] A mere glance at these categories tells us that they still permeate our own thought about the world at the profoundest levels, especially the notion of substance.

Reversing the Platonic hierarchy, Aristotle urges that universals (qualities, such as "redness" or "tallness") depend on particular things for their existence, not vice versa. Though Aristotle would agree with Plato that reason has access to a higher knowledge than our senses, he insists that the senses are the starting point and the source of knowledge. He attempts to balance Plato's unilateral emphasis on reason with due attention to our actual experience and to close observation of the world. In a broad sense, the history of Western thought has often emerged as a conflict between these two visions: the idealistic Platonic vision which views reality as above and beyond our own world, and the more empirical Aristotelian view which seeks to find reality within our world.

Aristotle's logic

Aristotle's greatest contribution to philosophy lies in the realm of logic. Aristotle was the first philosopher to formalize the rules and methods of logic. The basis of his logic, which acted as the foundation of the discipline for over 2000 years, was the syllogism. This typically consists of a major premise, a minor premise, and an inferred conclusion, as in the classic example: "All men are mortal; Socrates is a man; therefore, Socrates is mortal." Aristotle classified a number of different kinds of syllogism, ranging from this simple "if ... then" structure to far more complex formats.

Even more fundamental than the syllogism are the three so-called laws of logic (sometimes called the "laws of thought") as formulated by Aristotle and developed by numerous subsequent thinkers into our own day. The first of these is the law of identity, which states that A is A; the second is the law of non-contradiction, which dictates that something cannot be both A and not-A; and the third, the law of the excluded middle, holds that something must be *either* A *or* not-A. These "laws," which can be regarded as the same law expressed from three different perspectives, have served for over two millenia as the (almost) unshakeable foundation of Western thought. As such, they bear examination in a little more detail. What does it mean to say that A is A? Is this not an obvious and empty tautology? We can see that it is no trite proposition the moment we substitute any important term for the letter A. Let us, for example, use the term "man." When we say that "a man is a man," we are appealing to certain qualities which compose the *essence* of man; we are saying that this essence is fixed and unalterable; we are *also* saying that a man is somehow different from a woman, from an animal, from a plant, and so forth. We can quickly begin to see how our definition will have vast economic and political implications: if we define our "man" as rational, as political, as moral, and as free, it will seem natural to us that he should partake in the political process. The woman, whom we define as lacking these qualities, will by our definition be excluded. That this law of identity is highly coercive and hierarchical will become even clearer in the case of the terms "master" and "slave." The master might be defined in terms of attributes that collectively signify "civilized," while the slave is constricted within designations of "savage" (Aristotle, who owned many slaves, himself defines a slave as a "speaking instrument"). Such hierarchical oppositions have in history embraced the terms Greek and barbarian, Christian and Jew, white and black, noble and serf.

The second and third laws of logic will merely confirm our implicit degradation of the woman or slave. The second law, the law of non-contradiction, on which Aristotle insists,[4] tells us that something/someone cannot be both a man and not a man. Again, is this not obvious? Surely it tells us nothing new? In fact, we are stating a further implication of the law of identity: that a certain set of qualities is attributed to "man" and a *different* set of qualities is accorded to woman, there being no overlap between these two sets of qualities. According to this logic, we cannot speak of a person who might come in between these two poles: a man who had womanly qualities or a woman with manly attributes. The third law, the law of the excluded middle, explicitly forbids this middle ground (*Met. I–IX*, 1011b–23) in its urging that something must be *either* A *or* not-A. One must be either a man or not a man; either American or not-American; either Muslim or Jew; either good or bad; either for or against. Hence, these "laws," which unfortunately still largely govern our thinking today, are not only coercive but encourage a vision of the world as divided up sharply into categories, classes, nations, races, and religions, each with its own distinctive essence or character. So deeply rooted is this way of thinking that even attempted subversions of it, such as those issued from Marxism, feminism, deconstruction, and psychoanalysis, must operate within a broader network of complicity with what they challenge.

Aristotle's *Poetics*

In contrast with Plato, Aristotle sees poetry as having a positive function in the political state, which exists not merely for utilitarian purposes but to promote what Aristotle calls the "good life," or the achievement of virtue and *phronesis* or practical wisdom.[5] For Aristotle, poetry and rhetoric had the status of "productive" sciences; these disciplines had their place in a hierarchy of knowledge; and Aristotle viewed them as rational pursuits, as seeking a knowledge of "universal" truths (rather than of random "particular" things or events), and as serving a social and moral function. The entire structure of the Aristotelian system was governed by the notion of substance, from the lowest level to God as the First Cause, or Unmoved Mover. Each element within this hierarchical order had its proper place, function, and purpose. Aristotle's universe is effectively a closed system where each entity is guided by an internalized purpose toward the fulfillment of its own nature, and ultimately toward realization of its harmony with the divine. Poetry, in this system, is analyzed and classified in the same way as the other branches of human knowledge and activity. Our modern notions of poetic autonomy would have been meaningless to Aristotle. In *Nicomachean Ethics*, he states quite clearly concerning productive activity that "the act of making is not an end in itself, it is only a means, and belongs to something else." The purpose of art, like that of metaphysics, is to attain to a knowledge of universals.[6]

At the core of Aristotle's *Poetics* are two complex notions: imitation and action. Like Plato, Aristotle holds that poetry is essentially a mode of imitation. In contrast with Plato, Aristotle invests imitation with positive significance, seeing it as a basic human instinct and as a pleasurable avenue to knowledge.[7] Aristotle asserts that all the various modes of poetry and music are imitations. These imitations can differ in three ways: in the means used, in the kinds of objects represented, and in the manner of presentation. As against popular notions which equate poetry with the use of meter, Aristotle insists that the essential characteristic of the poet is imitation, in which all human beings take pleasure (*Poetics*, I). For Aristotle, the poet is an integral part of human society, rationally developing and refining basic traits which he shares with other human beings.

What is common to all arts, says Aristotle, is that they imitate men involved in action (*Poetics*, II). For Aristotle, "action" has a moral end or purpose. Art imitates human action; but human action must have as its ultimate purpose "the Supreme Good."[8] The actions imitated, says Aristotle, must be either noble or base since human character conforms to these distinctions (*Poetics*, II). Tragedy represents men as better than the norm; comedy as worse than the norm. Aristotle allows only two basic types: narration, where the poet speaks in his own person or through a character; and dramatic presentation, where the story is performed and acted out (*Poetics*, III).

Aristotle makes an important contrast between poetry and history. It is not the function of the poet to narrate events that have actually happened, but rather "events such as might occur ... in accordance with the laws of probability or necessity" (*Poetics*, IX). He infers that poetry is more "philosophical" and "serious" (*spoudaioteron*) than history because poetry expresses what is universal (*ta kathalou*), while history merely deals with individuals. Another way of putting this is to say that poetry yields general truths while history gives us particular facts and events. The poet expresses the inner structure of probability or causality which shapes events and, as such, is universalizable and applicable to other sets of events.

Later in the *Poetics* Aristotle seems to broaden his definition of poetic imitation. He says that the poet must imitate in one of three ways. He must imitate things that were, things that are now or things that people say and think to be, or things which ought to be. Aristotle's earlier definitions, we may recall, referred poetic imitation not to morality or realism but to probability and universality. The emphasis now, however, is upon realism: the poet represents events which happened in the past or occur in the present. Moreover, two important factors are introduced. The first is an appeal to the moral imperative of imitation, whereby the poet should represent an ideal state of affairs. The second is an appeal to conventional opinions. For example, while a poet may not represent the gods truthfully, he is justified in presenting them in accordance with prevailing opinions and myths which are told about the gods. This is a huge step toward suggesting that truth is not somehow transcendent and that it is realized within, not beyond, a human community. In his *Rhetoric*, Aristotle states that "truth is not beyond human nature."[9]

Aristotle's view of tragedy

Aristotle's analysis of tragedy remained influential until the eighteenth century. It is here that the connections between imitation, action, character, morality, and plot emerge most clearly, as in Aristotle's famous definition:

> Tragedy is, then, an imitation of an action that is serious, complete and of a certain magnitude – by means of language enriched with all kinds of ornament, each used separately in the different parts of the play: it represents men in action and does not use narrative, and through pity and fear it effects relief to these and similar emotions. (*Poetics*, VI.2–3)

The Greek word used for "action" is *praxis* which here refers not to a particular isolated action but to an entire course of action and events that includes not only what the protagonist does but also what happens to him. In qualifying this action, Aristotle again uses the word *spoudaios* which means "serious" or "weighty." This is essentially a *moral* seriousness. It seems, then, that the subject matter of tragedy is a course of action which is morally serious, presents a completed unity, and occupies a certain magnitude not only in terms of importance but also, as will be seen, in terms of certain prescribed constraints of time, place, and complexity. Moreover, since a tragedy is essentially dramatic rather than narrative, it represents men in action, and a properly constructed tragedy will provide relief or *katharsis* for various emotions, primarily pity and fear. Hence the *effect* of tragedy on the audience is part of its very definition.

The notion of "action" is central to Aristotle's view of tragedy because it underlies the other components and features, which include plot, character, diction, thought, spectacle, and song. These elements include the means of imitation (diction and song), the manner of imitation (spectacle), and the objects of imitation (actions as arranged in a plot, the character and thought of the actors). Aristotle also prescribes other requirements such as completeness of action, artistic unity, and emotional impact. The element of tragedy which imitates human actions is not primarily the depiction of character but the plot, which Aristotle calls the "first principle" and "the soul of tragedy" (*Poetics*, VI.19–20). Aristotle accords priority to action in poetic representation: tragedy is not a representation of men or of character; rather it represents a sphere "of action, of life" (*Poetics*, VI.12). Because tragedy is essentially dramatic, its basis cannot be the depiction of character; as Aristotle points out, one cannot have a tragedy without action, but a tragedy without character study is quite feasible (*Poetics*, VI.14–15). A tragedy must be based on a certain structure of events or incidents to which the specific actions of given characters contribute. This overall dramatic structure, the plot, is "the end at which tragedy aims" (*Poetics*, VI.13).

For Aristotle, the most important feature of the plot is *unity*: "the component incidents must be so arranged that if one of them be transposed or removed, the unity of the whole is dislocated and destroyed" (*Poetics*, VIII.4). Aristotle sees the entire complex as *one* unified action. How is such organic unity achieved? Aristotle offers the following definition: "A whole is what has a beginning and middle and end" (*Poetics*, VII. 2–3). A beginning, for Aristotle, is that which is not necessarily caused by anything else, but itself causes something else. A middle both follows from something else and results in something else. An end is what necessarily follows from something else but does not produce a further result. Hence the unity of the plot is based on a notion of causality (*Poetics*, VII.7). Aristotle's formulae concerning beginning, middle, and end have been profoundly influential, extending far beyond the confines of tragedy or drama, and deeply infusing modes of thinking and writing even into our own times.

Aristotle explains unity of plot in terms of both the plot's formal structure and the emotions produced in an audience. While he divides the formal structure of the plot into prologue, episode, exode, parode, and stasimon, it is clear that for him the real structure of the plot consists in the movement of the action. He divides plots into simple plots, which exhibit a continuous action, and complex plots – as exemplified in *Oedipus Rex* – whose action is marked by a movement through reversal, recognition, and suffering. Much later in his text, he divides the action into two parts, the "complication" which includes all of the events until the change in fortune, and the "denouement" or unravelling which proceeds from the change in fortune until the end of the play. In this way, the change in fortune is indeed placed at the center of the play: the action as divided both leads to it and flows from it; and it is in relation to it that reversal, recognition, and suffering take their significance. Aristotle prefers complex plots because it is through the processes of reversal, recognition, and suffering that the emotions of pity and fear are evoked, which themselves contribute to the plot's unity.

The plot's unity, then, integrates not only causality, probability, and change of fortune but also the emotions of fear and pity which are generated in an audience. Aristotle explains that pity is aroused by undeserved misfortune; fear is aroused when we realize that the man who suffers such misfortune is "like ourselves" (*Poetics*, XIII.4). Hence these emotions cannot be inspired by a wicked man prospering; nor can they issue from seeing the misfortune suffered by either an entirely worthy man or a thoroughly bad man (*Poetics*, XIII.2–4). Rather, the character in question must occupy a mean between these extremes: he must be a man "who is not pre-eminently virtuous and just, and yet it is through no badness or villainy of his own that he falls into the misfortune, but rather through some flaw in him" (*Poetics*, XIII.5–6).

The legacy of Aristotle's *Poetics*

The *Poetics* is usually recognized as the most influential treatise in the history of literary criticism. The legacy of Aristotle's aesthetics, like that of his philosophy as a whole, is a distinctly classical one. The most fundamental premise of Aristotle's classicism is a political one, namely that the individual achieves his or her nature and purpose only within a society and a state. Poetry, for Aristotle, does not express what is unique about individuals but rather their universal characteristics, what they share with other members of society. While Aristotle grants to poetry a certain autonomy, it yet occupies a definite place within the state as an instrument of education and moral edification. Poetry is not, as in Romantic thought, exalted to an eminence beyond other pursuits.

Poetry is also subject to the classical principles of Aristotle's philosophy in general. From the most minute level of diction to the highest level of plot construction, poetry is held to be a rational, deliberative activity which must always observe the central Aristotelian principle of moderation. Like philosophy, poetry seeks to express universal truths, which are not constrained by reference to particular situations. Its relation to reality is governed by the notions of probability and necessity. Also classical in outlook is Aristotle's insistence on distinguishing clearly between different genres in a hierarchical manner: comedy, which deals with "low" characters and trivial matter, ranks lowest; epic, which includes various plots and lengthy narration, falls below tragedy which is more concentrated and produces a greater effect of unity. Again, the insistence on propriety and consistency of character is classical.

Aristotle's notions anticipate developments in several areas of literary criticism: the issue of poetic imitation, the connection between art and reality, the distinction between genres as well as between high and low art, the study of grammar and language, the psychological and moral effects of literature, the nature and function of the audience, the structure and rules of drama, as well as the notions of plot, narrative, and character. All of these notions are still profoundly pervasive in our thinking about literature and the world. Above and beyond all of these influences, however, is his doctrine of substance, a notion that continues to underlie our thinking, and even our attempts to undermine conventional modes of thought.

Notes

1. *Frogs*, ll. 786, 796, in *Aristophanes Volume II: The Peace, The Birds, The Frogs*, trans. Benjamin Bickley Rogers, Loeb Classical Library (Cambridge, MA and London: Harvard University Press/Heinemann, 1968). Hereafter cited as *Frogs*.
2. *Republic*, in *Collected Dialogues of Plato*, ed. Edith Hamilton and Huntington Cairns (Princeton: Princeton University Press, 1969), 514a–c. Hereafter cited as *Republic*.
3. Aristotle, *The Categories; On Interpretation; Prior Analytics*, trans. Harold P. Cooke and Hugh Tredennick, Loeb Classical Library (Cambridge, MA and London: Harvard University Press/Heinemann, 1973), pp. 16–19.
4. Aristotle, *The Metaphysics I–IX*, trans. Hugh Tredennick, Loeb Classical Library (Cambridge, MA and London: Harvard University Press/Heinemann, 1947), 1011b–13. Hereafter cited as *Met. I–IX*.
5. Aristotle, *Politics*, trans. T. A. Sinclair (Harmondsworth: Penguin, 1986), VII.i.
6. *Nicomachean Ethics*, trans. H. Rackham, Loeb Classical Library (London and New York: Heinemann/Harvard University Press, 1934), VI.ii.5–VI.iii.4–6.
7. *Aristotle: Poetics; Longinus: On the Sublime; Demetrius: On Style*, trans. W. Hamilton Fyfe (Cambridge, MA and London: Harvard University Press/Heinemann, 1965), IV.2–3. Hereafter cited as *Poetics*.
8. Aristotle, *Posterior Analytics; Topica*, trans. Hugh Tredennick and E. S. Forster, Loeb Classical Library (Cambridge, MA and London: Harvard University Press/Heinemann, 1976), p. 171.
9. Aristotle, *The Art of Rhetoric*, trans. H. C. Lawson-Tancred (Harmondsworth: Penguin, 1991), 1355a.

Chapter 2

The Traditions of Rhetoric

The word "rhetoric" derives from the Greek word *rhetor*, meaning "speaker," and originally referred to the art of public speaking. This art embraced the techniques whereby a speaker could compose and arrange a speech that would be persuasive through its intellectual, emotional, and dramatic appeal to an audience. Over the last two millennia, rhetoric has been important in a number of spheres: the political sphere, where this art was born; philosophy, which has often placed rhetoric below logic and metaphysics; theology, which has used rhetoric for its own ends; education, where rhetoric has often assumed a central role, extending into our own composition classrooms; and, of course, literary criticism, which continues to draw upon rhetoric in its focus on language, tropes, and audience.

Greek Rhetoric

Rhetoric originated in ancient Greece in the fifth century BC. It owed its early development to the Sophists, Aristotle, and then, in the Roman world, to Cato, Cicero, and Quintilian. Classical rhetoric, as developed until the time of Cicero, had five parts or "offices": invention, arrangement, style, memory, and delivery. "Invention"(*heuresis*/*inventio*) referred to the content of a speech: a statement of the issue at stake and the means of persuasion, which embraced direct evidence, an account of the speaker's character, logical argument, consideration of the emotions of the audience as well as of the ethical and political premises of the speech. The second office was the "arrangement" (*taxis*/*dispositio*) of the speech into a given order. The speech would begin with an "introduction" to arouse audience interest and sympathy; then a "narration" of a given background and relevant facts; a "proof" which would include logical arguments and a refutation of objections or counterarguments; its "conclusion" might recapitulate the essential argument and appeal further to the emotions of the audience. The third office,

Literary Criticism from Plato to the Present: An Introduction   M. A. R. Habib
© 2011 M. A. R. Habib

"style" (*lexis/elocutio*), conventionally had two elements: diction (or word choice) and composition, which referred to various elements of sentence construction, such as structure, rhythm, and the use of figures.

These three offices were common to both public speaking and written composition. There were two further offices, identified by Aristotle, peculiar to speaking: "memory," which signified the memorization of the speech for oral performance; and "delivery," which embraced control of voice and gesture. Style was conventionally evaluated on the basis of four virtues of style formulated by Aristotle's student Theophrastus: correctness (of grammar and language usage); clarity; ornamentation (using tropes and figures of speech); and propriety. Styles were classified as grand, middle, and plain.

According to one tradition, the art of rhetoric was formally founded in 476 BC by a native of Syracuse, Corax, whose student Tisias transmitted his master's teachings to the mainland.[1] Rhetoric was an integral part of the political process in ancient Greece, especially in Athens and Syracuse of the fifth century BC. It has profound and perhaps intrinsic ties to the political system of democracy, since it presupposes the freedom for a range of view-points to be expressed in public discourse. On the ability to speak persuasively could depend the entire future of a state, family, or individual. On rhetoric often hung the balance of life or death, war or peace, prosperity or destruction, freedom or slavery.

Given that rhetoric was so vital in ancient Athens, there emerged a group of professional teachers, called Sophists (from *sophos*, meaning "wise"), who taught this art for use in the courts, the legislature, and political forums, as well as for philosophical reflection and debate. Through their influence, rhetoric came to assume a central role in Greek education. The most influential of the Sophists were Protagoras, Gorgias, Antiphon, Lysias, and Isocrates. Protagoras' most famous belief was that "man is the measure of all things." This was essentially a secular humanistic and individualistic idea. He also taught that every argument had two sides, which could be equally rational. Hence he encouraged relativism, skepticism, and agnosticism. Another powerful figure among the Sophists was Gorgias (ca. 485–380 BC), who stressed the need for rhetoric to borrow figures of speech from poetry. Like Protagoras, he subordinated the notion of truth to the presentation of a particular viewpoint and to the persuasion of a given audience. Isocrates (436–338 BC) was influential in his emphasis on rhetoric as the basis of education. He viewed the essential purpose of oratory as political, to train politicians in promoting the values and unity of Greek culture.

Plato's Critique of Rhetoric

Given the importance of rhetoric in Athenian public life, it is hardly surprising that this art was subject to abuse. The Sophists nurtured in their students an ability to argue both or many sides of a case; they were consequently accused of training people in "making the worse cause appear the better" and in thereby sacrificing truth, morality, and justice to self-interest. Aristophanes satirized the Sophists in his comedy *The Clouds*. A more serious, and permanently damaging, challenge was issued by Plato, especially in his dialogues *Gorgias* and *Phaedrus*.

Plato's critique of rhetoric in *Gorgias* (through the persona of Socrates) is premised on a sharp opposition between the spheres of philosophy and rhetoric. There are two kinds of persuasion, maintains Socrates: one which confers conviction without understanding and one which confers knowledge. Rhetoric, he insists, leads to conviction without educating people as to right and wrong.[2] He argues that the rhetorician is a non-expert persuading other non-experts. He never need know the actual facts of a situation; he needs no expertise, merely a persuasive ploy (*Gorgias*, 459a–c). Socrates' criticism is underlain by Plato's notion of truth as transcending human opinion. In the law courts, says Socrates, rhetoric relies on producing a large number of eminent witnesses; but such argument or refutation is worthless in the context of truth. In effect, suggests Socrates, the rhetorician and the politician are forced to pander to the existing power structure and the views of the majority (*Gorgias*, 481d–482c).

Aristotle and the Further Development of Rhetoric

Aristotle's influential treatise *Rhetoric* states that rhetoric is the "counterpart" of dialectic or logical argument. Whereas dialectic uses logical syllogisms, rhetoric uses the enthymeme, which is a syllogism whose premises are not certain or necessary but probable.[3] In contrast with Plato, Aristotle urges that rhetoric is a useful skill precisely because it can promote the causes of truth and justice. In fact, the true position is naturally superior and more easily argued (*Rhet.*, 1355b). Moreover, we need the capacity to argue contradictory positions so that we have a fuller understanding of the case and can refute unjust counterarguments (*Rhet.*, 1355a).

Again in pointed contrast with Plato, Aristotle contends that rhetoric, like dialectic, is not concerned with any single field. Whereas each of the other arts is persuasive and instructive about a special province, rhetoric deals with the element of persuasiveness in any field (*Rhet.*, 1355b). Aristotle classifies proof, the most important component of rhetoric, into three basic types, as these relate to (1) the character of the speaker, who must establish his credibility; (2) the audience, which must be induced into a certain emotional state; and (3) the persuasive nature of the speech itself (*Rhet.*, 1356a). To master these various proofs, one must master the syllogism, one must have a scientific understanding of character and virtue, and one must understand each emotion and how it is brought about. Given that rhetoric requires this broad mastery, Aristotle considers it to be an offshoot of dialectic and ethics. He in fact suggests that rhetoric "is quite properly categorized as political" (*Rhet.*, 1356a).

Aristotle distinguishes three genres of rhetoric. The first genre is "deliberative" rhetoric, whose province is politics, concerning which future actions should be taken by the state. "Forensic" rhetoric is used in the law courts; it concerns actions already performed in the past, and it employs prosecution and defense in its objective of achieving justice. The final genre is "display" rhetoric which focuses on the present and involves praise and denigration in its aim of displaying nobility (*Rhet.*, 1358b–1359a).

Aristotle urges that the chief virtue of "style" is to be clear and to be appropriate to the subject. Metaphor is a central element of style but must be used moderately (*Rhet.*, 1405a–b). Another prime attribute of style is propriety, which means that a given content must be expressed in a suitable manner. Also integral to propriety are the use of emotion and tailoring of the speech to the audience's character, as well as timeliness, the use of the appropriate expression at the appropriate time (*Rhet.*, 1408a–b). In the final section of the *Rhetoric*, concerning composition, Aristotle explains that a speech will have four parts: the introduction; the presentation or main narrative; the proof of the speaker's claims, which includes refutation of counterarguments; and finally a summarizing epilogue (*Rhet.*, 1414b).

Hellenistic Rhetoric

Classical Greek culture based on the *polis* or city-state effectively ended with the defeat of Athens by Philip of Macedon at the battle of Chaeronea in 338 BC. Shortly after Aristotle's death in 332 BC his "student" Alexander the Great, son of Philip, conquered the vast Persian Empire in its entirety. The Hellenistic period is said to begin with Alexander's death in 323 BC, after which his empire was divided up among his generals, who initiated various dynasties: Ptolemy in Egypt (and later Phoenicia and Palestine), Seleucus in Syria, Persia, and Mesopotamia, and Cassander in Macedonia. Notwithstanding these divisions, Greek language and culture were spread all across the conquered territories. This new Hellenistic era was characterized by a merging of Greek and Oriental traditions.

The great library and museum of Alexandria in Egypt was a center of scholarship in the fields of science, textual criticism, and poetic composition. Hellenistic scholars working here further systematized the content and rules of rhetoric. A major surviving text of this period is the *Rhetorica ad Alexandrum* (dedicated to Alexander the Great), written in Greek in the fourth century BC. Greek rhetoricians of this period include Theophrastus (ca. 370–285 BC) who may have initiated the study of figures of speech and figures of thought, and who may have founded the notion of three levels of style – high, middle, and plain. The most important Greek rhetorician of this time was Hermagoras of Temnos, who influenced Cicero and Quintilian, especially through his doctrine of *stasis*, which identified the "position" or "stance" toward the issue at stake in an argument.[4]

Roman Rhetoric

Greek rhetoric made its entry into Rome in the second century BC. Hermagoras had a great influence on two of the major early Roman texts of rhetoric, the *Rhetorica ad Herennium* (*Rhetoric for Herennius*, ca. 90 BC) and Cicero's *De inventione* (87 BC). The *Rhetorica*, attributed for several centuries to Cicero, is the first text to present a detailed discussion of the five-part system which was central to the Roman tradition of rhetoric.[5] The author defines these parts as follows: invention is the devising of matter which will make a given case convincing; arrangement is the ordering of the matter; style is the adaptation of words and sentences to the matter invented; memory is the firm retention in the mind of the content; and delivery refers to the regulation of voice, countenance, and gesture (*RH*, I.ii.3). The most complete argument, he tells us, has five parts: proposition, reason, proof of the reason, embellishment, and résumé or conclusion. A conclusion is tripartite, and includes summary, amplification, and appeal to pity.

The author suggests that there are three levels of style: the grand or high style, which uses ornate arrangements of impressive words; the middle style, which uses a lower class of words which, however, are not colloquial; and the simple or plain style, which uses the most current idiom of standard speech (*RH*, IV.viii.11). This concept of the three styles was adapted by critics in the Middle Ages, who saw the three levels respectively as applying to narratives about the court, the town, and the peasantry.

Finally, the author provides a long list of "figures of speech" and "figures of thought." The former are produced by an adornment of language; the latter by a distinction in the idea or conception itself (*RH*, IV.xii.18). Metonymy is defined as a figure which draws from an object closely akin to the intended object but substitutes a different name. Synecdoche occurs when the whole is understood from the part or vice versa, or when the singular is understood from the plural or vice versa (*RH*, IV.xxxii.43–xxxiii.45). Metaphor is said to occur when a word applying to one thing is transferred to another, on the basis of a given similarity; it is used to create vividness, brevity, to avoid obscenity, to magnify or diminish, or to embellish. Finally, allegory is defined as a manner of speech denoting one thing by the letter of the words but another by their meaning.

Cicero's Rhetorical Theory

Marcus Tullius Cicero (106–43 BC) is the most renowned of the classical rhetoricians. As a student in Rome, he entered an educational system which was centered on rhetoric and assigned exercises in writing, speaking, arguing a thesis, legislative and judicial declamations, the exercise of memory, and the proper delivery of a speech. He published his rhetorical treatise *De inventione* in the early part of the first century BC. This was followed by other rhetorical texts, *De oratore* (55 BC), *Brutus* (46 BC), a history of Roman oratory, *Orator* (46 BC), *De optimo genere oratorum* [*On the Ideal Classification of Orators*] (46 BC), and *Partitione oratoria* [*On the Divisions of Rhetoric*] (45 BC).

In *De inventione* Cicero stresses the political importance of rhetoric. He also affirms that the function of rhetoric is to help promote a society based on justice and common welfare rather than physical strength. As such, the speaker must possess not only eloquence but also wisdom.[6] Cicero divides a speech into six parts, beginning with the *exordium*, intended to make the audience well disposed, moving on to *body* which consists of a narrative of events, *argumentation*, *refutation* of counterarguments, then ending with a *peroration* which has three parts: a résumé of the speech's substantial points, arousal of animosity against the opponent, and the arousing of sympathy for one's own case. A peroration might also include personification as well as appealing to the pity of the jury (*DI*, I.80.100–105). Cicero considers delivery to be the supreme factor in successful oratory (*DI*, III.213). The orator is defined in general as someone who can express ideas clearly to an "ordinary" audience (*DI*, I.85).

What is most interesting about the *De oratore* is the way it addresses two important topics: the cultural value of rhetoric, and the connection between rhetoric, philosophy, and other forms of knowledge. Cicero maintains that the art of rhetoric has flourished especially in states which have enjoyed freedom, peace, and tranquility. Moreover, this art above all others distinguishes men from animals; it is this art which has brought unity and civilization to humanity.[7] Cicero also takes issue with Plato's criticism of rhetoric. Where Plato sees rhetoric as focused on style and divorced from philosophy, Cicero insists that the good rhetorician must speak on the basis of knowledge and understanding of his subject, and that philosophy and rhetoric are complementary.

Quintilian

It is reputed that Cicero's last words were "With me dies the republic!" Cicero's rhetorical successors saw the death of the Roman republic and the imposition of imperial rule, where one man, the emperor, had absolute power. There was a consequent decrease in personal and political freedom, including the ability to speak freely. This led to a general decline of rhetoric in the first century AD in Rome. Nonetheless, this era produced in Quintilian a figure whose *Institutio oratoria* was a major contribution to rhetorical and educational theory as well as to literary criticism; its influence has been vast, second only to Cicero's in the Renaissance, and reaching into our own educational systems.

In the *Institutio* Quintilian offers a program for the education of an ideal orator from childhood. He stresses what is perhaps the most original theme of his text, the dependence of true oratory on moral goodness: "the perfect orator ... cannot exist unless he is above all a good man."[8] Like Cicero, Quintilian opposes Plato's separation of rhetoric and philosophy. Quintilian's integration of these activities is based on morality: the orator cannot leave the principles of moral conduct to the philosophers because he is actively involved as a citizen in the various enterprises of the state, civil, legal, judicial, private, and public. Like Cicero, then, Quintilian views wisdom and eloquence as naturally and necessarily accompanying each other.

Quintilian urges that once a child has learned how to read and write, he must next learn grammar (*IO*, I.ii.31). He defines the province of grammar as comprising two parts, the art of speaking correctly and the interpretation of literature. Quintilian suggests that the passages chosen for reading should portray moral goodness. In analyzing poetry, the student must be taught to read closely, to specify the parts of speech, the feet and meter, to identify the correct usage of words, to know the various senses of a given word, to recognize all kinds of tropes, figures of speech, and figures of thought, to be acquainted with relevant historical facts, and, above all, to understand the merit in the way the whole work is organized (*IO*, I.viii.5–18). In general, the stories told by poets should be used to increase students' knowledge rather than simply treated as models of eloquence (*IO*, I.ix.2–6).

Quintilian's foremost point is that the teacher of rhetoric, receiving boys at an impressionable age, should be of exemplary morality:

> Let him [the teacher] adopt, then, above all things, the feelings of a parent toward his pupils ... Let him neither have vices in himself, nor tolerate them in others. Let his austerity not be stern, nor his affability too easy, lest dislike arise from the one, or contempt from the other ... Let him be plain in his mode of teaching, and patient of labor ... Let him reply readily to those who put questions to him, and question of his own accord those who do not ... In amending what requires correction, let him not be harsh, and, least of all, not reproachful ... Let him speak much every day himself, for the edification of his pupils. (*IO*, II.ii.4–8)

The best teachers, adds Quintilian, will be people of good sense who know how to adapt their teaching to the standards of their pupils. Above all, their command of their learning will enable them to achieve in their teaching the virtue of clarity, which is "the chief virtue of eloquence." The less able a teacher is, the more obscure and pretentious he will be (*IO*, II.iii.2–9). He must be practical, adaptable, kind, moderate, and maintain a Stoic sense of his duty to his country. In general, it can be seen that Quintilian's major contribution to the fields of rhetorical and educational theory lies in his insistence that all aspects of these fields are underlain by morality.

The Subsequent History of Rhetoric: An Overview

After the civil war in which Octavius defeated Antony at the battle of Actium, Octavius became emperor of the entire Roman world in 27 BC and ruled until AD 14. The Republic had permanently collapsed and Rome was ruled by emperors until its fall in AD 410. In this period, the freedom to speak – and the art of rhetoric – was profoundly constrained: speakers focused on style and delivery and rhetorical ornamentation rather than substance. The period is generally referred to as the Second Sophistic (27 BC–AD 410), named after a new generation of sophists who advocated a return to the language and style of classical Athens. The Second Sophistic produced no major rhetorical treatises, with the exception of Longinus' *On the Sublime*. Given that rhetoric had effectively been denuded of its social and political functions, it henceforth lost its public role, focusing increasingly on imitation of earlier models and the formalization of rules for literary composition, which was seen through the Middle Ages as part of the province of rhetoric.

By the end of the fourth century, Christianity had risen to a predominant status in the Roman Empire. This process had been initiated by a series of edicts issued by Emperor Constantine in AD 313 allowing Christianity to be tolerated; Emperor Theodosius I had issued a decree in 380 making Christianity the official religion of the Empire. A reaction set in against the use of Classical pagan methods and mythology in education. Augustine produced his *De doctrina christiana* in 426, in which he argued for the importance of rhetoric as an instrument of explaining and conveying the Christian message. Eventually, the Church adopted Cicero's rhetoric as a guide for preachers. Augustine thus provides a link between classical and medieval rhetoric.

In the Middle Ages rhetoric was one part of the educational "trivium," the other two components being grammar and logic. Rhetoric was concerned primarily with the means of persuasion of an audience, whereas the focus of grammar was on the rules of linguistic correctness, and that of logic on valid argumentation. The boundaries between poetics and rhetoric were somewhat blurred. In general, rhetoric in the Middle Ages took second place to the development of logic, especially in the hands of the scholastic theologians such as Thomas Aquinas.

In the Renaissance, which returned to classical sources, rhetoric enjoyed a revived centrality in the educational curriculum. The Renaissance humanists drew profusely on the teachings of Cicero[9] as well as Quintilian's newly recovered treatise, in their emphasis on *content* and the strategies of invention ("RP," 1048–1049). As the Renaissance progressed, however, rhetoric – itself reduced to style – was subsumed under poetics, inspired partly by the rediscovery of Aristotle's *Poetics*: the rhetorical concern with audience, modes of argumentation, and persuasion were all lost. Rhetoric as such was dead. Poetic invention of course retained its importance but it was not, as in traditional rhetoric, oriented primarily toward an audience. Rather, it became a private, meditative act, the composition of a solitary mind in isolation. The figures of speech were less directed toward the passions of an audience; composition was viewed more as a form of self-expression, an indication of the author's psyche, and began to be examined by the new discipline of psychology ("RP," 1049).

This mode of thinking achieved a new intensity in Romanticism, which offered a new account of poetic creation on the basis of the faculty of imagination. The Romantics tended to draw upon Plato and Longinus, attacking the remnants of Aristotelian poetics and rhetoric that infused neoclassical poetics. The profusion of written culture encouraged the theory and practice of invention and creativity as an isolated and solitary process. After the Renaissance, the rise of bourgeois economy and modes of thought in the late eighteenth and nineteenth centuries contributed to the disintegration of rhetoric in several ways, firstly through increasing specialization, whereby each area of inquiry aspired to a relative autonomy, possessing not only its own unique content but its own methods. Moreover, the predominance of rationalist, empirical, and experimental outlooks promoted a more straightforward and literal use of language, divesting language of its allegorical potential as so richly realized in medieval texts. By the end of the nineteenth century and indeed into present times, "rhetoric" became a derogatory term, signifying emptiness of content, bombast, and superfluous ornamentation. Nonetheless, as indicated below, rhetoric has experienced some significant revivals during the twentieth century.

The Legacy of Rhetoric

In the Western world, rhetoric has played a central role in politics and law; for two millennia rhetoric has been at the center of the educational system in Europe, and its influence in education is still visible in its continued domination of the teaching of composition. Approaches to teaching composition have begun to feel the reverberations of a rhetorical revival in literary studies. Rhetoric has recently exercised a renewed impact on cultural and critical theory, spanning numerous disciplines, especially those such as speech act theory which are directly concerned with the nature of communication. The influence of rhetoric on literary criticism and theory extends much further than the stylistic analysis of figures of speech. A rhetorical approach to a text must concern itself not only with the author's intentions but with all the features implicated in the text as a persuasive use of language: the structure of the text as a means of communication, the nature and response of the audience or reader, the text's relation to other discourses, and the social and political contexts of the interaction between author, text, and reader, as well as a historicist concern with the differences between a modern reception of the text and its original performative conditions. In short, a rhetorical approach views a literary text not as an isolated act (merely recording, for example, the private thoughts of an author) but as a *performance* in a social context.

In this broad sense, rhetoric has been an integral element in many approaches to literature and philosophy, ranging from Marxist and feminist perspectives through hermeneutic to reception theories. A study of the nature of language has been central to the project of much formalism, including the New Criticism. But as with earlier formalisms, this modern formalism – expressed partly in manifesto slogans such as "a poem should not mean, but be" – tended to undermine a rhetorical approach to literature as an effective form of communication, and to view the literary text as an isolated verbal structure. One of the figures associated with New Critical tendencies, I. A. Richards, produced a book, *Philosophy of Rhetoric* (1936), in which he made a distinction, deriving partly from John Locke, between poetry, which draws on the multiple meanings of words, rhetoric, designed to persuade, and expository language in which the meaning of each word should be clear and the language used neutral or impartial. Given the impossibility of avoiding polysemy or multiple meaning, Richards suggests that it is the task of rhetoric to examine the semantic richness of language.

To a large extent, Richards' insights gave way before the predominance of New Critical and other formalisms during the 1940s. A subsequent revival of rhetoric was heralded by Kenneth Burke's reaction against these various modern formalisms and his call for the renewal of a rhetorical approach to literary form and interpretation. Writers such as T. S. Eliot and Wayne Booth tended to focus on the author's relation to the text, as in Eliot's essay "The Three Voices of Poetry"; Northrop Frye's *Anatomy of Criticism* (1957) also ultimately rejected any sharp distinction between a literary or rhetorical use of language that made use of figures and tropes, and a philosophical and expository use of language. Reception and reader-response theorists, including Iser, Holland, and Fish, have focused on the role and situation of the reader; other critics, such as Burke, Jakobson, Lacan, Derrida, and Paul de Man, resurrected the idea of certain foundational rhetorical tropes such as irony, metaphor, and metonymy, some arguing that these tropes are integral to language and the process of thought. Linguists and structuralists such as Todorov, Genette, and Barthes have often modified rhetorical classifications of tropes. A rhetorical perspective is explicitly acknowledged in the so-called Law and Literature movement: the narrative of a prosecution or defense in a courtroom will employ many literary and rhetorical strategies. But the influence is not one-sided: literary and other texts can themselves be viewed in the light of rhetorical strategies designed for the courtroom. The entire arsenal of "literary" figures, in fact, was devised by rhetoricians. In this broad sense, then, rhetoric might be viewed as an inevitable component of all kinds of discourse.

This rhetorical heritage in Western literature and education has been countered by a long tradition of philosophy which has seen itself as devoted to the rational pursuit of truth, the definition of the good life, and happiness; in short, the mainstream Western philosophical tradition has tended to reject rhetorical considerations of style, passion, and effect on audience, in favor of an emphasis on content. This tradition was effectively inaugurated by Plato; it runs through medieval logic and theology, as well as disputes in the Middle Ages concerning the status of logic, grammar, and rhetoric in the educational trivium; it continues through Renaissance attempts to stress the formal elements of poetry as well as through Ramist logic in the seventeenth century into the empiricist and rationalist philosophy of the Enlightenment, as expressed in Locke's insistence that philosophical language be free of figures and tropes; it survives into the twentieth century in the analytic philosophy of G. E. Moore and Bertrand Russell, as well as logical positivism, speech act theory, and various branches of semiology. Interestingly, whereas the philosophical disparagement of rhetoric has usually aligned the latter with poetry, sometimes the advocates of poetry have themselves opposed the alleged rigidity and prescriptiveness of rhetoric, as in Romanticism, late nineteenth-century symbolism, and modern formalism. These struggles continue into the present day in conflicts between rhetoric and more conventional analytic and empirical modes of philosophizing. As against the latter, rhetoric holds that truth cannot be abstracted from all practical and political concerns but is intrinsically tied to prevailing political structures and an appeal to consensus.

Notes

1. George A. Kennedy, *A New History of Classical Rhetoric* (Princeton: Princeton University Press, 1994), p. 34.
2. Plato, *Gorgias*, trans. Robin Waterfield (New York and Oxford: Oxford University Press, 1994), 455a.
3. Aristotle, *The Art of Rhetoric*, trans. H. C. Lawson-Tancred (Harmondsworth: Penguin, 1991), 1355a. Hereafter cited as *Rhet.*

4. George A. Kennedy, ed., *The Cambridge History of Literary Criticism: Volume I: Classical Criticism* (Cambridge: Cambridge University Press, 1997), p. 198. Rawson (1997); V.V: *Volume V: Romanticism*, ed. Marshall Brown (2000).

5. [Cicero] *Ad C. Herennium: De ratione dicendi (Rhetorica ad Herennium)*, trans. Harry Caplan (Cambridge, MA and London: Harvard University Press/ Heinemann, 1968), I.ii.2. Hereafter cited as *RH*.

6. Marcus Tullius Cicero, *De inventione; De optimo genere oratorum; Topica*, trans. H. M. Hubbell, Loeb Classical Library (Cambridge, MA and London: Harvard University Press/Heinemann, 1968), I.5. Hereafter cited as *DI*.

7. Cicero, *De oratore*, in *Cicero on Oratory and Orators*, trans. J. S. Watson (Carbondale: Southern Illinois University Press, 1970), I.viii.

8. *Quintilian: On the Teaching of Speaking and Writing: Translations from Books One, Two, and Ten of the Institutio oratoria*, ed. James J. Murphy (Carbondale: Southern Illinois University Press, 1987), p. 6. Hereafter cited as *IO*.

9. Some of the insights in this section are indebted to the extremely learned article, "Rhetoric and Poetry," by Thomas O. Sloane in *The New Princeton Encyclopedia of Poetry and Poetics*, ed. Alex Preminger and T. V. F. Brogan (Princeton: Princeton University Press, 1993). Hereafter cited as "RP."

Chapter 3
Greek and Latin Criticism During the Roman Empire

Horace (65–8 BC)

The influence of Horace's *Ars poetica* has been vast, exceeding the influence of Plato, and in many periods, even that of Aristotle. Horace (Quintus Horatius Flaccus) is known primarily as a poet, a composer of odes, satires, and epistles. In the realm of literary criticism, he has conventionally been associated with the notions that "a poem is like a painting," that poetry should "teach and delight," as well as the idea that poetry is a craft which requires labor. Horace's text takes the form of an informal letter from an established poet giving advice to the would-be poets of the wealthy Piso family in Rome. Though the *Ars poetica* is technically a work of literary critical and rhetorical theory, it is itself written as a poem, a mode that was imitated by several men of letters, including the medieval writer Geoffrey de Vinsauf, the Renaissance writer Pierre de Ronsard, the neoclassical poets Nicolas Boileau-Despréaux and Alexander Pope, the Romantic poet Lord Byron, and twentieth-century poets such as Wallace Stevens. Horace was introduced by the poet Vergil to Gaius Maecenas, an extremely wealthy patron of the arts. Eventually, Horace enjoyed the patronage of the emperor Augustus himself.

Horace's text, though casual in tone, can be seen as focused on the following issues: (1) the relation of a writer to his work, his knowledge of tradition, and his own ability; (2) the moral and social functions of poetry, such as establishing a repository of conventional wisdom, providing moral examples through characterization, and promoting civic virtue and sensibility, as well as affording pleasure; (3) the contribution of an audience to the composition of poetry, viewed both as an art and as a commodity; (4) an awareness of literary history and historical change in language and genre. These are the largely conventional themes that preoccupy Horace's text, whose principles claim to be drawn from practical experience rather than theory.

Literary Criticism from Plato to the Present: An Introduction   M. A. R. Habib
© 2011 M. A. R. Habib

Among Horace's most salient views is his insistence on the moral function of literature. In drama, for example, the depiction of good character is indispensable. This function, he says, should be effected partly by the chorus.[1] He also stresses the then standard rhetorical principle of "decorum," which calls for a "proper" relationship between form and content, expression and thought, style and subject matter, diction and character (*AP*, 312–315). As against Plato, who had regarded the poet as necessarily distorting reality by offering a mere imitation of it, Horace insists that the "principal fountainhead of writing correctly is wisdom" (*AP*, 309) and he sees poetry as a repository of social and religious wisdom (*AP*, 396–407). In the depiction of character, the poet must be aware of the various characteristics of men from childhood, youth, manhood to old age (this repertoire of the ages of man is taken from rhetoric) (*AP*, 158–174). Hence, the poet's work must be based on knowledge; not bookish knowledge but a detailed empirical knowledge derived from acute observation of actual life. Horace demands a high degree of realism from the poet, as expressed in this statement: "My instruction would be to examine the model of human life and manners as an informed copyist and to elicit from it a speech that lives" (*AP*, 317–318).

In a famous statement, Horace remarks that

> a poet has matched every demand if he mingles the useful with the pleasant [*miscuit utile dulci*], by charming and, not less, advising the reader; that is a book that earns money for the Sosii [publishers]; a book that crosses the sea and, making its writer known, forecasts a long life for him. (*AP*, 342–346)

Horace's call for literature to be socially useful as well as pleasing was vastly influential; as was his insistence that a poem not only charm the reader but also offer moral advice. Horace stresses the amount of labor required for composing good poetry. Part of this labor is seeking out valid criticism of one's work from sincere and qualified people. Horace admonishes the poet to store his work away for nine years. He warns that, once a poem is published, the words used by the poet will forever become public property, part of a language inescapably social: "it will be permissible to destroy what you have not published: the voice once sent forth cannot return" [*nescit vox missa reverti*] (*AP*, 386–390). Horace's argument seems strikingly modern in rejecting an author's intention as the sole determinant or ultimate criterion of a poem's meaning. It may, indeed, be his combination of classical and newer attitudes, as well as his ability to give striking poetic and epigrammatic expression to a body of accumulated wisdom or "common sense," the critic speaking with the authority of a poet, that ensured the classic status of Horace's text.

Longinus (First Century AD)

After the period of the early Roman Empire, two broad intellectual currents emerged during the first four centuries. The first of these was known as the Second Sophistic (27 BC–AD 410), named after a new generation of sophists and rhetoricians who took for their model the classical language and style of Attic Greece. The second was the philosophy of Neo-Platonism, whose prime exponent Plotinus will be considered in the next section. The major rhetorical treatise of this period was written in Greek: entitled *peri hupsous* or *On the Sublime*, it is conventionally attributed to "Longinus," and dates from the first or second century AD. It was the most influential rhetorical text through much of the period of the Second Sophistic, and has subsequently exerted a pronounced influence on literary criticism since the seventeenth century, somewhat against the grain of the classical heritage derived from Aristotle and Horace. It has fascinated critics of the modern period on account of its treatment of the sublime as a quality of the soul or spirit rather than as a matter of mere technique. In the later classical period and the Middle Ages, the treatise appeared to be little known. Initially published during the Renaissance by Robotelli in 1554, it was subsequently translated into Latin in 1572 and then into English by John Hall in 1652. In modern times the concept of the sublime owed its resurgence to a translation in 1674 by Nicolas Boileau, the most important figure of French neoclassicism. The sublime became an important element in the broad Romantic reaction in Europe against neoclassicism as well as in the newly rising domain of aesthetics in the work of thinkers such as Immanuel Kant.

Longinus offers an initial definition, stating that the sublime consists "in a consummate excellence and distinction of language . . . the effect of genius is not to persuade the audience but rather to transport them out of themselves." He adds that "what inspires wonder casts a spell upon us and is always superior to what is merely convincing and pleasing."[2] We can control our reasoning but the sublime exerts a power which we cannot resist (I.4). Longinus distinguishes dramatically between other compositional skills and the sublime. Inventive skill and appropriate use of facts, for example, are expressed through an entire composition. But the sublime, he says, appears like a bolt of lightning, scattering everything before it and revealing the power of the speaker "at a single stroke" (I.4).

Longinus' subsequent definition of the sublime appeals to experience in a manner later echoed by Arnold, Leavis, and others. The true sublime will produce a lasting and repeated effect on "a man of sense, well-versed in literature" (VII.1–3). As with Arnold and Leavis, Longinus' view of greatness in literature appears to be an *affective* one: we judge it by its emotional effects on the reader or listener (the Latin *affectus* as a noun means "disposition" or "state," and as a verb, "affected by"). Longinus broadens his definition to say that the "truly beautiful and sublime ... pleases all people at all times" (VII.4).

According to Longinus, there are five "genuine sources" of the sublime: (1) the command of "full-blooded" or robust ideas (sometimes expressed by translators as "grandeur of thought"); (2) the inspiration of "vehement emotion"; (3) the proper construction of figures – both figures of thought and figures of speech; (4) nobility of phrase, which includes diction and the use of metaphor; (5) the general effect of dignity and elevation which embraces the previous four elements. More fundamental than anything else in creating sublimity is the arrangement of the various elements of a passage into a unified, single system. Longinus advocates an artistic organicism, using an analogy which has subsequently served countless writers: just as with the members of the human body, so it is with the elements of sublimity: "None of the members has any value by itself apart from the others, yet one with another they all constitute a perfect organism"(XL.1).

Longinus' examples of sublimity here are intended to express what might be viewed as his fundamental position: citing Homer, he reflects that "a great style is the natural outcome of weighty thoughts, and sublime sayings naturally fall to men of spirit" (IX.1–3). Those passages in Homer are sublime "which represent the divine nature in its true attributes, pure, majestic, and unique" (IX.8). Interestingly, Longinus also cites early passages from the Old Testament ("Let there be light...") as expressing "a worthy conception of divine power" (IX.9). In these passages Longinus seems to find sublimity in the expression of profound and appropriate religious sentiment which displays a sense of decorum and which justly marks the relation of divine and human. Great writers, then, achieve sublimity through their grandeur of thought, by expressing a vision of the universe that is morally and theologically elevated.

Indeed, in a famous passage, Longinus states that "Nature" has distinguished us over other creatures, and has

> from the first breathed into our hearts an unconquerable passion for whatever is great and more divine than ourselves. Thus within the scope of human enterprise there lie such powers of contemplation and thought that even the whole universe cannot satisfy them, but our ideas often pass beyond the limits that enring us. (XXXV.2–3)

Hence, the sublime embodies the highest purpose of humankind. This purpose, far from according with a classical Aristotelian recognition of our finitude and proper place in the cosmic scheme, is to strive beyond our own human nature toward the divine, on the wings of "unconquerable passion."

Longinus subsequently says that sublimity lifts men "near the mighty mind of God" (XXXVI.1).

The final surviving part of the manuscript is perhaps the most revealing of Longinus' world view. He laments that truly great or sublime literature is no longer being produced because of the "love of money, that insatiable sickness from which we all now suffer, and the love of pleasure," both of which "enslave us." He goes on to say that "men no longer then look upwards ... they value that part of them which is mortal and consumes away, and neglect the development of their immortal souls." Longinus' account is quite clear in its system of priorities: the soul over the body, the immortal, permanent and selfless over the perishable, transient, and self-interested. The world view is Stoic and Platonic – even Neo-Platonic – but also somewhat Christian in its emphasis. The parallels between Longinus' world view and those of the Romantics are clear. Moreover, if we view Longinus' influence as moving in a broadly "aesthetic" direction toward notions of relative artistic autonomy, we can see that the debate between classicism and Romanticism was played out not only from the eighteenth through the twentieth centuries but in the Hellenistic world itself and in the early Roman Empire. Especially influential was Longinus' recognition of the power of language – founded on grandeur of thought and the skillful use of figures – to attain sublimity, thereby transforming our perception of the world.

Neo-Platonism

The philosophy of Neo-Platonism was predominant during the third and fourth centuries of the Christian era. It derived some inspiration from the doctrines of Philo Judaeus and was developed systematically by Plotinus, the Syrian philosopher Porphyry, and Proclus. The Neo-Platonists held the classical authors in the highest esteem, and attempted to reconcile discrepancies between various classical authors such as Plato and Aristotle, as well as between philosophy and poetry; they attempted in particular to reconcile Plato's theories of poetry with the poetic practice of Homer and other poets. Their fundamental method of achieving this was through allegorical and symbolic modes of interpretation, opening the way for Christian medieval conceptions of allegory which viewed the physical world as inherently symbolic of a higher world. It was a Latin writer, Macrobius, who transmitted these essentially Greek developments in the art of interpretation to the Middle Ages. From a literary critical perspective, the great achievement of the Neo-Platonists was to reformulate Plato's metaphysical framework so as to rehabilitate and accommodate the arts. The three major exponents to be considered here are Plotinus, Macrobius, and Boethius.

Plotinus (AD 204/5–270)

The third-century philosopher Plotinus has been variously called the greatest metaphysician of antiquity, the founder of Neo-Platonism, and the most profound single influence on Christian thought. Neo-Platonism takes from Plato, but also modifies, the idea that ultimate reality subsists in a transcendent and spiritual realm, from which the physical world takes its existence and meaning. After Plotinus' death, his teaching was continued by his disciples Porphyry and Iamblichus; its last great expression as an independent philosophy was in the work of Proclus (411–485), after which it was integrated into Christian thought.[3] Plotinus' vast influence extends from Augustine, Macrobius, Boethius, and medieval Christian Platonism through Italian Renaissance humanism, the seventeenth-century Cambridge Platonists, and the Romantic poets to modern thinkers and critics such as William James, Henri Bergson, A. N. Whitehead, and Harold Bloom.

While Plotinus basically accepts Plato's division of the world into a higher intellectual realm of eternal Forms and a lower sensible world of time and change, what distinguishes his scheme from Plato's is his elaboration of a more refined hierarchy of levels of reality. His scheme can be represented as follows:

The One
Embodies: Unity/Truth/Origin/Good
Is Source of Essence and Existence

Eternal

Act/Utterance
Divine Mind: Presides Over
Intellectual Realm

"There"

Act/Utterance
Inner   Soul
All-Soul/World-Soul/Great Soul   Humans
Outer (Nature-Principle)   Body

"Here"   World of Matter, Sense, Time

According to Plotinus, all the phases of existence emanate from the divinity; the goal of all things is ultimately to return to the divine. Reality is basically divided into an eternal spiritual and intellectual realm (which consists of the One, the Intellectual Realm and the All-Soul), and a physical realm of matter, sense, space, and time. Human beings belong to both of these worlds: their souls belong to the higher realm of All-Soul, while their bodies occupy the spatial and temporal world of matter, sense, and extension. The task of philosophy is to facilitate the soul's transcendence of the physical realm, to rise to intellectual intuition and ultimately to attain an ecstatic and mystical union with the One.

In Plotinus' system, the divinity itself is a hierarchical triad expressed in three principles or "hypostases": the One, the Divine Mind or Intellect, and the All-Soul. The One can also be termed the Absolute, the Good, or the Father. From this One emanates the Divine Mind which presides over the realm of Divine Thought or Intellection (this intellectual realm is equivalent to Plato's Ideas or Forms). The intellectual forms in this realm are the archetypes of all that exists in the lower, sensible sphere. Moreover, the Divine Intelligence is an expression of the One which is unknowable by mere intellect or reason. From the Divine Mind emanates the All-Soul, or Soul of all things. The All-Soul has three phases: the intellective soul, which contemplates the Divine Thought of the intellectual realm; the Reasoning Soul, which generates the sensible universe on the model of the archetypes in the intellectual realm; and the Unreasoning Soul, which is the principle of animal life. Hence the All-Soul forms and orders the physical world. Unlike Plato, Plotinus does not view these relationships as imitation; rather each phase is an "emanation" from the preceding phase, retaining the latter's archetypal imprint as a goal to which it must return on its path toward its ultimate reunion with the One.

Plotinus' views of art and beauty must be understood in the context of his scheme as outlined above. In his essay "On the Intellectual Beauty," he establishes that beauty is ideal: in other words, it belongs essentially to the realm of ideas, rather than the realm of sensible, physical objects. And as an idea it is more beautiful in its pure form than when it is mingled with matter. Indeed, it is only as an idea that beauty can enter the mind. Hence, beauty is not in the concrete object but in "soul or mind" (*Enneads*, V.viii.2).

Plotinus explains the origin of beauty with reference to his cosmological hierarchy. The Nature, he says, which creates beautiful things must itself be produced by a "far earlier beauty." The "Nature-Principle" (which lies below the level of the All-Soul) contains "an Ideal archetype of the beauty that is found in material forms." But this archetype itself has its source in a still more beautiful archetype in Soul. And this archetype, in turn, has its source in the Intellectual-Principle, in the realm of pure intellectual Forms. Plotinus' term for this intellectual realm is "There." He designates the sensible world as "Here" (*Enneads*, V.viii.3). The world of "There" or the intellectual realm is a world of complete unity, where all the beings merge into an infinite divine identity. Moreover, the wisdom of "There" is "not a wisdom built up by reasonings but complete from the beginning." It is a unity, complete, self-enclosed, and acting as the measure of all subsequent wisdom. Plotinus calls this "wisdom in unity" (*Enneads*, V.viii.4, 6).

In the world of "Here," the sensible world, things are very different. Everything is "partial," including our knowledge, which exists as "a mass of theorems and an accumulation of propositions" (*Enneads*, V.viii.4). The kind of wisdom we possess is only an image of the original "wisdom in unity," an image that reproduces the original in discursive form, in language, using reasoning (*Enneads*, V.viii.6). The one exception to this limitation lies in art: the artist goes back to "that wisdom in Nature," enjoying a more direct intuitive access into that earlier wisdom than the philosopher or scientist (*Enneads*, V.viii.5). Earthly beauty, then, derives from the perfect beauty of the divine world. Whereas Plato sees poetry as appealing to man's lower nature, his desires and passions, Plotinus sees in art a means of access to the divine world, based on art's reproduction of the beauty of that world, a beauty discernible not to the senses and passions but to the intellect. Where Plato thought of art as imitating what was already an imitation (of eternal Forms), Plotinus sees art as directly imitating the Forms themselves, with a directness inaccessible to the discursive reasoning of philosophy.

Plotinus ends his treatise with what is perhaps one of the most beautiful and insightful passages ever composed by a philosopher. The perception of beauty is not a passive act, of gazing upon a beautiful object that is external to the spectator. If our souls are "penetrated by this beauty," we cannot remain mere gazers, mere spectators: "one must bring the vision within and see no longer in that mode of separation but as we know ourselves" (*Enneads*, V.viii.10). Plotinus offers an account of mystical union with God. If we submit ourselves to the vision of God, we will lose our own self, and be unable to see our own image; possessed by God, we will see our own image "lifted to a better beauty"; progressing further, we will "sink into a perfect self-identity," forming "a multiple unity with the God silently present" (*Enneads*, V.viii.11). Hence the first stage of this ascent to union with God is separation, a state in which we are aware of self; but if we turn away from sense and desire, we become "one in the Divine": instead of remaining in the mode of separation, of mere spectator, we ourselves become "the seen," the object of our own vision or self-knowledge. So, truly to know beauty is to *become* it: we must put behind us reliance on sense or sight, which "deals with the external." Plotinus states that we are "most completely aware of ourselves when we are most completely identified with the object of our knowledge" (*Enneads*, V.viii.11). In these passages, Plotinus anticipates not only numerous forms of mysticism, both Christian and Islamic, but also the thought of Kant and Hegel who regard all consciousness as self-consciousness. For Plotinus, knowledge – of beauty or anything else – is a form of interaction, a mode of unity rather than separation, a manner of internalizing the object and being transformed by it, a process of mutual adaptation of self and object, losing the one in the other, in a merged identity.

Macrobius (b. ca. 360)

Another influential Neo-Platonic vision and perspective toward literature is contained in two texts by Macrobius that were widely influential in the

Middle Ages, the *Saturnalia* (ca. 395) and *Commentary on the Dream of Scipio* (ca. 400). The latter came to be regarded for many centuries as an authoritative account of the significance of dreams. Much later, Freud was rightly to remark that ancient cultures attached various kinds of serious significance to dreams whereas modern science had relegated them to the realm of superstition.

Macrobius' *Commentary* takes as its starting point Cicero's work *De republica* (the *Republic*). The last book of this treatise narrates a dream of Scipio Africanus the Younger, a Roman general, in which he is visited by his grandfather Scipio Africanus the Elder, the famous general who defeated the Carthaginian leader Hannibal. Macrobius' text, while ostensibly analyzing Scipio's dream, engages far broader issues. Its explanation of the Neo-Platonic scheme of reality and knowledge was influential through the Middle Ages; it considers the connections between literary and philosophical language, between figurative or allegorical uses of language and their role in providing an avenue to the truths of the higher realm; finally, it provides a systematic account of the meaning of dreams.

Scipio's dream in Cicero's text offers a poignant summary of a medieval cosmology that was influential for many centuries:

> These are the nine circles, or rather spheres, by which the whole is joined. One of them, the outermost, is that of heaven; it contains all the rest, and is itself the supreme God, holding and embracing within itself all the other spheres; in it are fixed the eternal revolving courses of the stars. Beneath it are seven other spheres which revolve in the opposite direction to that of heaven. One of these globes is that light which on earth is called Saturn's. Next comes the star called Jupiter's, which brings fortune and health to mankind. Beneath it is that star, red and terrible to the dwellings of man, which you assign to Mars. Below it and almost midway of the distance is the Sun, the lord, chief, and ruler of the other lights, the mind and guiding principle of the universe, of such magnitude that he reveals and fills all things with his light. He is accompanied by his companions, as it were – Venus and Mercury in their orbits, and in the lowest sphere revolves the Moon, set on fire by the rays of the Sun. But below the Moon there is nothing except what is mortal and doomed to decay, save only the souls given to the human race by the bounty of the gods, while above the Moon all things are eternal. For the ninth and central sphere, which is the earth, is immovable and the lowest of all, and toward it all ponderable bodies are drawn by their own natural tendency downward.[4]

This vision was highly influential in the Middle Ages, underlying the widespread notion that occurrences in the world have not only a literal significance in earthly terms, but also an even greater significance that reverberates through the higher realms.

Boethius (ca. 480–524)

The Roman philosopher Boethius had a seminal impact on medieval thinking, especially in the field of logic. He translated the four logical treatises comprising Aristotle's *Organon*, and also translated and commented on Porphyry's *Introduction to the Categories of Aristotle*. He composed five essays on logic. Also of vast influence was *The Consolation of Philosophy* (524), where Boethius places his own life within the larger context of questions about God's providence, the injustice of the world, human free will and the order and purpose of the world. He expresses, through a character who personifies philosophy, the following poem which was widely influential through the Middle Ages:

> Oh God, Maker of heaven and earth, Who govern the world with eternal reason, at your command time passes from the beginning. You place all things in motion, though You are yourself without change. No external causes impelled you to make this work from chaotic matter. Rather it was the form of the highest good, existing within You without envy, which caused you to fashion all things according to the eternal exemplar. You who are most beautiful produce the beautiful world from your divine mind and, forming it in your image, You order the perfect parts in a perfect whole.
>
> You bind the elements in harmony so that cold and heat, dry and wet are joined, and the purer fire does not fly up through the air, nor the earth sink beneath the weight of water.
>
> You release the world-soul throughout the harmonious parts of the universe as your surrogate, threefold in its operations, to give motion to all things...
>
> ... The sight of Thee is beginning and end; one guide, leader, path, and goal.[5]

The characteristic medieval notions expressed here include: divine reason ruling the world; God as the "unmoved Mover"; the intrinsic beauty of the created world; the relation of the four elements; the Neo-Platonic notion of the World-Soul as intermediary between God and material things; and the circle of beginning and end, whereby God is not only the source but the end and goal of all created things. This vision remained deeply ingrained within the medieval psyche for many centuries.

Notes

1. Horace, *The Art of Poetry*, trans. Burton Raffel (Albany, NY: State University of New York Press, 1974), pp. 196–201. Hereafter cited as *AP*, using line numbers.

2. *Aristotle: Poetics; Longinus: On the Sublime; Demetrius: On Style*, trans. Stephen Halliwell, W. Hamilton Fyfe, Doreen C. Innes, and W. Rhys Roberts (Cambridge, MA and London: Harvard University Press/Heinemann, 1996), I.3–4.
3. "Introduction," in *The Essence of Plotinus: Extracts from the Six Enneads and Porphyry's Life of Plotinus*, trans. Stephen Mackenna, ed. Grace H. Turnbull (New York and Oxford: Oxford University Press, 1948), pp. xvi–xix. Hereafter cited as *Enneads*.
4. Cicero, *De re publica; De legibus*, trans. Clinton Walker Keyes (Cambridge, MA and London: Harvard University Press/Heinemann, 1966), VI.xvii.
5. Boethius, *The Consolation of Philosophy*, trans. Richard H. Green (New York: Dover, 2002), 53–54.

Part II

The Medieval Era

Chapter 4

The Early Middle Ages

Historical Background

Until quite recently, the Middle Ages were perceived as an era of darkness, ignorance, and superstition. The term "Middle Age" (*medium aevum*) was devised by Italian humanist thinkers who wished to demarcate their own period – of renaissance, rebirth, and rediscovery of classical thinkers – from the preceding era. The Renaissance humanists' rejection of medieval thought was reinforced by the Protestant Reformation which associated it with Roman Catholicism.[1] While it is true that the early Middle Ages, from the fall of Rome at the hands of Germanic tribes in the fifth century until around AD 1000, saw a reversion to various forms of economic and intellectual primitivism, recent scholarship has shown that much Renaissance thought and culture was in fact a development from the medieval period, which was by no means ignorant of the Classical Greek and Roman traditions.

A number of factors contributed to the making of the Middle Ages: the evolving traditions of Christianity; the social and political patterns of the Germanic tribes who overran the Roman Empire; vestiges of the Roman administrative and legal system; the legacy of the classical world; and contact with Islamic civilization (which lies beyond the scope of this study). The most powerful force in the development of medieval civilization was Christianity. Even before the fall of Rome in 410, Christianity had been increasingly tolerated, as stipulated in a series of edicts, initiated by the emperor Constantine, from 313 onward; by 381 it was recognized as the official religion of the Roman Empire.

Early Christianity had been heterogeneous, containing a large number of sects with disparate beliefs and practices. The Arians and Nestorians, for example, rejected the notion of the Trinity which was advocated by the Athanasians. The Docetae and Basilidans rejected the factuality of Christ's crucifixion. The Pelagians denied the notion of original sin and espoused human free will. In order to settle these doctrinal disputes, a number of

Literary Criticism from Plato to the Present: An Introduction   M. A. R. Habib
© 2011 M. A. R. Habib

worldwide Church councils were convened, beginning with the Council of Nicaea in 325, which condemned the views of most of these sects as heretical and established the Athanasian view of the Trinity as orthodox Christian doctrine. The doctrine of the Incarnation was not formally adopted until the Council of Chalcedon in 451. These debates were shaped by such figures as Athanasius of Alexandria (293–373), Gregory of Nyssa, St. Basil (ca. 330–379), Gregory of Nazianzus (ca. 330–ca. 389), John Chrysostom (ca. 347–407), Ambrose (ca. 339–397), and Augustine of Hippo (354–430). One of the greatest Christian thinkers of this period was Jerome (ca. 347–420), who translated the Bible from its original languages into Latin (known as the Vulgate edition). Other steps were taken to promote unity of belief and practice: the promulgation of standard sermons, the training of bishops, and the growth of the papacy in power and prestige into a focus of allegiance and obedience. Having said this, Christian doctrine was never fully formalized in the early Middle Ages, and many of the Eastern churches adhered to unorthodox beliefs. It took further ecumenical councils until 681 for major schisms between the churches at Rome and Constantinople to be healed.

Notwithstanding these difficulties, after the collapse of the empire it was left to the Church to preserve unity, order, and guidance in many spheres. It was the Church, increasingly sophisticated in its organization and increasingly dominated by the leadership of the pope in Rome, which promoted moral values, fostered appropriate social conduct, and transmitted classical learning. Latin remained the language of scholarship and law during the Middle Ages. One particularly important aspect of Christianity was monasticism, with its roots in early Christian asceticism. Founded in the East by St. Basil and in the West by St. Benedict, monasticism entailed a strict regimen of poverty, obedience, humility, labor, and devotion. It was largely monks who were responsible for writing books, transmitting early manuscripts and maintaining schools, libraries, and hospitals. The monks would later develop into the regular clergy (following a strict rule or *regula*), as opposed to the secular clergy who operated in the worldly sphere (*saeculum* meaning "world" or "time").

Another force which overwhelmed the Western Roman Empire was the Germanic tribes, who included Scandinavians, Goths, Vandals, Franks, and Anglo-Saxons. Many of these peoples had already settled in various parts of the Empire long before the fall of Rome. Eventually revolting against Roman rule, the Visigoths led by Alaric sacked Rome in 410 BC. The city was taken again by the Vandals in AD 455. The lifestyle, as well as the legal, economic, and political structure of the Germanic peoples, was primitive in many respects. This structure, amalgamating with the administrative legacy of the Roman Empire, eventually developed into the system of feudalism, which involved contractual obligations between rulers and subjects, lords and vassals, obligations based on values such as courage, honor, loyalty, protection, and obedience. We see these values repeatedly expressed in poems such as *Beowulf*, often in uneasy commerce with Christian values such as humility and trust in divine providence. In the early Middle Ages, commerce and industry declined, and land became increasingly concentrated in the hands of a few, with famine and disease often widespread. The economic system was limited largely to local trade. Ancient Roman culture gave way before a life centered on villages, feudal estates, and monasteries. This hierarchical and largely static way of life was sanctioned by the Church; the social order, where each person had his place, was seen as part of the larger, divinely established, cosmic order.

Intellectual and Theological Currents

Christianity and classicism

The intellectual currents of the early Middle Ages were driven by two broad factors: the heritage of classical thought, and the varying relation of developing Christian theology to this heritage. The secular critics of the late Roman period included some influential figures: Macrobius and Servius, who contributed to the prestige of Vergil and the knowledge of Neo-Platonism, Servius also being the author of the standard grammar of this period; the grammarian Aelius Donatus, who wrote handbooks entitled *Ars minor* and *Ars maior*, used throughout the Middle Ages; Priscian, whose *Institutio grammatica* was also widely used; and Diomedes, who produced an exhaustive account of grammatical tropes and poetic genres. Vergil was the basic text in schools of grammar, while Cicero held a privileged place in the teaching of rhetoric. One of the rhetoricians of the early fifth century, Martianus Capella, was known in the Middle Ages by his authoritative encyclopedia of the seven liberal arts. Later influential encyclopedias were produced by Cassiodorus and Isidore of Seville who transmitted "the sum of late antique knowledge to posterity."[2] These compendia anticipated the eventual formalization of the liberal arts curriculum at medieval universities. Of these developments, two were especially germane to the early Middle Ages: Neo-Platonism (which, beginning prior to the Middle Ages, is considered in the previous chapter) and the closely related Christian tradition of allegorical interpretation, as embodied in the work of Augustine, which will be considered below.

In the early Middle Ages, the Church's "other-worldly" disposition tended to subordinate the position of literature and the arts to the more pressing issues of salvation and preparation for the next life. In general, the widespread instability, insecurity, and illiteracy intensified religious feeling and promoted ideals of withdrawal from the world, condemning earthly life as worthless and merely a means of passage to the next life, to eternal salvation and bliss. As the theological content of Christianity developed, two broad approaches to classical literature emerged. The first of these sought to distance Christianity from paganism and accordingly frowned on the pagan origins of the arts in the cultures of Greece and Rome, while the second sought to continue the Christian appropriation of classical rhetoric and philosophy. The former stream of Christian thought, deriving from the third-century theologian Tertullian (ca. 160–ca. 225) and enduring until the last patristic author Pope Gregory the Great (540–604), laid stress on the authority of faith and revelation over reason. Both Tertullian and Gregory renounced all secular knowledge and viewed literature as a foolish pursuit. The ascetic dispositions of monasticism intensified Christian anxiety concerning worldly beauty and art: St. Jerome, St. Basil, St. Bernard, and St. Francis all turned away from the beauty of nature as a distraction from the contemplation of things divine. Christian thinkers such as Boethius also echoed Plato's concern that the arts expressed unsavory emotions and that they could seduce men from the righteous path. There was also in the eighth and ninth centuries an "iconoclastic controversy" concerning the portrayal of images. Christians held that it debased their spiritual doctrines to represent them to the senses. It was not until the Council of Nicaea in 787 that devotional images were deemed a legitimate resource for religious instruction.

The second stream of Christian thought, from its beginnings in the letters of St. Paul and the Gospel of St. John, through the third-century Alexandrian theologians Clement and Origen, displayed a rationalist emphasis and attempted to reconcile ancient Greek thought with the tenets of Christianity. Clement believed that reason was necessary for the understanding of scripture, and that the Greek philosophers had anticipated the Christian conception of God. Origen (ca. 185–ca. 254) was the Greek author of *On First Principles*, the first systematic account of Christian theology. The most renowned biblical scholar of the early Church, Origen formulated a vastly influential system of allegorical interpretation, according to three levels – literal, moral, and theological – corresponding to the composition of man as body, soul, and spirit. This stream of thought continued through Gregory of Nazianzus, Gregory of Nissa, John Chrysostom, and Ambrose, reaching unprecedented heights in the work of St. Augustine, St. Bonaventura, and St. Thomas Aquinas. These thinkers had a more accommodating view of classical learning and literature. While poetry and history gained some acceptance, the Church remained for a long time opposed to drama, as well as to visual art, which was associated with idolatry. Augustine referred to stage-plays as "spectacles of uncleanness[3]" whose speeches were "smoke and wind.[4]"

George Kennedy usefully suggests that the Christian Fathers writing prior to the Council of Nicaea in 325 exhibited a broad agreement on certain general principles: that a Christian must acquire literacy, which must entail some reading of classical texts; that examples can be taken from classical works, and read allegorically so as to accord with Christian teaching; that classical philosophy and literature do contain certain truths; and that the Bible, being divinely inspired, is true at a literal level, but also harbors moral and theological levels of meaning.[5] In fact, it might be argued that Christian allegory had its origins in the need to confront classical thought, as well as in the imperative to reconcile the Old and New Testaments. We can now consider how these attempts toward synthesis were given a classic formulation by St. Augustine.

St. Augustine (354–430)

It is in Augustine's work (along with that of later writers such as Aquinas and Dante) that the profoundest synthesis of classical and Christian notions occurred. More than any other early Christian thinker, Augustine influenced the traditions of both Roman Catholic and Protestant thought. Chief of the Latin Church Fathers, he was born in North Africa. After studying in Carthage, Rome, and Milan, he was made bishop of Hippo in 395. In his *Confessions* (400), Augustine described the long and arduous process of his conversion to Christianity, a path which had included belief in Manicheism and skepticism. He expounded his theology in *City of God* (412–427), where he viewed human history as the unfolding of a divine plan. Here he was essentially defending Christianity against those who attributed the fall of Rome to the abandonment of the pagan gods. Augustine's views often accommodate those of Plato, whom he regarded as the greatest philosopher. But he subordinated philosophy to divine revelation, urging that the task of reason was to promote a clearer understanding of things already accepted on faith. He affirmed the supreme importance of original sin as responsible for man's departure from God and the depraved state of human nature. The cause of original sin, he affirmed, was pride, which he equated with man's self-love and desire for self-sufficiency, whereby man regards himself as his own light. Augustine divided spiritual life into the "earthly city," characterized by "self-love reaching the point of contempt for God," and the "Heavenly city," which rests on "the love of God carried as far as contempt of self" (*CG*, XIV.10–14). Though Augustine does not deny human free will (since it was man's depraved will which led to the original sin), he is often characterized as believing in determinism since only those who belong to the heavenly city, the elect, will attain salvation. The elect are chosen not on account of their goodness but for unknown reasons. This deterministic doctrine, originating in St. Paul, was later revived by Calvin. Augustine asserts that only God can restore the natural state of goodness in which man was created. The vehicle for man's redemption from sin is the Incarnation; only through Christ, who is the "mediator between God and men," can man have access to grace.

In his *Confessions* Augustine had retrospectively regretted his own "foolish" immersion in classical literature (*Confessions*, I.xiii; III.ii). He condemned liberal studies, suggesting that only the scriptures were truly liberating. While he sympathized with Plato's arguments for banishing poets and dramatists on moral grounds, his views of poetry's connection with truth were somewhat different. He suggests that paintings, sculptures, and plays were necessarily false, not from any intention to be such but merely from inability to be that which they represent. Paradoxically, the artist cannot be true to his artistic intent unless he enacts falsehood. One of the problems of medieval aesthetics was to reconcile earthly beauty with spiritual preoccupations. For Augustine and other medieval philosophers such as Albertus Magnus and Bonaventura, beauty was not specifically concerned with physical objects; rather, it implied a relationship of harmony between certain terms, whether these were material, intellectual, or spiritual. Influenced by Cicero, Augustine viewed the essential elements of beauty as, firstly, harmonious wholeness and, secondly, unity of parts which are ordered in due proportion (*Confessions*, IV.xiii).

Augustine's aesthetics rely on a modified Platonic framework appealing to a higher spiritual realm to which the physical world is subordinated. As such, art, composed of sensuous elements, was assigned a lower degree of reality than spiritual life, far removed from God, the ultimate source of being, and the ultimate standard of reality. The early Church, then, harbored a metaphysical idealism descended in part from Plato, insisting that reality is spiritual and that sense-perception and observation of the world were not reliable avenues to truth. However, the world of matter was not rejected as unreal but was admitted into the divine scheme of creation, occupying nonetheless a humble position. The beauty of earthly things was viewed as an expression of their divine origin, and rested on their unity – a unity in diversity – which imitated the Oneness of God. This relation expressed the medieval Christian vision of the One and the Many: it is ultimately God's unity which confers unity and harmony on the vast diversity of the world. The world is God's poem which proclaims its beauty through harmony and correct proportion (*CG*, XI.18).

Augustine's strategy of adapting classical thought and literature to Christian purposes is expressed in his important work *De doctrina christiana* [*On Christian Doctrine*] (397–426). In this text are some surprisingly modern insights. Augustine initially distinguishes between signs and things: "every sign is also a thing . . . but not every thing is also a sign."[6] He asserts that some things are for use while others are for enjoyment. The only objects for pure enjoyment are God and those which are "eternal and unchangeable" (*DDC*, I.22). All other objects are for use, being merely the means whereby we arrive at enjoyment of God (*DDC*, I.22). The distinction between use and enjoyment embraces the distinctions of means and end, adjective and substantive, temporal and eternal, physical and spiritual, journey and goal. Essentially, these distinctions are based on a broad distinction of "this-worldliness" and "other-worldliness" that was central to Christian theology for centuries: this world can never rise above the status of a means; even the beauty of the world can never be an end in itself. The world is thus divested of any *literal* significance: its meaning resides not in its isolated parts nor even in the system of relations connecting all of its parts, but in its potential to point beyond itself to what it signifies in another realm, a transcendent goal. No object in the world can have any significance, importance, or meaning except in reference to God. Only God is to be loved for his own sake, and all other things are to be loved in reference to God (*DDC*, I.27).

Hence, according to Augustine, the world as experienced by a Christian is not essentially a thing or a series of things since it is transformed into a sign or a series of signs (*DDC*, I.13). Many centuries before Saussure, Augustine distinguished between natural and conventional signs, the former embodying no human intention (as when smoke signals fire) and the latter devised by human beings to communicate (*DDC*, II.1–2). Even the signs given by God in the scriptures, says Augustine, were made known through men, and need to be studied. The difficulties of scripture, he thinks, spring largely from two sources, unknown and ambiguous signs. The main remedy is knowledge of the languages of scripture (Latin, Hebrew, Greek); Augustine even admits that a diversity of interpretations is useful inasmuch as these will often throw light on obscure passages (*DDC*, II.11, 12). Nonetheless, we must "believe that whatever is there written, even though it be hidden, is better and truer than anything we could devise by our own wisdom" (*DDC*, II.7). Hence, knowledge is viewed as a closed system, bounded by God's omniscience and foreknowledge. What would otherwise be the conventional nature of human knowledge is forever a partial emulation of, and aspiration after, what is already known to God.

Augustine is concerned to furnish rules which will guide the reader in knowing whether to interpret given passages of scripture literally or figuratively. The general rule is that whatever passage taken literally is inconsistent with either "purity of life" or "soundness of doctrine" must be taken as figurative (*DDC*, III.10). Augustine warns against taking a figurative expression literally. It is "a miserable slavery of the soul," he says, "to take signs for things, and to be unable to lift the eye of the mind above what is corporeal and created, that it may drink in eternal light" (*DDC*, III.5). These comments throw an interesting light on the foundations of Christian allegory. Literal meaning, whereby "things are to be understood just as they are expressed" (*DDC*, III.37), corresponds with the realm of materiality and bodily sensation. Figurative expressions, "in which one thing is expressed and another is to be understood," attempts to raise perception toward a spiritual and intellectual realm. Literal meaning is arrested at the opacity of "things" whereby figurative meaning looks *through* things, treating them as only signs of more exalted levels of truth, abolishing the thinghood of the world and imbuing it with a symbolic significance which refers all of its elements to the life hereafter. Thus is laid the foundation of various levels of meaning in allegory. All significant knowledge and wisdom is contained in the scriptures, which were inspired by the Holy Spirit; men can use their human faculty of reason and various branches of secular knowledge to a certain degree in understanding the Word of God. But ultimately, this Word stands above human language and reason, and men must ascend allegorically from a literal understanding of their world to a symbolic view of it as a small part in a vast scheme which both subsumes and gives meaning to it. The *world* must be understood as the *Word* of God.

Augustine advises that pagan knowledge, if useful, should be appropriated for Christian use (*DDC*, II.31). But he cautions: "whatever man may have learnt from other sources than Scripture, if it is hurtful, it is there condemned; if it is useful, it is therein contained" (*DDC*, II.42). In the final book of *De Doctrina* Augustine establishes that it is lawful for a Christian teacher to use the art of rhetoric. However, while eloquence is useful to the Christian preacher, it is less important than wisdom, especially since the wisdom being dispensed is not human wisdom but a "heavenly wisdom which comes down from the Father," The Christian preacher, then, is but a minister of this higher wisdom (*DDC*, IV.5). If the preacher can speak with eloquence as well as wisdom, however, he will be of greater service. Augustine's view of truth itself as the basis of good style underlies his new, Christianized, definition of rhetoric (*DDC*, IV.28).

Notes

1. *Cambridge Companion to Aquinas*, ed. Norman Kretzmann and Eleonore Stump (Cambridge: Cambridge University Press, 1993), pp. 4–5.
2. Ernst Robert Curtius, *European Literature and the Latin Middle Ages*, trans. Willard R. Trask (London: Routledge and Kegan Paul, 1979), p. 23.
3. St. Augustine, *City of God*, trans. Henry Bettenson (Harmondsworth: Penguin, 1984), I.31. Hereafter cited as *CG*.
4. *The Confessions of St. Augustine*, trans. Rex Warner (New York: Mentor, 1963), I.xvii.
5. George Kennedy, ed., *The Cambridge History of Literary Criticism: Volume I: Classical Criticism* (Cambridge: Cambridge University Press, 1997), pp. 339–340.
6. Saint Augustine, *De Doctrina Christiana* (Calvin College: Christian Classics Ethereal Library, 2003), I.2. This translation, which I find to be particularly effective, is in the public domain and can be found in electronic format at: www.ccel.org/ccel/augustine/doctrine.iii.html. Hereafter cited as *DDC*.

Chapter 5

The Later Middle Ages

Historical Background

During the early Middle Ages it had largely been left to the Church (and certain rulers such as Charlemagne) to attempt some kind of social and moral cohesion and to preserve and transmit the various intellectual and literary traditions. The later Middle Ages, beginning around 1050, witnessed considerable progress on many levels. Most fundamentally, there was an economic revival. It was in this period that the system of feudalism achieved a relatively stable formation. The term "feudalism" derives from the word "fief" (the medieval term being *feudum* or "feud"), which means a piece of land held in "fee": in other words, the land was not owned, but a person had the right to cultivate it in return for rent or certain services performed for the landlord. Perry Anderson defines "fief" as "a delegated grant of land, vested with juridical and political powers, in exchange for military service."[1]

The basic contractual relation in feudal society was between a lord and a vassal: the lord, owning the land, would provide protection, in return for the vassal's obedience, taxes or rent, and military or other service. Usually, fiefs (tracts of land or certain offices) were hereditary, and the feudal system was in general a static hierarchy, ranging from the highest lord, the monarch, through the various ranks of nobility such as castellans, barons, counts, and principals to the knights. Hence, each member of this hierarchy was both a lord and a vassal, involved in an intricate nexus of relationships with those above and below him. In a broader sense, however, society was increasingly divided into two classes, the one a landed aristocracy and clergy, the other composed of the mass of peasants, with a small middle class of merchants, traders, and craftsmen. The peasantry itself existed as a hierarchy, from villeins or tenant farmers through serfs (who were bound to a particular tract of land) to the poorest people who hired out their labor on an occasional basis. Clearly, this legal and political structure, as Hegel would observe later, was not rational but an outgrowth of hereditary status, existing practices, traditions, and customs. The basic unit of production in

Literary Criticism from Plato to the Present: An Introduction   M. A. R. Habib
© 2011 M. A. R. Habib

the feudal system was the manor or manorial estate: this comprised the lord's manor house and demesne (that part of his land not held by tenants), the parish church, one or more villages, and the land divided into strips between a multitude of peasants. The manor was largely self-contained, self-governed, existing in relative economic isolation, with minimal foreign trade (*PF*, 137).

Another important element in feudalism was the city. By the later Middle Ages, significant urban communities had grown. Major European cities included Palermo, Venice, Florence, Milan, Ghent, Bruges, and Paris. Economically, the cities were dominated by two types of organizations – merchant guilds and artisan guilds – whose purpose was to regulate the means of production, attempting to preserve a stability and freedom from competition, with standard wages and prices, and even frowning on new technology or greater efficiency. The members of the artisan guilds formed a hierarchy composed of master craftsmen, who owned their own businesses, and the "journeymen" who worked for them, as well as the apprentices, for whose training and upbringing the masters were responsible. The guilds had a paternalistic attitude toward their members, sustaining them in times of hardship, providing for their widows and orphans, as well as exercising broader religious and social functions. The guild system rested partly on Christian doctrines, stemming from the Church fathers and Aquinas, which frowned on excessive wealth or private property, condemned usury or the taking of interest, advocated fair prices, and encouraged an orientation toward the welfare of the community as a whole rather than that of the individual. At least, these were the ideals in theory.

Intellectual Currents of the Later Middle Ages

The medieval curriculum

The major intellectual currents of this period were: various forms of humanism deriving from the classical grammatical tradition; the heritage of Neo-Platonism and allegorical criticism; and the movement known as scholasticism, based on a revived Aristotelianism mediated through Islamic thinkers such as Ibn Rushd (Averroës). These later intellectual streams were enabled by educational developments, primarily the rise of the cathedral schools and the universities.[2] The universities were usually composed of faculties of liberal arts as well as medicine, law, and theology. The notion of the liberal arts can be traced as far back as the Sophist Hippias of Elis, a contemporary of Socrates, as well as to the rhetorician Isocrates who opposed Plato's insistence on a purely philosophical training in favor of a broader system of education. The *locus classicus* for the system of *artes liberales* is a letter by the Roman thinker Seneca, who called these arts "liberal" because they are worthy of a free man, their purpose not being to make money.

By the end of antiquity, the number of the liberal arts had been fixed at seven, and arranged in the sequence that they were to retain through the medieval period. The first three – grammar, rhetoric, and dialectic (or logic) – were known from the ninth century onwards as the "trivium" ("three roads"); the remaining four mathematical arts – arithmetic, geometry, music, and astronomy – had been designated by Boethius as the "quadruvium" ("four roads"), later known as the "quadrivium." Of the seven liberal arts, the most exhaustively studied was grammar, which comprised the study of both language and the interpretation of literature. The authors studied included Vergil, Ovid, Donatus, Martianus Capella, Horace, Juvenal, Boethius, Statius, Terence, Lucan, Cicero, as well as Christian writers such as Juvencus, Arator, and Prudentius. This list continued to expand into the thirteenth century, with the pagan authors subjected to allegorical interpretation.

It was the authority of this curriculum which was dislodged by the dialectical or logical methods of the scholastic thinkers. As mentioned earlier, these rational methods had been fostered by the growth, from the beginning of the twelfth century, of the cathedral schools and the universities. The cathedral schools effectively displaced the surviving monasteries as centers of education. They were located in towns, the most renowned being at Paris, Chartres, and Canterbury. Perhaps the single greatest force animating these schools was the revival of philosophy, which, at the end of antiquity, had given way to the liberal arts. This revival was spearheaded in the late eleventh and early twelfth centuries by Anselm of Canterbury (1033–1109), the French theologian Roscelin (ca. 1045–ca. 1120), his student Peter Abelard (1079–1142), and the Italian theologian Peter Lombard (ca. 1100–1160). These were the pioneers of scholasticism. They drew on Boethius' logic to attempt a rational and coherent interpretation of Christian doctrine, viewing logic as the preeminent Christian science.

Even more important in this twelfth century "renaissance" of thought was the widespread growth of universities. Ancient universities had been largely devoted to the teaching of grammar and rhetoric. It was in the Middle Ages that our modern notion of the university was born, with various faculties, a regular curriculum and a hierarchy of degrees. The oldest universities were in Italy, France, and England, and included Bologna (1158), Oxford (ca. 1200), Paris (1208–1209), and Naples (1224). Through these universities swept the philosophy of the "new" Aristotle, the recently recovered works of Aristotle on natural history, metaphysics, ethics, and politics, made available to the West through translations from Arabic and Greek. The foremost of the Arab Aristotelian thinkers was Ibn Rushd (Averroës). At the instigation of the pope, the study of the "new" Aristotle was forbidden in 1215, but the stricture had little force. It was the Dominican scholars who attempted to reconcile the Christian faith with Greek philosophy.[3] Thus came into being the great impetus of scholasticism, reaching its height in Albertus Magnus and then his student Thomas Aquinas. By the efforts of the Dominicans at the University of Paris, "the dangerous Aristotle was purified, rehabilitated, and authorized. Even more: his teaching was incorporated into Christian philosophy and theology, and in this form has remained authoritative" (Curtius, 56). This new prominence of philosophy and theology pushed the study of grammar, rhetoric, and literature somewhat into the background.

A historical overview of medieval criticism

The various kinds of medieval criticism can be classified in terms of the broad divisions of knowledge in the curriculum. All three elements of the medieval *trivium – grammatica, rhetorica, dialectica –* were sciences of language and discourse, concerned with interpretation and signification; their boundaries often overlapped and the status and placement of literature was often disputed. Since the late classical era, poetry had been treated as a branch of rhetoric; in the later Middle Ages, the study of poetry was increasingly absorbed under grammar, but in the hands of scholastic thinkers it became part of the province of logic or dialectic. These various streams of medieval criticism can now be examined through one or two of the major writers representing each tendency. We can begin by considering the medieval disposition to situate literature within the entire scheme of knowledge, as in the work of Hugh of St. Victor. We can then consider the nature and value of the grammar curriculum (of which literature was an important part) in the work of John of Salisbury. We can then proceed to the placement of poetry first within rhetoric (in the texts of Geoffrey de Vinsauf) and then within logic (as expressed in the scholastic thinkers Ibn Rushd and Aquinas, as well as in Dante); and finally, we can see the placement of poetry as a part of philosophy or theology in the writings of Boccaccio and Christine de Pisan who effect a humanistic revival of allegorical traditions.

The Traditions of Medieval Criticism

Literature and grammar

Most of the intellectual currents of the Middle Ages are founded on the grammatical tradition of textual exegesis or interpretation, extended by Christian scholars to scriptural exegesis. Poetry was seen as a part of grammar, a fact which spawned three kinds of treatise. The first was the *commentary* or *gloss*. In medieval manuscripts the pages had wide margins to accommodate substantial commentary; this fostered a textual fluidity and a blurring of boundaries between text and commentary. The text was elaborately encoded – and even contained – within a broader system of meaning handed down by traditional interpretation.[4] A second type of grammatical treatise was the *ars metrica* (metrical art), since the grammar curriculum included prosody and a study of the standard poetic forms. Notable among medieval Latin treatises of this type was Dante's *De Vulgari Eloquentia* (ca. 1304–1307). The third type of grammatical treatise was the *accessus* or "prologue" to an author.

All three types of grammatical treatise – the commentary, the *ars metrica*, and the *accessus* – were vehicles of medieval humanism.[5] It should be said that medieval grammar or *grammatica* was much broader than our modern notion of "grammar," and has great importance in the entire scheme of medieval thought and ideology. As Martin Irvine has recently argued, from late classical times until the early Renaissance, grammar had a foundational role, furnishing a model of learning, interpretation, and knowledge. It was a social practice that provided exclusive access to literacy, the understanding of scripture, knowledge of the literary canon, and membership of an international Latin textual community. *Grammatica* was sustained by the dominant social and political institutions of medieval Europe; in turn, *grammatica* functioned in support of those institutions: the courts, cathedrals, and all the major centers of power. As such, the authority of *grammatica* was a textual reflex of religious and political authority (*GLT*, 2, 13, 20).

Anticipating modern literary theory, *grammatica* had many centuries earlier replaced the world of things by the world of signs; it had already reduced thinghood to language, in a vast and hierarchical system of signification that spanned many levels. This system was just as relational as any view of language to be found in Saussure. In other words, no element in that system was presumed to have any isolated or independent significance. In all these ways, medieval literary theory was far more sophisticated – and more foundational in our own ways of thinking – than was previously thought.

Literature in the Scheme of Human Learning: the Sacred Hermeneutics of Hugh of St. Victor (ca. 1097–1141)   The medieval tendency to situate literature as one component in an ordered and hierarchical scheme of learning was expressed in a widely influential educational treatise composed in the late 1120s by Hugh of St. Victor, the *Didascalicon* (a Greek word meaning "instructive" or "fit for teaching"). In general, Hugh argues that the ultimate purpose of all the arts is to "restore within us the divine likeness."[6] He provides a scheme for reading both secular texts and the sacred scriptures. Unlike many authors in the tradition of allegorical exegesis (such as Augustine, Bede, Aquinas, and Dante), Hugh proposes a threefold (rather than fourfold) understanding of scripture. Sacred scripture has "three ways of conveying meaning – namely, history, allegory and tropology." History represents the literal level of meaning; allegory refers to the spiritual or mystical sense; and tropology refers to the moral level of interpretation (*DHV*, V.ii).

Hugh insists that a literal or historical reading be mastered before proceeding to the other levels of allegorical interpretation. Summarizing the threefold layers of interpretation, he suggests that history provides "the means through which to admire God's deeds"; allegory, the means through which "to believe his mysteries"; and morality, the means to "imitate his perfection" (*DHV*, VI.iii). Hugh cautions against imposing our own opinion on the text: we should attempt to make our own thought identical with that of the scriptures, rather than coercing scripture into identity with our own thought (*DHV*, VI.xi). In all of these assumptions Hugh is effectively adhering to mainstream medieval literary critical practice: novelty and individuality are discouraged, and the meanings of words must be constrained ultimately by the semantic field circumscribed by scripture.

Defending and Defining the Grammar Curriculum: John of Salisbury (ca. 1115–1180)   The work of John of Salisbury was symptomatic of the broadening of the grammar curriculum in the twelfth century and the revived centrality of logic. John's *Metalogicon* (1159) is not only a defense of grammar, logic, and rhetoric, but also an attempt to define these disciplines and their interconnection. He articulates the overwhelming importance of the grammar curriculum: "Grammar is the cradle of all philosophy, and ... the first nurse of the whole study of letters ... it fosters and protects the philosopher from the start to the finish [of his pursuits]."[7] John insists that the study of poetry belongs to grammar. Moreover, it is precisely the system of grammar that is the index of civilization and its distinctness from barbarianism (*ML*, 51–52).

An important principle of analysis for John is that a text should be analyzed in such a way that "the author's meaning is always preserved." The text should be "studied with sympathetic mildness, and not tortured on the rack" (*ML*, 146, 148). Typically of medieval exposition, there is much emphasis on authorial intention. A further principle is the imitation of distinguished authors, in an endeavor to educate students not only in technical skills but also in fostering faith and morality (*ML*, 68–69). Also characteristic of medieval educational methods was obliging students to memorize passages from the eminent authors. Such emphasis on imitation of past masters means effectively that the authorized modes of viewing the world are already determined and classified; all the student can do is to emulate precisely and repeat these world views, not only installed within his memory but codified by grammar and rhetoric so as to determine from the depths of the classical past the fundamental features of any future composition (*ML*, 92).

John regards language as enjoying an intimate correspondence with reality or the world of objects, a correspondence authorized ultimately by God, by the "thoughts of the Most High" (*ML*, 262–263). Human learning and the human faculties of perception are gradated within this divine plan. Our knowledge of the material world, says John, begins with our senses; the imagination operates upon and orders the data received by sensation; our faculty of reason transcends sense-perception and contemplates heavenly things; our highest faculty is a kind of intuitive understanding which leads to a spiritual wisdom (*ML*, 227–230). Our reason itself is divinely endowed: we possess reason because we participate in the "original reason," which is the "wisdom of God" (*ML*, 225). Hence all human learning – which must be directed by our striving toward goodness and wisdom – is circumscribed, from the outset, by religious categories. And it is the original reason of God which "embraces the nature, development, and ultimate end of all things" (*ML*, 250). All in all, the *Metalogicon* provides us with a revealing picture not only of the medieval curriculum but also of the religious world view and the conceptions of human nature underlying this curriculum.

Literature and rhetoric

Much literary criticism of the classical period – including the work of Horace and "Longinus" – was actually rhetorical criticism applied to poetry. The heritage of rhetoric since late classical times included the system of the three styles (high, middle, low), the division of figures into schemes and tropes, the division of figures of thought from figures of speech, the relative importance of genius and art in poetic composition, the doctrine of imitation of the masterpieces, the distinction between content and language, as well as the concept of "decorum" or mutual suitability of form and content (*MLC*, 5). The concept of a sharp distinction between poetic and rhetoric was not even available until the renewed circulation of Aristotle's *Poetics* in the sixteenth century. The *artes poeticae* or manuals on the art of poetry were part of the grammar curriculum, even though they had been heavily influenced by rhetoric. One of the best examples of such manuals is Geoffrey de Vinsauf's *Poetria Nova*.

Geoffrey de Vinsauf (ca. 1200)   Geoffrey de Vinsauf derives his name (*de Vino Salvo* in Latin) from a treatise on the preservation of wine which was attributed to him. However, it was not wine but poetics which earned him renown.[8] His treatise *Poetria Nova* (*New Poetics*), designed to provide guidance in the rules and practice of poetry, along with the study and imitation of great poets, became one of the standard training manuals of poets in Europe from the thirteenth century until well into the Renaissance. Characteristically of medieval writers, Geoffrey viewed poetry as a branch of rhetoric, dividing his treatise according to the five rhetorical "offices" of invention, arrangement, style, memory, and delivery. Geoffrey's treatise *Poetria Nova* echoes the title of a rhetorical manual *Rhetorica Nova*, indicating that he wishes to propound a new poetics. It also echoes the title of Horace's *Ars poetica*, which was known in the Middle Ages as the *Poetria*. Like Horace's text, Geoffrey's treatise is written in Latin verse.

The bulk of Geoffrey's treatise is devoted to style and the various "ornaments" that create given styles in poetry. In contrast with the long tradition of aesthetics which saw poetry as mere imitation of nature, Geoffrey places considerable emphasis on the transformation of nature by poetry, and the need for the poet to attain novelty. The resources of art provide "a means of avoiding worn-out paths and of travelling a more distinguished route" (*PN*, IV.982–983). While much of Geoffrey's text clearly points to a more modern poetics, he nonetheless sustains the classical precepts of moderation, decorum, propriety, and the appeal to reason, as well as to the important classical distinction between prose and verse and a hierarchy of genres.

Literature and logic

Scholasticism initially worked with a commonly accepted background of Christian orthodoxy. However, during the twelfth and thirteen centuries the works of Aristotle, transmitted largely by the Islamic philosophers Ibn Rushd (Averroës) and Ibn Sina (Avicenna), were translated into Latin and became increasingly well known. Eventually, Aristotle was taken as the fundamental philosophical foundation of the scholastics, and he replaced Plato as the primary philosophical basis of Christian theology. The scholastic philosophers relied primarily on dialectic (logic) and syllogistic reasoning. By the fourteenth century, scholasticism was eclipsed by nominalism which, along with the work of thinkers such as Roger Bacon (ca. 1214–1294), paved the way for the more scientific tenor of Renaissance thought, and an increasing separation of philosophy and theology.

Scholasticism's emphasis on logic extended to its treatment of literature, which was seen as a branch of logic, an instrument for the manipulation of language. Literature was seen as a *form* rather than as having any specific content. This conception was heavily influenced by Islamic philosophers such as al-Farabi and Ibn Rushd, especially the latter's *Commentary on the Poetics of Aristotle*, translated into Latin in 1256. Significantly, Ibn Rushd's commentary – in its Latin rendering – was far more widely read in the Middle Ages than Aristotle's *Poetics* itself (translated in 1278 and 1536). As such, it was the most important theoretical literary critical statement of the scholastic period (*MLC*, 14–15). In viewing poetry as a branch of logic, the scholastics accorded it a definite place in a hierarchy of sciences crowned by theology. They eventually fostered a new and more liberal critical vocabulary, allowing for a more comprehensive treatment of author, material, style, structure, and effect. In this section, we will consider Ibn Rushd's *Commentary* as well as the aesthetics of Aquinas in the context of his vastly influential world view, and finally Dante's *Epistle to Can Grande della Scala*, which is one of the foremost practical applications of scholastic criticism.

Ibn Rushd (Averroës) (1126–1198) In the medieval West, the Islamic philosopher and jurist Ibn Rushd gained wide recognition among both Christian and Jewish scholars. Nearly all of his commentaries on Aristotle's major works were translated into Latin, and some into Hebrew. It was through Ibn Rushd that the main corpus of Aristotle's texts was transmitted to Europe. The central endeavor of Ibn Rushd's own major philosophical treatises was to reconcile philosophy and religion, reason and revelation. Ironically, and sadly, Ibn Rushd's influence on Islamic thought was far smaller than his impact on Christian Europe; he failed to convince Islamic theologians of the propriety of philosophy within their religious visions.[9]

In Ibn Rushd's *Commentary on the Poetics of Aristotle*, we can distinguish three broad themes (bearing in mind that these themes intersect at times only tangentially with the Greek text of Aristotle, and that Ibn Rushd's text is written in Arabic, its immediate audience comprising Arab scholars and writers): (1) poetry is defined broadly as the art of praise or blame, based on representations of moral choice; (2) the purpose of poetry is to produce a salutary effect upon its audience, through both excellence of imitative technique and performative elements such as melody, gesture, and intonation; and (3) poetry is viewed as a branch of logical discourse, which is compared and contrasted with rhetorical discourse.

Ibn Rushd's central thesis that "Every poem and all poetry are either blame or praise" is developed only tangentially from Aristotle's comment in the *Poetics* that the first forms of poetry were praises of famous men and satire. Ibn Rushd states that the subjects proper to poetry are those that "deal with matters of choice, both good and bad."[10] Like Aristotle, he holds that all action and character are concerned with either virtue or vice (*MLC*, 91). Regarding poetic imitation, he places great emphasis on realism. Like Aristotle, he suggests that the poet is close to the philosopher inasmuch as he speaks "in universal terms" (*MLC*, 99). But whereas Aristotle talks of the poet representing what is *probable*, Ibn Rushd insists that, just as "the skilled artist depicts an object as it is in reality . . . the poet should depict and form the object as it is in itself" (*MLC*, 105). It seems that Ibn Rushd prescribes a broader pursuit of poetic objectivity, which was strangely modern; he goes so far as to say that poetry is most truthful when it is based on direct experience: the poet "does best in reporting those things that he has understood for himself and almost seen first-hand with all their accidents and circumstances" (*MLC*, 110). The impact of these insights was restricted to the West, and did not extend to the majority of Islamic thinkers and poets.

Ibn Rushd's emphasis on truth may derive partly from the fact that, like many Islamic thinkers, he appears to treat the Qur'an as the archetypal text. He sees the Qur'an as exceptional in Arabic literature inasmuch as it praises "worthy actions of the will and blame of unworthy ones." The Qur'an, he states, prohibits "poetic fictions" except those which rebuke vices and commend virtues (*MLC*, 109). In a striking commensurability with much medieval poetics, then, Ibn Rushd's views might be said to have a scriptural foundation: just as Vergil and the Bible were revered as authoritative texts (stylistically and grammatically, as well as in their content), so the Qur'an is invoked as a literary exemplar. Hence, Ibn Rushd's treatise is archetypal of scholastic views of poetry, situating it as one form of discourse among a hierarchy of discourses, at whose pinnacle stood theology.

What would later medieval and Renaissance writers have gleaned about Aristotle from Ibn Rushd's text? Certainly an emphasis on the moral function and the truth value of poetry; in formal terms, a stress on unified poetic organization, and the need for poetry to produce a powerful impact on its audience. But Ibn Rushd fails to distinguish between drama and narrative, between tragedy and epic, a conflation also found in writers such as Dante and Chaucer (*MLC*, 85). Moreover, readers would have found in Ibn Rushd's text a highly un-Aristotelian description of the components of tragedy. Whereas Aristotle had insisted that the plot was the most important element and that action took priority over character, Ibn Rushd, characterizing tragedy along with epic as a "song of praise," sees as its most important component "character and belief." The reader would also seek in vain for Aristotle's characterizations of "reversal" and "recognition," though he would find the notion that pity and fear are inspired by the spectacle of undeserved misfortune (*MLC*, 102).

Notwithstanding these sometimes drastic alterations of Aristotle, Ibn Rushd's text was widely influential, met with the approval of figures such as Roger Bacon, and was used extensively by critics such as Benvenuto da Imola, the fourteenth-century commentator on Dante, who saw Dante's *Commedia* as essentially a work of praise and blame. It also influenced Petrarch's humanist disciple Coluccio Salutati, who also made use of the principle of praise and blame, as well as of Ibn Rushd's definition of imitation. The influence is traceable in sixteenth-century writers such as Savonarola, Robortelli, and Mazzoni, who all believed that poetry was to some degree a branch of logic, and who all cited Ibn Rushd in support of their own positions. Ibn Rushd's version of Aristotle was congenial to the moralistic attitudes of the humanists. Ironically, then, Ibn Rushd's version of Aristotle was for a long time given more credit than the views of Aristotle himself.

St. Thomas Aquinas (1224/5–1274) Aristotle also assumes a prominent position in the thought of Thomas Aquinas, the greatest of the scholastic philosophers as well as the greatest philosopher of the Roman Catholic Church. Eventually, Aquinas was proclaimed to be an official "doctor" of the Church and his works were deemed to be the expression of orthodox doctrine. His system is still widely taught in Catholic educational institutions. Aquinas was born into a noble family in 1224 or 1225 in Italy near the city of Naples, where he joined the order of the Dominican friars, whose central scholarly endeavor was to reconcile the teachings of Aristotle and Christ. Aquinas studied with the renowned Dominican Albertus Magnus. Through the efforts of such figures, the Church established Aristotle, rather than Plato (who had been promoted by the Church Fathers for many centuries), at the center of Christian thought.

Aquinas is known primarily for two major works. The first, *Summa contra Gentiles*, was written between 1259 and 1264. Its essential purpose was to defend the truth of Christianity against gentiles who did not accept the authority of the scriptures. In the first four books of the *Summa*, Aquinas relies, therefore, not on scripture but on "natural reason," which can be used to prove God's existence and the soul's immortality. The truths of the Incarnation, the Trinity, and the Last Judgment, however, are beyond the grasp of natural reason. Indeed the provinces of reason and revelation need, according to Aquinas, to be clearly distinguished. He holds that these two provinces, while distinct, cannot contradict and must accord with each other. Religious truths capable of demonstration (for the learned) can also be known by faith, as in the case of simple people or children.

Ironically, it was misinterpretations of Ibn Rushd's teachings by the Latin "Averroists" – who viewed him as believing that faith and reason were irreconcilable – that provoked the response of Aquinas' philosophy, which labored to harmonize these domains. Aquinas sees theology as a divine science, to which all of the other elements of human knowledge are hierarchically ordered. While his scheme places theology at the apex of the human sciences, it also accommodates these sciences and views them as preparatory for man's last end as an intellectual creature, which is to know God.[11]

In his second major work, *Summa Theologica*, Aquinas offers five proofs of the existence of God. The first is the argument of the unmoved mover: in order to avoid an infinite regress, there must be something which "moves" or sets into motion other things without being moved itself. Second is the argument from First Cause, which follows a similar logic: there must be a primal cause of the world, which itself is not caused. Thirdly, there must be a primal source of all necessity. Fourthly, the various types and degrees of perfection which actually exist in the world must have their source in something absolutely perfect. Finally, even lifeless things serve a purpose, which must be directed toward some being beyond them. Some of the major characteristics of God, according to Aquinas, are as follows: God is eternal, unchanging, and he has no parts or composition since he is not material. In God, essence and existence are identical, and there are no accidents or contingencies in God. He does not belong to any genus and cannot be defined. God's intellection is his essence; he understands himself perfectly and in so doing understands the various elements of the world, which are like him in certain ways. As Aquinas puts it, "God himself, in knowing Himself, knows all other things" (*MTA*, 114). God's knowledge is comprehensive, holistic, and instantaneous; it is not discursive, piecemeal, and rational. But Aquinas acknowledges that there is a "community of analogy" between God and human beings (*MTA*, 36). He believes that God created the world *ex nihilo* or out of nothing; and that God is the end or purpose of all things, which tend toward likeness of God. The human intellect, which aspires after God, is a part of each man's soul, the soul being the form of the body. On the questions of sin and predestination, Aquinas basically agrees with Augustine that only God's grace can redeem man from sin and that the election of some men for salvation is a mystery.

The picture of the world which emerges here is one which is rigidly coherent and closed off from all possible intrusion of accidence. It is also one which is balanced precariously on the narrow ground of overlap of revelation and reason, God's providence and natural law, essence and existence. Moreover, all things except God have their true being outside of themselves, in their end, which is God. And God effectively acts as the boundaries of the universe since all things are replicated – in their true significance – in the sphere of God, his self-knowledge encompassing knowledge of them. In other words, things achieve their true identity only in God, and then only in God's act of self-knowledge, in the coerced relation of dependence to him in which they are obliged to subsist. They achieve identity, then, not as objects of knowledge in their own right, but as projections or rather introjections of God's subjectivity. Man's ultimate happiness consists in contemplation of God. Hence God's essence delimits the world in several ways: as origin and purpose, as beginning and end, as subject and object, as knower and known, as center and circumference.

Aquinas' world view furnished the context of much medieval thought and aesthetics. In his study of Aquinas, Umberto Eco describes Aquinas as "the person who gave most complete expression to the philosophical and theological thinking of the age."[12] Influential in medieval conceptions of beauty were Aquinas' belief that God's creation is intrinsically beautiful, and his intellectual conception of beauty as requiring three components: integrity or perfection, right proportion or consonance (*consonantia*), and splendor of form (*claritas*) (*MTA*, 90–92).

Medieval Allegory and Aquinas   There was a widespread tendency throughout the medieval period to view all things in the world and the universe as essentially symbolic, as signs in a vast lexicon through which God speaks to humanity. Everything points beyond itself, beyond its immediate worldly significance, toward a higher level of significance in a more comprehensive pattern of events and divine purpose. Among the influential proponents of such a view were pseudo-Dionysius, the Roman writer Macrobius, and John Scotus Eriugena who wrote that "there is nothing among visible and corporeal things which does not signify something incorporeal and intelligible" (Eco, 139). Such all-embracing symbolism provided a vision of a world constrained by unity, order, and purpose. In such a vision, human beings are obliged to read and decipher the book of the world or the book of the universe.

Christian allegory arose initially from the attempts by writers such as Origen to reconcile the Old and New Testaments. Allegory also had its basis in the endeavor to restrict the potentially infinite meanings of the scriptures, by subjecting them to a code of interpretation. Hence the Church Fathers devised an allegorical theory of interpretation of the Bible, according to three levels of meaning: the literal, the moral, and the mystical. Later, this system was expanded to include four levels, summarized by Nicholas of Lyre: "The literal sense tells us of events; the allegorical teaches our faith; the moral tells us what to do; the anagogical shows us where we are going" (Eco, 145).

In his *Summa Theologica*, Aquinas explained allegory in a formulation which comprehends the foregoing tendencies:

> that first signification whereby words signify things belongs to the first sense, the historical or literal. That signification whereby things signified by words have themselves also a signification is called the spiritual sense, which is based on the literal, and presupposes it. Now this spiritual sense has a threefold division . . . so far as the things of the Old Law signify the things of the New Law, there is the allegorical sense; so far as the things done in Christ, or so far as the things which signify Christ, are types of what we ought to do, there is the moral sense. But so far as they signify what relates to eternal glory, there is the anagogical sense. (*Summa Theologica*, Q.I, Tenth Article)[13]

What is notable about Aquinas' definition of allegory is the movement from the signification of *things* to that of *words*. The literal or historical sense denotes the connection between language and the world. But the remaining levels of significance are contained within the realm of language and literary/biblical tradition. The most general name for this symbolism is the "spiritual sense." The three divisions of this comprehend Christianity's attempt to appropriate the pre-Christian past into its own historical and theological framework (the allegorical sense); they also affirm the moral authority of Christ's own example (the moral sense); finally, they stress the Christian view of the transient, partial, and finite nature of this world, which has significance only in relation to the totality of God's eternal scheme which is accessible only by revelation and not by human reason (the anagogical or mystical sense).

Aquinas held that poetry was *infima doctrina* or an inferior kind of teaching to that of scripture because it dealt with objects which were imagined or invented. But, as Eco observes, such a view does not imply contempt for poetry on Aquinas' part – it expresses his sense of the hierarchy of various modes of knowledge (Eco, 148–149). After Aquinas, thinkers began to stress the particularity and uniqueness, rather than the universal qualities, of beauty, a view realized in many modern conceptions of art which emphasized art as creation rather than merely imitation, and stressed the particularity and uniqueness of beautiful things (Eco, 215–216).

Dante Alighieri (1265–1321) and the Allegorical Mode   Allegory is integral to the work of Dante Alighieri (1265–1321), arguably the greatest poet the Western world has produced. He is best known for his epic poem *Divina Commedia* (1307–1321) and his earlier cycle of love poems published as *La Vita Nuova* (*The New Life*, ca. 1295), written in honor of Beatrice Portinari. Dante also wrote literary criticism. In *De Vulgari Eloquentia* (*Eloquence in the Vernacular Tongue*, ca. 1304–1308), he defended the use of the vernacular Italian as appropriate for the writing of poetry. In *Il Convivio* (*The Banquet*, 1306–1309), he produced a collection of 14 odes with prose commentaries, designed to clear him of the charge of "unrestrained passion" in these odes and to explain the principles of allegory. And in 1319 he wrote a now famous letter, also treating of allegory, to his patron Can Grande della Scala, though the authenticity of this has been questioned. In *Il Convivio*, Dante states that allegory has four senses:

> The first is called the literal, and this is the sense that does not go beyond the surface of the letter, as in the fables of the poets. The next is called the allegorical, and this is the one that is hidden beneath the cloak of these fables, and is a truth hidden beneath a beautiful fiction...
> The third sense is called moral, and this is the sense that teachers should intently seek to discover throughout the scriptures, for their own profit and that of their pupils...
>   The fourth sense is called anagogical, that is to say, beyond the senses; and this occurs when a scripture is expounded in a spiritual sense which, although it is true also in the literal sense, signifies by means of the things signified a part of the supernal things of eternal glory.[14]

Dante insists that, in allegorical explication, "the literal sense should always come first, as being the sense in whose meaning the others are enclosed." Literal meaning is the foundation of the other senses. He pictures the literal meaning as being on the "outside," enclosing the other senses which are within (*IC*, II.i.65–80). In insisting on including literal meaning, Dante is following many theologians who affirmed the truth of all four levels of meaning, as against rhetorical and poetic views of allegory which might view even the literal meaning as fictional. But, clearly, one of the functions of allegory is to express "darkly" and in a hidden manner what is otherwise ineffable concerning the mysteries of God, which even philosophy, the noblest human pursuit, cannot fathom (*IC*, III.xv.58–69).

In the "Letter to Can Grande" Dante dedicates his *Divine Comedy* to his patron and explains the allegorical structure of his poem. Dante begins by reiterating Aristotle's position that some things are self-sufficient, having being in themselves, while the being of other things is relational, lying beyond themselves in their connections with other things.[15] Dante explains that his text is "polysemous, that is, having several senses." The literal sense necessarily signifies beyond itself to higher senses which complete it. The non-literal senses, although they are called by various names (allegorical, moral, anagogical) "may all be called allegorical, since they are all different from the literal or historical" ("LCG," 7). Hence he sees the structure of allegory as broadly dualistic, the literal sense being a narrative of this world and the allegorical sense referring to the spiritual domain.

In accordance with this duality, Dante sees the subject of the poem as twofold, corresponding to literal and allegorical senses. The subject of the work, taken literally, "is the state of souls after death." Allegorically, "the subject is man, in the exercise of his free will, earning or becoming liable to the rewards or punishments of justice" ("LCG," 8). Dante views the end or ultimate aim of the work as spiritual, namely to lead souls from a state of sin and misery to a state of blessedness ("LCG," 15). The twofold structure of allegory as given in Dante's text informs every aspect of the reading process, from the author's intentions and use of language to the reader's response. Allegory expresses at its profoundest level a vision of the world in which the existence of things is not self-sufficient but always depends ultimately, through a series of mediating relationships, on God as the prime and absolutely self-sufficient existent. All worldly goals are subordinated to the ultimate goal of human life, which is to achieve blessedness by beholding God, the "Origin of Truth" ("LCG," 33).

Transitions: Medieval Humanism

Two medieval figures, Giovanni Boccaccio and Christine de Pisan, were important forerunners of the Renaissance humanism that eclipsed (but also grew out of) scholasticism. As will be seen in the accounts below, Boccaccio saw an urgent need to defend poetry and a humanistic curriculum against the onslaughts not so much of scholastics as of the rising mercantile classes who saw no practical value in literature and the arts. Christine was a powerful humanistic voice in the medieval era, who dared to enter into a literary debate with established male authorities.

The defense of poetry: Giovanni Boccaccio (1313–1375)

Boccaccio is most widely known for his *Decameron* (1358), a collection of 100, sometimes bawdy, stories told by 10 characters against the background of the bubonic plague which overtook Italy in 1348. Like Dante, he pressed the cause of Italian vernacular literature. Yet, through his scholarly works, written in Latin, he was an influential forerunner of Renaissance humanism. His *De Mulieribus Claris* (*Concerning Famous Women*) (1361) was a source of Christine de Pisan's *City of Ladies* (1405). In terms of literary criticism, his most influential work was *Genealogia Deorum Gentilium* (*Genealogy of the Gentile Gods*) (1350–1362), a huge encyclopedia of classical mythology in 15 books, the last two of which are devoted to a comprehensive defense of poetry.[16] Hence, this work is not only an endeavor to expound the virtues of classical literature but also an attempt by a practicing poet to defend his art, in a tradition that stretches from Horace, through Ronsard, Du Bellay, Sidney, Boileau, and Pope, to Wordsworth, Coleridge, Shelley, and Arnold.

Boccaccio defends poetry against charges that it is an "unprofitable" activity by urging that poetry rejects worldly pursuits and "devotes herself to something greater . . . she moves the minds of a few men from on high to a yearning for the eternal" (*GDG*, XIV.iv). He is modern in claiming that poetry is an inspired art, for which there can be no rigid rules and formulae, and also in defining poetry in terms of its effect (*GDG*, XIV.vii). As for the charge that poets are tale-mongers or liars, Boccaccio retorts that poetry is imbued with the classical functions of teaching and delighting. It is also imbued with a theological function, that of cloaking divine mysteries. Poets, he says, must "sacrifice the literal truth in invention" (*GDG*, XIV.xiii). But while he sees poetry as sharing some aims with philosophy and theology, he is nonetheless concerned to mark out its domain as an autonomous province, finally extricated from rhetoric: "oratory is quite different, in arrangement of words, from fiction, and that fiction has been consigned to the discretion of the inventor as being the legitimate work of another art than oratory" (*GDG*, XIV.xii). A large part of Boccaccio's endeavor is to show that poetry is not somehow contrary to the principles of Christianity. But, for all his defense of poetry, Boccaccio situates this art in a hierarchy wherein it is subservient to both philosophy and theology.

Feminism: Christine de Pisan (ca. 1365–1429)

Christine de Pisan was perhaps the most articulate and prolific female voice of the European Middle Ages. Being widowed at the age of 25 without an inheritance and with three children, she was obliged to earn her living as a writer. She was commissioned as biographer of Charles V. Her patrons included King Charles VI of France, King Charles of Navarre, and two dukes of Burgundy. Her publications, which were translated into English, Italian, and other languages, included *Epistle of the God of Love* (1399) where she impugned the misogynistic portrayals of women and the dearth of morality in the popular French work *Roman de la Rose*, an allegorical love poem written by Guillaume de Lorris and expanded by Jean de Meun. The controversial quarrel surrounding these texts was known as the *Querelle de la Rose*, with Christine and Jean Gerson, chancellor of the University of Paris, allied against the esteemed humanist royal secretaries Jean de Montreuil and Pierre Col. In a further work, *Christine's Vision* (1405), she complained against her fortune as a female writer and scholar burdened by the conventional obligations of womanhood. Another work produced in the same year, *Livre des Trois Vertus* (*Book of Three Virtues*), concerns the status and role of women in society. Her most renowned work was *The Book of the City of Ladies* (1405), which was influenced by Boccaccio's *Concerning Famous Women* (1361) and Augustine's *City of God* (to which Christine's title alludes). Almost uniquely among women of her time, Christine was enabled to obtain a fine education through her family's connections to the court of Charles V.[17] Christine also published a poem on Joan of Arc, *Ditie de la pucelle* (1429).

The *Book of the City of Ladies* attempts effectively to rewrite the history of women, its scope extending through past and future, as well as over pagan and Christian eras. Such rewriting entails an explosion of age-long male myths about women, such as their inability to govern, their unfitness for learning, and their moral deficiencies. The nature of Christine's feminism has been a disputed issue, with some scholars pointing to her conservatism, her espousal of the medieval class structure, her appeals to tradition, and above all to Christianity. But others have seen her invocation of Christianity as her very means of resisting oppression.

The *Book* is written as a conversation between Christine and three allegorical virtues: Reason, Rectitude, and Justice. Just as Virginia Woolf, some 600 years later, began *A Room of One's Own* by reflecting on the enormous number of books written about women by men, so Christine opens her text by wondering why so many treatises by men contain "so many wicked insults about women and their behavior." What puzzles Christine is the disparity between these male theories about women and her own practical experience of women of all social ranks, "princesses, great ladies, women of the middle and lower classes" (*BCL*, I.1.1). As Christine ponders, debilitated, by these thoughts, there appears to her a vision of "three crowned ladies" (*BCL*, I.2.1). The first of these, Lady Reason, explains that she and her two companions are embarked on a mission: to provide a refuge for "ladies and all valiant women" against the numerous assailants of the female sex. In this mission, she tells Christine that she must, with the help of the three ladies, build a city, "which has been predestined," and where only ladies of fame and virtue will reside (*BCL*, I.3.3). Christine was chosen for her "great love of investigating the truth" (*BCL*, I.3.2).

As against the disparagement of women by revered males such as Cicero and Cato, Lady Reason explains that woman was created from a rib of Adam, which signified that "she should stand at his side as a companion and never lie at his feet like a slave," and that woman "was created in the image of God." Lady Reason observes, regarding Cato: "You can now see the foolishness of the man who is considered wise" (*BCL*, I.8.3). Ironically, what the divine authorizes here is the validity of female experience. And the personification of "Reason" as a woman extricates the faculty of reason from its history of male appropriation and abuse. So Christine's appeal to Christianity might be viewed as broadly humanistic. In this manner, Christine's rewriting of history is conducted on several concurrent levels: theological exegesis, the literary tradition as defined by males, and the male appropriation of "reason."

Lady Reason also extols the virtues of experience: "there is nothing which so instructs a reasonable creature as the exercise and experience of many different things" (*BCL*, I.27.1). Again, what is remarkable about this statement is that, despite its ostensibly theological framework, it anticipates the major strands of Enlightenment thought, combining a proposed rationalism with actual experience of the variety of the world. Talking of writers who have disparaged women, Christine herself admonishes: "From now on let them keep their mouths shut" (*BCL*, I.38.4–5). Christine's stance has now become outspoken. She raises a variety of other charges brought against women by men, all of which are refuted by Lady Rectitude's appeal to experience and numerous examples. These include women's inconstancy, infidelity, coquettishness, and greed (*BCL*, II.66.1–67.2).

Eventually, Rectitude announces that she has finished building the houses and palaces of the city: "Now a New Kingdom of Femininity is begun" (*BCL*, II.12.1). She explains that after it has been populated with noble citizens – women of "integrity, of great beauty and authority" – Lady Justice leads in the high princesses and the "Queen of Heaven" who announces: "I am and will always be the head of the feminine sex. This arrangement was present in the mind of God the Father from the start, revealed and ordained previously in the council of the Trinity" (*BCL*, III.1.3).

Christine ends the book in a manner that must disappoint modern feminists. She advises the women not to "scorn being subject to your husbands" (*BCL*, III.19.1–2). If their husbands are good or moderate, they should praise God; if their husbands are "cruel, mean, and savage," they should display forbearance and attempt to lead them back to a life of reason and virtue (*BCL*, III.19.2). She admonishes: "all women – whether noble, bourgeois, or lower-class – be well-informed in all things and cautious in defending your honor" (*BCL*, III.19.6). Modern feminists might also view the city as a form of ghettoization, whereby women are protected from the evils of male institutions at the cost of foregoing any active and transformative partici-pation. The reverse side is that women are allowed the space they need, the room, to extricate themselves from the male writing of their history and to rearticulate that history without interference.

Notes

1. Perry Anderson, *Passages from Antiquity to Feudalism* (London: Verso, 1985), p. 140. Hereafter cited as *PF*.
2. "Introduction," in *Medieval Literary Theory and Criticism, c.1100–c.1375: The Commentary Tradition*, ed. A. J. Minnis, A. B. Scott, and David Wallace (Oxford: Clarendon Press, 1988), p. 5.
3. Ernst Robert Curtius, *European Literature and the Latin Middle Ages*, trans. Willard R. Trask (London: Routledge and Kegan Paul, 1979), pp. 54–55. Hereafter cited as Curtius.
4. See Martin Irvine, *The Making of Textual Culture: "Grammatica" and Literary Theory, 350–1100* (Cambridge and New York: Cambridge University Press, 1994), pp. 17–19. Hereafter cited as *GLT*.
5. See "Introduction," in *Medieval Literary Criticism: Translations and Interpretations*, ed. O. B. Hardison, Jr. (New York: Frederick Ungar, 1974), p. 10. Hereafter cited as *MLC*.
6. *The Didascalicon of Hugh of St. Victor*, trans. Jerome Taylor (New York: Columbia University Press, 1991), II.I. Hereafter cited as *DHV*.
7. *The Metalogicon of John of Salisbury: A Twelfth-Century Defense of the Verbal and Logical Arts of the Trivium*, trans. Daniel D. McGarry (Gloucester, MA: Peter Smith, 1971), pp. 9–12. Hereafter cited as *ML*.
8. "Introduction," in Geoffrey of Vinsauf, *Poetria Nova*, trans. Margaret F. Nims (Toronto and Wetteren, Belgium: Universa Press, 1967), pp. 10–11. Hereafter cited as *PN*.
9. See W. Montgomery Watt, *Islamic Philosophy and Theology* (Edinburgh: Edinburgh University Press, 1985), pp. 117–119.
10. Averroës, "The Middle Commentary of Averroes of Cordova on the *Poetics* of Aristotle," in *MLC*, 89.
11. *An Introduction to the Metaphysics of St. Thomas Aquinas: Texts Selected and Translated*, preface by James F. Anderson (Indiana: Regnery/Gateway, 1953), pp. 109–117. Hereafter cited as *MTA*.
12. Umberto Eco, *The Aesthetics of Thomas Aquinas*, trans. Hugh Bredin (Cambridge, MA: Harvard University Press, 1988), p. 140. Hereafter cited as Eco.
13. *Summa Theologica*, trans. Fathers of the English Dominican Province, 1920–1931.
14. Dante, *Il Convivio: The Banquet*, trans. Richard H. Lansing (New York and London: Garland, 1990), II.i.1, 20–60. Hereafter cited as *IC*.
15. "The Letter to Can Grande," in *Literary Criticism of Dante Alighieri*, trans. Robert S. Haller (Nebraska: University of Nebraska Press, 1973), par. 5. Hereafter cited as "LCG," with numbers referring to paragraphs.

16. Charles G. Osgood, "Introduction," in *Boccaccio on Poetry: Being the Preface and the Fourteenth and Fifteenth Books of Boccaccio's Genealogia Deorum Gentilium* (Indianapolis and New York: Bobbs-Merrill, 1956), p. xxx. Hereafter cited as *GDG*.
17. "Introduction," in Christine de Pizan, *The Book of the City of Ladies*, trans. Earl Jeffrey Richards (New York: Persea Books, 1982), pp. xix, xxvii. Hereafter cited as *BCL*.

Part III

The Early Modern Period to the Enlightenment

Chapter 6
The Early Modern Period

Historical Background

The period from around the fourteenth until the mid-seventeenth century has conventionally been designated as the Renaissance, referring to a "rebirth" or rediscovery of the values, ethics, and styles of classical Greece and Rome. The term was devised by Italian humanists who sought to reaffirm their own continuity with the classical humanist heritage after an interlude of over a thousand years, a period of alleged superstition and stagnation known as the Dark Ages and Middle Ages. In this view, the Renaissance overturned the medieval theological world view, replacing it with a more secular and humanist vision, promoting a newly awakened interest in the temporal world both in economic and in scientific terms, and according a new importance to the individual – all inspired by a rediscovery of the classics. This view has been somewhat shaken, with even the term "Renaissance" often being replaced by the broader and more neutral term "early modern." Historians and scholars now recognize that many developments in the Renaissance were in fact continuations or modifications of medieval dispositions. For example, medieval scholasticism and Renaissance humanism are no longer viewed as entirely distinct. Nonetheless, as David Norbrook argues, the term "Renaissance" may facilitate our understanding of how modernity changed the world.[1]

The early modern period certainly bore distinctive traits marking it as an era of profound transformation. The most dominant trait has conventionally been identified as "humanism," a term ultimately deriving from Cicero and used by Italian thinkers and writers to distinguish themselves from the medieval scholastics. The term "humanism" implies a world view and a set of values centered around the human rather than the divine, using a self-subsistent definition of human nature (rather than referring this to God), and focusing on human achievements and potential rather than theological doctrines and dilemmas; the term also retained its Ciceronian connection with the liberal arts (one of the original definitions of a humanist was a teacher

Literary Criticism from Plato to the Present: An Introduction   M. A. R. Habib
© 2011 M. A. R. Habib

of the humanities) and in general with secular and independent inquiry in all fields, as opposed to viewing these areas of study as hierarchically bound within a theological framework.

However, Renaissance humanism itself was only one manifestation of a more profound shift in sensibility, from a broadly "other-worldly" disposition – viewing this earthly life as a merely transitory phase, as a preparation for the life hereafter – to a "this-worldly" attitude which saw actions and events in this world as significant in their own right without referring them to any ultimate divine meaning and purpose. This shift from "other-worldliness" to "this-worldliness" both underlies and reflects the major transformations of the early modern period. The most fundamental of these changes were economic and political: the fundamental institutions of the later Middle Ages – the feudal system, the universal authority of the pope, the Holy Roman Empire, and the system of trade regulated by medieval guilds – were all undermined. As a result of large-scale investment of capital, booming manufacture, and expanding trade and commerce, the focus of economic life increasingly shifted away from the manorial estates of the feudal nobility to the newly emerging cities such as Florence, Milan, Venice, Rome, Paris, and London, whose affluence enabled their prominence as centers of cultural efflorescence. Many factors contributed to the decline of feudalism: the rise of monarchies and centralized governments; the weakening of the feudal nobility; the rise of an increasingly powerful middle class; and the birth of our modern secular conception of the state which promoted a new "civic consciousness," returning to classical political ideals of civic humanism.

These developments were decisive in shaping the literature and criticism of the period. There was a more pronounced focus on style and aesthetics, as opposed to theology or logic. Most of the literary and artistic accomplishments of this period were achieved by laymen rather than clergy, with secular patrons. Nearly all of the poets of this era were actively involved in the political process, and formed an important constituent of the "public sphere," the arena of public debate and discourse which began to emerge during the later Renaissance. English poets, for example, wrote vehemently in favor of both royalist and parliamentary sides during the English Civil War; Milton (1608–1674) was the leading literary advocate of the Puritan revolution, and his epic *Paradise Lost* celebrated the Protestant notion of the individual's moral responsibility, while his *Areopagitica* (1644) was a passionate defense of free speech.

Intellectual Background

Humanism and the Classics

The early modern period witnessed the growth of a new secular class of educated people and a more secular employment of the classics in fields such as rhetoric and law. The most distinguished humanists of this period included Albertino Mussato, who is credited with writing the first tragedy of this period, and, even more important, Francesco Petrarca (1304–1374), who outlined a curriculum of classical studies. A major difference between medieval and humanist attitudes to the classics was that the latter insisted upon a thorough knowledge of the classical languages: not only Latin, but also Greek. The humanists also insisted on the direct study – without glosses – of ancient texts, which were now far more widely disseminated. Finally, the monopoly of Latin as the language of learned discourse and literature was undermined, and in the works of Dante, Petrarch, Boccaccio, and many humanists, the rules of grammar and composition were adapted to theorize about vernacular tongues. In general, the humanists supplanted the scholastic aversion to poetry and rhetoric with an emphasis upon the moral value of these disciplines and upon worldly achievement in general.

The new poets not only theorized about the vernacular but wrote in it and cultivated its elegant expression. Petrarch's friend Giovanni Boccaccio (1313–1375) adapted classical forms to the vernacular, developing literary forms such as the pastoral, idyll, and romance. Through his best-known works such as the *Decameron*, Boccaccio provided models of Italian prose which influenced both Italian writers such as Tasso and writers in other countries such as Chaucer. The cultivation of prose – in narratives, epistles, and dialogues – was an important achievement of the humanists. A renowned example is Baldassare Castiglione's treatise entitled *The Courtier*, a discussion of attitudes toward love, and of the courtly behavior and education appropriate for a gentleman. The Renaissance epic reached its height in the *Orlando Furioso* of Ludovico Ariosto (1474–1533), which departs from the idealistic and moralistic nature of medieval epics. Historiography and political writing also achieved a new level of realism: Machiavelli wrote a history of Florence that was free of theological explanations and based upon "natural" laws. Machiavelli's political writings entirely undermined medieval notions of government: in his treatise *The Prince* (1513), he saw the state as an independent entity, whose prime goal was the promotion of civic rather than religious virtue, and self-preservation at any cost. An even more important figure in historiography was Francesco Guicciardini (1483–1540) whose *History of Italy* is characterized by realistic, detailed analysis of character, motive, and events. Lorenzo Valla (1406–1457) applied critical methods of scholarship and analysis to biblical texts, and he challenged the authenticity of certain authoritative documents, opening the way for later attacks upon Christian doctrine.

Humanism flourished also in other parts of Europe. The Dutch thinker Desiderius Erasmus (1466–1536) was renowned for his strong humanistic convictions in reason, naturalism, tolerance, and the inherent goodness of man, which led him to oppose dogmatic theology and scholasticism, and to propound instead a rational religion of simple piety based on the example of

Christ. His most famous work, *Encomium moriae* (*The Praise of Folly*, 1509), satirized theological dogmatism and the gullibility of the masses. France also produced notable figures such as François Rabelais (1490–1553), whose *Gargantua and Pantagruel* expounded a naturalistic and secular philosophy glorifying humanity and ridiculing scholastic theology, Church abuses, and all forms of bigotry. In England, the most renowned humanist was Sir Thomas More (1478–1535), whose *Utopia* (1516) was a thinly veiled condemnation of the social and economic defects of his time: religious intolerance, financial greed, the glaring discrepancy between rich and poor, the notions of conquest, imperialism, and war.

The humanist tradition was richly expressed in the rise of English vernacular literature of this period. Even Chaucer, often treated as a medieval writer, expressed a somewhat secular humanistic vision in his *Canterbury Tales*, which tends to bypass simple moralism in the interest of broader stylistic ends such as verisimilitude and realistic portrayal of character, situation, and motive. English drama achieved unprecedented heights in the work of Christopher Marlowe (1564–1593), Ben Jonson (1573–1637), and William Shakespeare (1564–1616). Marlowe's *Doctor Faustus* expresses an overwhelming craving for experience and a humanistic desire to subjugate the world to human intellection and ingenuity. Shakespeare's plays expressed not only a profound analysis of human character and emotion but embodied the vast struggle between the values of a declining feudal system and an emerging bourgeois structure of values. The rise of national consciousness in many countries during this period was reflected in the growth of vernacular literatures in Italy, England, France, Germany, and Spain.

Philosophy and science

As well as returning to classical rhetoric, the humanists promoted the revival of other ancient philosophies such as Platonism. In fact, the major philosophers of this period, such as Marsilio Ficino (1433–1499) and Pico della Mirandola (1463–1494), were Neo-Platonists. Other thinkers such as Lorenzo Valla revived the ancient movements of Epicureanism, Stoicism, and skepticism. In France, Michel de Montaigne (1533–1592) expounded a philosophy of skepticism. The most renowned English philosopher of this period was Sir Francis Bacon (1561–1626), who was the forerunner of the empiricist tradition in Britain, urging the use of the inductive method and direct observation as against scholastic reliance upon authority, faith, and deductive reasoning.

A major distinction between the medieval and early modern periods lies in a momentous transformation in scientific outlook. Medieval cosmology and scholastic theology were premised on a Ptolemaic geocentric view of the earth as being at the center of the universe, surrounded by a series of seven concentric spheres (the orbits of the planets), beyond which was the Empyrean and the throne of God, who was the "unmoved Mover" and the "First Cause" of all things. The universe was thought to be composed of four elements – earth, air, fire, and water – combined in varying proportions; and human beings were constituted by four "humors." The earth, as in Dante's *Divine Comedy*, was thought to be populated only in its northern hemisphere, which was composed of Asia, Africa, and Europe. This world view, based largely on the physics and metaphysics of Aristotle, was shattered in the early modern era by the heliocentric theory of Nicholas Copernicus (1473–1543), whose truth was demonstrated by Galileo Galilei (1564–1642), and thus paved the way for modern mechanistic (rather than spiritual) conceptions of the universe. A particularly significant invention of this time was that of printing, developed in Germany by Johannes Gutenberg and spreading quickly through Europe.

Religion

One of the most profound and vast transformations in the early modern period was the Protestant Reformation, erupting in 1517 and resulting in a major schism in the Christian world. Most of Northern Europe broke away from Roman Catholicism and the authority of the pope. There also occurred the Catholic Reformation (sometimes known as the Counter-Reformation) which reached its most fervent intensity in the mid-sixteenth century, changing the shape of Catholicism considerably from its medieval character. National consciousness played an even more integral role in the Reformation since the Protestant cause was affiliated with reaction against a system of ecclesiastical control at whose apex sat the pope.

While it may have been immediately incited by abuses within the Catholic Church – such as the amassing of wealth for private self-interests, the sale of indulgences, and the veneration of material objects as holy relics – the Protestant Reformation was directed in essence against some of the cardinal tenets of medieval theology, such as its theory of the sacraments, its elaborate ecclesiastical hierarchy of intermediation between God and human beings, and its insistence that religious faith must be complemented by good deeds. As seen earlier, medieval theology had been broadly propagated through two systems: the theology of the early Middle Ages had been based on the teachings of St. Augustine that man is fallen (through original sin), his will is depraved, and that only those whom God has so predestined can attain eternal salvation. This somewhat fatalistic system was largely supplanted in the twelfth and thirteenth centuries by the theologies of Peter Lombard and Thomas Aquinas, which acknowledged man's free will, but urged that he needed divine grace to attain salvation. Such grace was furnished to man through the sacraments, such as baptism, penance, and the Eucharist or mass.

It was the ecclesiastical hierarchy, tracing its authority all the way through the pope to the apostle Peter, which had the power to administer these sacraments and hence to gain access to divine grace.

The Protestant Reformers such as Martin Luther reacted against this complex system of intermediation between God and man, advocating a return to the actual doctrines of the scriptures and the writings of the Church Fathers such as Augustine. They rejected the theory of the priesthood as well as worship of the Virgin, the intermediation of the saints, and the reverence for sacred relics. In general, they returned to the Augustinian visions of original sin, the depraved state of man's will, and, in the case of Calvinism, a strong belief in predestination.

Martin Luther's central doctrine was "justification by faith": man's sins are remitted and his salvation achieved through faith alone, not through good works. In effect, Luther emphasized the primacy of individual conscience, and the directness of man's relation with God, unmediated by priests, saints, relics, or pilgrimages to shrines. Luther's views were denounced as heretical and in 1521 he was excommunicated. Germany was swept by a series of uprisings culminating in the Peasants' Revolt of 1524–1525. A Protestant Revolution in Switzerland was incited by Ulrich Zwingli (1484–1531) and the Frenchman John Calvin (1509–1564); the latter strongly reaffirmed the Augustinian doctrine of predestination, whereby God has already predestined his elect for salvation, and the remainder to damnation. However, Calvin taught that, while none can know whether he is of the elect or damned, a "sign" of election is a life of piety, good works, and abstinence. Ironically, as Max Weber was to argue, the influence of Calvin's world view and the "Protestant ethic" – which could be used to sanction the worldly activities of disciplined trading and commerce – played an integral role in the rise of capitalism. The Catholic Reformation resulted eventually in a redefinition of Catholic doctrines at the Council of Trent (1545–1563), convened by Pope Paul III.

These momentous religious transformations induced a vast schism in the Christian world: northern Germany and Scandinavia became Lutheran; England adopted a compromise, integrating Catholic doctrine with allegiance to the English crown; Calvinism held sway in Scotland, Holland, and French Switzerland. The countries still expressing allegiance to the pope now numbered only Italy, France, Spain, Portugal, Austria, Poland, Ireland, and southern Germany. The Protestant Reformation promoted not only individualism but also nationalism (as coextensive with independence from the Church at Rome), increased sanction for bourgeois thought and practice, as well as a broader education accessible to more of the masses. Many of the values of Protestantism and humanism overlapped or reinforced each other: these included self-discipline, industry, and intellectual achievement.

Literary criticism

Just as many of our own institutions are descended from the early modern period, much of our own literary criticism, and indeed the very notion of criticism as a relatively autonomous domain, derives from this era. In particular, the rise of the independent state and of a liberal bourgeoisie enabled the pervasive growth of humanist culture and of national sentiment; the literature and criticism of the period tends to reflect civic values, a sense of national identity, and a sense of place in history, especially as gauged in relation to the classics. The technology of the period, such as the development and dissemination of printing, transformed the conditions of reading, facilitating the process of editing (of especially classical texts), and vastly extending the sphere of the reading public. The innovative characteristics of Renaissance literary criticism included moving away from the scholastic fourfold allegorical structure to a view of language as historically evolving. Such a shift entailed new approaches to reading and interpretation.[2]

In our own day, and especially in Western culture, where poetry and good literature have been marginalized, it is easy to forget how deeply poetry and literary criticism were embroiled in the political process during the Renaissance. As David Norbrook explains, poets engaged fervently in the emerging "public sphere," a realm of debate in which citizens could participate as equals, independently of pressure from monopolies of power.[3] The expansion of the public sphere enabled the poet to create fictive and utopian worlds, to mold the image of public events (as in Marvell's "Horatian Ode"), and to assert an individualism that was also promoted by Protestantism; the translation of the Bible into vernacular languages shifted interpretative authority away from the clergy to the individual reader. In such a climate, poets and critics inevitably placed emphasis on the practical and social functions of poetry and its dependence on rhetorical strategies (*PBRV*, 9, 11, 13–15).

Indeed, much Renaissance criticism was forged in the struggle to defend poetry and literature from charges – brought within both clerical and secular circles – of immorality, triviality, and irrelevance to practical and political life. The types of criticism proliferating in the early modern period also included a large body of humanist commentary and scholarship on classical texts. The most influential classical treatises during the sixteenth and seventeenth centuries were Aristotle's *Poetics* and Horace's *Ars poetica*. A third important body of criticism in this period is comprised of commentaries on Aristotle's *Poetics* and debates between the relative virtues of the Aristotelian and Horatian texts as well as attempts to harmonize their insights. Alongside Aristotle and Horace, the influential rhetorical voices of Cicero and Quintilian were recovered in the early fifteenth century: Renaissance critics tended to adapt, and even distort, these voices to their own needs.

Almost all of these defenses, commentaries, and debates concern a number of fundamental notions: imitation (of both the external world and the tradition of classical authors); the truth-value and didactic role of literature; the classical "unities"; the notion of verisimilitude; the use of the vernacular; the definition of poetic genres such as narrative and drama; the invention of new, mixed genres such as the romantic epic and the tragicomedy; the use of rhyme in poetry; the relative values of quantitative and qualitative verse; and the place of literature and poetry in relation to other disciplines such as moral philosophy and history. In the sections below, we shall look at the treatment of these issues by some of the influential writers of the period. It will be useful to divide them into three broad categories. The first set of writers, all Italian (Giraldi, Castelvetro, Mazzoni and Tasso), are concerned to reformulate their connections with the classical tradition; the second group, comprising both French and English writers (Du Bellay and Sidney), endeavors to defend poetry and the use of the vernacular; the third, represented here by Gascoigne and Puttenham, aims to define the art of poetry, drawing on the traditions of rhetoric. In many of these writers, the promotion of the vernacular and the very definition of the poetic is intrinsically tied to their political and often nationalistic affiliations.

Confronting the Classical Heritage

A new and powerful stimulus to literary criticism arose when the Greek text of the *Poetics* was made available in 1508 and translated into Latin in 1536 (previously it had been available only through an Arabic commentary by the Islamic philosopher Ibn Rushd). A number of editions of Horace's *Ars poetica* were circulated. While poetics had overlapped increasingly with rhetoric, as evident in the work of Renaissance writers such as Minturno, Scaliger, Du Bellay, and Puttenham, the recovery of Aristotle's text fostered a new examination of literary form and organic unity that was not wholly grounded in rhetoric. Many commentaries on Aristotle appeared during the sixteenth century. Somewhat ironically (given the availability of the actual text of Aristotle's *Poetics*), many writers saw literature as Ibn Rushd had, as exercising a moral function through the depiction of virtue and vice; they combined this with Horace's precept that literature should also please; hence the formula that literature should "teach and delight" (used by Sidney) pervaded the thinking of this era.

Renaissance writers added the doctrine of the unity of place to Aristotle's original demand for the unity of action and time; debates over these unities encompassed the discussion of classical genres, notably the lyric, epic, tragedy, and comedy, as well as mixed genres such as the romantic epic and the tragicomedy. The newer, characteristically humanist, genres also included the essay and the dialogue form, as well as increasing focus on the epigram as an instrument of wit. As will be seen in the writers now to be examined, the treatment of these issues displayed emphatically how each writer's adaptation of classical norms was fueled by specific contemporary agendas.

Giambattista Giraldi (1504–1573)

The Italian dramatist, poet, and literary critic Giraldi advocated a new genre, the romance, a lengthy narrative poem which combined elements of the classical epic with those of medieval romances. The most noteworthy contemporary example of such a romance was Ariosto's *Orlando Furioso* (1516). Hence Giraldi was effectively involved in a quarrel between "ancients" and "moderns" which was to last for many centuries. Giraldi's leaning toward the modern is shown in a number of ways. To begin with, he tends to view literature in a historical context, which means that classical values are not necessarily applicable to all ages. He also reacted, both in his dramas and in his theory, against many of Aristotle's prescriptions for tragedy, such as unity of action and unity of time. His literary criticism, of which his *Discorso intorno al comporre dei romanzi* (1554; *Discourse on the Composition of Romances*) was the most controversial and influential, anticipates the views of Coleridge, Mazzoni, and Du Bellay.

In his *Discourse* Giraldi states unapologetically that romances directly contravene Aristotle's precept that an epic should imitate a single action. Romances deal not only with many actions but with many characters, building "the whole fabric of their work upon eight or ten persons."[4] Giraldi pointedly remarks that the romance came neither from the Greeks nor from the Romans but "laudably from our own language." The great writers of this language, he adds, gave to this genre "the same authority" that Homer and Vergil gave to their epics. Giraldi strikes a Romantic and modern tone when he insists that authors should not limit their freedom by restricting themselves within the bounds of their predecessors' rules (*DCR*, 39). His arguments here have a nationalistic strain: the Tuscan poets, he maintains, need not be bound by the poetic forms or literary confines of the Greeks and Romans (*DCR*, 40). As regards the civil function of the poet, Giraldi insists that poetry must "praise virtuous actions and censure the vicious" (*DCR*, 52). But the poet should observe the classical virtues of decorum and moderation in the use of figures such as allegory (*DCR*, 56, 67). Hence, Giraldi attempts a balance or compromise between classical virtues and contemporary artistic needs.

Lodovico Castelvetro (1505–1571)

Castelvetro is best known for his stringent reformulation of Aristotle's unities of time and place in drama, his rigid approach being subsequently endorsed by neoclassical writers. As against a long critical tradition, deriving in part from Horace, that the function of poetry was to be "useful" as well as to entertain, Castelvetro insisted, in a strikingly modern pose, that the sole end of poetry was to yield pleasure, especially for the common people. Moreover, the poet, he insisted, is made, not born or possessed by a Platonic furor: his creations are the product of study, training, and art.[5] In general, Castelvetro agrees with Aristotle's doctrine of the unities but offers a different rationale. On the unity of time, he agrees with Aristotle that a tragic plot must not exceed "one revolution of the sun," which Castelvetro takes to be 12 hours. But the real reason for this is not, as Aristotle held, the audience's limited memory, but the requirement of realism (*PA*, 82, 87).

Castelvetro accepts Aristotle's definition of the unity of a plot as consisting of a "single action of a single person" or, at most two actions which are closely interrelated (*PA*, 87, 89). But he finds no rationale in Aristotle for this; his own rationale is, firstly, that the temporal limitation of 12 hours on tragedy will not allow the representation of many actions; and, secondly, that the epic poet who restricts his representations to one action will all the more exhibit his "judgment and skill" (*PA*, 89–90). Moreover, Castelvetro appears to extrapolate the Aristotelian unity of time to extend to space: the action "must be set in a place no larger than the stage on which the actors perform and in a period of time no longer than that which is filled by their performance" (*PA*, 243). As this last sentence indicates, Castelvetro reformulates Aristotle's notion of the unities into a prescription for detailed realism. However, he agrees with Aristotle's general requirement that the poet represent the probable and the necessary.

Giacopo Mazzoni (1548–1598)

In his essay *Della difesa della Commedia di Dante* (1587; *On the Defense of the Comedy of Dante*), the Italian scholar Giacopo Mazzoni defended Dante's allegory against critics who condemned it as fantastic and unreal; he also formulated a comprehensive and systematic aesthetics of poetic imitation. Mazzoni draws upon a distinction made by Plato in his dialogue, the *Sophist*, between two kinds of imitation. The first, which imitates actual things, is "icastic"; the second, which imitates things of the artist's invention, is "phantastic."[6] In general, Mazzoni sees poetry as a "sophistic" or rhetorical art, whose proper genus is imitation, whose subject is the "credible," and whose end or purpose is delight (*DCD*, 85). According to Mazzoni, poetry can be viewed, in three different modes, as having three different ends or purposes: in its mode of imitation, its end is to provide a correct imitation or representation; considered as amusement, poetry's purpose is simply to produce delight; thirdly, it can be considered as "amusement directed, ruled, and defined by the civil faculty" (*DCD*, 95). In this mode, poetry has usefulness or moral betterment as its purpose: it "orders the appetite and submits it to the reason" (*DCD*, 98). Mazzoni uses this threefold definition of poetry to answer Plato's charges against poetry. The sort of poetry banished by Plato, says Mazzoni, was that which, unregulated by the civil faculty, produced a "free" delight which "disordered the appetite ... producing complete rebellion against reason and bringing damage and loss to a virtuous life" (*DCD*, 97).

A final strategy of Mazzoni's text is its attempt to rescue rhetoric from its scandalous reputation and to name poetry as a species of such a redeemed rhetoric. The redemption of both rhetoric and poetry rests upon Mazzoni's redefinition of their connection with truth; he deploys Aristotle's text to show that, as far as these disciplines are concerned, it is credibility rather than truth which stands as an appropriate ideal. In this insistence also, Mazzoni is modern, rescuing sophism, relativism, and author–audience interaction from the tyranny of absolute truth imposed by Plato and his successors.

Torquato Tasso (1544–1595)

Tasso is best known for his epic poem *Jerusalem Delivered* (1581), revised into a longer version, *Jersualem Conquered*. Tasso also wrote a long critical treatise *Discorsi del Poema Eroica* (1594; *Discourses on the Heroic Poem*), which defended his vernacular epic and which had a considerable impact not only on Renaissance but also on subsequent literary theory in Italy, England, and France.

In this text Tasso takes up the question of the relative merits of epic and tragedy, and of course, for him, it is the epic poem that must be accorded the higher honor. The epic poem provides its own distinctive delight, a delight produced through metaphor and the other figures of speech.[7] In arguing the superiority of epic, Tasso is challenging the authority of Aristotle who urged the superiority of tragedy given that it has all of the elements of epic but in greater concentration and unity. Tasso suggests that he is parting company with Aristotle in a few matters so that he "may not abandon him in things of greater moment, that is, in the desire to discover truth and in the love of philosophy" (*DHP*, 205). It is perhaps characteristic of his status as a Renaissance theorist that Tasso builds his own theory of epic on the foundation of Aristotle's poetics by refashioning that very foundation to serve his own purpose.

Defending the Vernacular

Notwithstanding the humanist reverence for the classics, many of the most illustrious minds of the Renaissance and Middle Ages, including such writers as Dante, Petrarch, Boccaccio, William Langland, John Gower, and Geoffrey

Chaucer, wrote in the vernacular; some of these, such as Petrarch and Dante, felt called upon to theorize and defend their practice. Ironically, humanism itself had done much to undermine the authority of *grammatica* by dismantling the edifice of late medieval scholasticism and the peculiar legacy of Aristotle informing it. Much of the impetus for this self-extrication from the imperial language of Latin lay in nationalist sentiment, and the sixteenth century witnessed the growth of national literatures in several countries, notably Italy, England, France, and Germany. The Protestant Reformation not only fueled such nationalist sympathy but fostered vernacular translations of the Bible as well as of liturgies and hymns, which in some cases laid broad foundations for the development of national languages. "National" epics were written by many of the major poets of the period, including Ariosto, Tasso, Ronsard, Spenser, and Milton. These writers were obliged to address controversial issues of meter, rhyming, and versification in vernacular tongues, as can be seen in the work of Du Bellay.

Joachim Du Bellay (ca. 1522–1560)

Du Bellay's *Defence and Illustration of the French Language* (1549) aimed to justify the French vernacular by basing it upon a new poetics such that it could match the gravity and decorum of the classical Greek and Latin languages. Du Bellay acknowledges that some languages have indeed become richer than others, but the reason for this is not their intrinsic virtue but the "artifice and industry of men."[8] He argues that the degradation of the French language is deeply rooted in a history of imperialism, not only in the military subjugation of other nations but in their cultural and linguistic subjugation. Du Bellay expresses the hope – no less political than cultural – that "when this noble and puissant kingdom will in its turn obtain the reins of sovereignty," the French language may "rise to such height and greatness, that it can equal the Greeks themselves and the Romans" (*NTC*, 283–284). Again, Du Bellay's text clearly connects cultural greatness with political and economic power. In a lengthy apostrophe to the future French poet, Du Bellay calls upon him to leave behind all popular verse forms and songs; to "turn the leaves of your Greek and Latin exemplars"; and, following Horace, to "mingle the profitable with the agreeable." For his subject matter, the poet should take praises of the gods and virtuous men, and the "immutable order of earthly things" (*NTC*, 289).

In some ways, Du Bellay's message is deeply conservative and traditional. While he calls for a renovation and enrichment of French language and literature, such elevation is focused entirely on a return to classical seriousness, gravity, and form. The only novel feature of his vision is the insistence that, by returning to the resources and archetypes of the classical languages, the French language might fulfill its potential to displace them and dislodge them from their positions of cultural sovereignty. Together with Ronsard and other members of the Pléiade, Du Bellay helped inaugurate a new era of French poetry.

Poetics and the Defense of Poetry

Following Boccaccio's and Du Bellay's endeavors, notable defenses of poetry were undertaken by many writers. Such apologiae and defenses have been obliged to continue through the nineteenth century into our own day, highlighting the fact that the category of the "aesthetic," as a domain struggling to free itself from the constraints of theology, morality, politics, philosophy, and history, was in part a result of Renaissance poetics. Integral to many of these defenses was a formula adapted from Horace that poetry must teach and delight, as in the work of Sidney.

Sir Philip Sidney (1554–1586)

Sir Philip Sidney is often cited as an archetype of the well-rounded "Renaissance man": his talents encompassed not only poetry and cultivated learning but the virtues of statesmanship and military service. He was involved in a war waged by Queen Elizabeth I against Spain and died from a wound at the age of 32. He wrote a pastoral romance, *The Countess of Pembroke's Arcadia* (1581), and he was original in producing a sonnet cycle in the English language, entitled *Astrophil and Stella* (1581–1582).

Sidney's *Apologie for Poetrie* (1580–1581) is in many ways a seminal text of literary criticism. While its ideas are not original, it represents the first synthesis in the English language of the various strands and concerns of Renaissance literary criticism, drawing on Aristotle, Horace, and more recent writers such as Boccaccio and Julius Caesar Scaliger. It raises issues – such as the value and function of poetry, the nature of imitation, and the concept of nature – which were to concern literary critics in numerous languages until the late eighteenth century. Sidney's writing of the *Apologie* as a defense of poetry was occasioned by an attack on poetry entitled *The School of Abuse* published in 1579 by a Puritan minister, Stephen Gosson.

In the *Apologie*, Sidney produces a wide range of arguments in defense of "poor Poetry," based on chronology, the authority of ancient tradition, the relation of poetry to nature, the function of poetry as imitation, the status of poetry among the various disciplines of learning, and the relationship of poetry to truth and morality. Sidney's initial argument is that poetry was the first form in which knowledge was expressed, the "first light-giver to ignorance," as bodied forth by figures such as Musaeus, Homer, Hesiod, Livius, Ennius, Dante, Boccaccio, and Petrarch.[9] His point is that an essential prerequisite of knowledge is pleasure in learning; and it is poetry that has made each of these varieties of knowledge – scientific, moral, philosophical, political – accessible by expressing them in pleasurable forms (*APP*, 218).

Sidney's second argument is an "argument from tradition" since it appeals to the ancient Roman and Greek reverence for poetry. The Roman term for the poet was *vates*, meaning "diviner, fore-seer, or prophet." The ancient Greek definition of poetry is even more important: the Greek origin of the English word "poet" was the word *poiein*, meaning "to make." Whereas other arts and sciences are constrained, examining a particular area or aspect of nature, the poet ranges freely "within the zodiac of his own wit." As such, the poet's "making" or production is superior to nature: "Nature never set forth the earth in so rich tapestry, as divers poets have done . . . Her world is brazen, the poets only deliver a golden" (*APP*, 219–221).

Sidney situates this human creativity in a theological context. Though man is a "maker" or poet, his ability derives from his "heavenly Maker . . . who having made man to his own likeness, set him beyond and over all the works of that second nature, which in nothing he showeth so much as in poetry: when with the force of a divine breath, he bringeth things forth far surpassing her doings." Sidney goes on to refer to original sin, as a result of which "our erected wit, maketh us know what perfection is, and yet our infected will, keepeth us from reaching unto it" (*APP*, 222). Significant here is the intrinsic connection between man's ability to "make" poetry and his status in relation to God. That man is made in the image of God is most profoundly expressed in man's replication, on a lower level, of God's function as a creator. It also implies that man is elevated above the world of physical nature (which Sidney calls "second nature").This God-like activity in man which exalts him above the rest of nature is expressed above all in poetry.

Sidney defines poetry as "an art of imitation, for so Aristotle termeth it in his word *mimesis*, that is to say, a representing, counterfeiting, or figuring forth: to speak metaphorically, a speaking picture: with this end, to teach and delight." Sidney suggests that there have been three kinds of poetic imitation. The first is religious, imitating "the inconceivable excellencies of God, as in the Old Testament. The second is effected by poetry that deals with subjects whose scope is philosophical, historical or scientific, such as the works of Cato, Lucretius, Manilius, or Lucan. The third kind, urges Sidney, is produced by "right poets . . . who having no law but wit, bestow that in colors upon you which is fittest for the eye to see." These are the poets who "most properly do imitate to teach and delight, and to imitate, borrow nothing of what is, hath been, or shall be: but range only . . . into the divine consideration of what may be, and should be" (*APP*, 223–224). Hence the poet is free of dependence on nature in at least two ways: firstly, he is not restricted to any given subject matter, any given sphere of nature. Secondly, his "imitation" does not actually reproduce anything in nature, since his concern is not with actuality but with portrayals of probability and of idealized situations.

The ultimate aim of this kind of poetry is moral: the poet imitates, says Sidney, in order "both to delight and teach." The object of both teaching and delighting is goodness. However, Sidney sees all learning, and not just poetry, as directed to this final end or purpose. While all sciences have "a private end in themselves," the "ending end of all earthly learning" is "virtuous action." In leading the soul toward good, poetry is superior to its chief competitors, moral philosophy and history. Both disciplines are one-sided: the philosopher sets down the "bare rule" in difficult terms that are "abstract and general"; the historian, conversely, lacks the force of generalization and is "tied, not to what should be, but to what is, to the particular truth of things." Sidney says that "the one giveth the precept, and the other the example." It is the "peerless poet," according to Sidney, who performs both functions: "he coupleth the general notion with the particular example." It is poetry which can strike the soul and the inward sentiments by means of "a true lively knowledge" (*APP*, 226–230). The power of poetry to move or influence people, says Sidney, "is of a higher degree than teaching." For all of these reasons, proclaims Sidney, we must set "the laurel crown upon the poet as victorious, not only of the historian, but over the philosopher." Sidney's tone is repeatedly triumphalistic and persistent in attempting to overturn the conventional hierarchy of knowledge: "of all sciences . . . is our poet the monarch" (*APP*, 235–236). The irony here is that Sidney uses a theological justification for poetry to dethrone theology and philosophy from their preeminent status. This is unmistakably a step in the direction of secular humanism.

Sidney now addresses the specific charges brought against poetry. One of the main charges is that poetry "is the mother of lies." Sidney's famous retort is that "the poet . . . nothing affirms, and therefore never lieth." Unlike the historian, the poet does not claim to be telling the truth; he is not relating "what is, or is not, but what should or should not be." He is writing "not affirmatively, but allegorically, and figuratively" (*APP*, 247–249). The most serious charge that Sidney confronts is that Plato banished poets from his ideal republic. He argues that Plato opposed the abuse of poetry rather than the art itself (*APP*, 253–255). Sidney concludes by admonishing the reader that "there are many mysteries contained in poetry, which of purpose were written darkly, least by profane wits, it should be abused." And he curses those who are possessed of "so earth-creeping a mind, that it cannot lift itself up, to look to the sky of poetry" (*APP*, 269–270). The metaphor here truly encapsulates the entire thrust of Sidney's text: formerly, sacred scripture was spoken of in this fashion, as written "darkly," so as to lie beyond the reach of unworthy eyes; in Sidney's text, poetry is elevated to that sacred status: in its very nature it is opposed to worldliness and "earth-creeping" concerns; it is the newly appointed heaven of human invention.

Poetic Form and Rhetoric

Until the recovery of Aristotle's *Poetics* which fostered a new examination
of literary form that was not wholly grounded in rhetoric, the domains of
poetics and rhetoric had increasingly overlapped. During the Renaissance,
rhetoric enjoyed a renewed centrality in educational institutions. Many of
the writers we have looked at, such as Du Bellay and Sidney, treated poetry
as a higher form of rhetoric and took from rhetorical theory an emphasis on
persuasiveness and the power to move an audience or reader. In returning to
classical precedents, Renaissance poets confronted other issues. They rejected the regular stress-based alliterative meter of medieval poets. Some
experimented with the idea of classical quantitative meters, based on length
of syllables rather than stress. In general, the humanists rejected rhyme as an
unclassical barbarism; the controversy over rhyme was salient in the debate
between Samuel Daniel, who wrote a *Defence of Rhyme* (1603), and
Thomas Campion, who rejected rhyme in favor of classical forms. The
aversion to rhyme on the part of figures such as William Webbe and George
Puttenham, who went so far as to affiliate the use of rhyme with a Roman
Catholic mentality, led to the search for a new metrical basis for English
poetry and eventually fueled the growth of blank verse. These tendencies,
including a rhetorical approach to poetic form, can now be considered as
they occurred on the English literary scene in the work of Gascoigne and
Puttenham.

George Gascoigne (1542–1577)

The poet and dramatist George Gascoigne is credited with having written the
first literary-critical essay in the English language, entitled "Certayne Notes of
Instruction Concerning the Making of Verse or Ryme in English" (1575).
Here, Gascoigne offers advice on a range of rhetorical issues, including
invention, prosody, verse form, and style. He stresses the need for "fine
invention," or the finding of appropriate theme and material. It is not enough,
he says, "to roll in pleasant words," or to indulge in alliterative "thunder."[10]
Gascoigne insists that the poet must employ "some depth of device in the
invention, and some figures also in the handling thereof," or else his work will
"appear to the skilful reader but a tale of a tub" (i.e., some trite or ordinary
matter) (*ER*, 163).

Gascoigne cautions against the use of "rhyme without reason" and advises
the poet to be consistent in his use of meter throughout a poem (*ER*, 164). He
admonishes the poet to situate every word such that it will receive its "natural
emphasis or sound . . . as it is commonly pronounced or used." He indicates
the three types of accent, *gravis* (\\) or the long accent, *levis* (/) or the short

accent, and *circumflexa* (∼) which is "indifferent," capable of being either long or short (*ER*, 164). He notes that the most common foot in English is the foot of two syllables, the first short and the second long (the iambic foot), and he encourages the use of the iambic pentameter (in which, as many other writers have noted, the English language seems naturally to fall). Also furthering the cause of a distinctive English verse is Gascoigne's advice that the poet avoid words of many syllables, since "the most ancient English words are of one syllable, so that the more monosyllables that you use the truer Englishman you shall seem, and the less you shall smell of the inkhorn" (*ER*, 166).[11] Gascoigne urges the poet to find a middle ground between "haughty obscure verse" and "verse that is too easy" (*ER*, 167). Much of the advice offered by Gascoigne moves in the direction of both standardizing certain English poetic and metrical practices and differentiating these from "foreign" practices.

George Puttenham (d. 1590)

A long and influential treatise entitled *The Arte of English Poesy*, published anonymously in 1589, is attributed to George Puttenham. The central purpose of this treatise is to justify the use of the vernacular language for poetry, and specifically to establish English vernacular poetry as an *art*, requiring serious study and labor. The *Arte* is divided into three books, the first justifying poetry as expressing the needs of individual and society; the second, "Of Proportion," devoted to the craft of poetry; and the third, "Of Ornament," offering a renaming of the figures and tropes of classical rhetoric. Puttenham was writing at the advent of a great period of English letters, and his text amply exhibits how early English criticism was tied to certain controversies over language (such as the desirability of importing terms from Greek, Latin, and other languages), as well as to the emerging perception of certain features of English verse, such as the emphasis on stress of syllables. It might be said that Puttenham's treatise not only contributed to the idea of a "standard" English, but also founded and enabled some of the terminology of early modern literary criticism in English. Terms such as "ode," "lyric," and "epigrammatist" were brought into standard currency partly through the agency and influence of Puttenham's text.[12]

Importantly, Puttenham sees the English line of verse as based on meter and rhyme, and moves toward a perception of the function of stress in English verse (*AEP*, 78–80). Classifying the various meters used at this time, he furnishes effectively the first English prosody. His chapter "Of Language" is a *locus classicus* of the issue of standard English. He sees a point at which a language achieves a general consensus and standardization, a point beyond which only minor changes are admissible. Like Sidney, Puttenham urges that poetry is unique among the arts inasmuch as it is enabled by "a cleare and bright phantasie and imagination." The poet, in fact, is "most admired when he is most naturall and least artificiall" (*AEP*, 307). Puttenham's text represents in many ways an important stage in the development of modern English criticism, long anticipating what will become Romantic reactions against neoclassicism, and even moving toward a notion of art as primarily offering pleasure. The overt emphasis on pleasure, as opposed to moral instruction, is an implicit – though not at this stage a consciously or precisely formulated – gesture toward poetic autonomy.

Notes

1. David Norbrook, "Introduction," in *The Penguin Book of Renaissance Verse 1509–1659*, ed. H. R. Woudhuysen (Harmondsworth: Penguin, 1993), pp. xxii–xxv. Hereafter cited as *PBRV*.
2. Glyn P. Norton, ed., *The Cambridge History of Literary Criticism: Volume III: The Renaissance* (Cambridge: Cambridge University Press, 1999), pp. 3–4.
3. David Norbrook, *Poetry and Politics in the English Renaissance*, revised edition (Oxford: Oxford University Press, 2002), p. 1. Hereafter cited as *PER*.
4. *Giraldi Cinthio on Romances: Being a Translation of the Discorso intorno al comporre dei romanzi*, trans. Henry L. Snuggs (Lexington: University of Kentucky Press, 1968), p. 11. Hereafter cited as *DCR*.
5. Castelvetro, *On the Art of Poetry: An Abridged Translation of Lodovico Castelvetro's Poetica d'Aristotele Vulgarizzata et Sposta*, trans. Andrew Bongiorno (Binghamton, NY: Medieval and Renaissance Texts and Studies, 1984), pp. 42–43. Hereafter cited as *PA*.
6. Giacopo Mazzoni, *On the Defense of the Comedy of Dante: Introduction and Summary*, trans. Robert L. Montgomery (Tallahassee: University Presses of Florida, 1983), p. 46. Hereafter cited as *DCD*.
7. "Introduction," in Torquato Tasso, *Discourses on the Heroic Poem*, trans. Mariella Cavalchini and Irene Samuel (Oxford: Clarendon Press, 1973), p. 172. Hereafter cited as *DHP*.
8. Joachim Du Bellay, *La Deffence et Illustration de la Langue Francoyse* (Paris: Société des Textes Français Modernes, 1997). Since the English translation, *The Defence and Illustration of the French Language* by Gladys M. Turquet, is not easily available, I have referred to the selections from this translation reprinted in *The Norton Anthology of Theory and Criticism*, ed. Vincent B. Leitch (New York and London: W. W. Norton, 2001). Hereafter cited as *NTC*.
9. *The Selected Poetry and Prose of Sir Philip Sidney*, ed. David Kalstone (New York and Toronto: New American Library, 1970), pp. 216–217. Hereafter cited as *APP*.
10. George Gascoigne, "Certayne Notes of Instruction," reprinted in *English Renaissance Literary Criticism*, ed. Brian Vickers (Oxford: Clarendon Press, 1999), p. 162. Hereafter cited as *ER*.

11. Around this time there was raging the "Inkhorn" controversy concerning the use of foreign words in English. The inkhorn was an inkwell, and came to signify figuratively a certain pedantry associated with foreign, often polysyllabic, words.

12. George Puttenham, *The Arte of English Poesie*, ed. Gladys Doidge Willcock and Alice Walker (1936; rpt. Cambridge: Cambridge University Press, 1970), p. xcii. Hereafter cited as *AEP*.

Chapter 7

Neoclassical Literary Criticism

Neoclassicism refers to a broad tendency in literature and art enduring from the early seventeenth century until around 1750. Most fundamentally, neoclassicism comprised a return to the classical models, literary styles, and values of ancient Greek and Roman authors. In this, the neoclassicists were to some extent heirs of the Renaissance humanists. But many of them reacted sharply against what they perceived to be the stylistic excess, superfluous ornamentation, and linguistic oversophistication of some Renaissance writers; they also rejected the lavishness of the Gothic and Baroque styles.

Many major medieval and Renaissance writers, including Dante, Ariosto, More, Spenser, and Milton, had peopled their writings with fantastic and mythical beings. Authors such as Giraldi had attempted to justify the genre of the romance and the use of the "marvelous" and unreal elements. Sidney and others had even proposed that the poet's task was to create an ideal world, superior to the world of nature. The neoclassicists, reacting against this idealistic tendency in Renaissance poetics, might be thought of as heirs to the other major tendency in Renaissance poetics, which was Aristotelian. This latter impetus had been expressed in the work of Minturno, Scaliger, and Castelvetro, who had all stressed the Aristotelian notion of probability, as well as the "unities" of action, time, and place.

However, whereas many Renaissance poets had labored toward an individualism of outlook, the neoclassicists were less ambiguous in their emphasis upon the classical values of objectivity, impersonality, rationality, decorum, balance, harmony, proportion, and moderation. Whereas many Renaissance poets were beginning to understand the importance of invention and creativity, the neoclassical writers reaffirmed literary composition as a rational and rule-bound process, requiring a great deal of craft, labor, and study. Where Renaissance theorists and poets were advocating new and mixed genres, the neoclassicists tended to insist on the separation of poetry and prose, the purity of each genre, and the hierarchy of genres (though, unlike

Literary Criticism from Plato to the Present: An Introduction   M. A. R. Habib
© 2011 M. A. R. Habib

Aristotle, they generally placed the epic above tragedy). The typical meters and verse forms of the neoclassical poets were the alexandrine in France and the heroic couplet in England. Much neoclassical thought was marked by a recognition of human finitude, in contrast with the humanists' (and, later, the Romantics') assertion of almost limitless human potential.

Two of the concepts central to neoclassical literary theory and practice were "imitation" and "nature," which were intimately related. In one sense, the notion of imitation – of the external world and, primarily, of human action – was a reaffirmation of the ideals of objectivity and impersonality. But it also referred to the imitation of classical models, especially of Homer and Vergil. In fact, these two aspects of imitation were often identified, as by Pope. The identification was based largely on the concept of "nature," which had a number of senses. It referred to the harmonious and hierarchical order of the universe, including the various social and political hierarchies within the world. In this vast scheme of nature, everything had its proper and appointed place. The concept also referred to *human* nature: to what was central, timeless, and universal in human experience. Hence, "nature" had a deep moral significance, comprehending the modes of action that were permissible and excluding certain actions as "unnatural" (a term often used by Shakespeare to describe the murderous and treacherous behavior of characters such as Lady Macbeth). Clearly, the neoclassical vision of nature was very different from the meanings later given to it by the Romantics. The neoclassical writers saw the ancients such as Homer and Vergil as having already expressed the fundamental laws of nature. Hence, the external world could best be expressed by modern writers if they followed the path of imitation already paved by the ancients. Invention was allowed but only as a modification of past models.

But some neoclassical writers, such as Ben Jonson, Corneille, and Dryden, were more flexible in their assimilation of classical values. Indeed, there raged at the beginning of the eighteenth century various debates over the relative merits of "ancients" and "moderns." The ancients were held to be the repository of good sense, natural laws, and the classical values of order, balance, and moderation. Such arguments were found in Jonathan Swift's *The Battle of the Books* (1710) and in the writings of Boileau and Pope. Proponents of the "modern" laid stress on originality of form and content, flexibility of genre, and the license to engage in new modes of thought.

The connection of neoclassicism to recent science and to the Enlightenment was highly ambivalent and even paradoxical. On the one hand, the neoclassical concept of nature was informed by Newtonian physics, and the universe was acknowledged to be a vast machine, subject to fixed analyzable laws. On the other hand, the tenor of most neoclassical thought was retrospective and conservative. On the surface, it might seem that the neoclassical writers shared with Enlightenment thinkers a belief in the power of reason. But, while it is true that some neoclassical writers, especially in Germany, were influenced by Descartes and other rationalists, the "reason" to which the neoclassical writers appeal is in general not the individualistic and progressive reason of the Enlightenment; rather, it is the "reason" of the classical philosophers, a universal human faculty that provides access to general truths and which is aware of its own limitations. Alexander Pope and others emphasized the finitude of human reason, cautioning against its arrogant and unrestricted employment. Reason announced itself in neoclassical thought largely in Aristotelian and sometimes Horatian terms: an adherence to the requirements of probability and verisimilitude, as well as to the three unities, and the principle of decorum (harmony of form and content). But the verisimilitude or realism that neoclassical writers sought was different from nineteenth-century realism: they sought to depict the typical elements and the universal truths about any given situation; their realism did not operate via accumulation of empirical detail or a random recording of so-called reality. It was reason in this Aristotelian sense that lay behind the insistence on qualities such as order, restraint, moderation, and balance.

This general tendency of neoclassicism toward order, clarity, and standardization was manifested also in attempts during the seventeenth and eighteenth centuries to regulate the use of language and the meanings of words. In France, the Académie Française was established for this purpose in 1635. Samuel Johnson's *Dictionary* was published in 1755. The impetus behind these endeavors was reflected in John Locke's theory of language, and his insistence on philosophy using "clear and distinct" ideas and avoiding figurative language. This ideal of clarity, of language as the outward sign of the operations of reason, permeated neoclassical poetry which was often discursive, argumentative, and aimed to avoid obscurity. This movement toward clarity has been variously theorized as coinciding with the beginnings of bourgeois hegemony, as reacting against a proliferation of vocabulary and meanings during the Renaissance, and as marking a step further away from a medieval allegorical way of thinking toward an attempted literalization of language. The following sections will consider some of the major figures of neoclassical literary criticism in the countries where it was most pronounced: France and England.

French Neoclassicism

Neoclassical literary criticism first took root in France from where its influence spread to other parts of Europe, notably England. The mission of the French Academy, founded in 1635, was partly to standardize language through the creation of a dictionary and grammar, and to foster an eloquence deemed necessary to the public sphere and the growth of civil society.[1] The major figures of French neoclassicism were Corneille, Racine, Molière, and La Fontaine. Corneille's theories grew out of the need to defend his dramatic practice against strict classicists such as Scudéry and Jean Chapelain. The most prominent theorists were Dominique Bouhours, René Rapin, and Nicolas Boileau.

Pierre Corneille (1606–1684)

Pierre Corneille's most important piece of literary criticism, *Trois Discours sur le Poème Dramatique* (*Three Discourses on Dramatic Poetry*, 1660), was produced in response to the charge that his play, *Le Cid* (1637), despite its popularity, violated the classical unities – of action, time, and place – as well as the Aristotelian precepts of probability and necessity, and thereby undermined the morally didactic function of drama.

In his third *Discourse*, entitled "Of the Three Unities of Action, Time, and Place," Corneille agrees with Aristotle that "there must be only one complete action," but he insists that "action can become complete only through several others ... which ... keep the spectator in a pleasant suspense."[2] As for the number of acts, this was not prescribed by Aristotle; and though Horace limits a play to five acts, we do not know for sure, says Corneille, how many acts ancient Greek plays contained ("TU," 107–108). Nor was there a rule for the unity of place; and the unity of time, prescribed by Aristotle as "one revolution of the sun," must be interpreted liberally according to what is practical on the stage and for the audience ("TU," 109, 114–115).

In general, Corneille explains that it is easy for critics to be strict in their censure; but if they themselves had to produce plays, if they themselves "recognized through experience what constraint their precision brings about and how many beautiful things it banishes from our stage," they might reconsider their own severity. The test, Corneille insists, is experience, actual practice. Corneille's overall aim, as he suggests, is to "make ancient rules agree with modern pleasures" ("TU," 115). In this endeavor, he is not so much making those rules more liberal as reformulating them in the light of the needs and requirements of the audience, especially the modern audience. Corneille effectively rescues the importance of performance from the peripheral status it meekly occupies in Aristotle's text.

Nicolas Boileau (1636–1711)

The French poet and critic Boileau had a pervasive influence not only on French letters (of the old-fashioned kind) but also on English and German poets and critics, notably Pope. His *L'Art Poétique* (*The Art of Poetry*), first published in 1674, was translated into English by John Dryden. Boileau's text represents a formal statement of the principles of French classicism and enjoyed such prestige that he was known as the *législateur du Parnasse*, credited with the formation of French literary taste. Just as Molière's plays effect a balance between religious belief and rationalism, arguing for an enlightened rather than authoritarian religion, so Boileau's *Art of Poetry* is marked by a central affirmation of the importance of reason, as well as observation. It reacts against Christian puritanism, submitting the claims of the latter to the judgment of reason. But, as with Molière and Pope, the "reason" espoused by Boileau is not the individualistic reason of the Enlightenment but a classical view of reason as a common human faculty which perceives what is universally true.

Boileau's text is written as a poem, in the tradition of Horace's *Ars poetica*. In canto I, he reiterates the Horatian formula:

> In prudent lessons everywhere abound,
> With pleasant join the useful and the sound;
> A sober reader a vain tale will slight,
> He seeks as well instruction as delight.[3]

Where Boileau's text moves beyond Horace is in its insistence on the centrality of reason to the poetic enterprise: "Love reason then; and let whate'er you write/Borrow from her its beauty, force, and light" (*APB*, I, ll. 37–38). Boileau is skillful in drawing out the widely varied ramifications of the reliance on reason, which enables poetic control, moderation, the unities of time and place, and the imitation of classical examples. For Boileau, reason also urges against the subjection of poetry to religious puritanism. He states: "Our pious fathers, in their priest-rid age, / As impious and profane abhorred the stage." But "At last right reason did his laws reveal, / And showed the folly of their ill-placed zeal (*APB*, III, ll. 79–80, 85–86). In his desire to return to classical models, Boileau countenances even those aspects of classical paganism that directly contradict Christian teaching, on the grounds that the gospels are not a fitting subject for verse and that removal of classical ornament will impoverish a poem.

Anticipating Pope, Boileau appeals to nature: "To study nature be your only care." The poet, he says, must know human nature and the "secrets of the heart." He must observe and be able to paint all kinds of people, at all stages in life. But even here, the following of nature is seen as obeying the rules of reason: "Your actors must by reason be controlled; / Let young men speak like young, old men like old" (*APB*, III, ll. 390–391). Reason has one final aspect in Boileau's text: a harmony with the passions, which it must "move" by entertaining them (*APB*, III. ll. 15–21, 25–26). Boileau is here repeating an old formula, used earlier by many Renaissance writers such as Sidney: inasmuch as poetry instructs, it must first delight.

Neoclassicism in England

The main streams of English neoclassical criticism were inspired by (and reacted against) the French example. French influence in England was intensified by the Restoration of 1660, whereby Charles II, exiled in France after the English Civil War, returned with his court to England. Boileau's influence was most pronounced on Pope; Dryden defended English drama against some of the French critics. As noted earlier, the France of Louis XIV had embarked upon a neoclassical program of national proportions. While neoclassical criticism in England was not so systematic, many saw the adoption of neoclassical ideals as integral to a stable and orderly political state. The classical tendency in England embraced a number of major prose writers who laid the foundations of the modern English novel such as Daniel Defoe (1660?–1731), Jonathan Swift (1667–1745), and Henry Fielding (1707–1754). In general, the critics ranging from Jonson to Dryden effectively advanced the notion of a viable English literary tradition.

John Dryden (1631–1700)

Samuel Johnson termed Dryden "the father of English criticism," and affirmed of his *Essay of Dramatic Poesy* (1668) that "modern English prose begins here." Dryden's critical work was extensive, treating of various genres such as epic, tragedy, comedy and dramatic theory, satire, the relative virtues of ancient and modern writers, as well as the nature of poetry and translation. Dryden was also a consummate poet, dramatist, and translator. He was appointed poet-laureate in 1668 and his major poems included the mock-heroic "Mac Flecknoe" (1682), and a political satire *Absalom and Achitophel* (1681). Dryden's *Essay of Dramatic Poesy* is written as a series of debates on drama conducted by four speakers – Eugenius, Crites, Lisideius, and Neander – who have conventionally been identified with four of Dryden's contemporaries, with Neander ("new man") representing Dryden himself.[4]

Like Tasso and Corneille, Dryden attempted to strike a compromise between the claims of ancient authority and the needs of the modern writer. In Dryden's text, this compromise subsumes a number of debates, concerning: the classical "unities," of time, place, and action; the rigid classical distinction between various genres, such as tragedy and comedy; classical decorum and propriety; and the use of rhyme in drama. Dryden also undertakes an influential assessment of the English dramatic tradition.

As against the neoclassical virtues of French drama, Neander urges the virtues of English tragi-comedy, thereby overturning nearly all of the ancient prescriptions concerning purity of genre, decorum, and unity of plot. Neander poignantly repeats Corneille's observation that anyone with actual experience of the stage will see how constraining the classical rules are. Neander states that Shakespeare "had the largest and most comprehensive soul." He was "naturally learn'd," not through books but by the reading of nature and all her images: "he looked inwards, and found her there." In an important statement he affirms that "Shakespeare was the Homer, or father of our dramatic poets; Johnson was the Vergil, the pattern of elaborate writing" (*DP*, 76–82). What Neander – or Dryden – effectively does here is to stake out an independent tradition for English drama, with new archetypes displacing those of the classical tradition. In the final debate, concerning rhyme, Dryden suggests that blank verse and rhyme are equally artificial: in everyday life, people do not speak in blank verse, any more than they do in rhyme (*DP*, 100–101).

If Dryden is neoclassical, it is in the sense that he acknowledges the classics as having furnished archetypes for drama; but modern writers, he says, are at liberty to create their own archetypes and their own literary traditions. Again, he might be called classical in insisting that the unity of a play, however conceived, be a paramount requirement; that a play present, through its use of plot and characterization, events and actions which are probable and express a semblance of truth; that the laws of "nature" be followed, if not through imitation of the ancients, then through looking inward at our own profoundest constitution; and finally, that every aspect of a play be contrived with the projected response of the audience in mind. But given Dryden's equal emphasis on the poet's wit, invention, and imagination, his text might be viewed as expressing a status of transition between neoclassicism and Romanticism.

Indeed, in his 1666 preface to *Annus Mirabilis*, he states that the "composition of all poems is, or ought to be, of wit; and wit . . . is no other than the faculty of imagination in the writer" (*DP*, 14). Again, the emphasis here is on wit and imagination rather than exclusively on the classical precept of imitation. In fact, Dryden commends rhyme for the delight it produces: "for delight is the chief, if not the only, end of poesy: instruction can be admitted but in the second place, for poesy only instructs as it delights." If in such statements Dryden appears to anticipate certain Romantic predispositions, these comments are counterbalanced by other positions which are deeply entrenched in a classical heritage. Later in the "Defence" he insists that "moral truth is the mistress of the poet as much as of the philosopher; Poesy must resemble natural truth, but it must *be* ethical."[5] Hence, notwithstanding the importance that he attaches to wit and imagination, Dryden still regards poetry as essentially a rational activity, with an ethical and epistemological responsibility. This stance effectively embodies both Dryden's classicism and the nature of his departure from its strict boundaries.

Alexander Pope (1688–1744)

Pope's *An Essay on Criticism* (1711) is perhaps the clearest statement of neoclassical principles in any language. It expresses a world view which synthesizes elements of a Roman Catholic outlook with classical aesthetic principles and with deism. The prevailing anti-Catholic laws constrained many areas of Pope's life: he could not obtain a university education, hold public or political office, or even reside in London. However, Pope was privately taught and moved in an elite circle of London writers which included the dramatists Wycherly and Congreve, the poet Granville, the critic William Walsh, as well as the writers Addison and Steele, and the deistic politician Bolingbroke. Pope produced some of the finest verse ever written. His most renowned publications include several mock-heroic poems such as *The Rape of the Lock* (1712; 1714), and *The Dunciad* (1728). His philosophical poem *An Essay on Man* (1733–1734) was a scathing attack on human arrogance or pride in failing to observe the due limits of human reason, in questioning divine authority and seeking to be self-reliant; Pope espouses an ethic based on an ordered and hierarchical universe yet depicts this order in terms of Newtonian mechanism and expresses a broadly deistic vision.

An Essay on Criticism is written in verse, in the tradition of Horace's *Ars poetica*. Pope here not only delineates the scope and nature of good literary criticism, but redefines classical virtues in terms of "nature" and "wit," as necessary to both poetry and criticism. Pope's call for a "return to nature" is complex. On a cosmic level, nature signifies the providential order of the world and the universe, a hierarchy in which each entity has its proper assigned place. In *An Essay on Man* Pope expounds the "Great Chain of Being," ranging from God and the angels through man and the lower animals to plants and inanimate objects. Nature can also refer to what is normal, central, and universal in human experience, encompassing the spheres of morality and knowledge, the rules of proper moral conduct as well as the archetypal patterns of human reason. The word "wit" in Pope's time could refer in general to intelligence; it also meant "wit" in the modern sense of cleverness, as expressed in figures of speech and especially in discerning unanticipated similarities between different entities. By Pope's time, literature generally had come to be associated with wit and had come under attack from the Puritans, who saw it as morally defective and corrupting.

While Pope cautions that the best poets make the best critics, and while he recognizes that some critics are failed poets (l. 105), he points out that both the best poetry and the best criticism are divinely inspired: "Both must alike from Heav'n derive their Light" (ll. 13–14). Pope sees the endeavor of criticism as a noble one, provided it abides by Horace's advice for the poet:

> But *you* who seek to *give* and *merit* Fame,
> And justly bear a Critick's noble Name,
> Be sure *your self* and your own *Reach* to know,
> How far your *Genius*, *Taste*, and *Learning* go;
> Launch not beyond your Depth...
>
> (ll. 46–50)

Apart from knowing his own capacities, the critic must be conversant with every aspect of the author whom he is examining. Pope insists that the critic base his interpretation on the author's intention: "In ev'ry Work regard the Writer's *End*, / Since none can compass more than they *Intend*" (ll. 233–234, 255–256).

Pope specifies two further guidelines for the critic. The first is to recognize the overall unity of a work, and thereby to avoid falling into partial assessments based on the author's use of poetic conceits, ornamented language, meters, as well as judgments which are biased toward either archaic or modern styles or based on the reputations of given writers. Finally, a critic needs to possess a moral sensibility, as well as a sense of balance and proportion, as indicated in these lines: "Nor in the *Critick* let the *Man* be lost! / *Good-Nature* and *Good-Sense* must ever join (ll. 523–525). Pope ends his advice with this summary of the ideal critic:

> But where's the Man, who Counsel *can* bestow,
> Still *pleas'd* to *teach*, and yet not *proud to know*?
> Unbiass'd, or by *Favour* or by *Spite*;
> Not *dully prepossest*, nor *blindly right*;
> Tho learn'd, well-bred; and tho' well-bred, sincere;
> ... Blest with a *Taste* exact, yet unconfin'd;
> A *Knowledge* both of *Books* and *Humankind*;
> Gen'rous *Converse*; a *Soul* exempt from *Pride*;
> And *Love* to *Praise*, with *Reason* on his Side?
>
> (ll. 631–642)

It is clear that these qualities of a good critic are primarily attributes of humanity or moral sensibility rather than aesthetic qualities. Indeed, the only specifically aesthetic quality mentioned here is "taste." The remaining virtues might be said to have a theological ground, resting on the ability to overcome pride. Pope effectively transposes the language of theology ("soul," "pride") to aesthetics. The "reason" to which Pope appeals is (as in Aquinas and many medieval thinkers) a universal archetype in human nature, and is a corollary of humility. It is the disposition of humility – an aesthetic humility, if you will – which enables the critic to avoid the foregoing faults.

Now comes Pope's central advice to both poet and critic, to "follow Nature," whose restraining function he explains:

> Nature to all things fix'd the Limits fit,
> And wisely curb'd proud Man's pretending Wit;
> ... One Science only will one Genius fit;
> So vast is Art, so narrow Human Wit...
>
> (ll. 52–53, 60–61)

Hence, even before he launches into any discussion of aesthetics, Pope designates human wit generally as an instrument of pride, as intrinsically liable to abuse. In the scheme of nature, however, man's wit is puny and occupies an apportioned place. It is in this context that Pope proclaims his famous maxim:

> First follow NATURE, and your Judgment frame
> By her just Standard, which is still the same:
> *Unerring Nature*, still divinely bright,
> Once *clear*, *unchang'd*, and *Universal* Light,
> Life, Force, and Beauty, must to all impart,
> At once the *Source*, and *End*, and *Test* of Art.
>
> (ll. 68–73)

The features attributed to nature include permanence or timelessness and universality. Ultimately, nature is a force which expresses the power of the divine, not in the later Romantic sense of a divine spirit pervading the physical appearances of nature but in the medieval sense of expressing the order, harmony, and beauty of God's creation. As such, Nature provides the eternal and archetypal standard against which art must be measured.

Pope does not believe, like many medieval rhetoricians, that poetry is an entirely rational process. In poetry, as in music, he points out, are "*nameless* Graces which no Methods teach" (l. 144). Indeed, geniuses can sometimes transgress the boundaries of judgment and their very transgression or license becomes a rule for art (ll. 152–156). Pope here seems to assert the primacy of wit over judgment, of art over criticism, viewing art as inspired and as transcending the norms of conventional thinking in its direct appeal to the "heart." The critic's task here is to recognize the superiority of great wit. While this emphasis strides beyond many medieval and Renaissance aesthetics, it must of course be read in its own poetic context: he immediately warns that modern writers should not rely on their own insights but draw on the common store of poetic wisdom, established by the ancients, and acknowledged by "*Universal* Praise" (l. 190).

Pope's exploration of wit aligns it with the central classical virtues, which are themselves equated with nature: "*True Wit* is *Nature* to Advantage drest, / What oft was *Thought*, but ne'er so well *Exprest*" (ll. 297–298). Pope subsequently says that expression is the "*Dress of Thought*," and that "true expression" throws light on objects without altering them (ll. 315–318). The lines above are a concentrated expression of Pope's classicism. If wit is the "dress" of nature, it will express nature without altering it. The poet's task here is twofold: not only to find the expression that will most truly convey nature, but first to ensure that the substance he is expressing is indeed a "natural" insight or thought. What the poet must express is a universal truth which we will instantly recognize as such. This classical commitment to the expression of objective and universal truth is echoed a number of times through Pope's text. For example, he admonishes both poet and critic: "Regard not then if Wit be *Old* or *New*, / But blame the *False*, and value still the *True*" (ll. 406–407).

Another classical ideal urged by Pope is that of organic unity and wholeness. The expression or style must be suited to the subject matter and meaning: "The *Sound* must seem an *Eccho* to the *Sense*" (l. 365). An essential component in such unity and proportion is the classical virtue of moderation. Pope advises both poet and critic to follow the Aristotelian ethical maxim: "Avoid *Extreams*." Those who go to excess in any direction display "*Great Pride*, or *Little Sense*" (ll. 384–387). And, once again, the ability to overcome pride – humility – is implicitly associated with what Pope calls "right Reason" (l. 211). Indeed, the central passage in the *Essay on Criticism*, as in the later *Essay on Man*, views all of the major faults as stemming from pride:

> Of all the Causes which conspire to blind
> Man's erring Judgment, and misguide the Mind,
> ... Is *Pride*, the *never-failing Vice of Fools*.
>
> (ll. 201–204)

It is pride which leads critics and poets alike to overlook universal truths in favor of subjective whims; pride which causes them to value particular parts instead of the whole, pride which disables them from achieving a harmony of wit and judgment, and pride which underlies their excesses and biases. As in the *Essay on Man*, Pope associates pride with individualism, with excessive reliance on one's own judgment and failure to observe the laws laid down by nature and by the classical tradition.

Pope's final strategy in the *Essay* is to equate the classical literary and critical traditions with nature, and to sketch a redefined outline of literary history from classical times to his own era. Pope insists that the rules of nature were merely discovered, not invented, by the ancients: "Those Rules of old *discover'd*, not *devis'd*, / Are *Nature* still, but *Nature Methodiz'd*" (ll. 88–89). Pope's advice, for both critic and poet, is clear: "Learn hence for Ancient *Rules* a just Esteem; / To copy *Nature* is to copy *Them*" (ll. 139–140). Pope traces the genealogy of "nature," as embodied in classical authors, from Aristotle through the Roman authors Horace, Petronius, Quintilian, and Longinus. After these, a dark age ensued with the collapse of the western Roman Empire at the hands of the Vandals and Goths, an age governed by "tyranny" and "superstition," an age where "Much was *Believ'd*, but little *understood*" (ll. 686–689). What is interesting here is that, even though he was himself a Catholic, Pope sees the Catholic medieval era as a continuation of the so-called Dark Ages. Even more striking is his subsequent praise of the

Renaissance humanist thinker Erasmus, who "drove those *Holy Vandals* off the Stage" (ll. 693–694).

Pope's implicit allegiance to Erasmus (and in part to contemporary figures such as Bolingbroke) points in the direction of a broad deism which, on the one hand, accommodates the significance of pride in secular, rather than theological, contexts, and, on the other hand, accommodates reason within its appropriate limits. His historical survey continues with praises of the "Golden Days" of the Renaissance, and suggests that the arts and criticism thereafter flourished in Europe, especially in France which produced the critic and poet Nicolas Boileau (1636–1711). Given Boileau's own impact on Pope's critical thought, we can see that Pope now begins to set the stage for his own entry into the history of criticism. The writers Pope now cites were either known to him or his tutors. All in all, Pope's strategy here is remarkable: in retracing the lineage of good criticism, as based on nature and the true use of wit, he traces his own lineage as both poet and critic, thereby both redefining or reaffirming the true critical tradition and marking his own entry into it.

Aphra Behn (1640–1689)

Aphra Behn was a pioneer in many respects. Because of her family circumstances and her husband's early death, she was obliged to support herself as a writer – one of the first women to do so. She is one of the founders of the English novel; her extended stay in Surinam inspired her to write *Oroonko* (1688), the first novel to oppose slavery. And her experience as a female playwright exposed her to the enormous obstacles faced by a woman in this profession, resulting in her highly unorthodox and controversial views about drama. These views are expressed largely in the prefaces to her plays, such as *The Dutch Lover* (1673), *The Rover* (1677), and *The Lucky Chance* (1687). If figures such as Pierre Corneille took a step away from the authority of classical rules by appealing to experience, Aphra Behn's appeal to experience – to specifically female experience – was far more radical. Moreover, she (perhaps unwittingly) elevates to a newly important status the performative dimensions of drama, such as the ability and integrity of the actors.

In one of her prefaces, Behn strikes a tone of utter defiance. She defends the value of drama by contrasting it favorably with traditional learning as taught in the universities.[6] But equally, she denies that dramatic poets can perform a moral function: "no Play was ever writ with that design." Behn's own, carefully unstudied, opinion is that drama represents the best entertainment that "wise men have"; to discourse formally about its rules, as if it were "the grand affair" of human life, is valueless. Behn's own purpose, in writing her play *The Dutch Lover*, was "only to make this as entertaining as I could," and the judges of her success will be the audience (*Behn*, I, 223).

Behn now takes up the murky issues surrounding female authorship. She heaps a barrage of insulting criticism ("ill-favour'd, wretched Fop" and more) upon a man who warned the audience for her play to expect "a woful Play . . . for it was a womans." Replying to his presumption, she asserts that women, if given the same education as men, are just as capable of acquiring knowledge and in as many capacities as men. Further, given that "affectation hath always had a greater share both in the actions and discourse of men than truth and judgment have," women might well reach the heights attained by men" (*Behn*, I, 224). The classical rules of drama she dismisses in a breath: these "musty rules of Unity, . . . if they meant anything, they are enough intelligible, and as practicable by a woman" (*Behn*, I, 224). With no apology, she ends with: "Now, Reader, I have eas'd my mind of all I had to say" (*Behn*, I, 225).

In her preface to *The Lucky Chance*, written some 15 years later, Behn states that she will defend her comedy against "those Censures that Malice, and ill Nature have thrown upon it, tho' in vain."[7] It is the very success of her play, she exclaims, that caused critics to "load it with all manner of Infamy." And they heap upon it, she says, "the old never failing Scandal – That 'tis not fit for the Ladys" (*Behn*, III, 185). She hastens to point out that many works of poetry have long treated the subject of women in an indecent fashion, but the offense is overlooked "because a Man writ them." She admonishes her critics not simply to condemn her work because it is a woman's; but to "examine whether it be guilty or not, with reading, comparing, or thinking" (*Behn*, III, 185). Moreover, she points out several great plays with allegedly indecent scenes which are artistically justified (*Behn*, III, 186).

What Behn effectively does here is to place the virtues of good judgment, critical reading, and thinking, beyond the pale of traditional masculine learning and the conventional male literary establishment, which have both, on account of their transparent bias and maliciousness, forfeited their right to speak with authority. Behn presents another voice, a woman's voice, speaking not from a position below that establishment but rather from above; she takes no great pains to dislodge male assumptions about women writers; rather, she appropriates for woman's use the categories of common sense and reason, extricating them from the tradition of male prejudice in which they have been abused and occluded.

Behn's originality lies as much in the way she speaks as in what she speaks: her texts adopt a tone and a style unprecedented in the history of literary criticism. Defiant, unapologetic, and placing herself entirely outside of the traditional canons of male learning and literature (an externality achieved often by her very tone), her writing does not follow a logical pattern; it seems to be punctuated, rather, by the movement of her righteous anger, her deliberate outpourings of emotion, the nodal points of her rebuttals of insubstantial criticism, and the flow of particularity or detail – of names, and particular circumstances – which itself infuses her general statements with substance in a newly immediate and transparent manner, the general being treated as on the same level as the particulars which it comprehends rather than loftily coercing particulars (in what she would regard as a conventionally male fashion) into the exemplifying service of its own pre-determined and prescriptive nature.

Samuel Johnson (1709–1784)

Samuel Johnson is perhaps best remembered for his two-volume *Dictionary of the English Language*, first published in 1755. Of almost equal renown are his *Lives of the English Poets* (1783) and his eight-volume edition of Shakespeare (1765). His most famous poem is *The Vanity of Human Wishes* (1749), a speculation on the emptiness of worldly pursuits. He also wrote drama and a fictional work, *The History of Rasselas* (1759), as well as numerous essays in periodicals such as *The Rambler*, *The Adventurer*, and *The Idler*. Johnson's own biography was recorded by his friend James Boswell, who published his celebrated *Life of Samuel Johnson* in 1791. Johnson's "Preface" to, and edition of, Shakespeare's plays played a large part in establishing Shakespeare's reputation; his account of the lives of numerous English poets contributed to the forming of the English literary canon and the defining of qualities such as metaphysical "wit"; his remarks on criticism itself were also to have an enduring impact.

In his fictional work, *The History of Rasselas*, Johnson expresses through one of his characters called Imlac a statement which has often been regarded as a summary of neoclassical principles. The business of the poet, says Imlac, is "to examine, not the individual, but the species; to remark general properties and large appearances . . . He is to exhibit in his portraits of nature such prominent and striking features, as recall the original to every mind." The poet must "divest himself of the prejudices of his age or country; he must consider right and wrong in their abstract and invariable state . . . and rise to general and transcendental truths, which will always be the same."[8]

Johnson's classical commitment to reason, probability and truth was complemented by his equally classical insistence on the moral function of literature. In 1750 he urged that modern writers require not only the learning that is to be gained from books but also "that experience which . . . must arise from general converse, and accurate observation of the living world."[9] However, the prime concern of the author should not be verisimilitude but moral instruction (*Rambler*, 11). Johnson acknowledges that "the greatest excellency of art" is to "imitate nature; but it is necessary to distinguish those parts of nature, which are most proper for imitation" (*Rambler*, 12–13). The author must not "confound the colors of right and wrong," and must indeed help to "settle their boundaries." Vice must always produce disgust, not admiration; and virtue must be shown in the most perfect form that probability will allow (*Rambler*, 14–15). Like Aristotle, Johnson desires literature to express truth in general and universal terms, but its choice of material and manner should be circumscribed by moral imperatives. However, he acknowledges that rules should be drawn from reason rather than from mere precedent (*Rambler*, 197–199).

Johnson's "Preface" to his edition of Shakespeare's plays is informed by three basic concerns: how a poet's reputation is established; the poet's relation to nature; and the relative virtues of nature and experience of life as against a reliance on convention. Inquiring into the reasons behind Shakespeare's enduring success, Johnson makes an important general statement: "Nothing can please many, and please long, but just representations of general nature."[10] Once again, by "general nature," Johnson refers to the avoidance of particular manners or customs and the foundation of one's work on universal truths. Shakespeare, above all writers, is "the poet of nature: the poet that holds up to his readers a faithful mirrour of manners and of life." His characters are not molded by the accidents of time, place, and local custom; rather, they are "the genuine progeny of common humanity," and they "act and speak by the influence of those general passions and principles by which all minds are agitated" (Preface, 62).

Johnson acknowledges that Shakespeare's plays "are not in the rigorous and critical sense either tragedies or comedies." Shakespeare "has united the powers of exciting laughter and sorrow not only in one mind but in one composition" (Preface, 66–67). It is here, in his defense of tragicomedy, that Johnson appeals to nature as a higher authority than precedent. He allows that Shakespeare's practice is "contrary to the rules of criticism ... but there is always an appeal open from criticism to nature. The end of writing is to instruct; the end of poetry is to instruct by pleasing. That the mingled drama may convey all the instruction of tragedy or comedy cannot be denied, ... and approaches nearer than either to the appearance of life" (Preface, 67).

Johnson does concede, however, that Shakespeare had many faults: the looseness of his plots, the lack of regard for distinction of time or place, the grossness and licentiousness of his humor; the coldness and pomp of his narrations and set speeches; and a digressive fascination with quibbles and wordplay (Preface, 71–74). He argues that Shakespeare does observe unity of action, but he had no regard for the unities of time and place, a point on which Johnson defends Shakespeare by questioning these unities themselves. Johnson concludes that these unities are "to be sacrificed to the nobler beauties of variety and instruction," the greatest virtues of a play being "to copy nature and instruct life" (Preface, 80). In this text, Johnson's appeal to nature and direct experience and observation over classical precedents and rules, as well as his assessment of Shakespeare as inaugurating a new tradition, effectively set the stage for various broader perspectives of the role of the poet, the poet's relation to tradition and classical authority, and the virtues of individualistic poetic genius.

Another area in which Johnson exerted great influence on his successors was that of biography and comparative estimation of the poets in the English canon. In his *Lives of the English Poets* (1781), he raises biography to an art: far from being slavishly adherent to facts, Johnson's text is replete with all the apparatus of imaginative texts: figures of speech, imaginative insights, hypothetical argumentation, vivid descriptions, and speculative judgments; he appeals not only to the intellects of his readers but to their emotions, backgrounds, and moral sensibilities.

Notes

1. Glyn P. Norton, ed., *The Cambridge History of Literary Criticism: Volume III: The Renaissance* (Cambridge: Cambridge University Press, 1999), p. 500.
2. Pierre Corneille, "Of the Three Unities of Action, Time, and Place," trans. Donald Schier, in *The Continental Model: Selected French Critical Essays of the Seventeenth Century, in English Translation*, ed. Scott Elledge and Donald Schier (Ithaca and London: Cornell University Press, 1970), pp. 101–102. Hereafter cited as "TU."
3. Nicolas Boileau, *The Art of Poetry*, IV, ll. 86-89. The text used here is the translation by William Soame and John Dryden. It is reprinted in *The Art of Poetry: The Poetical Treatises of Horace, Vida, and Boileau*, trans. Francis Howes, Christopher Pitt, and Sir William Soames, ed. Albert S. Cook (Boston: Ginn, 1892). Hereafter cited as *APB*.
4. John Dryden, "Defence of *An Essay of Dramatic Poesy*," in *Essays of John Dryden: Volume I*, ed. W. P. Ker (New York: Russell and Russell, 1961), p. 133. Hereafter cited as *DP*.
5. *Essays of John Dryden: Volume II*, ed. W. P. Ker (New York: Russell and Russell, 1961), pp. 113, 121.
6. *The Works of Aphra Behn: Volume I*, ed. Montague Summers (New York: Benjamin Blom, 1967), p. 221. Hereafter cited as *Behn*, I.
7. *The Works of Aphra Behn: Volume III*, ed. Montague Summers (New York: Benjamin Blom, 1967), p. 185. Hereafter cited as *Behn*, III.
8. Samuel Johnson, *The History of Rasselas, Prince of Abyssinia* (Harmondsworth: Penguin, 1986), ch. X.
9. Samuel Johnson, *Essays from the Rambler, Adventurer, and Idler*, ed. W. J. Bate (New Haven and London: Yale University Press, 1968), p. 10. Hereafter cited as *Rambler*.
10. *The Yale Edition of the Works of Samuel Johnson: Volume VII: Johnson on Shakespeare*, ed. Arthur Sherbo, introd. Bertrand H. Bronson (New Haven and London: Yale University Press, 1968), p. 61. Hereafter cited as Preface.

Chapter 8

The Enlightenment

Historical and Intellectual Background

The Enlightenment was a broad intellectual tendency, spanning philosophy, literature, language, art, religion, and political theory, which lasted from around 1680 until the end of the eighteenth century. Conventionally, the Enlightenment has been called the "age of reason," though this designation fails to comprehend the various intellectual trends of the period. The Enlightenment thinkers were by no means uniform in their outlooks, but in general they saw themselves as initiating an era of humanitarian, intellectual, and social progress, underlain by the increasing ability of human reason to subjugate analytically both the external world of nature and the human self. They viewed it as their mission to rid human thought and institutions of irrational prejudice and superstition, as well as to foster a society free of feudal caprice, political absolutism, and religious intolerance, where human beings could realize their potential through making moral and political choices on the foundations of rationality and freedom. In political and economic terms, Enlightenment thought was integral to the rise of liberalism and the French Revolution of 1789, which initiated the displacement of the power of the king and nobility by the power of the bourgeoisie or middle classes. The feudal world was characterized by values of static hierarchy, loyalty, reverence for authority, and religious faith. These were increasingly displaced by bourgeois ideology, which was predominantly secular, stressing reason, individual experience, efficiency, usefulness, and, above all, political liberalism based on a free rational economy aided by technology and science.

The main streams of the Enlightenment continue to have a profound effect on our world. Much Enlightenment thought was underlain by a new scientific vision of the universe inspired by the work of the English mathematician Sir Isaac Newton (1642–1727): this conception of a mechanical universe ordered by laws which were scientifically ascertainable eventually displaced the view of the universe as ordered and historically directed by a benevolent divine

Literary Criticism from Plato to the Present: An Introduction   M. A. R. Habib
© 2011 M. A. R. Habib

providence. The very concept of reason issued a profound challenge to centuries-old traditions of thought and institutional practice. Reliance on reason was in itself nothing new; the classical philosophers such as Plato and Aristotle had urged reason as the faculty through which we could gain access to truths which were universal and certain. Medieval Christian philosophy acknowledged that reason was a necessary component of a proper spiritual disposition, but it was only one element and needed to be balanced by faith and revelation. What was novel to the Enlightenment was its insistence on reason as the primary faculty through which we could acquire knowledge, and on its potentially limitless application. The exaltation of man's individual capacity for reasoning effectively undermined reliance on any form of authority, whether it be the authority of the Church, the state, or tradition. This way of thinking is particularly marked in modern democracies even today: as Alexis de Tocqueville noted about America, people in general prefer to rely on their own insight (however uninformed) rather than submit to the authority or testimony of others, even of experts.

Three seminal precursors of Enlightenment thought were the English thinker Francis Bacon (1561–1626), the French rationalist philosopher René Descartes (1596–1650), and the Dutch rationalist thinker Benedict (or Baruch) Spinoza (1632–1677). Bacon's major philosophical works were *The Advancement of Learning* (1605) and *The New Organon* (1620), where he formulated the method of induction whereby we generalize on the basis of actual observation of a number of particular occurrences. He favored induction, as the method of modern science, over the medieval reliance on deduction and *a priori* reasoning, whose premises were handed down by tradition. For centuries, Bacon warns, the human mind has been misled by four classes of "idols" or false notions. The first type are "Idols of the Tribe," or the distorted impressions of nature caused by common human deficiencies of sense and understanding; the next are "Idols of the Cave": each man has a private cave or den – his subjective background and experience – from which he sees the world; the third kind of idols are those of the "marketplace," the vulgar notions formed through social intercourse. Finally, there are "Idols of the Theatre," the philosophical systems which are "merely stage plays" because they represent "worlds of their own creation" rather than the actual world.[1] The upholders of these previous systems urge us to view the world through those fictions rather than experiencing it directly for ourselves.

René Descartes (1596–1650) is often called the "father" of modern philosophy. Like Bacon, Descartes challenged the basic principles of medieval philosophy. In his *Discourse on Method* he began his thinking in a skeptical mode, doubting all things, including his own senses, understanding and the reality of the external world, until he could find a secure and certain foundation of knowledge. He imagined that the entire world might be a delusion. But Descartes realized that he could not doubt that very element in himself which was engaged in doubting or thinking, hence his conclusion "I think, therefore I am." Descartes proceeded to identify his essential nature or self with the process of thinking, calling himself a "thinking being." In this way, he made his famous dualism or distinction between mind and body. The mind is a thinking substance, whereas the body belongs to the world of space, time, and material extension. Descartes inferred as a general rule that the things which we conceive very "clearly and very distinctly" are all true.[2] He took mathematics as his model of knowledge given that its ideas were clear and distinct and that its truths were certain.

The third seminal figure, Spinoza, was a Jew born in Amsterdam, whose own rationalist and unorthodox views led to his expulsion from the Jewish community in 1656 for heresy. Like Descartes, he believed in the primacy of deduction and in a mechanistic view of the universe; however, he did not adopt Cartesian dualism, arguing instead that the universe is composed of a single substance, which he viewed as God, and which is refracted differently in the attributes of mind and matter. In his major work, the *Ethics* (1677), he urged that the highest good consists in the rational mastery over one's passions and ultimately in the acceptance of the order and harmony in nature, which is an expression of the divine nature. Subsequent Enlightenment thinkers, such as John Locke (1632–1704) and David Hume (1711–1776) in Britain, Voltaire (1694–1778), Diderot, and d'Alembert in France, as well as Gotthold Lessing (1729–1781) in Germany, encouraged more skeptical, rational, and tolerant approaches to religion. The most common approach was "deism," which saw divine laws as natural and rational, and dismissed all superstition, miracles, and sacraments.

It is worth looking briefly at the empiricist philosopher John Locke (1632–1704), whose most influential works were *An Essay Concerning Human Understanding* and *Two Treatises on Civil Government*, both published in 1690. In the *Essay* Locke denied Descartes' view that the mind has "innate ideas," ideas that it is simply born with. Rather, the mind is initially a *tabula rasa* or blank slate upon which our experience of the world is written.[3] Locke argues that all our ideas come from experience, through either sensation or reflection. We receive distinct ideas of the objects in the external world through our senses, such as the ideas of yellow, white, hard, cold, or soft; we also receive ideas through reflection on the internal operation of our own minds; these ideas include perception, thinking, doubting, reasoning, and believing. These two operations, he says, are "the fountains of knowledge" and there is no other source of knowledge or ideas (*Essay*, 89–90, 348).

The Scottish philosopher David Hume (1711–1776) developed some of Locke's empiricist notions toward more radical, skeptical, conclusions. Where Locke had urged that our minds know the external world through ideas, Hume argued that we know *only* ideas, not the external world itself. We can know external objects only by the "perceptions they occasion" whether they indeed are real or merely "illusions of the senses."[4] In fact, Locke himself acknowledged that the real essence of things is unknowable (*Essay*, 271–273, 287, 303). Both Locke and Hume rejected the Aristotelian concept of "substance" or essence as the underlying substratum of reality. Hume develops the skepticism implicit in Locke's rejection of substance: there are no essences actually in the world, whether we are talking of external objects such as a table, or human identity, or moral concepts such as goodness. All of these are ultimately constructions of our minds, informed largely by custom and habit. Indeed, in Hume's view, even the human self or human identity was not a fixed datum but a construction through a "succession of perceptions" (*THN*, 135). In Hume's eyes, the law of causality, on which modern science was based, has merely a conventional validity, based on nothing more than the authority of custom or the habitual, "constant conjunction" of phenomena (*THN*, 316).

In France, the main figures of the Enlightenment were Voltaire (1694–1778), Denis Diderot (1713–1784), and Jean d'Alembert. Perhaps more than anyone else, Voltaire popularized the ideas of Newton and Locke. His numerous works included the *Philosophical Dictionary* (1764) and a fictional philosophical tale, *Candide* (1759), in which he promulgated the necessity of reason and experience, and the notion that the world is governed by natural laws. He mocked the optimism, determinism, and rationalism of the German philosopher Gottfried Leibniz who believed in a preestablished harmony in the world, lampooning the latter's position in the phrase "Everything is for the best in this best of all possible worlds." The implication is that abstract reason of itself does not comprehend the infinite variety of human situations. In this sense, reason is held up as a kind of comforting fiction, pandering to the human need for order. Voltaire satirizes the "rational" justifications for war, the intolerance of religions, the institutions of inequality, the search for a utopia, the greed which undermines human contentment, the gullibility of the masses, and the strength of human self-deception; one of the two stark lessons to emerge is the need to experience the world directly: "to know the world one must travel," concludes Candide. The other lesson is the need to work, in order to stave off the "three great evils, boredom, vice and poverty." In general, Voltaire championed liberty and freedom of speech, though his sympathies did not extend to the common man. The other French Enlightenment rationalists, Diderot and d'Alembert, were the leading members of the group which produced the *Encyclopedia*, a compendium of the latest scientific and philosophical knowledge. In Germany, the tendencies of the Enlightenment were expressed by Gotthold Lessing (1729–1781) and Moses Mendelssohn (1729–1786) who both propounded philosophies of religious tolerance.

In political terms, several Enlightenment philosophers drew up a theory of the ideal state or "social contract," the contract that might be agreed upon by citizens of a state so that social life would be governed by laws and that both the ruler's power and the rights of his subjects would be defined. Many of these thinkers postulate what men would be like in a state of nature, prior to the formation of a social contract. Hobbes' view of this state, as expressed in his *Leviathan* (1651) is bleak: men would be in a perpetual state of war. There would be merely "continual fear, and danger of violent death; and the life of man, solitary, poor, nasty, brutish, and short." The most important philosopher in the formulation of political liberalism was John Locke, and certain Enlightenment philosophies had a formative influence on the ideals behind the French Revolution. Locke's *Second Treatise of Civil Government* (1690) condemned despotic monarchy and the absolute sovereignty of parliaments, affirming that the people had a right to resist tyranny. Voltaire advocated an enlightened monarchy or republic governed by the bourgeois classes. Baron de Montesquieu (1689–1755) also influenced the French Revolution, advancing a liberal theory based on a separation of executive, legislative, and judicial powers. Jean-Jacques Rousseau (1712–1778) exerted a powerful impact on the more radical stages of the Revolution through his theories of democracy, egalitarianism, and the evils of private property, as advocated in his *Social Contract* and *Discourse on the Origin of Inequality*. However, in some ways, Rousseau hardly belongs to the main trends of rationalist Enlightenment thought; he is often hailed as the father of Romanticism on account of his exaltation of the state of nature over civilization, and of the emotions and instincts over reason and conventional learning.

In general, the major tendencies of Enlightenment philosophy were toward rationalism, empiricism, pragmatism, and utilitarianism; these formed the core of liberal-bourgeois thought. The main philosophical assumptions behind this tradition of thought were: that the world is composed of particular things which are distinct and separate from one another (philosophical pluralism); that consciousness (the human self) and the world are mutually distinct, and there is an external reality independent of our minds; and that general ideas are formed from the association and abstraction of particular ones (in other words, general ideas are constructions of our minds and are not found in the world). It is these assumptions that underlie the other trends of Enlightenment thinking: that the world is a machine, subject to laws; that human society is an aggregate of atomistic or separate individuals; that the individual is an autonomous and free rational agent; that reliance on reason and experience or observation will enable us to understand the world, the human self, and enable historical progress in humanitarian, moral, religious, and political terms.

These assumptions not only permeate Enlightenment discussions of literature, but have continued to inform many literary critical perspectives, ranging from the experiential theories of literature advanced by figures such as Matthew Arnold and Henry James to the New Criticism and other movements of the twentieth century such as neo-Aristotelianism. The rationalist disposition of the Enlightenment has in various modifications informed the aesthetics of Kant, Hegel, Marx, and Croce. Equally, much criticism flowing from the Romantics and French symbolists, as well as from thinkers such as Schopenhauer, Nietzsche, Bergson, Heidegger, and Sartre, has urged the problematic nature of Enlightenment assumptions. The psychoanalytic criticism inspired by Freud and Jung, and more recent movements such as structuralism, deconstruction, and postcolonial criticism have subjected Enlightenment rationalism and empiricism to searching intellectual and ideological scrutiny. They have questioned the idea that entities exist independently, the epistemological validity of subject–object dualism, the idea of an independent external world, and the notion that language somehow reflects or corresponds with reality. It should be remembered, however, that many of these critiques were initiated by the Enlightenment philosophers themselves and were most articulately expressed by Hegel long before the advent of more modern developments.

Enlightenment Literary Criticism: Language, Taste, and Imagination

A very direct connection between Enlightenment philosophy and literary criticism occurs through the various philosophies of language in the eighteenth century, the most important being the theory of John Locke. Many scholars have argued that Locke's empiricism stimulated in literature a relatively novel preoccupation with sensory detail, scientific description, and particularity. This influence undermined the neoclassical conception, stretching all the way back through Renaissance and medieval writers to Aristotle, that poetry speaks a universal language and expresses general truths. Also influential were the psychological aspects of empiricism, presenting the mind as not merely receiving ideas passively from the external world but as *active* in constructing experience through associating those ideas in various combinations. Poetry attempted to express human psychology and to register the mind's association of ideas. In fact, the doctrine of "associationism," running through thinkers such as Locke, Hume, Hartley, and Condillac, became a force in literary critical discussions of poetic language.[5]

The philosophical assumptions of the Enlightenment can now be examined in the literary and cultural criticism of some major thinkers. We can consider the views of language formulated by Locke and Vico; the popularization of Locke's ideas and their integration with neoclassical and even precursive Romantic notions in the work of Addison; the theories of taste and judgment offered by Hume and Burke (whose thinking, specifically opposed to many

Enlightenment values, can fruitfully be considered here); and the analysis of women's social and educational status undertaken by Mary Wollstonecraft, who effectively extends Enlightenment ideals to the notion of gender.

John Locke (1632–1704)

John Locke laid the foundations of classical British empiricism, and his thought is often characterized as marked by tolerance, moderation, and common sense. The implications of Locke's empiricism are still with us: many ideological forces still encourage us to look at the world as an assemblage of particular facts, yielding sensations which our minds then process in arriving at abstract ideas and general truths.

Locke's philosophy of language anticipates a great deal of modern literary critical thinking about language. His fundamental endeavor is to show how closely language is connected with the process of thought and he therefore urges the need to use language in the most precise way so as to avoid unnecessary confusion in our concepts. In an influential passage that impinges profoundly on literature, Locke makes his famous distinction between two faculties, wit and judgment:

> men who have a great deal of wit, and prompt memories, have not always the clearest judgment or deepest reason. For wit lying most in the assemblage of ideas, and putting those together with quickness and variety . . . thereby to make up pleasant pictures and agreeable visions in the fancy; judgment, on the contrary, lies quite on the other side, in separating carefully, one from another, ideas wherein can be found the least difference, thereby to avoid being misled . . . This is a way of proceeding quite contrary to metaphor and allusion; wherein for the most part lies that entertainment and pleasantry of wit, which strikes so lively on the fancy. . . (*Essay*, II, xi, 2)

Locke effectively revives the age-old antagonism between philosophy and poetry (or rhetoric). The domain of poetry is governed by wit, which sees identities and affinities between disparate things, an imaginative and fictive operation designed to please the fancy. The realm of philosophy, on the other hand, is presided over by judgment, by the clear, cool ability to *separate* what does not belong together, to distinguish clearly between things, in the interests of furthering knowledge. The impulse of one lies toward confusion and conflation, while the impetus of the other is toward clarity. The poetic realm is the realm of fancy, of figurative language, of metaphor and allusion; the language of philosophy shuns adornment, and engages with the real world. Locke attempts to dismantle the poetic effort of many centuries to fuse the claims of delight and instruction, viewing these as opposed rather than allied.

Indeed, Locke urges that figurative speech comprises one of the "abuses" of language, and calls rhetoric a "powerful instrument of error and deceit" (*Essay*, III, x, 34). Locke defines language as "the instrument of knowledge" (*Essay*, III, ix, 21). The imperfection of words lies in the uncertainty of what they signify. He lists a number of willful faults which contribute to the failure of communication: the use of words without "clear and distinct ideas," or the use of "signs without anything signified"; affecting obscurity, by using words in new and unusual ways; and using obscurity to cover up conceptual difficulties and inadequacies (*Essay*, III, x, 2–22). Locke speculates that if there were a dictionary to standardize and clarify all language usage, many of the current controversies would end (*Essay*, III, xi, 9–26). Locke is effectively calling for a literalization of language, an extrication of words from their metaphorical and allegorical potential, a potential accumulated over many centuries. Locke's voice is perhaps the most pronounced sign of the bourgeois refashioning of language into a utilitarian instrument, a scientistic tendency that still infects some of our composition classrooms to this day.

Locke's seemingly harsh views of figurative speech need to be appraised in the context of his skeptical empiricism. Anticipating Saussure and many modern theorists of language, Locke emphasizes that the connection between signs (words) and ideas is not natural but is made by "a perfectly arbitrary imposition" which is regulated by "common use, by a tacit consent" (*Essay*, III, ii, 8). He emphasizes that "general" and "universal" do not belong to "real existence" or to "things themselves": they are inventions of the human mind, designed to facilitate our understanding of the world (*Essay*, III, iii, 11–12). The essence of any general idea such as "man" is not found in the world; it is a purely verbal essence; Locke denies that there are in the world any "real essences" that we can know (*Essay*, III, iii, 13). Nature itself contains only particulars, and its apparent regularity and order are projections of our own thought processes whose medium is language.

All of this points to a "coherence" theory of language, whereby language is not referential (referring to some external reality), but acquires meaning only through the systematic nature and coherence of its expression of our perceptions. Indeed, Locke's urgent desire for linguistic clarity is perhaps a reaction to the failing system of referentiality: the entire edifice, the entire equation and harmony of language and reality, promulgated through centuries of theological building on the notion of the Logos (embracing the idea of God as both Word and the order of creation expressed by this), is about to crumble.

Joseph Addison (1672–1719)

Joseph Addison contributed much to the development of the essay form, which, like the literary form of the letter, flourished in the eighteenth century. Together with his friend and colleague Richard Steele, he authored a series of articles in the periodicals *The Tatler* (1709–1711) and *The Spectator* (1711–1714). Steele referred to his age as "a corrupt Age," devoted to luxury, wealth, and ambition rather than to the virtues of "good-will, of Friendship, of Innocence."[6] He urges that people's actions should be directed toward the public good rather than merely private interests, and that these actions should be governed by the dictates of reason, religion, and nature (*Spectator*, 68–70).

In *The Spectator* there are several essays or articles dealing with specifically literary-critical issues, such as the nature of tragedy, wit, genius, the sublime, and the imagination. As far as tragedy goes, Addison and Steele advise following the precepts of Aristotle and Horace. Their general prescription is to follow nature, reason, and the practice of the ancients (*Spectator*, 87). Addressing themselves to a broad middle-class public immersed in the materialist and pragmatist ideologies of bourgeois thought, their insistence on classical values might be seen as part of their endeavor to cultivate the moral, religious, and literary sensibilities of this class; they were nonetheless obliged to accommodate the more recent attitudes toward beauty and the imagination, attitudes gesturing in the direction of Romanticism, which equally undermined the conventional values of this political class.

Giambattista Vico (1668–1744)

The Italian philosopher Vico articulated a historical view of the progress of human thought, language, and culture that anticipates the evolutionary perspectives of Hegel, Marx, and others. His major work was *Scienza nuova* (*New Science*), first published in 1725. He was affiliated with a group of radical intellectuals who reacted against the central tenets of medieval philosophy and who espoused the rationalist and empiricist values of the Enlightenment. He urges that the "new science" must be "a rational civil theology of divine providence," demonstrating in its analysis of human institutions, "what providence has wrought in history."[7]

In a strikingly new fashion, Vico's insights into poetry form an integral part of his attempt to explain the origins and development of human society. Vico sees the progression of wisdom or knowledge as moving from the senses (the province of poetry) through reason (the sphere of philosophy) to revelation. The first poets, says Vico, not having our power of abstraction, used a "poetic logic" of four basic tropes: metaphor, metonymy, synecdoche, and irony (*NS*, para. 409, p. 131). In their initial use among primitive peoples, these four tropes represented the *only* engagement with the world, which had no underlying literal basis. As the human mind developed, a more rational, scientific, and literal expression of our relationship with the world was established and the tropes were reduced to a figurative status, articulated in relation to this literal level. They remained, however, as integrally related to the literal and endured as its foundation. Thus, Vico attributes two important historical functions to poetry, or what he calls "poetic wisdom": on it were founded the religious and civil institutions of the first peoples; and it provided the embryonic basis for all further learning.

David Hume (1711–1776)

As noted earlier, the Scottish empiricist and skeptical philosopher David Hume was one of the major figures of the Enlightenment. His essay "Of the Standard of Taste" (1757) raises questions about the standards of aesthetic judgment that are still pertinent today: how do we reconcile people's conflicting judgments about taste? Can we arrive at an objective standard? Hume stresses that the rules of art are not fixed by *a priori* reasonings but by experience, by "general observations, concerning what has been universally found to please in all countries and all ages."[8] True taste, according to Hume, is a rational process; we rely on good sense to check our prejudices, and reason is requisite to the formation of good taste in a number of ways. We must be aware of the structure of the work, of the way the various parts relate to the whole, of the "consistence and uniformity of the whole," as well as the end or purpose of the work of art. Even poetry, says Hume, "is nothing but a chain of propositions and reasonings ... however disguised by the colouring of the imagination." Hence the poet himself needs not only taste and invention but judgment; likewise, the "same excellence of faculties" is required by the critic who would achieve good taste ("OST," 494). The standard of taste, then, is not objective; rather, it is based on subjective consensus – but only the consensus of "qualified" people.

In attempting to rescue artistic taste from mere subjectivism, Hume appeals to a number of factors, all of which are based on experience. First, there is a canon of literature and art that has survived the judgment of various times and cultures, a canon established by consensus. Next, this consensus points to a common human nature which responds universally to certain features of art, such as elegance and organic unity. Finally, this consensus is the consensus of a qualified elite of critics who, through their ability to reach a disinterested aesthetic perspective, are authorized to act as the arbiters of true taste, as the voice of that common human nature in its intact, cultivated, and unbiased state.

Edmund Burke (1729–1797)

Edmund Burke is best known for his political writings and his activities as a statesman. By far his most famous work was his *Reflections on the Revolution in France* (1790), a scathing attack on numerous aspects of the French Revolution of 1789. Here Burke expresses a desire to conserve the essential economic and political fabric of feudalism. He appeals to the authority of the past and opposes the collective wisdom and experience of the past to what he sees as the abstract rationalism of the French revolutionists. Like all conservatives, he maintains that, in reforming society, we must adopt a policy of gradual change, and our starting point must be the actual status quo rather than an idealistic and abstractly rational set of principles which may not be related at all to actual social and economic conditions. He insists on the validity and legitimacy of the feudal hierarchy, a hereditary monarchy, with a hereditary nobility and clergy occupying dominant positions. And finally, he insists that liberty is indissolubly tied to social responsibility and duty.

These political dispositions are somewhat anticipated in Burke's much earlier text, *A Philosophical Enquiry into the Origins of Our Ideas of the Sublime and Beautiful* (1757). Burke is here writing in a tradition that goes back to Longinus' treatise *On the Sublime* (which Burke had read), and which was revived in the eighteenth and nineteenth centuries largely under the auspices of Kant and Romantic writers. Burke's essay draws on the insights of Addison and Hume, and like these thinkers, he adopts a broadly empiricist perspective. Burke's comments on the sublime and beautiful anticipate in some respects the account later offered by Kant. He says that whatever excites ideas of pain, danger, and terror is a source of the sublime; and the sublime is the "strongest emotion which the mind is capable of feeling," far more powerful than emotions of pleasure.[9] Ultimately, pain is so potent in force because it is "an emissary" of death, the "king of terrors." It is when we are able to distance ourselves from such pain and terror that we can find them delightful; and it is this feeling which is sublime (*PE*, 550). The sublime differs from the beautiful in fundamental ways: sublime objects are vast, rugged, obscure, dark; beautiful objects are small, smooth, light, and delicate. Sublime objects are founded on pain while beautiful objects give pleasure (*PE*, 550).

Mary Wollstonecraft (1759–1797)

Acknowledged as one of the first feminist writers of modern times, Mary Wollstonecraft was a radical thinker whose central notions were framed by the French Revolution of 1789. Her *Vindication of the Rights of Men* (1790), like Thomas Paine's *The Rights of Man*, was a defense of the Revolution against the scathing attacks expressed in Burke's *Reflections on the Revolution in France* (1790). Wollstonecraft has rightly been characterized as an Enlightenment thinker, propounding arguments in favor of reason, against hereditary privilege and the entire inequitable apparatus of feudalism. Yet Wollstonecraft added to these conventional Enlightenment elements an important concern for the economic and educational rights of women, as expressed in the work for which she is best known, *A Vindication of the Rights of Woman* (1792).

Wollstonecraft's troubled life reflects and underlies her ideological dispositions. One of six children, she suffered, with the rest of her family, at the hands of a somewhat despotic father. She experienced first hand the economic disadvantages to which women were subject, attempting to earn a living in the conventional female occupations as a governess and lady's maid; she was a victim of unfortunate romantic encounters, first with the painter Henry Fuseli and then with an American businessman, Gilbert Imlay, with whom she conceived a child and whose infidelity led her to two suicide attempts; she eventually married the political philosopher William Godwin (whose *Political Justice* appeared in 1793); a few days after giving birth to a daughter (who would marry the poet Shelley and write the novel *Frankenstein*), she died. Notwithstanding her turbulent life, she mixed with some of the prominent radical figures of her day: the dissenter Dr. Richard Price (who initially provoked Burke's anti-revolutionary sentiments), Thomas Paine, and of course William Godwin himself.

The issues Wollstonecraft raises in *A Vindication of the Rights of Woman* have remained crucial to much feminist literary criticism. Her central argument is that if woman "be not prepared by education to become the companion of man, she will stop the progress of knowledge and virtue; for truth must be common to all."[10] She points out that woman can cooperate in this enterprise only if she understands why she ought to be virtuous, and only if "freedom strengthens her reason till she comprehends her duty," part of which is to be a "patriot." If the rights of man merit consideration, claims Wollstonecraft, then by a "parity of reasoning," women's rights also claim attention. These claims are founded on two fundamental principles: firstly, that not only men but also women have "the gift of reason"; and secondly, that no authority can simply coerce women into fulfilling a given set of duties (*VRW*, 86–88). Like Christine de Pisan many centuries earlier, Wollstonecraft endeavors to redeem the notion of reason from its history of male abuse. For many centuries "deeply rooted prejudices have clouded reason, and . . . spurious qualities have assumed the name of virtues." Wollstonecraft sees the entire history and structure of feudalism as based on irrational expediency and prejudice, rather than on reason: "Such, indeed has been the wretchedness that has flowed from hereditary honours, riches, and monarchy" (*VRW*, 91–93). Wollstonecraft makes a powerful assertion: "the rights of Woman may be respected, if it be fully proved that reason calls for this respect, and loudly demands JUSTICE for one-half of the human race" (*VRW*, 89). What she is essentially appealing to are the Enlightenment principles of reason, duty, freedom, self-determination, and even patriotism; her feminism consists in the demand that these same principles extend to women; she is not, like later feminists, devaluing these principles themselves as outgrowths of a patriarchal history.

Women are taught, says Wollstonecraft, to nurture qualities such as cunning, an appearance of weakness, and a duplicitous "outward" obedience; they are encouraged to develop "artificial graces" whereby "their sole ambition is to be fair, to raise emotion instead of inspiring respect." Such attributes, they are advised, will earn them the "protection of man" (*VRW*, 100, 121). Even Rousseau, whom Wollstonecraft otherwise admires, suggests that woman should exercise cunning and coquetry to make herself "a more alluring object of desire." Wollstonecraft's retort is simple: "What nonsense!" (*VRW*, 108). A more recent example of such "nonsense" is to be found in John Gregory's handbook on proper female behavior, entitled *A Father's Legacy to his Daughters* (1774). Gregory advises women to cultivate such "virtues" as a "fondness for dress," a capacity for dissimulation, and the avoidance of "delicacy of sentiment" (*VRW*, 111, 116). Wollstonecraft also attacks female writers such as Hester Lynch Thrale Piozzi, Mme. de Staël and the celebrated French writer Mme. Felicité Genlis, as effectively reiterating "masculine sentiments" (*VRW*, 202–205).

Underlying all of these prescriptions for female behavior, Wollstonecraft sees one fundamental principle, rooted in educational strategy: an endeavor to "enslave women by cramping their understandings and sharpening their senses" (*VRW*, 104). In Wollstonecraft's view, women are effectively constrained within particularity, forced to look at the world as a series of discrete and unrelated phenomena, whose connections might as well be random. In being deprived of the ability to generalize, women are, in effect, deprived of the ability to think (*VRW*, 116, 118). There are degrading and injurious consequences of women being given such a haphazard education: women are unable to act as genuine moral agents: without the power of reason, they cannot make moral choices and are disposed to blind obedience of whatever power structure can claim authority over them. Another prerequisite of moral action is freedom; Wollstonecraft wisely states that liberty "is the mother of virtue" (*VRW*, 121).

Hence, the national education of women is of the "utmost consequence" (*VRW*, 297). Wollstonecraft recommends national day schools which will be free to all classes of society, and where both sexes will be educated together. Such a system will cultivate friendship and love between the sexes. Instead of rote-learning of what they do not comprehend, children must be encouraged to think for themselves, by exchanging and testing their ideas against those of their peers. Religion, history, and politics "might also be taught by conversations in the Socratic form" (*VRW*, 283–288). Such intellectual independence bears similarities with her view of the artist's independence. The true artist does not simply make a "servile copy" of nature but uses an "exalted imagination, ... fine senses and enlarged understanding" to form an ideal picture or harmonious whole. As a result of the education she prescribes, woman will acquire a "dignified beauty . . . physical and moral beauty ought to be attained at the same time" (*VRW*, 290–291). Wollstonecraft here effectively *redefines* female beauty as an integral product of a rational, affectionate, and independent disposition, a quality behind which lies not merely the accident of appearance but a revolutionizing of gender relations. She also urges: "Make women rational creatures and free citizens, and they will quickly become good wives and mothers" (*VRW*, 299).

Hence, Wollstonecraft seeks to extend to women the Enlightenment principle of basing both knowledge and morality upon reason, which itself presupposes access to the right kinds of information, a nurturing of coherent thinking, and, above all, the freedom to think and judge for themselves. Wollstonecraft implicitly rejects any sharp distinction between the private, "domestic" sphere of women and the public sphere of men. Later feminists have often diverged from Wollstonecraft's views of marriage, her view that morality and virtue should be founded on eternal principles and even her appeal to reason. What is enduring about her vision, however, is its insistence that female equality in any sphere depends ultimately on a radical restructuring of the social and political order; her arguments for education remain pertinent today; and her view that genuine morality cannot be based on ignorance and blind obedience retains its inspiring force.

Notes

1. Francis Bacon, *The New Organon*, ed. Fulton H. Anderson (Indianapolis: Bobbs-Merrill, 1960), pp. 47–50.
2. *The Philosophical Works of Descartes: Volume I*, trans. E. S. Haldane and G. R. T. Ross (NP: Dover Publications, 1955), p. 101.
3. John Locke, *An Essay Concerning Human Understanding*, ed. A. D. Woozley (Glasgow: Fontana/Collins, 1975), p. 89. Hereafter cited as *Essay*.
4. David Hume, *A Treatise of Human Nature: Book One*, ed. D. G. C. Macnabb (Glasgow: Fontana/Collins, 1978), pp. 113, 130–131. Hereafter cited as *THN*.
5. William Keach, "Poetry, after 1740," in *The Cambridge History of Literary Criticism, Volume IV: The Eighteenth Century*, ed. H. B. Nisbet and Claude Rawson (Cambridge: Cambridge University Press, 1997), pp. 129–133.
6. Addison and Steele, *Selections from the Tatler and the Spectator*, ed. Robert J. Allen (New York: Holt, Rhinehart, and Winston, 1961), pp. 67–68. Hereafter cited as *Spectator*.
7. *The New Science of Giambattista Vico*, revised translation of third edition, Thomas Goddard Bergin and Max Harold Fisch (Ithaca and New York: Cornell University Press, 1968), para. 364, p. 110. Hereafter cited as *NS*.

8. David Hume, "Of the Standard of Taste," in David Hume, *Four Dissertations* (New York: Garland, 1970), para. 488. Hereafter cited as "OST"; numbers refer to paragraphs.

9. Edmund Burke, *A Philosophical Enquiry into the Origins of Our Ideas of the Sublime and Beautiful* (New York and Oxford: Oxford University Press, 1990), p. 549. Hereafter cited as *PE*.

10. Mary Wollstonecraft, *Vindication of the Rights of Woman*, ed. Miriam Brody Kramnick (Harmondsworth: Penguin, 1985), pp. 85–86. Hereafter cited as *VRW*.

Chapter 9

The Aesthetics of Kant and Hegel

Immanuel Kant (1724–1804)

Much modern literary and cultural theory has encouraged us to view literature and art within their historical and ideological contexts. However, in both academia and popular culture, we are still today very familiar with terms such as "art for art's sake" and we still hear poetry, music, and art spoken of as "ends in themselves," to be enjoyed for their own sake. The idea behind such expressions is that literature must be free from any specific moral obligations, or political purposes: its primary purpose is to give pleasure. Most thinkers from Plato to the eighteenth century would have been puzzled or exasperated at such an idea: while they might admit that one function of literature is to "delight" us, they would insist that literature has an important moral, religious, or social dimension.

The idea of literature as autonomous, as having no purpose beyond itself, received its first articulate expression by a philosopher, Immanuel Kant, in his *Critique of Judgment* (1790). This book proved to have a vast influence on subsequent aesthetics and poetry, extending into our own day. Kant is usually considered, along with G. F. W. Hegel, as one of the two greatest philosophers of modern times. By far the most important and groundbreaking of Kant's works was the *Critique of Pure Reason* (1781). Kant himself saw this work as initiating a "Copernican Revolution" in philosophy, in virtue of its threefold endeavor: firstly, Kant wished to define the boundaries of human reason and knowledge: what kinds of things can reason tell us about and what kinds of things are beyond its grasp? Secondly, he wished to establish a secure foundation for metaphysics. The empiricist philosophers Locke and Hume had argued that, since all of our knowledge comes from experience, this knowledge cannot be grounded on any necessary laws. In the wake of Hume's skepticism – a skepticism which, as Kant recalls, aroused him from his "dogmatic slumbers" – Kant was concerned to ground metaphysics on principles which were *a priori* (independent of experience) and necessary.

Literary Criticism from Plato to the Present: An Introduction   M. A. R. Habib
© 2011 M. A. R. Habib

In other words, such knowledge as we do have must be shown to possess absolute certainty. Finally, Kant made a distinction between phenomena and noumena. Phenomena refer to the world of objects which we experience, objects as they *appear* to us; noumena, or objects as they might be in themselves, are objects which are merely "thinkable" and outside of our possible experience. This distinction served not only to secure the world of phenomena on a sure foundation but also to provide a feasible basis for the world of morality which for Kant is the noumenal realm (the project of Kant's next work, the *Critique of Practical Reason*, 1788), and which he wishes to protect against the rationalist and empiricist onslaught of the Enlightenment thinkers. Kant held that only the phenomenal world, grounded in sense experience, could be known by the intellectual faculty of pure reason. The noumenal entities, which he named as God, freedom, and immortality, were a function of the "practical" moral faculty, the will. Causality indeed reigns in Kant's phenomenal realm, which is effectively the world bequeathed by modern science; but its grasp cannot extend into the noumenal world, which is essentially the domain of morality and faith.

The nature of aesthetic judgment

In his *Critique of Judgment*, Kant acknowledges the subjective character of our aesthetic judgments but wishes to show that they are still based on necessary and universal principles. Central to his view of aesthetic judgment is the concept of "purposiveness." This refers to the fact that we must assume a certain coherence and connection among the appearances of the external world or nature so that we can reflect coherently upon it. We presuppose a harmony between nature and our cognitive powers, as if they were suited or adapted to each other. It is this presumed harmony, which Kant calls "purposiveness," which gives us pleasure.[1] According to Kant, when we make an aesthetic judgment, we make a judgment about the *form* of an object (not its content as given through our senses); the object's form gives rise to pleasure because it exhibits a harmony with our cognitive powers, namely our understanding and imagination. We then call the object "beautiful" and our ability to judge the object by such a pleasure is "taste" (*CJ*, 30). An aesthetic judgment is not a judgment of cognition; it does not refer to the object and gives us no knowledge of it. It refers only to the perceiving subject, to our self and its feeling of pleasure or displeasure. It tells us only about how we, as subjects, are affected by our mental representation of the object.

There are, according to Kant, certain distinctive features of aesthetic judgment as we use it in describing an object as beautiful. To begin with, a judgment of taste is "disinterested." In other words, when we judge an object to be beautiful, we have no *interest*, no ulterior motive, in the object's actual existence. We do not care if the object produces certain effects in the world, or if it has some kind of utility or even a positive moral value. In Kantian terms, we have no interest in the object's practical *purpose* in the world. In an aesthetic judgment we regard an object or any aspect of nature as having "purposiveness without purpose." We are content simply to contemplate the object and to take pleasure in it. As Kant says, beautiful things have no meaning, and he defines beauty as the object of a disinterested judgment of taste.

Do aesthetic judgments have universal validity?

However, if aesthetic judgment is subjective, if our perception of beauty says nothing about the object but reflects merely our feeling of pleasure, how can we make others agree with our judgment? Kant's answer to this dilemma reverberates through much of modern literary theory. If our judgment of an object's beauty is *disinterested*, this means that our judgment doesn't rest on any subjective inclination or private conditions, a feature which implies a ground of pleasure for all people. For example, if I like a particular portrait, I cannot base this liking on the fact that the portrait reminds me of my father, or that I see a certain moral significance in it: these would be private motives which obviously cannot apply to everyone. My judgment of the portrait as beautiful must be free of all such private reasons and conditions. According to Kant, we *can* claim that our judgment is universal – i.e., that others must agree with our judgment – if we separate from it everything which has to do with mere sensory pleasure (which is based on private feeling) or with our ideas of the morally good (*CJ*, 379).

Kant also states that taste is a kind of *sensus communis*, a sense shared by all of us. The principles of this "common sense" are to think for oneself, in an unbiased way; to think from the perspective of everyone else; and to think consistently. We can thereby override the private conditions of our judgment and reflect on our own judgment from a "universal" point of view (*CJ*, 160–161). However, aesthetic judgments have merely a *subjective* universality (*CJ*, 378). Even though we speak of beauty as though it were a characteristic of the object, what we are really claiming is that the connection between the object and the subject's feeling of pleasure will be the same in everyone. Kant offers a related insight here which is still highly pervasive today: no rule or rational argument can enforce our recognition of beauty. In aesthetic judgments we always want to submit the object to our own eyes, to see whether or not *we* find it beautiful (*CJ*, 59). We can see here not only the overwhelming importance Kant attaches to direct experience in aesthetic judgments, but the grounds he establishes for arriving at a notion of beauty based on consensus. An object we consider beautiful will give rise to a harmonious interplay of the cognitive powers, imagination and understanding, in everyone. Such harmony between these two faculties, he says, is required not only for aesthetic judgments but for cognition in general, hence we can assume that this harmony is a universal feature of our subjective apparatus (*CJ*, 62, 159).

The role of imagination in aesthetic judgment

Kant's account of the role of imagination in an aesthetic judgment laid the foundation for a great deal of Romantic theory and literary practice. He defines an aesthetic judgment as an ability to judge an object in reference to the "free lawfulness" of imagination (*CJ*, 91). In our everyday knowledge of objects, imagination is *reproductive*: it reproduces the information given to us by our senses into images; and this reproduction is subject to certain laws of association, and to the rules of the understanding. However, when we approach the world from an aesthetic perspective, our imagination is not required to undergo the same constraints. In this case, understanding serves imagination rather than vice versa (*CJ*, 91–92). The imagination can now be *productive* and spontaneous; it can combine images differently from their sequence in our ordinary experience, to yield new and surprising combinations. What gives us pleasure is this free play of imagination. However, even in this creative role, imagination is not entirely free: its creations must still not violate the *basic* laws of understanding. This is why Kant refers to the "free lawfulness" of the imagination: it is a lawfulness (an adherence to the basic laws of understanding) which is not imposed on the imagination but self-exercised, even in its free play. This seems to be what Kant means when he talks of a subjective harmony of imagination and understanding, which he equates with a "purposiveness without purpose." It is this *felt* harmony between our cognitive powers which gives us aesthetic pleasure. Because it is felt, each person must experience it for herself and there can be no objective rule as to what constitutes beauty. Kant defines beauty as "the form of the *purposiveness* of an object, so far as this is perceived *without any representation of a purpose*" (*CJ*, 384–386). He is not somehow averse to using art and literature for moral purposes; he is simply concerned to establish that these spheres have a certain autonomy and that, when they are connected with other spheres such as morality and practical usefulness, the nature of the connection be clearly understood. We see here an important departure on Kant's part from Enlightenment thought, indeed a point of transition to Romantic thought. Not only is an aesthetic judgment freed from the bondage of morality, not only is art transformed into an autonomous province, but it is also made the province of subjective experience, at the heart of which stands imagination in its supremely creative role, triumphing to some extent over our conceptual faculty.

The sublime

To grasp Kant's vastly influential views on the sublime, we need to consider some important statements he makes in the *Critique of Pure Reason*: just as the concepts of the understanding give unity to the data of sense experience, so the concepts of reason (which Kant calls *ideas*) give unity to the concepts of the understanding. The concepts of reason are "transcendental" ideas because they are not derived from experience and indeed they transcend experience. For example, the idea of "virtue" or the idea of "humanity" is an idea of reason, not derived from experience, but held up by reason as an ideal to be aimed at. Reason sets forth an ideal of unity and totality toward which the understanding can aspire.

Kant acknowledges that the beautiful and the sublime are similar in that they are both concerned with pleasure rather than knowledge, a pleasure that arises from the way in which the object is presented to us (rather than the object itself). However, there are striking differences. To begin with, beauty concerns the *form* of an object, which consists of definite boundaries; the sublime concerns *formless* objects, which represent boundlessness. Beauty is accompanied by a feeling of charm, of the furtherance of life, as well as by the play of our imagination; the sublime gives rise to a different response: we feel a momentary checking of our vital powers and then a stronger outflow of them. Kant characterizes our feeling about the sublime as a "negative pleasure": we feel not charm or love but admiration or respect (*CJ*, 386–387).

These differences between the beautiful and the sublime rest on the connection between understanding and reason: when we judge natural beauty as beautiful, we attribute to it a formal "purposiveness" whereby the object in nature seems to be preadapted to our cognitive powers, producing a harmonious interplay between our imagination and understanding that gives pleasure. But the sublime presents a challenge to our cognitive faculties: nature appears as contrapurposive: in its might and magnitude, it seems beyond the reach and control of our mental apparatus. But this very inadequacy of our imagination to represent such a magnitude of disordered nature forces us to realize that we have another faculty, namely reason, which transcends the entire world of nature and whose ideas are supersensible (above the sphere of sensation). As Kant puts it, we realize that we have a faculty of mind which surpasses every standard of sense. It is this realization or ability to which Kant gives the name "sublime." So the sublime is not in fact a quality of nature but of our own minds. When nature appears to us as infinite, this intuition excites in us the realization of an infinite power in ourselves, namely the power of reason. Kant equates this feeling of the sublime with moral feeling and with respect for our own supersensible or spiritual destination. Our judging nature as sublime, says Kant, may initially excite our fear, since we recognize our physical impotence as natural beings;

but in consequence our imagination is elevated by referring itself to reason; hence we call forth our strength, "to regard as small the objects of our natural concerns, such as property, health and life" (*CJ*, 388–391).

The legacy of Kant

Kant's philosophy and aesthetics have had vast influence, especially on Romantic thought and Romantic conceptions of the literary imagination. His notions of aesthetic freedom, artistic form, genius, and the non-utilitarian, non-moral character of art exerted, for example, a profound impact on his contemporaries Goethe and Schiller, as well as on Coleridge, the American transcendentalists, and Poe. Both Romantic and non-Romantic thought attempted to overcome Kant's absolute distinction between phenomena and noumena: the noumenal world was brought back within the grasp of imagination and intellect. Indeed, in Kant's work lay the very possibility of Hegel's system whose profound influence encompassed philosophy and aesthetics. The philosophical problems raised by Kant heavily influenced Anglo-American idealists such as Josiah Royce, and inspired the growth of the Marburg School, whose prominent members included Ernst Cassirer (1874–1945) and Rudolph Stammler (1856–1938). Kant's ideal of aesthetic "disinterestedness" was applied by subsequent writers such as Matthew Arnold and T. S. Eliot to the sphere of literary criticism, which they saw as an activity ideally unencumbered by immediate political and social exigencies. The influence of Kant's aesthetics extended to Russian criticism, in the views of Leo Tolstoy and others. In their emphasis upon form and artistic autonomy these aesthetics also held considerable attraction for late nineteenth-century proponents of aestheticism, modernist writers and the New Critics. Kant's treatment of the sublime is an important component in the work of more recent writers such as Paul de Man and Jean-François Lyotard. In more general terms, Kant's philosophy has been profoundly influential in its distinction of phenomena and noumena, its insistence that the world is in fundamental ways our own construction, and its grounding of morality on rationality and freedom. Finally, in Kant's thought, the notion of substance – the metaphysical foundation of Christian theology – is subjectivized and reduced to one of 12 basic categories of human understanding, thereby reduced to one of the viewpoints through which the world can be apprehended.

Hegel (1770–1831)

Historical context of Hegel's thought

The Hegelian philosophical system occupies a central place in the history and genesis of modern Western thought. Hegel's system was initially inspired by the French Revolution of 1789 which for him embodied the revolutionary struggle of the bourgeois class throughout Europe to gain supremacy over the feudal aristocracies and the clergy, and to replace the decaying and irrational hierarchy of feudalism with a society based on reason, where both social institutions and the human community embodied a rational outlook. Revolutionary bourgeois philosophy and ideals received their most articulate expression in Hegel's work. In this sense, Hegel is a product of the Enlightenment, stressing as he does the supreme value of reason, which he brings into confluence with the other main impulse of Enlightenment philosophy, empiricism, or the doctrine that knowledge derives from experience. However, Hegel's system, while not itself Romantic, is also deeply informed by certain attributes derived from Romanticism: a commitment to the idea of unification or totality and a concomitant belief that subject and object, the human self and the world, are created and determined in their nature by each other. Hence Hegel's thought effects a vast synthesis of two major currents in European intellectual and social history, the Enlightenment and Romanticism, which are conventionally seen to be opposed in many respects. In its inheritance of both of these trends, Hegel's philosophy was profoundly influenced by the work of Kant.

The historical and philosophical consequences of Hegel's thought were even more momentous. His system influenced a wide range of philosophies whose effects are still with us today: Marxism, the Anglo-American idealism of the late nineteenth and early twentieth centuries, various branches of existentialism, as well as the thought of many twentieth-century theorists ranging from feminists such as Simone de Beauvoir and Julia Kristeva to so-called "poststructuralist" thinkers such as Jacques Lacan and Jacques Derrida. Hegel's doctrines have informed much Protestant theology, and his philosophy of history has profoundly affected numerous disciplines, including political and cultural theory. Equally, the Hegelian system has provoked much opposition to itself, in the form of the nineteenth-century positivism of Auguste Comte and Émile Durkheim, the early twentieth-century realism of Bertrand Russell, G. E. Moore, and others, as well as the logical positivism, the analytic philosophies and the various brands of empiricism which have survived through the twentieth century.

Hegel's first major publication was *The Phenomenology of Spirit* (1807), perhaps the most difficult philosophical work ever written; this was followed by his three-volume *Science of Logic*, published between 1812 and 1816. His subsequent *Encycoplaedia of the Philosophical Sciences* was essentially a restatement of his philosophy as a whole; and the final work published in his lifetime was his *Philosophy of Right* (1821). After his death, his students and disciples edited and published his lectures on various subjects, including *Lectures on the Philosophy of History*, *Lectures on Aesthetics*, *Lectures on the Philosophy of Religion*, and *Lectures on the History of Philosophy*.

The Hegelian dialectic

All aspects of Hegel's philosophy, logical, metaphysical, political, and aesthetic, are intimately tied to his philosophy of history. Hegel was the most articulate and influential advocate of what was later called "historicism," the belief that nothing can be examined in abstraction from its particular history, its causes, its effects, and its specific position in a broader historical scheme, a scheme often said to be driven toward specific goals through the operation of inexorable laws. In general, Hegel sees human history as a progress of absolute mind or consciousness toward self-conscious freedom. The movement toward freedom is equated by Hegel with a movement toward greater rationality, in both the operations of the human mind and the social and political arrangements which express these. Essentially, when our own minds have become rational and the laws and institutions that we live under are also rational, we shall freely consent to live by those laws. Hegel also characterizes this general movement as toward *self*-consciousness; in other words, as consciousness moves to higher levels, it perceives increasingly that what it previously took as the external world, as something alien and foreign to it, is in fact essentially constituted, at its deepest rational core, by its own operations. What was previously confronted as *substance* is now recognized as *subjectivity*. Hence Hegel also describes this entire movement as a progression from substance to subject.[2]

The most comprehensive avenue into understanding Hegel's philosophy as a whole is the notion of the dialectic, a notion which operates on three broad levels: logical, phenomenological (the forms taken by consciousness), and historical. The dialectic moves through three stages. Initially an object is viewed in its given particularity as self-identical. In the second stage the object's "identity" is viewed as externalized or dispersed through the totality of its social and historical relations: it is viewed in its universal aspect. In the third stage the object's identity is viewed as mediated (rather than immediately given) and as a combination of universal and particular. Hence the dialectic is a mode of thinking that recognizes that the self and world stand in necessary connection, that thought is not a static system of classification but a self-criticizing process, and that the world as simply given to our senses is not worthy of the name "reality." Things in the world are to a large extent defined by their relations; they cannot be understood in isolation, abstracted from their connections with other things, but must be understood within their historical contexts. As Hegel states in his *Philosophy of Right*, "What is real is rational, and what is rational is real." Reality is not simply a vast and possibly incoherent assemblage of unrelated and unalterable facts (as crude empiricism would have it); rather, in its core, it is rational, historically progressive, and potentially unified, answering to the deepest demands of our own rational selves. Hence the dialectic is a mode of thought that is not only rational but relational and historical.[3] In fact, the dialectic as formulated by Hegel is a historically cumulative process. As he states in his *Lectures on the History of Philosophy*, Hegel sees this movement toward freedom operating historically, from the Oriental world, where only one person – the emperor – is free, to the Greek and Roman world, where some people are free, to the modern world where all are free.[4]

Hegel's aesthetics

Hegel's aesthetics are very closely tied to his philosophy of history. As we have seen, Hegel sees human history as a progress of absolute mind or consciousness toward self-conscious rationality and freedom. Hegel sees art as one of the stages traversed by the absolute idea or spirit on this journey. Art, like religion and philosophy, is one of the modes through which spirit is expressed. Like Kant, Hegel sees art and beauty as a realm that belongs to "*sense*, feeling, intuition, imagination." Its sphere is essentially different from that of thought, and it is "precisely the *freedom* of production and configurations that we enjoy in the beauty of art … the source of works of art is the free activity of fancy which in its imaginations is itself more free than nature is."[5] True art, Hegel says, must be free (*IA*, 7). Rather than subserving the ends of religion or morality, it must, like religion and philosophy, be a valid mode of expressing the universal truths of the spirit:

> in this its freedom alone is fine art truly art, and it only fulfils its supreme task when it has placed itself in the same sphere as religion and philosophy, and when it is simply one way of bringing to our minds and expressing the *Divine*, the deepest interests of mankind, and the most comprehensive truths of the spirit. (*IA*, 7)

In other words, art must fulfill the same functions and ends as these other disciplines in its own way, and stand with relative independence, rather than its end falling within those other disciplines. What distinguishes art from other modes of expression is its ability to present even the most abstruse ideas in sensuous form, such that our feelings and senses will be affected. Hence art reconciles the worlds of sense and intellect, nature and thought, the external and the internal. Art actually helps us to perceive reality by organizing the chaos and contingency of the world such that we can see the "true meaning" of appearances (*IA*, 9). Hence the reality embodied in art is higher than "ordinary reality," infected as the latter is with contingency and chance. Like Aristotle and Sidney, Hegel points out that history is burdened with the "contingency of ordinary life and its events," whereas art evinces the universal and "eternal powers that govern history" (*IA*, 9). Hegel is careful to point out, however, that art is not the highest mode of expressing the truths of the spirit; in this function, it is superseded by both religion and philosophy (*IA*, 9–10). Hegel here appears to suggest that art no longer serves the "real" functions of being the primary form through which we can apprehend truth, morality, cultural history, and ambition. And we no longer rely on art to shape our view of the world, to shape our very modes of feeling and perception.

Art's vocation, Hegel says,

> is to unveil the *truth* in the form of sensuous artistic configuration, to set forth the reconciled opposition [between the worlds of thought and sense] . . . and so to have its end and aim in itself. For other ends, like instruction, purification, bettering, financial gain, struggling for fame and honour, have nothing to do with the work of art as such, and do not determine its nature. (*IA*, 55)

Within the context of Hegel's overall thesis that art must express the truths of spirit, he nonetheless insists on the autonomy of art: its expression of spiritual truth is not in the interests of pleasure, morality, or instruction; rather, this expression of truth is an end in itself, the end and purpose of art.

Hegel considers how the absolute idea has been expressed historically in particular forms of art. He cites three progressive configurations or stages of art: symbolic, classical, and romantic. At the first stage, that of *symbolic* art, the spiritual content or idea is still indefinite, obscure, and not well understood. Spiritual meaning is attached randomly to objects in nature, and a true correspondence between content and form does not occur. For example, a block of stone might symbolize the divine but it does not truly represent it. This art exaggerates natural phenomena, distorting them into grotesqueness, hugeness, and diversity in attempting to raise them to a spiritual level. The spirit, says Hegel, "persists sublime above all this multiplicity of shapes which do not correspond with it" (*IA*, 76–77). Hegel characterizes this stage as the "artistic pantheism" of the Orient, which attempts to coerce any object, however trivial, into bearing a spiritual significance. This, then, is the first, symbolic, form of art, "with its quest, its fermentation, its mysteriousness, and its sublimity" (*IA*, 77).

The second form is *classical* art which, says Hegel, annuls the twofold defect of symbolic art: the indeterminate nature of the Idea embodied in it, and the inadequate nature of this embodiment itself, the inadequate "correspondence of meaning and shape" (*IA*, 77). In contrast, classical art "is the free and adequate embodiment of the Idea in the shape peculiarly appropriate to the Idea itself in its essential nature" (*IA*, 77). Hegel sees this "appropriate" shape as the human form, his reasoning being that God, or the "original Concept," created the human form as an expression of spirit. Hence art advances to anthropomorphism and personification, since the human form is the only sensuous expression appropriate to spirit (*IA*, 78). Such personification, however, constitutes precisely the limitation of classical art: "here the spirit is at once determined as particular and human, not as purely absolute and eternal" (*IA*, 79). In other words, while the human form is the most appropriate to expressing spirit, it nonetheless expresses it in a limited manner, weighed down by its particular and material nature.

This defect demands a transition to a higher stage, the *romantic* form of art. The unity which had been achieved between the idea and its reality is here cancelled or annulled once again; and the opposition or difference of these is reinstated, though at a higher plane than that of symbolic art. Hegel acknowledges that the classical mode is the "pinnacle" of artistic form, and its limitation is inherent in art itself, which must use sensuous forms to express a spiritual content. For spirit, Hegel reminds us, is pure thought or ideality whose infinite and organic expansiveness cannot be restrained or expressed by outward, sensuous means (*IA*, 79). Hence romantic art cancels the "undivided unity" of classical art because it expresses a higher content, it expresses spirit or idea at a higher stage of self-development, coinciding with Christianity's view of God, a stage of self-conscious knowledge that enables man to rise above his animal nature and to know himself as spirit (*IA*, 80).

If, then, we are confronted with spirit at this higher stage, what could be the appropriate form for its embodiment or expression? The medium which will express such spiritual content can no longer be sensuous and material; rather, it must be the "*inwardness of self-consciousness.*" In this way, Hegel suggests, "romantic art is the self-transcendence of art." In this third stage, then, the object or subject matter of art is subjectivity itself, the inner world of emotion, spirituality, and thought (*IA*, 81). And yet, even if the romantic artist is concerned to express the depths of human subjectivity, how can she do this without an external, material medium of expression? Hegel's answer is that an external medium is indeed utilized but is recognized as "inessential and transient," a merely contingent circumstance employing expedient devices such as plot, character, action, incident, as devised by the imagination (*IA*, 81). What Hegel appears to be saying here is that elements of the external world are used by the romantic artist not for their own meaning but symbolically and metaphorically to express human thoughts and emotions; they are recognized as merely contingent occasions for expressing the inner world of subjectivity.

Hegel now passes on to the third part of his subject, which concerns the realization of the three general forms of art in specific arts, namely, architecture, sculpture, painting, music, and poetry. The first (and lowest) of the specific arts is architecture, which manipulates external organic nature as "an external world conformable to art," thereby making this world cognate with spirit. Hence architecture is the fundamentally symbolic art because spirit cannot be realized in such material. However, architecture levels a space for the god and builds his temple, an enclosure for spiritual congregation (*IA*, 84). The next phase of art is contained in sculpture: into this temple, the "god enters himself as the lightning-flash of individuality striking and permeating the inert mass" (*IA*, 84). So sculpture, embodying the spirit, fundamentally expresses the classical form of art: through sculpture, the spirit stands in bodily form, in immediate unity with it (*IA*, 85).

So far, then, architecture has built the temple, and sculpture has set up therein the image of the god. In the third stage, the spirit moves to a higher level: instead of being embodied in material form, God – as spiritual knowledge – passes into the subjectivity of the community, into the beliefs, thoughts, and feelings of the community. God is seen as alternating between his own "inherent unity" and his realization in the knowledge of the individuals within a community. This third phase of God's development coincides with romantic art, for the object of artistic representation is now the inner world of human thought and feeling (*IA*, 85–86).

The sensuous material used in romantic art must be appropriate to such "subjective inwardness." What is this material? It is of three broad types: color, musical sound, and "sound as the mere indication of inner intuitions and ideas." The modes of art corresponding to these materials are, respectively, painting, music, and poetry. The third and highest realization of romantic art is poetry, which completes the liberation of spirit from sensuousness that was begun by painting and music (*IA*, 88). Hegel sees the proper element of poetic representation as the imagination; and poetry itself "is the universal art of the spirit," which is not bound by sensuous material; instead, "it launches out exclusively in the inner space and the inner time of ideas and feelings" (*IA*, 89). And it is precisely at this stage that "art now transcends itself ... and passes over from the poetry of the imagination to the prose of thought" (*IA*, 89).

The legacy of Hegel's aesthetics

Hegel's aesthetics have had a pervasive influence on both literature (as, for example, on the dramas of Friedrich Hebbel) and criticism. The late nineteenth-century thinker and aesthetician Wilhelm Dilthey was profoundly influenced by Hegel in his historicism; the modern aestheticians Benedetto Croce and Giovanni Gentile developed many of Hegel's insights. Hegel anticipated some of the insights of Freud concerning the development of identity, and the insights of Saussure concerning the nature of language. The work of the Hungarian philosopher and aesthetician György Lukács is informed by an intimate knowledge of the entire corpus of Hegel's work. The leading members of the Frankfurt School, such as Max Horkheimer, Walter Benjamin, Theodor Adorno, Herbert Marcuse, and Jürgen Habermas, have stressed the debt of Marxism to certain features of Hegel's thought, such as the role of consciousness in creating the world, and have developed

Marxist critique in aesthetic, cultural, and linguistic dimensions. Hegel's thought was fundamental to the articulation of existentialism, as in the work of Jean-Paul Sartre, and of feminism, as expounded by Simone de Beauvoir. Jacques Lacan, Jacques Derrida, and Jean Lyotard have continued to develop or react against the insights originally offered by Hegel. Much of this recent criticism has reacted against what it sees as the totalizing nature of Hegel's vision, stressing instead the local, the particular, and the notion of "difference." But it was Hegel who first articulated the notion of difference, of relatedness, of human identity as a reciprocal and social phenomenon, of the world as a social and historical human construction, of identity as intrinsically constituted by diversity, of language as a system of human perception, and of the very idea of otherness or alterity as it informs much modern thought.

Notes

1. Immanuel Kant, *Critique of Judgment*, trans. Werner S. Pluhar (Indianapolis and Cambridge: Hackett, 1987), pp. 22–25. Hereafter cited as *CJ*.
2. G. W. F. Hegel, *Phenomenology of Spirit*, trans. A. V. Miller (Oxford: Clarendon Press, 1979), p. 17. Hereafter cited as *PS*.
3. *Hegel's Science of Logic*, trans. A. V. Miller (London and New York: George Allen and Unwin/Humanities Press, 1976), pp. 128–132, 479.
4. *Hegel's Lectures on the History of Philosophy, III*, trans. E. S. Haldane and Frances H. Simson (London and New York: Routledge and Kegan Paul/Humanities Press, 1963), pp. 217–218, 295, 363–369, 427–428.
5. *Hegel's Introduction to Aesthetics: Being the Introduction to the Berlin Aesthetic Lectures of the 1820s*, trans. T. M. Knox (Oxford: Oxford University Press, 1979), p. 5. Hereafter cited as *IA*.

Part IV

Romanticism and the Later Nineteenth Century

Chapter 10

Romanticism

Romanticism was a broad intellectual and artistic disposition that arose toward the end of the eighteenth century and reached its zenith during the early decades of the nineteenth century. The ideals of Romanticism included an intense focus on expressing human subjectivity, an exaltation of nature, of childhood and spontaneity, of primitive forms of society, of human passion and emotion, of the poet, of the sublime, and of imagination as a more comprehensive and inclusive faculty than reason. The most fundamental philosophical disposition of Romanticism has often been seen as irony, an ability to accommodate conflicting perspectives of the world. Developing certain insights of Kant, the Romantics often insisted on artistic autonomy and attempted to free art from moralistic and utilitarian constraints.

It was in the fields of philosophy and literature that Romanticism – as a broad response to Enlightenment, neoclassical, and French Revolutionary ideals – initially took root. Romanticism bore a complex connection to the predominating bourgeois world views, which were broadly rationalist, empiricist, individualist, and utilitarian. Some of the Romantics, such as Blake, Wordsworth, and Hölderlin, initially saw the French Revolution as heralding the dawn of a new era of individual and social liberation. Schiller and Goethe in their own ways exalted the struggle for human freedom and mastery of knowledge. Shelley, Byron, Heine, George Sand, and Victor Hugo were passionate in their appeals for justice and liberation from oppressive social conventions and political regimes. Underlying nearly all Romantic views of literature was an intense individualism based on the authority of experience and, often, a broadly democratic orientation, as well as an optimistic and sometimes utopian belief in progress. Moreover, the Romantics shared Enlightenment notions of the infinite possibility of human achievement, and of a more optimistic conception of human nature as intrinsically good rather than as fallen and theologically depraved. In all these aspects, there was some continuity between Enlightenment and Romantic thought.

Literary Criticism from Plato to the Present: An Introduction   M. A. R. Habib
© 2011 M. A. R. Habib

However, many of the Romantics, including some of the figures cited above such as Blake, Wordsworth, Shelley, and Byron, reacted against certain central features of the new bourgeois social and economic order. Appalled by the squalor and the mechanized, competitive routine of the cities, as well as by the moral mediocrity of a bourgeois world given over to what Shelley called the principles of utility and calculation, they turned for spiritual relief to mysticism, to nature, to Rousseauistic dreams of a simple, primitive, and uncorrupted life, which they sometimes located in an idealized period of history such as the Middle Ages. Wordsworth held that the poet should emulate the language of real life; he, along with Blake and Coleridge, exalted the state of childhood and innocence of perception, untainted by conventional education; and many Romantic writers – in tune with growing nationalistic sentiments – revived primitive forms such as the folktale and the ballad. Nature, for the Romantics, departed from the conception of nature held by neoclassical writers such as Pope, for whom the term signified an eternal unchangeable and hierarchical order of the cosmos as well as certain criteria for human thought and behavior. For the Romantics, nature was transfigured into a living force, held together as a unity by the breath of the divine spirit. It was infused with a comprehensive symbolism resting on its profound moral and emotional connection with human subjectivity. Coleridge referred to nature as the "language of God."

Perhaps the most fundamental trait of all Romanticism was its shift of emphasis away from classical objectivity towards subjectivity: in the wake of the philosophical systems of Fichte, Schelling, and, above all, of Hegel, the worlds of subject and object, self and world, were viewed as mutually constructive processes, human perception playing an active role rather than merely receiving impressions passively from the outside world. Such an emphasis placed a high value on uniqueness, originality, novelty, and exploration of ever-expanding horizons of experience, rather than the filtering of experience through historically accumulated layers of tradition and convention. The emphasis on uniqueness is amply exemplified in Rousseau's *Confessions*. Moreover, the "self" which is exalted in Romanticism was a far cry from the bourgeois individualistic notion of the self as an atomistic (and economic) unit. The Romantic self was a profounder, more authentic ego lying beneath the layers of social convention, a self which attempted through principles such as irony to integrate the increasingly fragmented elements of the bourgeois world into a vision of unity. The Romantics exalted the status of the poet, as a genius whose originality was based on his ability to discern connections among apparently discrepant phenomena and to elevate human perception toward a comprehensive, unifying vision.

The most crucial human faculty for such integration was the imagination, which most Romantics saw as a unifying power, one which could harmonize the other strata of human perception such as sensation and reason. It should be noted that Romanticism is often wrongly characterized as displacing Enlightenment "reason" with emotion, instinct, spontaneity, and imagination. To understand what is at issue here, it is necessary to recall that much Romantic thought took Kant's philosophy (which itself was not at all Romantic) as its starting point, notably his distinction between phenomena and noumena, his treatment of imagination, and his establishing of a relative autonomy for the category of the aesthetic. Kant declared that the categories of the understanding applied throughout the phenomenal world, but did not extend into the world of "noumena." The only objects in the noumenal realm – God, freedom, and immortality – were merely *presuppositions* required for our moral behavior. Kant had, moreover, viewed imagination as a mediating principle which reconciled sense-data with the categories of the understanding. The Romantics, like Hegel (who himself was not a Romantic), placed the noumenal realm within the reach of human apprehension, and often exalted the function of imagination, viewing it as a vehicle for the attainment of truths beyond the phenomenal world and beyond the reach of reason alone. But they did not attempt to dismiss or discard the findings of logic and reason, merely to place these within a more embracing scheme of perception. Shelley even saw imagination as having a moral function, as a power enabling the self to situate itself within a larger empathetic scheme, as opposed to reason which expressed the selfish constraints of the liberal atomistic self. Hence the relation between Romanticism and the mainstreams of bourgeois thought, which had risen to hegemony on the waves of the Enlightenment, the French Revolution, and the Industrial Revolution, was deeply ambivalent. Our own era is profoundly pervaded by this ambivalent heritage.

This ambivalent connection of Romanticism to bourgeois thought operated through both the notion of imagination and the equally archetypal notion of Romantic irony. By the end of the eighteenth century, irony had risen from being a mere rhetorical device to an entire way of looking at the world. Schlegel's *Fragments* of 1797 accords irony an epistemological and ontological function, seeing it as a mode of confronting and transcending the contradictions of the finite world. The theorizing of irony in this direction was furthered by numerous writers including Heine, Kierkegaard, and Nietzsche. At the core of irony as formulated by most nineteenth-century thinkers was a Romantic propensity to confront, rather than overlook, the obstinate disorder, contingency, flux, and mystery of the world. In this sense, an ironic vision accepts that the world can be viewed from numerous irreconcilable perspectives, and rejects any providential, rational, or logical foreclosure of the world's absurdity and contradictions into a spurious unity. Yet such Romantic irony is not entirely negative: while it rejects the "objective" order imposed upon experience or the word by religious or rational means, it seeks a higher transcendent unity and purpose, grounded ultimately in subjectivity.

Irony was essentially an idealistic reaction against the reductively mechanistic, utilitarian, and commercial impetus of bourgeois thought. Irony was a means of reinvesting the world with mystery, of limiting the arrogant claims of reason, of denying the ideals of absolute clarity and definition, of reaffirming the profound interconnection of things, and of seeking for the human spirit higher and more spiritual forms of fulfillment than those available through material and commercial efficiency. Yet irony could merely voice subjective protests against colossal historical movements which were already in process of realization. The Romantics' only recourse was to an ironic vision which insisted that reality is not confined to the here and now but embraces the past or is located in a Platonic ideal realm.

Germany

During the 1760s and 1770s, Germany witnessed the rise of the *Sturm und Drang* ("Storm and Stress") movement in which writers and critics such as Johann Gottfried von Herder (1744–1803), Goethe, and Schiller experimented with new subjective modes of expression. The major figures of Romanticism included Schiller and Heinrich Heine (1797–1856), who were both critics of conservatism and staunch advocates of freedom. The greatest poet of this period was Friedrich Hölderlin (1770–1843), whose view of history was mythical. The poetry and prose of Friedrich Novalis (1772–1801) explored the preconscious depths of human nature and looked back to the Middle Ages as an ideal. Another towering figure, Johann Wolfgang von Goethe (1749–1832) was in some respects an advocate of classicism; yet some of his major works, such as *Faust* and *The Sorrows of Young Werther*, express human subjectivity, creativity, passion, and the thirst for boundless experience with a Romantic intensity. The dramas of Ludwig Tieck (1773–1853) expressed a Romantic ironic vision. Many poets looked back to primitive and fantastic forms of literature such as folktale and romance.

It was in Germany that Romantic philosophy and literary criticism achieved their foundation, in the work of Kant and Friedrich von Schlegel. The poet Schiller, influenced by Kant, viewed the aesthetic *per se* as a mode of freedom. The philosopher Johann Gottlieb Fichte (1762–1814) saw Kant's distinction of phenomena and noumena as harboring an irreconcilable chasm between appearance and reality, as well as between self and world; to overcome this, Fichte posited the ego or self as the primary reality, and held that the external world was posited by this as its appearance or projection. This notion profoundly influenced the Romantics. The main philosopher of Romanticism, however, was Friedrich Schelling (1775–1854), who argued in his *System of Transcendental Idealism* (1800) that consciousness essentially knows only itself, and its knowledge of the external world is a mediated form of self-consciousness. The systems of both Fichte and Schelling effectively merge the realms of subject and object, self and nature. Schelling held that the mind achieves its highest self-consciousness in art, in a process of intuition. Schelling's influence extended to Coleridge and the other English Romantics. Hegel's philosophy offered a historicized account of the construction of the world by human categories, as well as of the progress of art through various forms, symbolic, classical, and romantic. Hegel was influenced by Goethe, Schelling, and Solger, and his impact extended to many literary figures, beginning with the literary history written by Gervinus. Hegel's friend Friedrich Hölderlin also emphasized the historical dimensions of aesthetic experience.

It is clear, then, that one lineage of Romantic thought went back to Kant, pursuing the nature of subjectivity, examining aesthetics and the notion of the imagination. Another, overlapping, strand, can be traced to Friedrich von Schlegel, whose influential definition of Romantic irony occurs as a recasting of Socratic irony: "In this sort of irony, everything should be playful and serious, guilelessly open and deeply hidden … It contains and arouses a feeling of indissoluble antagonism between the absolute and the relative, between the impossibility and the necessity of complete communication."[1] Hence, irony harbors a movement between shifting perspectives of the world, relative and absolute, instinctive and rational, held together not by some higher order of harmony but by an acknowledgment of contradiction and paradox. In an essay of 1800, Schlegel speaks of the "irony of irony" which pervades discourse at such a profound level that "one can't disentangle oneself from irony anymore." Schlegel's general point is that the communication of ideas can never occur unequivocally and completely.[2] His notion of irony as informing even philosophy and literary criticism is reenacted in the hermeneutic theory of Friedrich Schleiermacher. The work of Schiller and Schleiermacher can now be considered briefly.

Friedrich von Schiller (1759–1805)

Schiller was a poet, dramatist, and literary theorist; writing in the aftermath of the most violent phase of the French Revolution (known as the Reign of Terror, 1793–1794), he saw art and letters as the solution to the malaise of a world corrupted by the principles of mechanism and utility; he was a staunch advocate for freedom. His two most well-known pieces in the realm of literary theory are *On the Aesthetic Education of Man* (1795) and *On Naive and Sentimental Poetry* (1795–1796). In the former, Schiller urges that his own epoch is not conducive to art: it is mired beneath the "tyrannical yoke" of material needs: "*Utility* is the great idol of the time, for which all powers slave and all talents should pay homage."[3] What is needed, says Schiller, is to place "Beauty before Freedom": the political problem must be approached "through the aesthetical, because it is beauty, through which one proceeds to freedom" ("AEM," 226).

Schiller draws an idealistic but astute contrast between the ancient Greek world and modern civilization. The Greeks, he says, combined both imagination and reason "in a glorious humanity" ("AEM," 232). In the modern world, however, these aspects are fragmented, with not only individuals but entire classes developing only one part of their potential while the rest remains stunted. Greek society, says Schiller, received its form from "all-uniting Nature," whereas modern culture is based on "all-dividing understanding" ("AEM," 232). Schiller blames this divisiveness and fragmentation on the process of civilization itself. As knowledge increased, and modes of thought became more precise, sharp divisions between the various sciences, ranks and occupations ensued, shattering the "inner bond of human nature" ("AEM," 233). In the Greek world there was a harmony between individual and state, an organic wholeness; in contrast, the modern world is torn by fundamental dualisms:

> the state and church, the laws and the customs, were now torn asunder; enjoyment was separated from work, the means from the end, the effort from the reward. Eternally chained to only a single fragment of the Whole, man only develops himself as a fragment . . . and eternally the state remains foreign to its citizens. ("AEM," 234)

Schiller anticipates the ideas of both Hegel and Marx on "estrangement" or alienation.

Schiller's text is a seminal point of many important Romantic doctrines. Foremost is his urging of the artist to turn away from reality, to seek inspiration from an ideal world or from a bygone golden age, and to recreate the world in the artistic image of such ideality. Such a process lies at the core of Romantic irony. Also characteristic of much Romantic thought is Schiller's retreat from political solutions and his effective substitution of art for religion, his delineation of the realm of art as possessing moral and spiritual functions. This recourse will be found also in later critics such as Matthew Arnold and F. R. Leavis.

Friedrich Schleiermacher (1768–1834)

The German philosopher and Protestant theologian Friedrich Scheiermacher laid the foundations of modern hermeneutics, or the art of systematic textual interpretation. His *Hermeneutics and Criticism* (1838) formulates principles for the textual interpretation of the New Testament. These principles had a profound effect on the work of both contemporaries such as Ralph Waldo Emerson and later thinkers such as Wilhelm Dilthey (1833–1911),

Martin Heidegger, Hans Georg Gadamer, and twentieth-century thinkers such as Lyotard, Rorty, and Derrida.

In *Hermeneutics and Criticism* Schleiermacher offers a "formula" for interpretation, whereby we can identify with the author's overall situation, a formula which includes: *objective historical* reconstruction, which considers how a given utterance relates to language as a whole, and how the knowledge in a text is the product of language; *objective divinatory* reconstruction, which conjectures how the utterance or discourse itself will contribute to the language's development; *subjective historical* reconstruction, which examines a discourse as a product of an individual writer's mind; and, finally, *subjective divinatory* reconstruction, which assesses how the process of composition affects the speaker. Strikingly modern in his apparently anti-intentionalist insight, Schleiermacher asserts that the task of hermeneutics is to understand the text or utterance "just as well and then better than its author." All our knowledge of him is not immediate (like his own) but mediated; and we can therefore attempt to make conscious elements of which he may have been unconscious. By attaining such knowledge of the language as he himself had, we will possess a more exact understanding of it than even his original readers had.[4]

Schleiermacher expounds the famous "hermeneutic circle" of interpretation or understanding: "Complete knowledge is always in this apparent circle, that each particular can only be understood via the general, of which it is part, and vice versa" (*HC*, p. 24). The point is that, since the particular is integrally part of a totality, knowledge of the general and knowledge of the particular presuppose each other. We must initiate, therefore, a "provisional understanding," based on the knowledge we obtain about particulars from a general knowledge of the language (*HC*, p. 27).

The principles of hermeneutics as formulated by Schleiermacher include important insights into language and the construction of meaning: that language is historically determined; that any element of a text must be situated not only within the text as a totality but in the context of the writer's work and historical situation as a whole; that the cultural and psychological constitution of the subject has an active role in the creation of meaning; that an author's work is to a large extent determined by his location within the history of language and literature, while he himself may exert a reciprocal influence on the development of both; and that our knowledge itself moves in endless circles such that we must often acknowledge its provisional and progressive nature.

France

One of the founders of Romanticism, its so-called "father," was the French thinker Jean-Jacques Rousseau (1712–1778), who espoused a return to nature and equated the increasing refinement of civilization with corruption, artificiality, and mechanization. Rousseau's *Social Contract* espouses democratic principles and begins with the famous sentence "Man is born free, and everywhere he is in chains." This statement was as important for Romanticism as it was for the French Revolution. Romanticism eventually triumphed over attempted classical revivals, and was expressed in the work of Germaine de Staël (1766–1817) and François de Chateaubriand (1768–1848). De Staël, influenced by Schlegel, essentially rejected classical ideals as outdated, and identified Romantic notions as progressive, working in her literary criticism toward cultural relativism and historical specificity. Charles Augustin Sainte-Beuve (1804–1869) developed a biographical criticism which attempted "scientifically" to contextualize the creative work of given individuals. His criticism embodies an amalgam of Romantic notions such as a belief in genius with neoclassical principles of order and decorum. Chateaubriand, effectively opposed to Enlightenment principles, promoted a Catholic revival, but exalted the life of the lowly strata of society. George Sand (1804–1876) also made heroes and heroines of peasants and rustics in her novels; and Victor Hugo (1802–1885), in *Les Misérables*, reflects his relentless opposition to social injustice and oppression. Hugo insisted, as against the conservatives such as Désiré Nisard (1806–1883) and Gustave Planche (1808–1857), that art and poetry must be autonomous and free, not restricted by classical constraints. In the famous preface to his *Mademoiselle de Maupin* (1835), Théophile Gautier offered his theory of "art for art's sake," deriding any utilitarian conception of art.[5]

Germaine de Staël (1766–1817)

Mme. de Staël was one of the heirs of Enlightenment thought; her writings offended Napoleon, who exiled her from Paris. Politically, she espoused a constitutional monarchy; in letters she advanced the cause of Romanticism while anticipating later developments in realism; she was a staunch believer in freedom and the notion of historical progress. She published two novels, *Delphine* (1802) and *Corinne, or Italy* (1807); her important contributions to literary criticism are contained in her "Essay on Fictions" (1795) and her longer work *On Literature Considered in its Relationship to Social Institutions* (1800). In the latter, de Staël examines the various social obstacles to the success of women writers. She urges that women must be enlightened and taught together with men, in order to establish any "permanent social or political relationships." The development of reason in women will promote "both enlightenment and the happiness of society in general." She explains that women "are the only human beings outside the realm of political interest and the career of ambition, able to pour scorn on base actions, point out ingratitude, and honor even disgrace if that disgrace is caused by noble sentiments."[6] She here sees women not only as occupying a position of externality to the public sphere, but one of disinterestedness, whereby they can act as a voice of conscience in this sphere since they have no direct interests vested in it.

England

The early English Romantics included Thomas Gray, Oliver Goldsmith, and Robert Burns. Like their European counterparts, the English Romantics reacted at first favorably to the French Revolution and saw their own cultural and literary program as revolutionary. The first major figure of English Romanticism, William Blake (1757–1827), had recourse to mysticism and a mythical vision of history; he saw the world as inherently harboring opposites and contradictions, which it was the poet's task to harmonize. His own idiosyncratic religious views were presented in poems such as *The Marriage of Heaven and Hell* (1793). In other poems, he expressed powerfully a vision of the new urban world as plagued by social injustice, and he railed against what he saw as the oppressive rationality embodied by figures such as Voltaire and Rousseau. English Romanticism reached its most mature expression in the work of William Wordsworth (1770–1850), who saw nature as embodying a universal spirit, and Samuel Taylor Coleridge who, drawing on the work of Kant, Fichte, and Schelling, gave archetypal formulation to the powers of the poetic imagination. The other English Romantics included Dorothy Wordsworth (1771–1855), who authored letters, poems, and a series of journals, and who had a considerable influence on her brother and Coleridge; John Keats (1795–1821); Percy Bysshe Shelley (1792–1822); Mary Shelley (1797–1851), author of *Frankenstein* (1818); and George Gordon Lord Byron (1788–1824). Shelley's *Defence of Poetry* is a beautifully expressed manifesto of Romantic principles, detailing the supremacy of imagination over reason, and the exalted status of poetry. Keats's brief literary-critical insights are notable. He suggests that, in poetic creation, the poet acts as a catalyst for the reaction of other elements, stating that "Men of Genius are great as certain ethereal Chemicals operating on the Mass of neutral intellect ... they have not any individuality, any determined Character."[7] Deploying what Keats calls the "negative capability" of abstaining from particular positions or dogmas, the poet's mind loses itself wholly among the objects and events of the external world which are its poetic material (*Letters*, 184, 386–387). Many of these issues can now be examined in the literary theories of Wordsworth and Coleridge.

William Wordsworth (1770–1850)

It was Wordsworth who in 1809 wrote the famous lines about the French Revolution as it first appeared to many of its sympathizers: "Bliss was it in that dawn to be alive,/... When Reason seemed the most to assert her rights" (*Prelude*, XI, 108–113). But, later, as he became disillusioned with the effects of the revolution – such as the "terror" and France's war with England – he returned, guided by nature, to his "true self," his fundamental identity as a poet. The most elemental factor in Wordsworth's return to nature was imagination. In the *Prelude* he made his celebrated declaration that there are in our existence "spots of time," or moments of imaginative insight, whereby our minds are "nourished" and renovated above the "deadly weight" of trivial and present occupations (XII, 127–136, 203–206, 222–223). In "Lines Composed a Few Miles above Tintern Abbey," Wordsworth also recalls his progress from a merely sensual to an imaginative apprehension of nature, which allows him to see the unity of nature in itself as well as the unity of humankind with nature: he perceives in "the round ocean and the living air,/And the blue sky, and in the mind of man:/A motion and a spirit, that impels/All thinking things, all objects of all thought,/And rolls through all things" (*Tintern Abbey*, 95–102). The human mind here is no longer regarded as a passive receiver of external impressions but as active in the construction of its world.

Wordsworth's most important contribution to literary criticism is his controversial *Preface* to *Lyrical Ballads*, a collection of poems published jointly by Wordsworth and Coleridge in 1798.[8] Wordsworth's *Preface* advances what have now become classic statements of Romantic aesthetic doctrine. He stresses that his poems attempt to present "the real language of men in a state of vivid sensation" (*PLB*, 119). What Wordsworth is calling for is a return to a kind of realism, a descent of poetic language from its stylized status, from its self-created world of metaphorical expression and artificial diction to the language actually used by human beings in "common life," especially those engaged in "rustic life," who speak a purer language than those mired in the squalor and corruption of city life. But he adds that the poet should throw over these incidents from common life "a certain colouring of imagination, whereby ordinary things should be presented to the mind in an unusual aspect" (*PLB*, 123–125, 160–162).

In Wordsworth's characterization, the poet is "a man speaking to men"; but he has a "disposition to be affected more than other men by absent things as if they were present; an ability of conjuring up in himself passions," passions that are closer to those produced by real events than those that most men can otherwise reproduce (*PLB*, 138). The power to which Wordsworth alludes here is imagination, or the "image-making" power (*PLB*, 138). In a sense, the very faculty which characterizes the poet – imagination – is not a faculty orientated toward realism in our modern sense; rather, in its very nature, it is a transformative faculty which uses the "real" world as its raw material. And yet, the imaginary world created by the poet must "resemble" that real world (*PLB*, 139). In support of such realism, Wordsworth cites a classical authority: "Aristotle, I have been told, has said, that Poetry is the most philosophic of all writing: it is so: its object is truth, not individual and local, but general, and operative; not standing upon external testimony, but carried alive into the heart by passion; truth which is its own testimony" (*PLB*, 139). Though Wordsworth's *Preface* is viewed as archetypally Romantic, his ideal here is a classical one: poetry does not so much express private emotions and the particulars of a given situation as the universal truths underlying these. Wordsworth insists that the poet "converses with general nature," and directs his attention to the knowledge and sympathies shared by all human beings (*PLB*, 140). Again, in classical fashion, Wordsworth sees poetry as concerned with what is central and universal in human experience. In transcending his time, the poet reestablishes the unity of humankind, reaffirming the relationship and unity of all things.

Also classical is Wordsworth's insistence on poetry as a rational art: he speaks of the pleasure that "a Poet may rationally endeavour to impart" (*PLB*, 119). His statement that "all good poetry is the spontaneous overflow of powerful feelings" has often been torn from its context to illustrate an allegedly Romantic view of poetic creation as an expression of immediate feelings. Yet Wordsworth proceeds to say that "our continued influxes of feeling are modified and directed by our thoughts, which are indeed the representatives of all our past feelings" (*PLB*, 127). Wordsworth sees such a close connection between thought and feeling that these can actually pass into each other. What the poet expresses then is neither thought nor feeling alone but a complex of both; and what appears as spontaneity is the result of long reflection and practice.

This view of poetry as a meditated craft is elaborated in Wordsworth's other renowned comment in the *Preface* that poetry

> takes its origin from emotion recollected in tranquillity: the emotion is contemplated till, by a species of re-action, the tranquillity gradually disappears, and an emotion, kindred to that which was before the subject of contemplation, is gradually produced, and does itself actually exist in the mind. In this mood successful composition generally begins. (*PLB*, 149)

To put it another way, we leave behind the current emotion as mediated by thought and retrospection, returning to it in its immediate state. In this sense, poetic composition *begins* in feeling, but this feeling will be subsequently modified again by thought.

Wordsworth presses these classical views, however, toward a more Romantic aesthetic purpose. The poet's essential focus is not on the external world, or supposedly "objective" events and actions, but on the *connection* between the inner world of human nature and the world of external nature. Archetypally Romantic is his view that these two worlds are created by mutual interaction. He also diverges from Aristotle and other classical thinkers in his view that the purpose of poetry is to give "immediate pleasure" (*PLB*, 139). But the principle of pleasure is more profound than at first appears: it is founded on "the pleasure which the mind derives from the perception of similitude in dissimilitude" (*PLB*, 149). This ability signifies a broader capacity for seeing the world in a new light: we discern patterns in nature, as well as in thought, emotion, and experience, that were hitherto overlooked. Wordsworth sees the whole of life as governed by this principle, from our sexuality to our moral sensibility. So the poet's task, in giving "pleasure," is a difficult one, that of searching for the universal "truths" which have been clouded by convention, authority, and prejudice. But where classical thinkers regarded such truths as objective and accessible to reason, Wordsworth sees them as discernible only through poetic insight.

Samuel Taylor Coleridge (1772–1834)

The genius of Samuel Taylor Coleridge extended over many domains. In poetry he is best known for compositions such as "The Rime of the Ancient Mariner," "Frost at Midnight," "Christabel," and "Kubla Khan," as well as *Lyrical Ballads* (1798) which he co-authored with Wordsworth. He also wrote on educational, social, political, and religious matters in his *Lectures on Politics and Religion* (1795), *Lay Sermons* (1816), and *On the Constitution of the Church and State* (1829). Much of his thinking on philosophical issues is contained in his *Logic*. His literary criticism includes detailed studies of Shakespeare and Milton, and a highly influential text *Biographia Literaria* (1817), an eclectic work, combining intellectual autobiography, philosophy, and literary theory.

Two experiences were central to Coleridge's development as a poet and thinker: the first was his meeting with the poet Wordsworth in 1795, resulting in a friendship that lasted until 1810. Coleridge and his wife Sara lived close to Wordsworth and his sister Dorothy from 1796; in 1800 they all moved to the Lake District, which proved to be a rich source of poetic inspiration. The other experience was travel (with the Wordsworths) to Germany in 1798 where Coleridge studied the work of Kant and the German Romantic thinkers. Like Wordsworth, Coleridge was at first of radical mind, inspired by the promise of the French Revolution to write such poems as *Ode on the Destruction of the Bastille* (1789).[9] However, like Wordsworth, Coleridge became disillusioned with the revolutionary movement, as he records in

Biographia[10] and in his poem "France: An Ode," where he finds the spirit of liberty ultimately not in any form of government but in the mind's contemplation of its own individuality and the surrounding sublime objects of nature, as pervaded by the love of God. Shortly after his disillusionment with French revolutionary principles, he also questioned his own unorthodox Unitarian views, and by 1805 he had made positive overtures toward trinitarianism. Coleridge eventually took his place in the tradition of English conservatism, on which he exerted considerable influence.

At the heart of Coleridge's conservatism was his insistence, similar to Edmund Burke's, that truth cannot be reached by focusing on the present alone. Rather, both men appealed to what they called universal principles that would comprehend past, present, and future. Both men reacted against the prevailing philosophies of the Enlightenment, and especially against what they saw as the principle of "abstract reason" governing French and other revolutionary attempts to reform society according to "abstract" principles rather than on the basis of actual history and culture. Coleridge bemoaned the modern spirit of commerce and speculation that had thwarted the diverse potential of human beings.[11] Coleridge sought the antidote to these evils in the universal principles of truth and morality as contained in the Bible, which he advocated as the "end and center of our reading" (*LS*, 17, 70). In a formulation which proved to have great impact on later writers such as Poe and Baudelaire, Coleridge returned to the medieval idea of the Book of Nature, whereby the world of nature itself contained the "correspondences and symbols of the spiritual world" (*LS*, 70). He made a distinction between symbol and allegory, defining the latter as merely a "translation of abstract notions into a picture-language." A symbol, on the other hand,

> is characterized by a translucence of the Special in the Individual or of the General in the Especial or of the Universal in the General. Above all by the translucence of the Eternal through and in the Temporal. It always partakes of the Reality which it renders intelligible; and while it enunciates the whole, abides itself as a living part in that Unity, of which it is the representative.

Central to Coleridge's project are his views of the imagination. He seems to follow Kant (and much eighteenth-century thought) in viewing the imagination as a faculty which unites what we receive through our senses with the concepts of our understanding; but he goes further than Kant in viewing imagination as a power which "completes" and enlivens the understanding so that the understanding itself becomes a more comprehensive and intuitive (rather than merely discursive) faculty. The Romantics, including Coleridge, are often characterized as extolling imagination as the supreme human faculty. Nonetheless, Coleridge appears to view reason as the supreme faculty, one which contains all the others: "the REASON without being either the SENSE, the UNDERSTANDING or the IMAGINATION contains all three within itself, even as the mind contains its thoughts, and is present in and through them all" (*LS*, 69–70). Hence, just as imagination combines sense with understanding, so reason, placed at a higher vantage point, unites the knowledge derived from all three of these. Coleridge insists that each individual partakes of the light of a reason which is universal and divine.

In *Biographia Literaria*, Coleridge makes his famous distinction between fancy and imagination:

> The IMAGINATION then I consider either as primary, or secondary. The primary IMAGINATION I hold to be the living Power and prime Agent of all human Perception, and as a repetition in the finite mind of the eternal act of creation in the infinite I AM. The secondary I consider as an echo of the former, co-existing with the conscious will, yet still as identical with the primary in the *kind* of its agency, and differing only in *degree*, and in the *mode* of its operation. It dissolves, diffuses, dissipates, in order to re-create; or where this process is rendered impossible, yet still at all events it struggles to idealize and to unify. It is essentially *vital*, even as all objects (*as* objects) are essentially fixed and dead.
>
> FANCY, on the contrary, has no other counters to play with, but fixities and definites. The Fancy is indeed no other than a mode of Memory emancipated from the order of time and space; and blended with, and modified by that empirical phenomenon of the will, which we express by the word CHOICE. But equally with the ordinary memory it must receive all its materials ready made from the laws of association. (*BL*, I, 304–305)

What Coleridge designates as the primary imagination is roughly equivalent to what Kant views as the "reproductive" imagination: it operates in our normal perception, combining the various data received through the senses into a unifying image, which can then be conceptualized by the understanding. Even in this primary role, however, imagination as formulated by Coleridge evokes a wider, cosmic context: the very act of perception "repeats" on a finite level the divine act of creation. In other words, human perception actively recreates or copies elements in the world of nature, reproducing these into images that can be processed further by the understanding. There is no originality in the primary imagination: like Kant's reproductive imagination, it is bound by what we actually experience through the senses.

It is the secondary imagination which is poetic: like Kant's "productive" or spontaneous imagination, this is creative and forms new syntheses, new and more complex unities out of the raw furnishings of sense-data, following its own rules. Coleridge also stresses in this passage the voluntary and controlled nature of the secondary or poetic imagination. Nonetheless, this poetic imagination is still dependent for its raw material on the primary imagination. Another way of putting this might be to say that even the creative poetic imagination is ultimately rooted in our actual perceptions of the world: it cannot simply create from nothing, or from the insubstantiality of its own dreams. For, ultimately, the secondary imagination is perceiving the world at a higher level of truth, one that sees beneath the surface appearances of things into their deeper reality, their deeper connections, and their significance within a more comprehensive scheme that relates objects and events in their human, finite significance to their symbolic place in the divine, infinite order of things.

Fancy has a degree of freedom in the way it recalls and combines images; it is not restricted to the original order of images in time and space. Unlike the primary imagination, then, fancy is not merely a perceptual agent; rather, it is a creative power but operates at a lower level of creativity than the secondary or poetic imagination which has the power to dissolve perceptions entirely and create new combinations. Elsewhere, Coleridge calls imagination a "shaping and modifying power," and fancy "the aggregative and associative power" (*BL*, I, 293 and n. 4). Indeed, Coleridge refers to imagination as the "esemplastic" power, a term he derives from the Greek *eis hen plattein* meaning "to shape into one" (*BL*, I, 168). Collectively, these statements suggest that imagination unifies material in an internal organic matter, changing the very elements themselves that are united, whereas the combinations produced by fancy are aggregative, comprising merely external addition, as in the placing of images side by side.

Coleridge's views on the nature of poetry and poetic language are intrinsically tied to his views of poetic imagination. He holds that poetry is distinguished from other disciplines such as science and history "by proposing for its *immediate* object pleasure, not truth"; it furnishes such pleasure through its organic unity, whereby each part is integrated into the whole (*BL*, II, 12–13). Coleridge sees this pleasure as derived not only from truth as the *ultimate* goal but "by the attractions of the journey itself" (*BL*, II, 14). This view anticipates many modern conceptions of poetry and poetic autonomy: the primary purpose of poetry is not referential, but rather to draw attention to itself as a linguistic and material construct, to the journey or *means* whereby truth is achieved. Coleridge's renowned definition of "poetic faith" as a "willing suspension of disbelief" helps explain this poetic autonomy: the images in poetry have a force and logic of their own that urge the reader to enter the world of poetic illusion and to suspend judgment as to whether the images of that poetic world have a real existence.

Coleridge's most comprehensive definition of the activity of the poet sees it as relying on the unifying power of imagination, which

> reveals itself in the balance or reconciliation of opposite or discordant qualities: of sameness, with difference; of the general, with the concrete; the idea, with the image; the individual, with the representative; the sense of novelty and

freshness, with old and familiar objects; a more than usual state of emotion, with more than usual order; judgment ever awake and steady self-possession, with enthusiasm and feeling profound or vehement. (*BL*, II, 16–17).

What the mere understanding can perceive only in terms of opposites – such as general and concrete – imagination has the power to reconcile in a higher vision of unity. This power distinguishes poetry from prose or from any discursive activity that brings us conventional perceptions of the world: the imagination can not only reassemble whatever elements the world presents to our senses but also see the profounder connection of those elements.

Given Coleridge's views of the unique status of the poet, it is hardly surprising that he takes issue with Wordsworth's insistence that the poet adopt the "real" language of men, found in its purest form in rustic life. Coleridge retorts that language varies in every country and every village; given such variety, what would "real" language mean? Hence, for "real," thinks Coleridge, we should substitute the term "ordinary" or *lingua communis* (*BL*, II, 55–56). More importantly, the rustic's discourse would be impoverished (*BL*, II, 55–56). The best part of language, according to Coleridge, "is derived from reflection on the acts of the mind itself" (*BL*, II, 54). But, like Wordsworth, Coleridge uses classical Aristotelian precepts – in this case, the poetic expression of universal truths – toward Romantic ends. What allows the poet to communicate general and essential truths is the unifying power of imagination which sees the connections between particular and general, concrete and abstract, individual and representative.

America

Romanticism in America flowered somewhat later than in Europe, embroiled as the new nation was in the struggle for self-definition in political, economic, and religious terms. It was American independence from British rule, achieved in 1776, that opened the path to examining national identity and developing a distinctly American literary tradition in the light of Romantically reconceived visions of the self and nature. The major American Romantics included Ralph Waldo Emerson, Walt Whitman, Nathaniel Hawthorne, Margaret Fuller, Henry David Thoreau, and Herman Melville. While some of these writers were influenced by European Romantics and philosophers, nearly all of them were inspired by a nationalistic concern to develop an indigenous cultural tradition and a distinctly American literature. Indeed, they helped to define – at a far deeper and more intelligent level than the crude definitions offered by politicians since then until the present day – the very concept of American national identity. Like the European Romantics, these American writers reacted against what they perceived to be the mechanistic and utilitarian tenor of Enlightenment thinking and the industrial, urbanized world governed by the ethics and ideals of bourgeois commercialism. They sought to redeem the ideas of spirit, nature, and the richness of the human self within a specifically American context.

It was Emerson who laid the foundations of American Romanticism. Utilizing the ideas of Wordsworth, Coleridge, and Thomas Carlyle, he developed organicist ideas of nature, language, and imagination. Both Emerson and Whitman referred to America as a "poem" which needed to be written. In the preface to his *Leaves of Grass* (1855), Whitman saw himself as writing "the great psalm of the republic." Like Emerson, he reacted against the strictures of genre and form and wrote in a freer form using colloquial speech, or what Whitman called "the dialect of common sense," intended to convey the vastness of the American spirit. He saw the "genius" of the United States as residing in the common people, and thought that the redemption of America from its rotten commercialism lay in the realization of its authentic self.[12] Whitman's *Song of Myself* begins with the line "I celebrate myself." But this narrative "I" is symbolic ("In all people I see myself"). Whitman celebrates the divine in all dimensions of this common humanity which he locates in both soul and body, spurning didactic aims and conventional morality, as in his questioning "What blurt is it about virtue and about vice?" (l. 468). Whitman moves toward a total acceptance of humanity, free from the artifice of conventional perception, and the false imposition of coherence: "Do I contradict myself?/Very well then ... I contradict myself;/I am large ... I contain multitudes" (ll. 1314–1316). Whitman saw the human personality as integrating and accommodating all kinds of development, scientific, artistic, religious, and economic.

Another major figure was Henry David Thoreau (1817–1862). In *Walden* (1854), based on his sojourn at Emerson's property at Walden pond, he advocated a life free of social artifice, routine, and consumerism, simplified in its needs, devoted to nature and art, imaginatively exploring the depths of the self, and developing an authentic language. Thoreau's highly Romantic and eccentric vision was also expressed in opposition to oppression; he was a fervent abolitionist, and his essay "Resistance to Civil Government" (1849; later entitled "Civil Disobedience") influenced Mohandas K. Gandhi and Martin Luther King, Jr. Margaret Fuller (1810–1850) also voiced fervent opposition to what she saw as a society soiled by material greed, crime, and the perpetuation of slavery. Influenced at various times by Goethe, Carlyle, Mary Wollstonecraft, and George Sand, and being a friend of Emerson's, she edited the transcendentalists' journal the *Dial* from 1840 to 1842. She also published a notable feminist work *Woman in the Nineteenth Century* (1844), in which she argued that the development of men and women cannot occur in mutual independence, there being no wholly masculine man, or purely feminine woman. This text can be read as an effort to make Emersonian self-reliance an option for women. Nathaniel Hawthorne drew upon Emerson's theories, Enlightenment philosophy, and Coleridge's views on imagination to define the genre of romance fiction as a locus where the real and the imaginary intersect and influence each other, in a unified vision. Both Hawthorne and his friend and admirer Herman Melville reacted, like the other American Romantics, against the mechanism and commercialism at the core of American life.

Ralph Waldo Emerson (1803–1882)

Emerson, the most articulate exponent of American Romanticism, was a poet; but he was distinguished primarily by his contributions to literary and cultural criticism. He was the leading advocate of American "transcendentalism" with its insistence on the value of intuition, individuality of perception, the goodness of human nature, and the unity of the entire creation. His views of nature and self-reliance not only influenced American literary figures, as noted above, but also left their mark on European writers such as George Eliot and Nietzsche, as well as the American pragmatist philosophers William James and John Dewey. Emerson's most renowned essays include "Nature" (1836), "The American Scholar" (1837), the "Address Delivered before the Senior Class in Divinity College" (1838) (where he criticized institutional religion for thwarting individual self-discovery), "History," "Self-Reliance," and "The Poet."

Emerson's essay "Nature" is one of the most powerful and succinct expressions of a Romantic world view. Emerson sees the universe as composed of "Nature" and the "Soul," taking up a distinction of Carlyle and Fichte between the "self" and the "not-self."[13] Characteristically of Romanticism, he believes that nature is apprehensible not to most adults but to the "eye and the heart of the child" (*RWE*, 25). He stresses that nature is part of God and through it circulate the "currents of the Universal Being" (*RWE*, 26). Whatever is furnished to our senses by nature Emerson calls "commodities." A higher gift of nature is the love of beauty, which we know in its lowest form through our senses (*RWE*, 29–30). Such nature reflects a higher and divine beauty which inspires man to virtue. The highest form under which beauty may be viewed is when it becomes "an object of the intellect," which "searches out the absolute order of things as they stand in the mind of God" (*RWE*, 32). Hence the beauty in nature "is not ultimate. It is the herald of inward and eternal beauty" (*RWE*, 33).

Nature also gives us language, which is "the vehicle of thought" in three ways. Firstly, words are "signs of natural facts" (*RWE*, 33). Secondly, "it is not words only that are emblematic; it is things which are emblematic. Every natural fact is a symbol of some spiritual facts. Every appearance in nature corresponds to some state of the mind" (*RWE*, 34). For example, light and darkness are familiarly associated with knowledge and ignorance. Nature taken in itself is a mere catalogue of facts. But once it is married to human history, it becomes alive, expressing a "radical correspondence between visible things and human thoughts." In this sense, nature is an "interpreter." It remains for wise men and poets to redeem language from its corruption and to "fasten words again to visible things" (*RWE*, 35–36). Emerson goes on to explain that the "world is emblematic. Parts of speech are metaphors, because the whole of nature is a metaphor of the human mind" (*RWE*, 36). Hence things in the world are themselves signs, are themselves allegorical enactments of higher truths; nature or the world does not exist in and for itself but as a vehicle of man's spiritual expression. Like Wordsworth, Emerson advocates the life of the country, a withdrawal from "the roar of cities or the broil of politics," in order to facilitate such a rejuvenation of language.

The poet, says Emerson, "proposes Beauty as his main end," whereas the philosopher proposes Truth. Nonetheless, they both seek to ground the world of phenomena in stable and permanent laws, in an *idea* whose beauty is infinite. Hence, the "true philosopher and the true poet are one, and a beauty, which is truth, and a truth, which is beauty, is the aim of both" (*RWE*, 47). Whereas later writers such as Poe will subordinate truth and morality to the overarching aim of beauty, Emerson holds these together in a precarious balance flown into the modern world directly from Plato's Athens.

It is Emerson's essay "The American Scholar" that perhaps best articulates some of the distinctive concerns of American Romanticism. Emerson declares that America's "day of dependence" on foreign learning is drawing to a close (*RWE*, 58). He outlines the duties and virtues of the scholar: all of these, he says, are comprised in "self-trust," a notion that includes being "self-relying and self-directed," being constrained neither by tradition or religion, nor by fashion and the opinion of popular judgment. Indeed, the scholar seems to stand in a relation of "virtual hostility" to society (*RWE*, 67). The task of Emerson's heroic scholar, unlike that of Nietzsche's overman who rises above common morality, is to reaffirm and reestablish man's lost connections with his universal, unified self, to reveal what is "universally true" (*RWE*, 68). It is the scholar who wakes people from their sleep-walking dream in search of money and power, leading them to this fundamental lesson: "The world is nothing, the man is all; in yourself is the law of all nature ... in yourself slumbers the whole of Reason" (*RWE*, 70–71).

As for the *particular* duties of the American scholar, Emerson famously declares: "We have listened too long to the courtly muses of Europe" (*RWE*, 73). He ends with an eloquent call for an independence that is based on relation, on integration within a totality: "We will walk on our own feet; we will work with our own hands; we will speak our own minds ... A nation of men will for the first time exist, because each believes himself inspired by the Divine Soul which also inspires all men" (*RWE*, 74). Emerson's is a powerful

voice attempting to situate American ideals such as self-reliance and independence (at both national and individual levels) within a pre-capitalist
harmony of self and world, a harmony equated with attunement to the
workings of the divine and thereby precariously balanced between secular
and religious visions.

In his essay "The Transcendentalist" (1842), Emerson explains that
transcendentalism (a term he adapts from Kant) is a form of idealism, and
that the transcendentalist's experience "inclines him to behold the procession
of facts you call the world, as flowing perpetually outward from an invisible,
unsounded center in himself ... necessitating him to regard all things as
having a subjective or relative existence" (*RWE*, 142). Transcendentalists,
says Emerson, are characterized by their withdrawal from society, their
disinclination even to vote, and their passion for "what is great and extraordinary" (*RWE*, 146, 148). Their attachment is to "what is permanent"
(*RWE*, 153–154). For Emerson, then, "transcendental" betokens a transcendence that refuses to take the bourgeois world as real, that seeks to locate
reality itself in another, higher, realm insulated from space, time, and history.

In "The Poet" (1844), Emerson defines the poet as a transcendentalist. His
province is language, and he uses the things in nature as types, as symbols;
hence, objects in nature acquire a second value, and nature "is a symbol, in the
whole, and in every part" (*RWE*, 192). Emerson explains that the "Universe is
the externization of the soul," and that its symbolic value lies in its pointing
beyond itself, toward the supernatural (*RWE*, 193). The poet, by "ulterior
intellectual perception," is able to see the connectedness of things, especially
the symbolic connection between material and spiritual elements. Such
insight is effected by the faculty of imagination, which is effectively "the
intellect released from all service and suffered to take its direction from its
celestial life" (*RWE*, 196–199). In other words, the intellect is freed from its
bondage to the restrictive bodily sphere of practical interests and survival.

Emerson concludes by calling for poetic universality to comprehend what is
peculiarly American. There exists, as yet, no poet of genius in America: "Yet
America is a poem in our eyes ... and it will not wait long for meters" (*RWE*,
204). Emerson's words proved prophetic in Whitman's: "I sing America."
Emerson calls on the poet to "leave the world, and know the muse only." The
poet is he for whom "the ideal shall be real" (*RWE*, 206). Emerson is true to
the Romantic inversion of the categories of the bourgeois world: that world
is insular, incomplete, and denuded of all relation, all context in which it
would find its true meaning. To redeem such relation is the poet's task.

Edgar Allen Poe (1809–1849)

Poe was the first major American writer explicitly to advocate the autonomy
of poetry, the freeing of poetry from moral or educational or intellectual

imperatives. He viewed poetry not as an object but as a series of effects on the reader or listener. Poe's image as an outcast, his emphasis on beauty rather than morality or truth, his view of poetry as affording us a glimpse of an ideal world, as well as his insistence on the close union of poetry and music, exerted a considerable fascination and impact on writers such as Baudelaire, who translated a number of his tales, and Mallarmé, who translated his poems, as well as Lacan who in 1966 published his seminar on Poe's story, "The Purloined Letter." Poe's most famous tales include "The Black Cat," "The Fall of the House of Usher" (1839), and "The Cask of Amontillado" (1846). Some of Poe's radical insights into poetry are expressed in his essay "The Philosophy of Composition" (1846), which purports to explain the origins of his own widely popular poem "The Raven" (1842). Other critical essays include "The Poetic Principle" and "The Rationale of Verse."

Poe's essay "The Poetic Principle" (1850) urges that a "totality of effect or impression" is the "vital requisite" in all works of art.[14] He attempts to undermine what he calls "the heresy of *The Didactic*," which refers to the view that "the ultimate object of all Poetry is Truth" and that every poem "should inculcate a moral." As against this, Poe insists that the most dignified and noble work is the "poem *per se* – this poem which is a poem and nothing more – this poem written solely for the poem's sake" ("PP," 892–893). Poe makes a sharp distinction between "the truthful and the poetical modes" ("PP," 893). In somewhat Kantian fashion, Poe divides the mind into three aspects: "Pure Intellect, Taste, and the Moral Sense." He places taste in the middle, acknowledging that it has "intimate relations" with the other two aspects, but he observes a distinction between these three offices: the intellect is concerned with truth; taste apprehends the beautiful; and moral sense disposes us toward duty ("PP," 893). Poe admits that the precepts of duty or even the lessons of truth can be introduced into a poem; but they must subserve the ultimate purpose of art, and must be placed "in proper subjection to that *Beauty* which is the atmosphere and the real essence of the poem" ("PP," 895).

Hence poetry should not be realistic, merely copying or imitating the beauties that lie before us. Poe defines the "poetic principle" in Platonic terms as "the Human Aspiration for Supernal Beauty," a quest for an excitement of the soul that is distinct from the intoxication of the heart or the satisfaction of reason. Poe defines poetry as

> *The Rhythmical Creation of Beauty*. Its sole arbiter is Taste ... In the contemplation of Beauty we alone find it possible to attain that pleasurable elevation, or excitement, *of the soul*, which we recognize as the Poetic Sentiment, and which is so easily distinguished from Truth, which is the satisfaction of the Reason, or from Passion, which is the excitement of the Heart. ("PP," 895)

What is not Platonic is Poe's isolated exaltation of beauty over truth and goodness; the Platonic harmony between these has disintegrated into a desperate craving for a beauty that is not found in the actual world, and a retreat from the increasingly troubled realms of truth and morality. Nonetheless, the poet, according to Poe, recognizes in many phenomena "holy impulses ... generous, and self-sacrificing deeds" ("PP," 906). Hence, the very morality that is expelled from the poet's quest for beauty returns as the very ground of this quest, resurrected in aesthetic form on the ground of its own beauty. In other words, morality becomes an integral part of the aesthetic endeavor, and becomes justified on aesthetic grounds. Once again, art is seen as salvific, displacing the function of religion in serving as our guide to the world beyond.

Notes

1. "Critical Fragments," 108, in Friedrich von Schlegel, *Philosophical Fragments*, trans. Peter Firchow (Minneapolis and Oxford: University of Minnesota Press, 1991), p. 13.
2. Friedrich von Schlegel, "On Incomprehensibility," in *German Aesthetic and Literary Criticism: The Romantic Ironists and Goethe*, ed. Kathleen M. Wheeler (Cambridge and New York: Cambridge University Press, 1984), pp. 33–38.
3. "On the Aesthetic Education of Man," in *Friedrich Schiller: Poet of Freedom*, trans. William F. Wertz, Jr. (New York: New Benjamin Franklin House, 1985), p. 225. Hereafter cited as "AEM."
4. Friedrich Schleiermacher, *Hermeneutics and Criticism and Other Writings*, trans. and ed. Andrew Bowie (Cambridge: Cambridge University Press, 1998), pp. 23–24. Hereafter cited as *HC*.
5. Théophile Gautier, "Preface," in *Mademoiselle de Maupin* (1835; rpt. Paris: Garnier, 1955), pp. 2–3, 11, 22–24.
6. *An Extraordinary Woman: Selected Writings of Germaine de Staël*, trans. Vivian Folkenflik (New York: Columbia University Press, 1987), pp. 204–205.
7. *The Letters of John Keats: Volume I*, ed. Hyder Edward Rollins (Cambridge, MA: Harvard University Press, 1958), p. 184. Hereafter cited as *Letters*.
8. *The Prose Works of William Worsdworth: Volume I*, ed. W. J. B. Owen and Jane Worthington Smyser (Oxford: Clarendon Press, 1974). Hereafter cited as *PLB*.
9. *Coleridge: Poetical Works*, ed. Ernest Hartley Coleridge (New York and Oxford: Oxford University Press, 1973), p. 11.
10. *The Collected Works of Samuel Taylor Coleridge. VII: Biographia Literaria*, ed. James Engell and W. Jackson Bate (Princeton: Princeton University Press, 1983), p. 187. Hereafter cited as *BL*.
11. *The Collected Works of Samuel Taylor Coleridge: Lay Sermons*, ed. R. J. White (Princeton and London: Princeton University Press/Routledge and Kegan Paul, 1972), p. 169. Hereafter cited as *LS*.

12. Walt Whitman, "Introduction," in *Leaves of Grass: The First (1855) Edition*, ed. Malcolm Cowley (Harmondsworth: Penguin, 1986), pp. 5, 8, 23.
13. "Nature," in *Ralph Waldo Emerson and Margaret Fuller: Selected Works*, ed. John Carlos Rowe (Boston and New York: Houghton Mifflin, 2003), p. 24. Hereafter cited as *RWE*.
14. "The Poetic Principle," in *Complete Tales and Poems of Edgar Allen Poe* (New York: Vintage Books, 1975), p. 889. Hereafter cited as "PP."

Chapter 11

Realism, Naturalism, Symbolism, and Aestheticism

Historical Background: The Later Nineteenth Century

In the second half of the nineteenth century, the vast unifying systems of thinkers such as Hegel, as well as the unifying visions of the Romantics, collapsed into a series of one-sided systems, such as utilitarianism, positivism, and social Darwinism. To be sure, there were a number of movements that continued the oppositional stance of Romanticism to mainstream bourgeois and Enlightenment ideals: Matthew Arnold criticized the philistinism of bourgeois society, while Thomas Carlyle promoted his own version of German idealism, and John Ruskin perpetuated a Romantic idealization of the Middle Ages. A tradition of alternative philosophy ran from Schopenhauer through thinkers such as Nietzsche, Kierkegaard, and Bergson. More politically forceful were the various movements of socialism inspired by Marx, Engels, and others.

But the values and ideals of the mainstream bourgeois Enlightenment prevailed. In the later nineteenth century, these values were increasingly attuned to the rapid progress of science and technology. As the culmination of a historical pattern beginning in the Renaissance, science effectively displaced religion and theology as the supreme arbiter of knowledge. The institutional demise of religion was intensified by broadly scientific endeavors. Charles Darwin's *Origin of Species* (1859) was held by some to undermine the biblical accounts of creation; the rise of the German Higher Criticism subjected the gospels to a searching "scientific" scrutiny, exposing many inconsistencies and contradictions. David Strauss' *The Life of Jesus* (1835) saw Christ in terms of myth rather than fact; Ernest Renan's book of the same title (1863) effectively denied the originality of Christ, viewing him as emerging from a religious context already prepared.

As such, the natural sciences became the model and the measure of other disciplines. The broadest name for this emulation of science is "positivism,"

Literary Criticism from Plato to the Present: An Introduction   M. A. R. Habib
© 2011 M. A. R. Habib

which derives its name from the self-proclaimed "positive" philosophies of thinkers such as Auguste Comte and Émile Durkheim in France, and Herbert Spencer in England. These thinkers wished to exclude from investigation all hypotheses that were not empirically verifiable, and they rejected as "metaphysical" all inquiries that were not amenable to supposedly scientific terms of analysis, such as "matter," "motion," and "force." In political terms, Herbert Marcuse has shown how positivism, or "positive philosophy," was essentially a conservative reaction against the "negative philosophy" of Hegel.[1] Hegel's entire dialectic had been premised on a rejection of the world as given and an imperative to transform the world in the image of our own rationality. In one sense, positivism was a reaction against the very principles of Hegelian unity and totality as achieved by some spiritual agency or absolute idea. Ideologically, positivism, in its manifold guises, was an attempt to confirm the reality and propriety of the world as given; in other words, these were essentially conservative modes of thought, sanctioning the status quo. Positivism pervaded many domains: sociology (as exemplified by Durkheim, who attempted to isolate a distinctly "social" fact), psychology (as shown in Freud's obsession with the scientific status of his work), and social thought (expressed in the evolutionism of Herbert Spencer). Realism and naturalism are the literary expressions of this general tendency.

Realism and Naturalism

A tendency toward realism arose in many parts of Europe and in America, beginning in the 1840s. The major figures included Flaubert and Balzac in France, Dostoevsky and Tolstoy in Russia, George Eliot and Charles Dickens in England, as well as William Dean Howells and Henry James in America. The most general aim of realism was to offer a truthful, accurate, and objective representation of the real world, both the external world and the human self. To achieve this aim, realists resorted to a number of strategies: the use of detail; avoidance of what was imaginary and mythical; adherence to the requirements of probability; inclusion of characters and incidents from all social strata, dealing not merely with rulers and nobility; focusing on contemporary life rather than longing for some idealized past; and using colloquial idioms and everyday speech. Underlying all these was an emphasis on direct observation, factuality, and experience. Realism was thus a broad reaction against the idealization, historical retrospection, and imaginary worlds of Romanticism. Moreover, realism – to this day – has been not just a literary technique but, as Fredric Jameson states, "one of the most complex and vital realizations of Western culture, to which it is ... well-nigh unique."[2]

Naturalism was the ancient term for the physical sciences or the study of nature. Modern naturalism explicitly endeavors to emulate the methods of the physical sciences, drawing heavily on the principles of causality, determinism, explanation, and experimentation. Some naturalists also drew on Darwinian notions of the struggle for survival. Hence naturalism can be viewed as a more extreme form of realism, extending the latter's scientific basis still further to encompass extremely detailed methods of description, a deterministic emphasis upon the contexts of actions and events (which are seen as arising from specific causes), upon the hereditary psychological components of their characters, experimenting with the connections between human psychology and external environment, and refusing to accommodate any kind of metaphysical or spiritual perspective. It was the literary historian Hippolyte Taine (1828–1893) who laid the theoretical foundations of naturalism and Émile Zola who first formulated its manifesto.

In Germany, a radical group called the Young Germans, whose prominent members included Heinrich Heine (1797–1856) and Carl Gutzkow (1811–1878), voiced their opposition to the perceived reactionary Romanticism of Goethe and Schlegel. Later proponents of realism included Julian Schmidt (1818–1886), the novelist Gottfried Keller (1819–1890), the dramatist Friedrich Hebbel (1813–1863), and Friedrich Theodor von Vischer (1807–1887), who endeavored to express a theoretical basis for realism. The naturalist movement, arising in the 1880s through the influence of Zola, was advanced by Arno Holz (1863–1929), Heinrich (1855–1906) and Julius Hart (1859–1930), Wilhelm Bolsche (1861–1939), the social novelist Theodor Fontane (1819–1898), and Wilhelm Scherer (1841–1886), who attempted to base literature on scientific principles.

Realism became a force in France during the 1850s. Edmond Duranty began a journal called *Réalisme* in 1856, in which realism was equated with truthfulness, sincerity, and the modern. Duranty believed that novels should reflect the lives of ordinary middle-class or working-class people. In 1857 Jules-François-Félix Husson (know as Champfleury) urged the need for scrupulous documentation and freedom from moral constraints. Positivism in France took on a more overt aspect in the work of Taine who sought a totalizing explanation of the causal operations governing both human beings and the world. In the famous introduction to his *History of English Literature* (1863–1864), he advocated, following Sainte-Beuve, an ideal of scientific exactness in literary criticism, urging that the task of the critic was to discover the master characteristic of a writer's work, as determined by three broad factors: race, milieu, and moment. The underlying assumption was that art expresses not only the psychology of its author but also the spirit of its age. Taine was a major influence on Zola and Ferdinand Brunetière (1849–1906). In 1880, Zola, Guy de Maupassant, Joris-Karl Huysmans, and others jointly published a volume of naturalistic fiction entitled *Les Soirées de Meda*.

In England, realism had in varying degrees informed the numerous types of novel – political, historical, religious – which had been written by major figures such as Thackeray and Dickens during the nineteenth century. But it was with the novels of George Eliot, Anthony Trollope, George Meredith, and Thomas Hardy that realism flowered. George Eliot's views were influenced by Ludwig Feuerbach and Auguste Comte. Eliot's domestic partner George Henry Lewes examined human psychology as intimately related to social conditions. Two other notable realists of this period were George Gissing (1857–1903) and George Moore (1852–1933), both influenced by Zola. The subsequent development of photography and the ideal of photographic accuracy had considerable significance for realism in both art and literature.

While realism in America reacted against the fundamental tendencies of Romanticism, it perpetuated the latter's concern with national identity and defining a native tradition. The foremost theorist was William Dean Howells, a powerful advocate of verisimilitude in fiction. In his manifesto *Crumbling Idols* (1894), Hamlin Garland propounded "veritism," a version of naturalism, which would express social concerns while respecting local traditions and individual qualities. The novels of both Theodore Dreiser and Stephen Crane bear the impact of Zola's naturalism and social Darwinism. Frank Norris' influential essay "A Plea for Romantic Fiction" (1901) was a defense of naturalism which accommodated some Romantic qualities. Another seminal figure in realist theory was Henry James. What follows is an analysis of central statements of realism and naturalism made in England, France, and America.

George Eliot (1819–1880)

One of the most succinct yet poignant statements of realism was made by the major Victorian novelist George Eliot, the latter being the pseudonym of Mary Ann Evans. Her novels include *Adam Bede* (1859), *The Mill on the Floss* (1860), *Silas Marner* (1861), *Middlemarch* (1871–1872), and *Daniel Deronda* (1874–1876). Her translation of David Strauss' controversial work *The Life of Jesus* appeared in 1846. She also translated Ludwig Feuerbach's *The Essence of Christianity* (1854). These thinkers promoted a humanistic and tolerant, as opposed to a rigidly religious, conception of human nature.

This newer conception is expressed in *Adam Bede*, where the narrator explains that as a novelist she wishes to "give a faithful account of men and things as they have mirrored themselves in my mind ... as if I were in the witness-box narrating my experience on oath."[3] Hence, the first principle of Eliot's realism is the artistic pursuit of truth, based on direct experience of the world. She is aware, however, of the difficulty of such an enterprise: "Falsehood is so easy, truth so difficult" (*AB*, 151–152). Indeed, she imagines the reader asking for the characters to be portrayed as unproblematically good or bad, so that they can be admired or condemned "at a glance," and without the "slightest disturbance" of their prepossessions or assumptions (*AB*, 150–151). So the second principle of her realism is that the representation of experience must be authentic, refusing to pander to current prejudices and popular taste.

A third principle of Eliot's realism is its moral basis: we should accept people in their actual, imperfect, state, rather than holding them up to impossible ideals: "These fellow-mortals, every one, must be accepted as they are: you can neither straighten their noses, nor brighten their wit, nor rectify their dispositions" (*AB*, 151). Hence Eliot's artistic focus on ordinary people and events has both an epistemological basis – the reliance on one's own experience – and a moral basis of sympathy or "fellow-feeling" with other human beings. This sympathy points to a fourth principle of realism, given in Eliot's redefinition of beauty as existing in "deep human sympathy," whereby we should "see beauty in these commonplace things" (*AB*, 153). Hence, Eliot cleverly presents her realism not merely as pertaining to literary technique but as encompassing an entire way of looking at the world: the pursuit of truth, the reliance on one's own experience, the acceptance of people as they are, the perception of beauty in ordinary things were all aspects of this vision; and these are all underlain by a religious disposition which itself is humane and based on human sympathy rather than endless doctrine and unrealistic ideals.

Émile Zola (1840–1902)

Zola was the leading figure of French naturalism. His essay *The Experimental Novel* (1880) attempted a justification of his own novelistic practice, and became the seminal manifesto of naturalism. In it Zola argues for a literature "governed" by an experimental or scientific method, a method which over-turns and rejects all previous authority and proclaims the liberty of thought.[4] A major principle of science, according to Zola, is the belief in "absolute determinism": there is no phenomenon, no occurrence in nature, which does not have a determining cause or complex of causes (*EN*, 3). Zola neatly situates literature within the general context of scientific advance:

> the experimental novel is a consequence of the scientific evolution of the century ... it substitutes for the study of the abstract and the metaphysical man the study of the natural man, governed by physical or chemical laws, and modified by the influences of his surroundings; it is in one word the literature of our scientific age, as the classical and romantic literature corresponded to a scholastic and theological age. (*EN*, 23)

Hence, the experimental novel must consider man in both social and psychological aspects, taking account of heredity and social conditions (*EN*, 21). Notwithstanding his scientism, Zola attempts to redeem the moral function of literature. He sees science as progressing toward a state where humanity will be in control of life and be able to direct nature, ultimately toward a moral purpose: "We shall enter upon a century in which man, grown more powerful, will make use of nature and will utilize its laws to produce upon the earth the greatest possible amount of justice and freedom. There is no nobler, higher, nor grander end" (*EN*, 25). Zola's position might well be seen as an attempt to reincarnate the classical idea of the "highest good" as the purpose to which all science and art are ultimately directed. This function of the novel, then, coheres with the paths of science and is also integrated with the efforts of legislators and politicians "toward that great object, the conquest of nature and the increase of man's power" (*EN*, 31).

William Dean Howells (1837–1920)

William Dean Howells' chief fictional work was *The Rise of Silas Lapham* (1885), and his subsequent novels, such as *A Hazard of New Fortunes* (1890) and *The World of Chance* (1893) move toward both socialism and social realism, whereby he conducted a critique of American capitalism and imperialism. Howells' reputation as the major American theorist of realism was established by his book *Criticism and Fiction* (1891), where he formulates a "democratic" theory of realism: the true realist "finds nothing insignificant" and "feels in every nerve the equality of things and the unity of men; his soul is exalted, not by . . . ideals, but by realities, in which alone the truth lives." For such a person, "no living man is a type, but a character."[5] Howells indicts current critical practice, based on personal feelings and impressions and a blind adherence to past models (*CF*, 311). What we need is a "dispassionate, scientific" study of literature, a study which is restricted "to the business of observing, recording, and comparing; to analyzing the material before it, and then synthesizing its impressions. Even then, it is not too much to say that literature as an art could get on perfectly well without it" (*CF*, 311, 314).

Howells directly equates democratic political beliefs with a democratic aesthetic: the political state, he says, was built "on the affirmation of the essential equality of men in their rights and duties . . . these conditions invite the artist to the study and appreciation of the common . . . The arts must become democratic, and then we shall have the expression of America in art" (*CF*, 339). In the spirit of this democratic mission, Howells urges: "let fiction cease to lie about life; let it portray men and women as they are, actuated by the motives and the passions in the measure we all know . . . let it speak the dialect, the language, that most Americans know – and there can be no doubt of an unlimited future, not only of delightfulness but of usefulness, for it" (*CF*, 328). Such is the circuitous historical route by which literary aesthetics returns to the principles of Horace, that the work of art must delight and teach.

Henry James (1843–1916)

Henry James, brother of the pragmatist philosopher William James, is best known for his novels, which include *The American* (1877), *The Europeans* (1878), *Daisy Miller* (1879), *The Portrait of a Lady* (1881), *The Ambassadors* (1903), and *The Golden Bowl* (1904). His influence extended to figures such as Ezra Pound and T. S. Eliot. In his essay "The Art of Fiction" (1884), James is concerned, firstly, to establish the novel as a serious art form. Secondly, he denies that rules can be somehow prescribed for fiction. James' central claim is that the novel must be free from moral and educational requirements and constraints.

This novelistic freedom is first worked out in relation to the kind of realism on which James insists: "The only reason for the existence of a novel is that it does attempt to represent life ... as the picture is reality, so the novel is history."[6] A novel produces the "the illusion of life" (*AF*, 173). James suggests as a broad definition that the novel is "a personal, a direct impression of life," and it is successful inasmuch as it reveals a particular and unique mind (*AF*, 170). Moreover, the enterprise of realism is vastly complex. The writer should indeed possess "a sense of reality" but "reality has a myriad forms" and cannot be encompassed within some formula (*AF*, 171). Like reality, experience is a complex concept. Experience "is never limited, and it is never complete; it is an immense sensibility, a kind of huge spiderweb of the finest silken threads suspended in the chamber of consciousness ... It is the very atmosphere of the mind" (*AF*, 172). A mere glimpse of a situation can afford a perspicacious novelist an entire perspective based on deep insight. Indeed, James identifies the very freedom of the novel with its potential for realistic – which for him might well read "metonymic" – correspondence: the novel has a "large, free character of an immense and exquisite correspondence with life" (*AF*, 179). Notwithstanding the complex nature of both reality and experience, James states that "the air of reality (solidity of specification) seems to me to be the supreme virtue of a novel" (*AF*, 173). He insists that "the province of art is all life, all feeling, all observation, all vision ... it is all experience." As such, nothing can be forbidden for the novelist, nothing can be out of bounds (*AF*, 177–178). Finally, in arguing that the novel must be free of all moral obliga-tions, he offers the apparently simple reasoning that "questions of art are questions ... of execution; questions of morality are quite another affair." If art has a purpose, that purpose is artistic: it must aim at perfection (*AF*, 181).

Symbolism and Aestheticism

Even as the currents of realism and then naturalism held sway in European literature, there was also fermenting in the works of poets such as

Charles Baudelaire an alternative set of concerns: with language, with poetic form, with evocation of mental states and ideal worlds, and the most intimate recesses of human subjectivity. To some extent, these concerns were inherited from the Romantics, as was the antagonism toward an urban life regulated by the cycles of modern industry and commerce. The followers of Baudelaire eventually became associated with a series of reactions against realism and naturalism: symbolism, aestheticism, and impressionism, which have sometimes, and in varying combinations, fallen under the label of "decadence."

This broad anti-realist and anti-bourgeois disposition had already surfaced in many writers and movements: in the Pre-Raphaelite Brotherhood of artists formed in 1848 in England which looked back to the direct and morally serious art of the Middle Ages prior to the advent of the Renaissance artist Raphael; in the Parnassian poets of France, inspired by Théophile Gautier and Leconte de Lisle (1818–1894), who adopted an ethic of "art for art's sake"; and in Poe's theories of poetic composition. Baudelaire and his successors, such as Paul Verlaine (1844–1896), Arthur Rimbaud (1854–1891), and Stéphane Mallarmé (1842–1898), were the heirs of these aesthetic tendencies; and they have all been associated with French symbolism. This affiliation is retrospective since the symbolist movement as such arose somewhat later, its manifesto being penned by Jean Moréas in 1886. The other symbolists included the poets Jules Laforgue, Henri de Regnier, Gustave Kahn, the novelist Joris-Karl Huysmans, the dramatist Maurice Materlinck, and the critic Remy de Gourmont. This movement reached its zenith in the 1890s and thereafter declined, being often derisively viewed as a form of decadence and affectation. It is the precursors of the symbolists – Baudelaire, Verlaine, Rimbaud, and Mallarmé – rather than the symbolists themselves who have had a vast and enduring influence, extending from major poets such as W. B. Yeats and T. S. Eliot, through writers of fiction such as Marcel Proust, James Joyce, and Virginia Woolf, and dramatists such as August Strindberg, to philosophers of language and modern literary theorists such as Roland Barthes, Jacques Derrida, and Julia Kristeva.

Mallarmé's *Divagations* (1897) was another important statement of symbolist aesthetics. Mallarmé rejected the realist assumption that language was referential, that words were the signs of a pregiven reality. Reality is an interpretation from a particular perspective, and for Mallarmé, a poem is part of reality and indeed helps to create reality. He also rejected the Romantic idea of a poem as expressing an author's subjectivity; rather, the poet enters the world of language which determines both his consciousness and the world. Mallarmé drew attention to the material dimensions of words, their sounds, their combinations on the page, and their ability to create new shades of meaning and perception. The major critic of the symbolist movement was Remy de Gourmont, who urged the ideals of subjectivity and artistic purity.

He asserted that "only mediocre works are impersonal"[7] and advocated a "pure art" which was "concerned exclusively with self-realization."[8]

In general, the symbolists refused to take the material world they had inherited as the real world. Drawing on Platonic philosophy, they saw the present world as an imperfect reflection of a higher, infinite, and eternal realm which could be evoked by symbols. Hence they rejected the descriptive language of the realists and naturalists in favor of a more suggestive, symbolic, and allusive language that could evoke states of consciousness. They also drew on Baudelaire's notion of "correspondences" between the senses to elaborate an aesthetic of synaesthesia, and their predominant analogy for poetry was with music. French symbolism was introduced into England through Arthur Symons' book *The Symbolist Movement in Literature* (1899), which characterized it as a "revolt against exteriority, against rhetoric, against a materialistic tradition."[9]

A more extreme development of this attitude of negation was in aestheticism, the doctrine that art exists for its own sake, or for the sake of beauty. The phrase "l'art pour l'art" (art for art's sake) had been coined by the philosopher Victor Cousin in 1818; this doctrine reverberated through the aesthetics of Kant, many of the Romantics, the Pre-Raphaelites, the Parnassians, the symbolists, the decadents, and the critical programs of the twentieth-century formalists. The work of some of the seminal figures of symbolism and aestheticism – Baudelaire, Pater, and Wilde – can now be considered.

Charles Baudelaire (1821–1867)

Known as the founder of French symbolism (though not himself part of the movement), Baudelaire was born in Paris where he lived a Bohemian life, adopting the artistic posture of a dandy, devoted to beauty, disdainfully aloof from the vulgar bourgeois world of materialism and commerce. He also assumed the pose of the *flâneur*, frequenter and consumer of the city streets. Baudelaire expressed a modernistic vision of the sordidness, sensuality, and corruption of city life, which influenced modernist writers such as T. S. Eliot. Baudelaire's infamous collection of poems, *Les Fleurs du Mal* (*The Flowers of Evil*) (1857), became the subject of an "obscenity" trial for including lesbian poems. He contracted syphilis and was paralyzed by a stroke before his death. Notwithstanding his lifestyle and his artistic views, Baudelaire was a believer in original sin, and viewed the modern world as fallen. In his *Journaux intimes* he stated that man is "*naturally* depraved," and he ridiculed the idea of progress, viewing commerce as "in its very essence, *satanic*."[10]

Baudelaire's famous sonnet "Correspondences" is a succinct expression of his symbolist aesthetic, seeing the material world as a "forest of symbols" which point to an ideal world. He regards the earth and its phenomena as a "revelation" of heavenly correspondences, and it is the poet who must decipher these. In an essay he states that "poetry is what is most real, what is completely true only in *another world*." The present world, he maintains, is merely a "dictionary of hieroglyphics" pointing to the world beyond.[11] Much of Baudelaire's important criticism is contained in his *Salons*, which were reviews of yearly exhibitions at the Louvre museum. In his "Salon" of 1846 he insisted that criticism of poetry "should be biased, impassioned, partisan," though it should be written from a point of view "that opens up the widest horizons" (*BLC*, 87–88). Baudelaire sanctions Poe's fundamental views: that an essential function of art is to produce a unity of impression or effect, that poetry "has no other goal than itself" and as such must not be subjected to the heresies of "*teaching ... of passion, of truth*, and of *morality*." Baudelaire acknowledges, however, that poetry can "ennoble manners" and raises "man above the level of vulgar interests" (*BLC*, 130–131). He accepts Poe's formulation of the "poetic principle" as "human aspiration toward a superior beauty." In fact, he adapts Poe's notion into the statement that the "immortal instinct for the beautiful ... makes us consider the earth and its spectacles as a revelation, as something in correspondence with Heaven" (*BLC*, 132).

Baudelaire notes that for Poe, "Imagination is the queen of faculties." Baudelaire's own definition implies again a system of correspondences that is not formulated in Poe's work: "Imagination is an almost divine faculty which perceives immediately and without philosophical methods the inner and secret relations of things, the correspondences and the analogies" (*BLC*, 127). Like Coleridge, Baudelaire sees the imagination as destroying conventional associations and recreating according to primordial imperatives found within human subjectivity, within the soul itself. But Baudelaire also states that "Imagination is the queen of truth," and that "it plays a powerful role even in morality" (*BLC*, 182). Hence, even though truth and morality are rigidly expelled by Poe and Baudelaire from the province of the aesthetic, they are effectively subsumed under the control of the very power which creates the aesthetic, the power of imagination. Baudelaire states that the "whole visible universe is but a storehouse of images and signs to which imagination will give a relative place and value; it is a sort of food which the imagination must digest and transform" (*BLC*, 186). What arranges the world, then, is not divine providence or the canons of truth or morality; all of these are now subjected to the aesthetic power of imagination which is newly invested with the functions of truth and morality in their subjectively reconstituted and reauthorized form.

Walter Pater (1839–1894)

Walter Pater is best known for his phrase "art for art's sake." In his insistence on artistic autonomy, on aesthetic *experience* as opposed to aesthetic *object*, and on experience in general as an ever-vanishing flux, he is a precursor of modern views of both life and art. His works included *Studies in the History of the Renaissance* (1873), *Marius the Epicurean* (1885), *Imaginary Portraits* (1887), and *Plato and Platonism* (1893).

In the preface to his *Studies*, Pater advocates a literary criticism based on subjective experience and impressions. Subverting Arnold's prescription that the critic must know the "object as . . . it really is," Pater insists that as a critic, one must "know one's own impression as it really is, to discriminate it, to realise it distinctly." [12] The kinds of questions we should ask are: "What is this song or picture . . . to *me*? What effect does it really produce on me?" (*Ren.,* viii). Pater's views of aesthetic experience are rooted in his account of experience in general. Given the brevity of our life, experience must be undertaken for its own sake: "Not the fruit of experience, but experience itself, is the end . . . To burn always with this hard, gem-like flame, to maintain this ecstasy, is success in life" (*Ren.,* 236–237). Such intense experience is furnished foremost by "the poetic passion, the desire of beauty, the love of art for its own sake" (*Ren.,* 239).

We have here reached a point in Western culture where experience is dirempted and abstracted from any kind of constraint whatsoever. Hegel would have regarded such experience as an abstract category, not even possible; but Pater expresses a desperate attempt to redeem experience from the weight of centuries of oppression and coercion and molding into various socially acceptable forms; he effectively aestheticizes experience, equating the fullness of experience with beauty. Experience is raised from the mereness of means to the exaltation of end, a celebration of purposelessness, indirection, relativism, and randomness.

Oscar Wilde (1854–1900)

Another figure in the aestheticist vein, who struck an even more decadent and dandyish posture, was Oscar Wilde. A dazzling wit and brilliant conversationalist, he was the author of several plays which took the London stage by storm, as well as of poetry, novels, and criticism. His most notable dramas were *Lady Windemere's Fan* (1892), *An Ideal Husband* (1895), and, most successful of all, *The Importance of Being Earnest* (1895). These plays powerfully satirized the morals and mores of the English middle classes; Wilde's own homosexual practices brought him into conflict with these moral standards, and he was imprisoned for two years with hard labor. Wilde's subversiveness has been a source of inspiration for gay and lesbian studies, and his refusal of absolutes aligns him not only with figures such as Pater but also with Nietzsche and indeed the entire heterological tradition.

In the famous preface to his novel *The Picture of Dorian Gray* (1890–1891), Wilde offers a brief and provocative manifesto of his aesthetic outlook. He states that the "artist is the creator of beautiful things."[13] Wilde continues, there "is no such thing as a moral or an immoral book" and "No artist has ethical sympathies." Moreover, no "artist desires to prove anything . . . Books are well written, or badly written. That is all." Wilde emphasizes that "All art is quite useless." And he effectively redefines its imitative function: "It is the spectator, and not life, that art really mirrors" (*OW*, 17). This statement and in fact Wilde's entire account of criticism anticipates reader-response and some historicist theories.

"The Critic as Artist" (1891) sets forth Wilde's most important views of art and criticism. Any proposed antithesis between art and criticism, says Wilde, is "entirely arbitrary. Without the critical faculty, there is no artistic creation at all worthy of the name" (*OW*, 1020). He insists that "Criticism is itself an art." And, just as the creative act is critical, so criticism is creative. It is also independent: "the highest Criticism, being the purest form of personal impression, is in its way more creative than creation, as it has least reference to any standard external to itself, and is . . . in itself, and to itself, an end" (*OW*, 1027). What this statement makes us realize is the length of the journey undertaken by literary criticism since Plato and Aristotle. We have now moved even beyond the demand that art itself be extricated from moral, religious, and ideological constraints. The demand for autonomy, having traversed the sphere of art, has now emerged in the realm of criticism, a demand that threatens to subvert not only previous conceptions of criticism but also the basic tenets of Western philosophy.

What, then, is the self-contained aim of criticism? Like Pater, Wilde rejects Arnold's definition of criticism's task as attempting "to see the object as in itself it really is." On the contrary, criticism "is in its essence purely subjective" and must express personal impressions (*OW*, 1028). Wilde insists that it is through the critic that the performative potential of the art is realized; it is the critic who gives voice to the work of art. Moreover, it is the critic who is "always showing us the work of art in some new relation to our age. He will always be reminding us that great works of art are living things" (*OW*, 1034). But criticism has a broader and more basic import. Wilde accepts Arnold's claim that criticism is responsible for creating the "intellectual atmosphere" and culture of an age (*OW*, 1055). It is criticism that gives us a sense of unity, that enables us to reconstruct the past, that enables us to rise above provincialism and prejudice into true cosmopolitanism (*OW*, 1053). Anticipating important modern insights, Wilde states that it

> is Criticism that, recognizing no position as final, and refusing to bind itself by the shallow shibboleths of any sect or school, creates that serene philosophic temper which loves truth for its own sake . . . Anything approaching to the free play of the mind is practically unknown amongst us . . . The artistic critic, like the mystic, is an antinomian always. (*OW*, 1057)

180 *Romanticism and the Later Nineteenth Century*

Notes

. Herbert Marcuse, *Reason and Revolution: Hegel and the Rise of Social Theory* (London: Routledge and Kegan Paul, 1977), pp. 232–388.
2. It is worth consulting Jameson's entire discussion, *The Ideologies of Theory: Essays 1971–1986. Volume II: The Syntax of History* (London: Routledge, 1989), pp. 118–122.
3. George Eliot, *Adam Bede*, ed. John Paterson (Boston and New York: Houghton Mifflin, 1968), p. 150. Hereafter cited as *AB*.
4. Émile Zola, *The Experimental Novel and Other Essays*, trans. Belle M. Sherman (New York: Haskell House, 1964), pp. 2, 26, 44. Hereafter cited as *EN*.
5. *Criticism and Fiction*, reprinted in *W. D. Howells: Selected Literary Criticism. Volume II: 1886–1869*, ed Donald Pizer and Christoph K. Lohmann (Bloomington and Indianapolis: Indiana University Press, 1993), pp. 302–303. Hereafter cited as *CF*.
6. Henry James, *The Art of Criticism*, ed. William Veeder and Susan M. Griffin (Chicago and London: University of Chicago Press, 1986), pp. 166–167. Hereafter cited as *AF*.
7. Remy de Gourmont, *Selected Writings*, trans. and ed. Glenn S. Burne (New York: University of Michigan Press, 1966), p. 124.
8. Remy de Gourmont, *Decadence and Other Essays on the Culture of Ideas*, trans. William Bradley (1922; rpt. London: George Allen and Unwin, 1930), p. 31.
9. Arthur Symons, *The Symbolist Movement in Literature* (1908; rpt. New York: Haskell House, 1971), pp. 4, 9.
10. *Intimate Journals*, trans. C. Isherwood, introd. T. S. Eliot (New York and London: Blackamore Press, 1930), pp. 48, 51.
11. *Baudelaire as a Literary Critic: Selected Essays*, trans. Lois Boe Hyslop and Francis E. Hyslop, Jr. (Pennsylvania: Pennsylvania State University Press, 1964), pp. 87–88. Hereafter cited as *BLC*.
12. Walter Pater, *The Renaissance: Studies in Art and Poetry* (London: Macmillan, 1913), p. viii. Hereafter cited as *Ren.*
13. *The Complete Works of Oscar Wilde: Stories, Plays, Poems, Essays*, introd. Vyvyan Holland (London and Glasgow: Collins, 1984), p. 17. Hereafter cited as *OW*.

Chapter 12

The Heterological Thinkers

The main streams of modern European and American thought, such as rationalism, empiricism, utilitarianism, and pragmatism, stemmed from the Enlightenment, the American and French Revolutions, as well as the ongoing Industrial Revolution. Hegel's philosophy had amalgamated the entire thrust of modern bourgeois thought from Descartes and Hobbes through the Enlightenment to Kant. There was, however, an important strand of thought which reacted against Hegel's philosophy as the embodiment of bourgeois principles. This was the "heterological" or alternative tradition initiated by Schopenhauer, who launched a radical critique of Enlightenment notions. The tradition was continued by Nietzsche, Kierkegaard, Bergson, Freud, Husserl, Heidegger, Derrida, and modern feminists. These thinkers challenged the very discipline of philosophy and its claims to arrive at truth through reason. They emphasized instead the role of emotion, the body, sexuality, the unconscious, as well as of pragmatic interests. This tradition exhibits some historical continuity with the Romantics, the symbolists, and decadents, as well as affiliations with humanists such as Irving Babbitt in America and Matthew Arnold in England. The aesthetic views of four figures from this heterodox line of thinking will be considered below in the context of their world views: Schopenhauer, Nietzsche, Bergson, and Arnold. These thinkers continue to influence literary debate in our own day at the profoundest levels.

Arthur Schopenhauer (1788–1860)

Schopenhauer – who is the most widely read philosopher in Germany today – offered an incisive critique of the bourgeois world and its self-abasement before the "crass materialism" of science.[1] He was especially contemptuous of attempts to historicize and rationalize the evils of the bourgeois world as part of an ordered teleological plan; he dismissed Hegel's "philosophy of absolute nonsense" as comprised of "three-quarters cash and one-quarter crazy notions" (*PW*, 79, 81). He saw history as exhibiting no unity beyond eternal recurrence of the same miserable patterns of events (*PW*, 108, 290). Schopenhauer argued that the intellect or reason so hypostatized by Enlightenment thought was actually in bondage to the practical motives of the will to live, a will concentrated in the sexual act, in the unconscious and irrational desire to perpetuate life. Schopenhauer viewed will as a force which operated (1) largely unconsciously, (2) often repressively, and (3) in intimate conjunction with memory and sexuality.

At the heart of Schopenhauer's philosophy and aesthetics is an attitude which continues through Nietzsche, Arnold, Bergson, and others: that rational knowledge can never be adequate to ideas of perception; and that poetry is the paradigm of disinterested and objective knowledge. As in so many nineteenth-century theories, epistemology – the science of knowing – here becomes aestheticized, and the aesthetic becomes a privileged category of human perception, elevated to a final resource for seeking harmony, unity, and order in the world. The harmony which was objectively fragmented in the late industrial world is now internalized as a subjective capacity: it is left to the aesthetic to attempt what religion, philosophy, and science can no longer accomplish. The aesthetic is *defined* as a form of perception of reality: poetry could no longer take for granted the reality it was to express.

Friedrich Nietzsche (1844–1900)

Friedrich Nietzsche is most often associated with the announcement that "God is dead" (which in fact is first found in Hegel's *Phenomenology*); he is also remembered by phrases such as the "will to power," as well as the idea of the "overman" or "superman" (*übermensch*) who gloriously rises above the common herd mentality and morality promoted by modern liberal states. His ideas have sometimes been aligned with anti-Semitism and Nazism, and with both extreme individualism and self-annihilating mysticism. Nietzsche himself saw the apparatus of both Church and state as coercing people into a mediocre conformity; he called for a new conception of humanity, based on self-creation, passion, power, and subjugation of one's circumstances.

Nietzsche's thought stresses the Dionysian side of human nature, fueled by unconscious impulses and excess, as a counter to the Apollonian side which is conscious, rational, and individuated; it subverts conventional notions of truth; it unashamedly displays scorn for women; and it undermines modern liberal political visions of democracy. Effectively, it challenges the fundamental assumptions of Western philosophy at epistemological, moral, political, and spiritual levels; for these reasons, as well as for his style – poetic, ironic, discontinuous, intimate – it has exerted an enormous influence on modernism, existentialism, the Frankfurt School of Marxism, the philosophy of science, and various branches of poststructuralism, such as those associated with Derrida and Foucault. Nietzsche's works include *The Birth of Tragedy* (1870–1871), *Ecce Homo* (1888), *The Antichrist* (1895), and his notebooks published posthumously as *The Will to Power* (1901).

Nietzsche's call for a new vision of humanity was profoundly atheistic: reality, truth, the world, even the self, are constructions, projections of human needs and interests. His definition of reality is pragmatic: he states that the world of appearance is created by our "practical instincts" and "is essentially a world of relationships . . . its being is essentially different from every point." He defines an object as "only a kind of effect produced by a subject upon a subject – a *modus of the subject*." Like Schopenhauer, Nietzsche views our pursuit of knowledge as not impartial but as one manifestation of our "will to power," our fundamental motive of self-assertion, subjugation, and conquest, as well as of our need for security.[2]

The text of Nietzsche's with the most bearing on literature and criticism is *The Birth of Tragedy* (1870–1871), which offers two major theses, one purporting to explain the origins of tragedy and the other the death of tragedy at the hands of what Nietzsche calls "Socratism," a rational and scientific outlook toward the world taught first by Socrates then by his disciple Plato. Hence in a treatise ostensibly about tragedy, Nietzsche effectively attempts to undermine the entire tradition of Western philosophy. Nietzsche's first thesis is that the evolution of art is based upon a broad conflict between two dispositions, represented respectively by the Greek gods Apollo and Dionysus. As a moral deity, Apollo demands self-control, self-knowledge, moderation; in short, he demands due respect and observance of the limits and status of the individual.[3] Dionysus, on the other hand, represents a condition in which this principle is shattered, a state where the "individual forgets himself completely," and all previous social and religious barriers are annulled, in a universal harmony (*BT*, 23). These two forces, the Apollonian and the Dionysian, are creative tendencies which developed side by side "usually in fierce opposition . . . until . . . the pair accepted the yoke of marriage and, in this condition, begot Attic tragedy, which exhibits the salient features of both parents" (*BT*, 19).

Nietzsche explains that, in order to endure the "terrors and horrors of existence," the Greeks had to create "the shining fantasy of the Olympians." The Greek deities answered to the Apollonian need for a beautiful and comforting illusion through this "aesthetic mirror" (*BT*, 30, 32). Hence the ancient Greek, though open to the deepest suffering, was "saved by art" (*BT*, 50–51). One of the "realities" from which art saves us is the Dionysiac realization, embodied in Hamlet, that no action of ours can alter the "eternal condition of things . . . Understanding kills action, for in order to act we require the veil of illusion" (*BT*, 51). Once we pierce to the truth of existence, we see its "ghastly absurdity" and are invaded by "nausea" (*BT*, 52).

Nietzsche here anticipates the views and terminology – absurdity, nausea – of existentialism. He sees such absurdity as a perennial human condition, which we must always repress. Art is the supreme mechanism at our disposal in achieving this illusion: our justification of life is ultimately neither religious nor moral but aesthetic.

Nietzsche's second thesis has wide-ranging implications for philosophy and literary and cultural theory. Greek tragedy, he suggests, "died by suicide," in the hands of Euripides who, viewing tragedy as a rational matter of conscious perceptions, attempted to eliminate altogether the Dionysiac strain, battling against the works of Aeschylus and Sophocles (*BT*, 75–76, 80). In so doing, he killed both myth and music (*BT*, 69). What spoke through Euripides in his endeavor to rebuild the drama on the basis of a non-Dionysiac art was a new and powerful daimon. His name was Socrates (*BT*, 77). From this point on, says Nietzsche, the real antagonism was between the Dionysiac spirit and the Socratic spirit, and "tragedy was to perish in the conflict" (*BT*, 77). Euripides and Socrates both were unable to understand tragedy; both viewed it as chaotic and irrational; and both condemned it along with its underlying ethics (*BT*, 82–83). In its place, Euripides must have seen himself "as the first rational maker of tragedy" (*BT*, 81).

As for Socrates: who, asks Nietzsche, was this man who dared single-handedly to "challenge the entire world of Hellenism"? His power, exerted primarily through his disciple Plato, was such that it forced poetry into a new status of subordination to philosophy (*BT*, 88). Nietzsche raises the question, as indeed Plato had himself, whether "art and Socratism are diametrically opposed to one another" (*BT*, 90). Socrates is the "despotic logician," the prototype "of an entirely new mode of existence," the *theoretical man* who delights in the very process of unveiling truth, thereby assuring himself of his own power (*BT*, 92). In Socrates is the first manifestation of a deep-seated "grand metaphysical illusion," that thought can "plumb the farthest abysses of being," to make "existence appear intelligible and thereby justified" (*BT*, 93). In this sense, Socrates is "the vortex and turning point of Western civilization" (*BT*, 94–95).

And yet there is hope. Modern man has begun to realize the limits of Socratic curiosity. And there are, thinks Nietzsche, certain forces that promise a rebirth of tragedy, as based on myth, on a "deeper wisdom" ineffable in words and concepts (*BT*, 103). Nietzsche points to a gradual reawakening of the Dionysiac spirit in the "German soul," as expressed in music from Bach through Beethoven to Wagner, as well as in the philosophies of Kant and Schopenhauer (*BT*, 98, 101, 119). Both movements have "authoritatively rejected science's claim to universal validity" and thereby initiated a culture of the tragic (*BT*, 111). In our present age, man is stripped of myth, and "stands famished among all his pasts," in the grip of a hunger that signifies "the loss of myth, of a mythic home, the mythic womb" (*BT*, 137).

Henri Bergson (1859–1941)

Schopenhauer's thought impinges considerably not only on the thought of Nietzsche but also on Bergson's ideas and his theories of art and humor. Bergson's philosophy influenced modernist writers such as Proust, T. S. Eliot, and Virginia Woolf. This philosophy was expressed in *Creative Evolution* (1907), where Bergson had argued that what is most real is precisely what philosophers since Plato have condemned as unreal: time. Plato, Plotinus, and Christian theology considered the temporal world as a degradation of the eternal. In affirming the reality of time rather than of eternity, Bergson was returning to the immediacy and authenticity of experience as against the conceptual and linguistic reduction of such experience to conventional categories, whether in the name of feudal Christianity, Enlightenment reason, or conservative humanism. Bergson's notion of *durée* placed emphasis on the human personality as the locus of the primary reality: "There is at least one reality which we all seize from within, by intuition and not by simple analysis. It is our own person in its flowing through time, the self which endures."[4]

Schopenhauer, Nietzsche, the French symbolists, and Bergson, as well as the modernists who were influenced by this tradition, opposed the idea of literal language, which embodied bourgeois positivism, scientism, and mechanism. For all of these writers, a subversion of literal language was the vehicle of access into a deeper reality. They tend to emphasize language as a temporal process rather than viewing it as a spatialized system of conventional concepts. According to Bergson, language is inescapably general; it can never express the true individuality of an object or situation. The most basic premise of Bergson's aesthetics is that art creates novelty. Whereas language is spatial, art is temporal, expressing duration, expressing the authentic flow of experience which is encrusted over by language. The poet's business is to rebel against the generality and conventionality of language. She individuates by deploying the materiality of language, treating words as sharing the same individual material status as other objects in the world rather than as universal meanings or atemporal signs of objects. The reality suggested by a poem is one where the "knowledge" offered by the intellect clashes with our sensory experience. For these thinkers, poetry is effectively the conclusion and resting place of philosophy.

Matthew Arnold (1822–1888)

Matthew Arnold has been regarded by some as one of the founding figures of modern English criticism. He raised many classical questions about the function of literature and criticism in the context of a modern industrial society, and they remain with us today. Arnold was not only a cultural critic but also a poet and an educator. In 1851 he became an inspector of schools and was deeply concerned with the kind of education suitable for middle-class and working-class students. In 1857 he was appointed Professor of Poetry at Oxford. Arnold's poetry, of which "Dover Beach" is perhaps the most famous example, expresses isolation and near-despair in a world seemingly abandoned by divine providence, a world on the brink of disastrous wars, a world in which the only faith is in other human beings. He described himself as "wandering between two worlds, one dead,/The other powerless to be born." Arnold's literary and social criticism was produced largely in the 1860's, comprising *Essays in Criticism*, first series (1865) and *Culture and Anarchy* (1869). A second series of *Essays in Criticism* was published in 1888. In the 1870s Arnold wrote on religious and educational matters; he considered his most important prose work to be *Literature and Dogma* (1873).

Central to Arnold's literary criticism is the problem of living adequately in late industrial society. Arnold's world view is deeply humanist, in a tradition that will run through figures such as F. R. Leavis and survives to this day. Arnold's central terms and phrases – "sweetness and light," "perfection," "inwardness," "the best that has been thought and said" – all derive ultimately from his analysis of the spiritual and moral malaise of modern culture. He deplored the narrow moralism and mercantilism of the bourgeoisie, whom he termed "philistines."[5] His essay "The Function of Criticism" is concerned to counteract the philistinism of the English bourgeoisie, enshrined in its obsession with practicality, utility, and reason.

In this essay, Arnold holds that, while the "critical faculty is lower than the inventive," it nonetheless creates the conditions in which creative genius can be realized (*SP*, 132–133). It is also the business of criticism "in all branches of knowledge . . . to see the object as in itself it really is" (*SP*, 134). He is calling for criticism to be "disinterested," an attitude whose recent deficiency he attributes partly to the French Revolution. Unlike previous major movements such as the Renaissance and the Reformation, which were "disinterestedly intellectual and spiritual movements," the French Revolution "took a political, practical character" (*SP*, 136). While Arnold concedes that this Revolution was "the greatest, the most animating event in history," it was characterized by a "fatal" exaltation of reason, a "fatal" mania for giving "an immediate political and practical application" to the ideas of reason (*SP*, 137). Arnold's argument is that, while we must value ideas "in and for themselves," we cannot "transport them abruptly into the world of politics and practice" (*SP*, 138). The "fatal" result, as Arnold states in *Culture and Anarchy*, is an inordinate and spiritually stunting "[f]aith in machinery," a utilitarian reduction of the world to a practical mechanism (*SP*, 209). Arnold's logic here, like Burke's, is that abstract ideas cannot simply be imposed upon a people's constitution or way of life (*SP*, 139).

Arnold suggests that criticism must be "disinterested" by keeping aloof from "the practical view of things," by "following the law of its own nature, which is to be a free play of the mind on all subjects which it touches. Criticism must attempt to know "the best that is known and thought in the world, and by in turn making this known, to create a current of true and fresh ideas . . . but its business is to do no more" (*SP*, 142). And the purpose of criticism? To lead man "towards perfection, by making his mind dwell upon what is excellent in itself" (*SP*, 144). Finally, Arnold cautions that if the critic is truly devoted to expanding the stock of true ideas, he will move beyond insularity, recognizing that much of the "best that is known and thought" will come from outside England. Criticism must regard "Europe as being, for intellectual and spiritual purposes, one great confederation" (*SP*, 156). This statement, in the view of tradition it implies, echoes Burke and anticipates T. S. Eliot.

In *Culture and Anarchy* (1869) Arnold redefines "culture" as "*a study of perfection*. It moves by the force, not merely or primarily of the scientific passion for pure knowledge, but also of the moral and social passion for doing good" (*SP*, 205). Culture, then, has an intellectual and an ethical component, and the aims of culture, according to Arnold, are identical with those of religion, which Arnold calls "the greatest and most important of the efforts by which the human race has manifested its impulse to perfect itself, – religion, that voice of the deepest human experience." What they have in common also is the cultivation of inwardness: religion preaches that "The Kingdom of God is within you," and culture "places human perfection in an *internal* condition" (*SP*, 208). Culture expands our gifts of thought and feeling, and fosters growth in wisdom and beauty. But culture advances beyond religion, according to Arnold, because, through a "disinterested study of human nature," it fosters a "harmonious expansion of *all* the powers which make the beauty and worth of human nature." The implication is, of course, that religion stresses the moral over the aesthetic, whereas culture promotes their harmony. Because culture represents for Arnold an inward condition of the mind and not outward circumstances, he regards its function as especially crucial in our modern civilization which is "mechanical and external" as well as strongly individualistic (*SP*, 209). In uniting beauty and intelligence, culture effects a harmony of "sweetness and light," terms taken from Jonathan Swift's *Battle of the Books* (1704). The task of both criticism and culture, then, is to place the pragmatic bourgeois vision of life in a broader historical and international context.

Arnold's essay "The Study of Poetry" (1880) is one of the most influential texts of literary humanism; it insists on the social and cultural functions of literature, its ability to civilize and to cultivate morality. According to Arnold, the status of religion has been increasingly threatened by science, by the ideology of the "fact." Philosophy he regards as powerless since it is hopelessly entrenched in unresolved questions and problems. It is, he claims, to poetry that we must turn, not merely for spiritual and emotional support and consolation but to interpret life for us. He defines poetry as a criticism of life. Poetry's high function is actually to replace religion and philosophy (*SP*, 340).

If poetry is to serve this exalted office, we must be even more certain, says Arnold, of our capacity to distinguish good from bad poetry. His essay contains also the notions of the "classic" and "tradition," which will be further developed by writers such as T. S. Eliot and F. R. Leavis. Arnold suggests that, in the first place, we need to be sure that our estimate of poetry is "real" rather than based on historical or personal considerations (*SP*, 341). How do we arrive at this real estimate of what constitutes a classic? Arnold's answer is to offer not a *theory* but a *practice*, of using "touchstones." We cannot say abstractly what comprises great poetry but we know we are in its presence when we experience and feel its power. Arnold cites a number of lines of "great" poets in various languages to illustrate his point. We know when we are in the presence of a great work because it exhibits truth and seriousness (*SP*, 348–349). What is interesting here is Arnold's lack of engagement with formal qualities. He implies that if the content is sufficiently true and serious, it will automatically be expressed in an appropriate form. Also lacking is any sense of engagement in historical context. His reliance on some ineffable literary sensibility which somehow knows how to judge is an appeal to so-called experience and to making judgments on the basis of a sensibility which defies articulation.

Notes

1. Arthur Schopenhauer, *Philosophical Writings*, ed. Wolfgang Schirmacher (New York: Continuum, 1994), pp. 20–22, 69, 86. Hereafter cited as *PW*.
2. Friedrich Nietzsche, *The Will to Power*, trans. W. Kaufmann and R. J. Hollingdale (Harmondsworth: Penguin, 1978), pp. 277–278, 306–307.
3. Friedrich Nietzsche, *The Birth of Tragedy and The Genealogy of Morals*, trans. Francis Golffing (New York: Doubleday, 1956), p. 34. Herafter cited as *BT*.
4. Henri Bergson, *The Creative Mind: An Introduction to Metaphysics* (New York: Philosophical Library, 1946), p. 162.
5. Matthew Arnold, *Selected Prose* (Harmondsworth: Penguin, 1970), pp. 177, 179. Hereafter cited as *SP*.

Part V

The Twentieth Century:
A Brief Introduction

Introduction

The twentieth century was marked by certain colossal events which profoundly shaped the worlds of literature and criticism. These events included the Bolshevik Revolution of 1917 in Russia, World War I (1914–1918), the great economic depression of the 1930s, World War II (1939–1945), the Cold War between the capitalist nations and the communist bloc, decolonization of many nations around the mid-century, the predominance of America as a world power, the emergence of the so-called "third world," the social and political unrest of the 1960s, and a general swing in the West toward right-wing politics in the 1980s. Many of these developments culminated in the collapse of the communist bloc and the Soviet Union by 1991. The 1990s witnessed a concerted awareness of environmental destruction, while the beginning of the new century has overseen the emerging narratives of a "New World Order" and the "war on terror," as capitalism emerges into a global phenomenon.

The devastating impact of World War I, fought between Germany and Austria on the one side (joined by Turkey and Bulgaria), and France, Russia, and Britain on the other (allied with Japan, Italy, and America), was unprecedented in history. Eric Hobsbawm states that this war "marked the breakdown of the (western) civilization of the nineteenth century."[1] The ideals of the Enlightenment, embodied in the various institutions of the capitalist world, and its ideologies of rational, scientific advance, material and moral progress, individualism, and the economic and cultural centrality of Europe, had culminated in a catastrophe on many levels, economic, political, and moral. The consequent psychological and material devastation led thinkers in all domains to question both the heritage of the Enlightenment and the very foundations of Western civilization. Long-held assumptions – concerning reason, historical progress, and the moral autonomy of human beings – were plunged into crisis.

Subsequently, the Great Depression of the 1930s represented "a world economic crisis of unprecedented depth." Hobsbawm remarks that liberal democratic institutions declined between 1917 and 1942, as fascism and various authoritarian regimes rose to power. World War II, waged by the allies (Britain, America, and France) to contain the expansionist ambitions of Nazi Germany (aided by the totalitarian regimes of Italy and Japan), wrought not only a second wave of wide-scale destruction but, in its aftermath, the disintegration of the huge colonial empires of Britain, France, Belgium, and the Netherlands, which had subjugated one-third of the world's population. Notwithstanding the formation of the United Nations in 1945, and NATO in 1949, the twentieth century "was without doubt the most murderous century of which we have record" (*AE*, 11). All of these phenomena – the two world wars, the rise of fascism, the depression, and decolonization – had a profound impact on literature and criticism.

Then followed a long period, from 1947 to 1973, of considerable growth and prosperity, which harbored the greatest and most rapid economic and cultural transformations in recorded history (*AE*, 11). Apart from the unprecedented technological advances, whereby most of the world's population ceased to live in agricultural economies, this era witnessed numerous political and social revolutions, whose principles were variously expressed by Che Guevara in Latin America, Frantz Fanon in Algeria, and the philosopher Herbert Marcuse, who inspired radical intellectuals in America and Europe. Political revolutions and movements against colonialism erupted in many parts of Africa; the earlier black militancy in America, inspired by figures such as Marcus Garvey and later Malcolm X, broadened into the civil rights movement of the 1950s and 1960s, whose leaders included Martin Luther King, assassinated in 1968. Many of the sentiments behind these movements were powerfully expressed in African-American literature and criticism. In the Middle East, things were no less turbulent. The termination of the British mandate in Palestine and the creation of the state of Israel in 1948 led to persistent conflict between Israel and the Arab nations, fought out in bitter wars in 1948, 1956, 1967, and 1973. This conflict has profoundly shaped the literature and criticism of the entire region; it was analyzed in the work of the Palestinian-American scholar Edward Said, as well as of recent thinkers such as Slavoj Žižek.

Throughout this period, Western capitalism pursued the path of increasing monopoly and consolidation, often employing the principles advocated by economists such as John Maynard Keynes, who thought that the inequities of capitalism could be remedied, and prosperity brought to all, using monetary control rather than the nineteenth-century principles of laissez-faire. A generation of students in America and Europe, however, reacted against what they saw as the repressive, unjust, sexist, racist, and imperialist nature of the late capitalist world, epitomized for many by American involvement in the

Vietnam War. In May 1968, left-wing uprisings of students and workers shook the University of Paris, as well as Berkeley, San Francisco State, Kent State, and elsewhere. Much literary theory in France and America, including feminism, took its impetus from this atmosphere of unrest and agitation. The later twentieth century brought a new awareness of ecology and the extent to which modern industrial life and production had damaged the environment.

As we enter a new century, the Cold War has been replaced by a new dynamic, which itself has served as the foundation for much recent criticism and theory. The relatively stable international system of communism was succeeded by local ethnic, tribal, and religious conflicts in Yugoslavia and areas of the former Soviet Union. Since the early 1990s, the core of this new dynamic has been underlain by America's unopposed predominance as *the* major world power, fueled by formulations of a "New World Order." The relative impotence of the political left has left its mark on the nature of theory, and on what is viewed as radical or conservative. What has occupied center stage since the attacks of September 11, 2001 on the World Trade Center has been the "war on terror." Hobsbawm states three ways in which the world has changed from the beginning to the end of the twentieth century: it is no longer Eurocentric, though America, Europe, and Japan are still the most prosperous; the world has in certain important ways become a "single operational unit," primarily in economic terms, but also increasingly in terms of mass culture; and, finally, there has been a massive disintegration of previous patterns of human relationships, with an unprecedented rupture between past and present. Capitalism has become a permanent and continuous revolutionary force that perpetuates itself in time and extends its empire increasingly in space (*AE*, 14–16). Modern criticism and theory has broadened to encompass all of these developments.

Note

1. Eric Hobsbawm, *The Age of Extremes: A History of the World, 1914–1991* (New York: Pantheon, 1994), p. 6. Hereafter cited as *AE*.

Chapter 13

From Liberal Humanism to Formalism

At the end of the nineteenth century, criticism in Europe and America had been predominantly biographical, historical, psychological, impressionistic, and empirical. With the establishment of English as a separate discipline in England, many influential critics, such as George Saintsbury, A. C. Bradley, and Arthur Quiller-Couch assumed academic posts. By far the most influential of this early generation of academic critics was A. C. Bradley. In *Shakespearean Tragedy* (1904), Bradley's central thesis, influenced by Hegel, saw Shakespearean tragedy as a dialectic whereby the moral order and harmony of the world were threatened (by the tragic hero) and then reestablished.

In America, influential theories of realism and naturalism had been propounded by William Dean Howells, Hamlin Garland, and Frank Norris. An important concern of American critics such as John Macy, Randolph Bourne, and Van Wyck Brooks was to establish a sense of national identity through tracing a specifically American literary tradition. In France, the most pervasive critical mode was the *explication de texte*, based on close readings which drew upon biographical sources and historical context. In the humanist tradition of Matthew Arnold, much of this *fin-de-siècle* criticism saw in literature a refuge from, or remedy for, the ills of modern civilization.

The humanist tradition of the late nineteenth century, as expressed by figures such as Matthew Arnold, vociferously reacted against the commercialism and philistinism of bourgeois society. This tradition was continued and intensified in the polemic of the "New Humanists," as well as by certain neo-Romantic and formalistic critics. Led by Harvard professor Irving Babbitt and including figures such as Paul Elmer More, Norman Foerster, and Stuart Sherman, the New Humanists were conservative in their cultural and political outlook, reacting against the predominant tendencies stemming from the liberal-bourgeois tradition: a narrow focus on the present at the expense of the past and of tradition; unrestrained freedom in political, moral, and aesthetic domains; a riot of pluralism, a mechanical exaltation of facts and an uninformed worship of science.

Literary Criticism from Plato to the Present: An Introduction   M. A. R. Habib
© 2011 M. A. R. Habib

Also reacting against the industrialism and rationalism of the bourgeois world were the neo-Romantic critics in England, including D. H. Lawrence, G. Wilson Knight, John Middleton Murry, Herbert Read, and C. S. Lewis. Lawrence (1885–1930) was an avowed irrationalist, who saw the modern industrial world as sexually repressive and as having stunted human potential. Lawrence advocated a vitalism and individualism which often had parallels in the views of Nietzsche and Freud. Lawrence anticipates the stress on the unconscious, the body, and irrational motives in various areas of contemporary criticism. Of the other neo-Romantic critics, G. Wilson Knight (1897–1985), a Shakespeare scholar, is best known for his *The Wheel of Fire* (1930), which interprets Shakespeare's plays in terms of certain recurring symbols and motifs. Another significant critic in this broad Romantic-religious tradition was C. S. Lewis (1898–1963) whose major critical work, *The Allegory of Love* (1936), contributed to his mission of promoting understanding of the formality and didacticism of the literature of the Middle Ages and the Renaissance. Finally, mention should be made of the scholar of Milton and Shakespeare, E. M. Tillyard (1889–1962), who engaged in a debate with C. S. Lewis in *The Personal Heresy* (1939) and whose most influential work was *The Elizabethan World Picture* (1943). New Critical trends were also anticipated in America where W. C. Brownell attempted to establish literary criticism as a serious and independent activity, and where James Gibbons Huneker and H. L. Mencken insisted on addressing the aesthetic elements in art as divorced from moral considerations.

Hence, the critical movements of the early twentieth century were already moving in certain directions: the isolation of the aesthetic from moral, religious concerns, and indeed an exaltation of the aesthetic (as transcending reason and the paradigms of bourgeois thought such as utility and pragmatic value) as a last line of defense against a commercialized and dehumanizing world; and a correlative attempt to establish criticism as a serious and "scientific" activity. This broadly humanist trend is far from dead; it has not only persisted through figures such as F. R. Leavis but also has often structured the very forms of critical endeavors which reject it.

The Background of Modernism

Modernism comprised a broad series of movements in Europe and America that came to fruition roughly between 1910 and 1930. Its major exponents and practitioners included Marcel Proust, James Joyce, Ezra Pound, T. S. Eliot, William Faulkner, Virginia Woolf, Luigi Pirandello, and Franz Kafka. These various modernisms were the results of many complex economic, political, scientific, and religious developments over the nineteenth century, which culminated in World War I (1914–1918). The vast devastation, psychological demoralization, and economic depression left by the war intensified the already existing reactions against bourgeois modes of thought and economic practice. Rationalism underwent renewed assaults from many directions: from philosophers such as Bergson, from the sphere of psychoanalysis, from neoclassicists such as T. E. Hulme, the New Humanists in America, and neo-Thomists such as Jacques Maritain. These reactions were often underlain by a new understanding of language, as a conventional and historical construct. The modernist writer occupied a world that was often perceived as fragmented, where the old bourgeois ideologies of rationality, science, progress, civilization, and imperialism had been somewhat discredited; where the artist was alienated from the social and political world, and where art and literature were marginalized; where populations had been subjected to processes of mass standardization; where philosophy could no longer offer visions of unity, and where language itself was perceived to be an inadequate instrument for expression and understanding.

A distinct group of artist-critics associated with modernism was the highly iconoclastic "Bloomsbury Group." This circle included Virginia Woolf and her sister Vanessa, daughters of the critic and agnostic philosopher Leslie Stephen, the art critics Roger Fry and Clive Bell, the economist John Maynard Keynes, the biographer Lytton Strachey, and the novelist E. M. Forster. Most members of the group fell under the influence of the Cambridge philosopher G. E. Moore's *Principia Ethica*. They saw this text as affirming an "aesthetic" approach to life inasmuch as it stressed the value of allegedly timeless states of consciousness which facilitated the enjoyment of beauty. The group inevitably fell under many of the influences that had shaped modernism, such as the notion of time advanced in the philosophy of Bergson. It was during this period also that the foundations of the New Criticism were laid by figures such as William Empson and I. A. Richards; the latter's *Principles of Literary Criticism* (1924) and *Practical Criticism* (1929) were widely and enduringly influential. Here, too, the literary artifact was treated as an autonomous and self-contained verbal structure, insulated from the world of prose, as in Richards' distinction between emotive and referential language. In France also, the somewhat positivistic earlier mode of criticism, the *explication de texte*, was opposed by influential figures such as Bergson, whose novel conceptions of time and memory, and whose view of art as uniquely transcending the mechanistic concepts of bourgeois society, profoundly influenced Proust and other modernists. Paul Valéry (1871–1945) formulated a criticism drawing on the earlier French symbolists, one which prioritized the aesthetic verbal structure over historical and contextual elements.

The Poetics of Modernism: W. B. Yeats, Ezra Pound, and T. S. Eliot

What underlies modernistic literary forms is an awareness that the definition of reality is complex and problematic. Modernists came to this common awareness by different paths: Yeats drew on the occult, on Irish myth and legend, as well as the Romantics and French symbolists. Proust drew on the insights of Bergson; Virginia Woolf, on Bergson, G. E. Moore, and others; Pound drew on various non-European literatures as well as French writers; T. S. Eliot, whose poetic vision was profoundly eclectic, drew on Dante, the metaphysical poets, Laforgue, Baudelaire, and a number of philosophers.

In general, literary modernism was marked by a number of features: (1) the affirmation of a continuity between the self and the world, which are viewed as shaping each other; (2) a perception of the complex roles of time, memory, and history in the mutual construction of self and world. Time is not conceived in a static model which separates past, present, and future as discrete elements in linear relation; rather, it is viewed as dynamic, with these elements influencing and changing one another; (3) a breakdown of any linear narrative structure: modernist poetry tends to be fragmented, creating its own internal "logic" of emotion, image, sound, symbol, and mood; (4) a self-consciousness regarding the process of literary composition. This embraces both an awareness of how one's own work relates to the literary tradition as a whole, and also an ironic stance toward the content of one's own work; (5) finally, and most importantly, an awareness of the problematic nature of language. Modernists display an aversion to so-called "literal" language which might presume a one-to-one correspondence between words and things; modernist poetry relies more on suggestion and allusion, aiming to construct alternative visions of reality.

Twentieth-century modernism, as manifested in the work of the Irish poet and critic W. B. Yeats (1865–1939), the American poet Ezra Pound, and the Anglo-American poet and critic T. S. Eliot, was deeply influenced by symbolism, whether that of the English Romantics such as Blake, Coleridge, Wordsworth, and Shelley, or French symbolism as developed in the work of Baudelaire, Mallarmé, Verlaine, and Rimbaud. French symbolism was introduced to English and American audiences largely through Arthur Symons' book *The Symbolist Movement in Literature* (1899), which saw French symbolism as a reaction against nineteenth-century scientism and materialism, and as affirming the reality of a higher, spiritual realm which could be divined not by rational thought but only in glimpses through a pure poetic language divested of any representational pretension.

Perhaps the most important modernist critic was the poet T. S. Eliot (1888–1965), whose main critical contributions were (1) to combat provincialism by broadening the notion of "tradition" to include Europe; (2) to advocate, as against the prevailing critical impressionism, a closely analytical and even objective criticism which situated literary works alongside one another in the larger context of tradition. In this, he contributed to the development of notions of artistic autonomy which were taken up by some of the New Critics; and (3) to foster, by his own revaluation of the literary tradition (reacting against the Romantics, for example, and highlighting the virtues of the metaphysical poets), a dynamic notion of tradition as always in the process of change. Eliot's criticism was in part a manifesto of literary modernism, characteristically infused with political conservatism.

Formalism

The emphasis on poetic form reached a new intensity not only in European modernism but also in the critical theories of the early twentieth century, beginning with the Formalist movement in Russia, extending subsequently to the New Criticism in England and America and later schools such as the neo-Aristotelians. In general, an emphasis on form parenthesizes concern for the representational, imitative, and cognitive aspects of literature. Literature is no longer viewed as aiming to represent reality or character or to impart moral or intellectual lessons, but is considered to be an object in its own right, autonomous (possessing its own laws) and autotelic (having its aims internal to itself). In this formalist view, literature does not convey any clear or paraphrasable message; rather it communicates what is otherwise ineffable. Literature is regarded as a unique mode of expression. Critics have variously theorized that preoccupation with form betokens social alienation, a withdrawal from the world, an acknowledgment of political helplessness, and a retreat into the aesthetic as a refuge of sensibility and humanistic values.

Russian Formalism

Along with movements in futurism and symbolism, the Russian Formalists were a group of writers who flourished during the period of the Russian Revolution of 1917. The Formalists and the futurists were active in the fierce debates of this era concerning art and its connections with ideology. The Formalists and futurists found a common platform in the journal LEF (Left Front of Art). The Formalists, focusing on artistic forms and techniques on the basis of linguistic studies, had arisen in pre-revolutionary Russia but now saw their opposition to traditional art as a political gesture, allying them somewhat with the revolution. However, all of these groups were attacked by the most prominent Soviet theoreticians, such as Trotsky, Nikolai Bukharin

(1888–1937), Anatoly Lunacharsky (1875–1933), and Voronsky, who decried the attempt to break completely with the past and what they saw as a reductive denial of the social and cognitive aspects of art. V. N. Volosinov and Bakhtin later attempted to harmonize the two sides of the debate, viz., formal linguistic analysis and sociological emphasis, by treating language itself as the supreme ideological phenomenon, as the very site of ideological struggle. Other groups, called "Bakhtin Circles," formed around this enterprise.

There were two schools of Russian Formalism. The Moscow Linguistic Circle, led by Roman Jakobson, was formed in 1915; this group also included Osip Brik and Boris Tomashevsky. The second group, the Society for the Study of Poetic Language (*Opoyaz*), was founded in 1916, and its leading figures included Victor Shklovsky, Boris Eichenbaum, and Yuri Tynyanov. Other important critics associated with these movements included Leo Jakubinsky and the folklorist Vladimir Propp.

The Russian Formalists' emphasis on form and technique was far more theoretical than that of the later New Critics who were more concerned with the practice of close reading of individual texts. Though Russian Formalism as a school was eclipsed with the rise of Stalin and the official Soviet aesthetic of social realism, its influence was transmitted through the structuralist analyses of figures such as Jakobson and Tzvetan Todorov to writers such as Roland Barthes and Gerard Genette.

Shklovsky (1893–1984) became a founding member of one of the two schools of Russian Formalism, the Society for the Study of Poetic Language, formed in 1916. His essay "Art as Technique" (1917) introduces defamiliarization, one of the central concepts of Russian Formalism: as our normal perceptions become habitual, they become automatic and unconscious. According to Shklovsky, habituation can devour work, clothes, furniture, one's wife, and the fear of war. It is against this background of ordinary perception in general that art assumes its significance:

> art exists that one may recover the sensation of life; it exists to make one feel things, to make the stone *stony* ... The technique of art is to make objects "unfamiliar," to make forms difficult, to increase the difficulty and length of perception because the process of perception is an aesthetic end in itself and must be prolonged. *Art is a way of experiencing the artfulness of an object; the object is not important.*[1]

Boris Eichenbaum (1886–1959)

Like Shklovsky, Eichenbaum was one of the leaders of the Russian Formalist group known as the Society for the Study of Poetic Language, founded in 1916. His essay "The Theory of the 'Formal Method' " (1926, 1927) explains that formalism is "characterized only by the attempt to create an independent science of literature which studies specifically literary material."[2] In the context of early twentieth-century Russia, where there was much pressure on literature to be revolutionary, Eichenbaum sees *this* strategy as revolutionary, as attempting to free art from serving ideological and political ends.

Eichenbaum also argued that poetry uses words differently from their function in ordinary speech, disrupting "ordinary verbal associations" ("TFM," 129). The suggestion here is that poetry comprises a kind of speech of its own, which is cumulatively developed by a tradition of poets. Also, the Formalists adopted a new understanding of literary history which rejected the idea of some linear, unified tradition. Rather, literary tradition involves struggle, a destruction of old values, competition between various schools in a given epoch, and persistence of vanquished movements alongside the newly dominant groups. The Formalists insisted that literary evolution had a distinctive character and that it "stood alone, quite independent of other aspects of culture" ("TFM," 134–135). Such a model of literary history anticipates later theories such as those of Pound and T. S. Eliot.

Mikhail M. Bakhtin (1895–1975)

Bakhtin is perhaps best known for his radical philosophy of language, as well as his theory of the novel, underpinned by concepts such as "dialogism," "polyphony," and "carnival," themselves resting on the more fundamental concept of "heteroglossia." Bakhtin's writings were produced at a time of momentous upheavals in Russia: the Revolution of 1917 was followed by a civil war (1918–1921), famine, and the dark years of repressive dictatorship under Joseph Stalin. While Bakhtin himself was not a member of the Communist Party, his work has been regarded by some as Marxist in orientation, seeking to provide a corrective to the abstractness of extreme formalism.

Bakhtin's major works as translated into English include *Art and Answerability: Early Philosophical Essays* (1990), *Rabelais and his World* (1965; trans. 1968), *Problems of Dostoevsky's Poetics* (1929; trans. 1973), *The Dialogic Imagination: Four Essays* (1930s; trans. 1981), and *Speech Genres and Other Late Essays* (1986). The authorship of some further publications, such as *Marxism and the Philosophy of Language* (1929, 1930), which was published under the name of V. N. Volosinov, is still in dispute.

Bakhtin's major achievements include the formulation of an innovative philosophy of language and "theory" of the novel. His essay "Discourse in the Novel," furnishes an integrated statement of both endeavors. Indeed, this text also offers a radical critique of the history of philosophy and an innovative explanation of the nature of subjectivity, objectivity and the very process of understanding. Bakhtin defines the novel as a "diversity of social speech types (sometimes even diversity of languages) and a diversity of individual voices, artistically organized."³ Bakhtin's view of the novel is dependent upon his broader view of the nature of language as "dialogic" and as comprised of "heteroglossia." In order to explain the concept of dialogism, we first need to understand the latter term: "heteroglossia" refers to the circumstance that what we usually think of as a single, unitary language is actually comprised of a multiplicity of languages interacting with, and often ideologically compet- ing with, one another. In Bakhtin's terms, any given "language" is actually stratified into several "other languages" ("heteroglossia" might be translated as "other-languagedness"). It is this heteroglossia, says Bakhtin, which is "the indispensable prerequisite for the novel as a genre" (*DI*, 263).

"Dialogism" refers to the fact that the various languages that stratify any "single" language are in dialogue with one another; Bakhtin calls this "the primordial dialogism of discourse," whereby all discourse has a dialogic orientation (*DI*, 275). We might illustrate this using the following example: the language of religious discourse does not exist in a state of ideological and linguistic "neutrality." On the contrary, such discourse might act as a "rejoinder" or "reply" to elements of political discourse. The political discourse might encourage loyalty to the state and adherence to material ambitions, whereas the religious discourse might attempt to displace those loyalties with the pursuit of spiritual goals. Even a work of art does not come, Minerva-like, fully formed from the brain of its author, speaking a single monologic language: it is a response, a rejoinder, to other works, to certain traditions, and it situates itself within a current of intersecting dialogues (*DI*, 274). Its relation to other works of art and to other languages (literary and non-literary) is dialogic.

Bakhtin has a further, profounder, explanation of the concept of dialogism. He explains that there is no direct, unmediated relation between a word and its object: "no living word relates to its object in a *singular* way." In its path toward the object, the word encounters "the fundamental and richly varied opposition of . . . other, alien words about the same object" (*DI*, 276–277). Even before we utter the word with our own signification, it is already invested with many layers of meaning, and our use of the word must accommodate those other meanings and in some cases compete with them. Our utterance will in its very nature be dialogic: it is born as one voice in a dialogue that is already constituted; it cannot speak monologically, as the only voice, in some register isolated from all social, historical, and ideological contexts. The word itself becomes the site of ideological conflict: language is not somehow neutral and transparent: it is the very medium and locus of conflict.

In formulating this radical notion of language, Bakhtin is also effecting a profound critique not only of linguistics and conventional stylistics but also of the history of philosophy: all postulate a unitary language (*DI*, 263–64, 269). Their historical project has been deeply ideological, exalting certain languages over others, incorporating "barbarians and lower social strata into a unitary language of culture," canonizing ideological systems and directing attention away "from language plurality to a single proto-language." Nonetheless, insists Bakhtin, these centripetal forces are obliged to "operate in the midst of heteroglossia" (*DI*, 271). Even as various attempts are being made to undertake the project of centralization and unification, the processes of decentralization and disunification continue (*DI*, 272).

Even literary language is stratified in its own ways, according to genre and profession (*DI*, 288–289). The various dialects and perspectives entering literature form "a dialogue of languages" (*DI*, 294). It is precisely this fact which, for Bakhtin, marks the characteristic difference between poetry and the novel. Most poetry is premised on the idea of a single unitary language; poetry effectively destroys heteroglossia; it strips the word of the intentions of others (*DI*, 297–298). In the novel, on the contrary, this dialogization of language "penetrates from within the very way in which the word conceives its object" (*DI*, 284). Bakhtin sees the genres of poetry and the novel as emblematic of two broad ideological tendencies, the one centralizing and conservative, the other dispersive and radical. The "novel" rejects any concept of a unified self or world; it acknowledges that "the" world is actually formed as a conversation, an endless dialogue, through a series of competing and coexisting languages; it even proposes that "truth" is dialogic. Hence, truth is redefined not merely as a consensus (which by now is common in cultural theory) but as the product of verbal-ideological struggles, struggles which mark the very nature of language itself (*DI*, 300).

Roman Jakobson (1896–1982)

The work of Roman Jakobson occupies a seminal place in formalism and structuralism. Essentially a linguist, Jakobson co-founded the Moscow Linguistic Circle in 1915. He was also involved in a second Russian Formalist group, the Society for the Study of Poetic Language, formed in 1916. The Formalists were in some ways precursors of structuralism: in 1926 Jakobson founded the Prague Linguistic Circle which engaged critically with the work of Saussure. And, fleeing from Nazi occupation, he moved to America in 1941 where he became acquainted with Claude Lévi-Strauss; in 1943 he co-founded the Linguistic Circle of New York. His ideas proved to be of greatest impact first in France and then in America.

In his paper "Linguistics and Poetics" (1958) Jakobson argues that poetics is an integral part of linguistics.[4] He argues that, whereas most language is concerned with the transmission of ideas, the poetic function of language focuses on the "message" for its own sake (*LL*, 69). Jakobson's essay "Two Aspects of Language and Two Types of Aphasic Disturbances" (1956) suggests that language has a bipolar structure, oscillating between the poles of metaphor and metonymy. This dichotomy, he urges, "appears to be of primal significance and consequence for all verbal behavior and for human behavior in general" (*LL*, 112). The development of any discourse takes place along two different semantic lines: one is metaphoric, where one topic leads to another through similarity or substitution. The other is metonymic, where one topic suggests another via contiguity (closeness in space, time, or psychological association). In normal behavior, says Jakobson, both processes operate, but one is usually preferred, according to cultural and personal conditions (*LL*, 110–111). In verbal art, also, while the two processes richly interact, one is often given predominance; for example, the primacy of metaphor in literary Romanticism and symbolism has been widely acknowledged. Jakobson notes that a competition between metaphoric and metonymic devices occurs in any symbolic process, for example in dreams. Here Jakobson anticipates Lacan's analysis of Freud's contrast between condensation and displacement in terms of metaphor and metonymy.

The New Criticism

In the Anglo-American world, formalistic tendencies were most clearly enshrined in the New Criticism. Some of the important features of this critical outlook originated in England during the 1920s in the work of T. S. Eliot and Ezra Pound, as well as in a further generation of professional critics who helped to rejuvenate the study of English literature. The most prominent of these, associated with the new English curriculum at Cambridge University, were I. A. Richards and his student William Empson. In his *Principles of Literary Criticism* (1924) and his *Science and Poetry* (1926), Richards attempted to establish a systematic basis for the study of literature. He distinguished, most fundamentally, the emotive language of poetry from the referential language of non-literary disciplines. In 1929 he published a book, *Practical Criticism*, whose influence still endures. Using samples of students' often erratic attempts to analyze poetry, he aimed to foster the skills and techniques necessary for the close reading of literature. The practice of close reading, sensitive to the figurative language of literature, as established by Richards later had a profound impact on the New Critics who facilitated its academic institutionalization. While William Empson himself was not a New Critic, he produced a book, *Seven Types of Ambiguity* (1930), which had an impact on the New Criticism in virtue of its close reading of literary texts and its stress on ambiguity as an essential characteristic of poetry. Richards' *Principles of Literary Criticism* advanced literary-critical notions such as irony, tension, and balance, as well as distinguishing between poetic and other uses of language.

Across the Atlantic, New Critical practices were also being pioneered by American critics, known as the Fugitives and the Southern Agrarians who promoted the values of the Old South in reaction against the alleged dehumanization of science and technology in the industrial North. Notable among these pioneers were John Crowe Ransom and Allen Tate, who developed some of the ideas of Eliot and Richards. Ransom edited the poetry magazine the *Fugitive* from 1922 to 1925 with a group of writers including Tate, Robert Penn Warren, and Donald Davidson. Other journals associated with the New Criticism included the *Southern Review*, edited by Penn Warren and Cleanth Brooks (1935–1942), the *Kenyon Review*, run by Ransom (1938–1959), and the still extant *Sewanee Review*. During the 1940s, the New Criticism became institutionalized as the mainstream approach in academia and its influence, while pervasively undermined since the 1950s, still persists. Some of the central documents of New Criticism were written by relatively late adherents: W. K. Wimsatt and Monroe Beardsley's essays "The Intentional Fallacy" (1946) and "The Affective Fallacy" (1949); Austin Warren's *The Theory of Literature* (1949); and W. K. Wimsatt's *The Verbal Icon* (1954). It is worth noting also the enormous influence of E. D. Hirsch's book *Validity in Interpretation* (1967), which equated a text's meaning with its author's intention.

John Crowe Ransom (1888–1974)

The seminal manifestos of the New Criticism, however, had been proclaimed earlier by Ransom, who published a series of essays entitled *The New Criticism* (1941) and an influential essay, "Criticism, Inc.," published in *The World's Body* (1938). This essay succinctly expresses a core of New Critical principles underlying the practice of most "New Critics," whose views often differed in other respects. As Ransom acknowledges, his essay is motivated by the desire to make literary criticism "more scientific, or precise and systematic"; it must become a "serious business."[5] He urges that the emphasis of criticism must move from historical scholarship to aesthetic appreciation and understanding.

In short, Ransom's position is that the critic must study literature, not *about* literature. Hence criticism should exclude: (1) personal impressions, because the critical activity should "cite the nature of the object rather than its effects upon the subject"(*WB*, 342); (2) synopsis and paraphrase, since the plot or story is an abstraction from the real content of the text; (3) historical studies, which might include literary backgrounds, biography, literary sources, and analogues; (4) linguistic studies, which include identifying allusions and meanings of words; (5) moral content, since this is not the whole content of the text; (6) "Any other special studies which deal with some abstract or prose content taken out of the work" (*WB*, 343–345). Ransom demands that criticism, whose proper province includes technical studies of poetry, metrics, tropes, and fictiveness, should "receive its own charter of rights and function independently" (*WB*, 346). Finally, Ransom insists on the ontological uniqueness of poetry, as distinct from prose. "The critic should," he urges, "regard the poem as nothing short of a desperate ontological or metaphysical manoeuvre," which cannot be reduced to prose (*WB*, 347–349). All in all, he argues that literature and literary criticism should enjoy autonomy both ontologically and institutionally. His arguments have often been abbreviated into a characterization of New Criticism as focusing on "the text itself" or "the words on the page."

William K. Wimsatt, Jr. (1907–1975) and Monroe C. Beardsley (1915–1985)

The critic Wimsatt and the philosopher Beardsley produced two influential and controversial papers that propounded central positions of New Criticism, "The Intentional Fallacy" (1946) and "The Affective Fallacy" (1949). In the first of these, they refuse to accept the notion of design or intention as a standard of literary-critical interpretation.[6] Their central argument runs as follows:

> If the poet succeeded in doing it, then the poem itself shows what he was trying to do. And if the poet did not succeed, then the poem is not adequate evidence, and the critic must go outside the poem – for evidence of an intention that did not become effective in the poem.

They repeat the American poet Archibald MacLeish's statement that a "poem should not mean but be." Wimsatt and Beardsley explain this statement as follows: "A poem ... simply *is*, in the sense that we have no excuse for inquiring what part is intended or meant. ... In this respect poetry differs from practical messages, which are successful if and only if we correctly infer the intention" (*VI*, 4–5). This is an effective statement of the New Critical position that the poem is an autonomous verbal structure which has its end in itself, which has no purpose beyond its own existence as an aesthetic object. It is not answerable to criteria of truth, accuracy of representation or imitation, or morality (*VI*, 5).

Wimsatt and Beardsley's later essay "The Affective Fallacy" (1949) is motivated by the same presupposition, namely that literature or poetry is an autonomous object, independent not only of author psychology, biography, and history but also of the reader or audience that consumes it. The word "affection" is used by philosophers to refer to emotion, mental state, or disposition. Hence, the "affective fallacy" occurs, according to Wimsatt and Beardsley, when we attempt to explicate or interpret a poem through recourse to the emotions or mental state produced in the reader or hearer. Just as the intentional fallacy "is a confusion between the poem and its origins," so the affective fallacy "is a confusion between the poem and its *results* ... The outcome of either Fallacy, the Intentional or the Affective, is that the poem itself, as an object of specifically critical judgment, tends to disappear."[7]

Notes

1. Victor Shklovsky, "Art as Technique," in *Russian Formalist Criticism: Four Essays*, trans. Lee T. Lemon and Marion J. Reis (Lincoln: University of Nebraska Press, 1965), pp. 5, 11–12.
2. Boris Eichenbaum, "The Theory of the 'Formal Method,' " in *Russian Formalist Criticism*, trans. Lemon and Reis, p. 103. Hereafter cited as "TFM."
3. M. M. Bakhtin, *The Dialogic Imagination: Four Essays*, ed. Michael Holquist, trans. Caryl Emerson and Michael Holquist (Austin: University of Texas Press, 1981), p. 262. Hereafter cited as *DI*.
4. "Linguistics and Poetics," in Roman Jakobson, *Language in Literature*, ed. Krystyna Pomorska and Stephen Rudy (Cambridge, MA and London: Harvard University Press, 1987), p. 63. Hereafter cited as *LL*.
5. John Crowe Ransom, *The World's Body* (Baton Rouge: Louisiana State University Press, 1968), p. 329. Hereafter cited as *WB*.
6. W. K. Wimsatt, Jr. and Monroe C. Beardsley, "The Intentional Fallacy," in W. K. Wimsatt, Jr., *The Verbal Icon* (Lexington: University of Kentucky Press, 1967), p. 4. Hereafter cited as *VI*.
7. W. K. Wimsatt, Jr. and Monroe C. Beardsley, "The Affective Fallacy," in *VI*, p. 21.

Chapter 14

Socially Conscious Criticism of the Earlier Twentieth Century

F. R. Leavis

With the Great Depression of the 1930s and the rise of fascism, literature and criticism in both Europe and America took a turn away from formalism toward a more socially conscious mode, as in socialist and Marxist criticism, and in the work of many poets. A central figure in English literary criticism, associated with the new English at Cambridge, was F. R. Leavis (1895–1978), who might broadly be placed in the moralistic and humanistic tradition of Matthew Arnold. Leavis edited the journal *Scrutiny* from 1932 to 1953. His major works, *New Bearings in English Poetry* (1932), *Revaluation* (1936), and *The Great Tradition* (1948), demoted Victorian and Georgian verse and sought to increase general appreciation of Eliot, Yeats, and Pound; he argued that the main stream of English poetry flowed through Donne, Pope, Johnson, and Eliot; and he traced the main tradition of fiction from Jane Austen, George Eliot, Henry James, and Joseph Conrad.

Leavis shared with Eliot and the New Critics the idea that literary criticism should be a separate and serious discipline. He insisted that we cannot go to literature in an "external" manner, treating it merely as a social document: "literature will yield to the sociologist, or anyone else, what it has to give only if it is approached as literature."[1] What separated him from the New Critics, however, was an equally forceful counter-insistence that literary criticism must go well beyond looking at "the words on the page": the study of literature, he said, is "an intimate study of the complexities, potentialities, and essential conditions of human nature." In his essay "Sociology and Literature" he affirmed that "a real literary interest is an interest in man, society and civilization, and its boundaries cannot be drawn" (*CP*, 184, 200).

Literary Criticism from Plato to the Present: An Introduction   M. A. R. Habib
© 2011 M. A. R. Habib

Marxist and Left-Wing Criticism

During the 1930s Marxism became a significant political force. Socially conscious criticism had a long heritage in America, going back to figures such as Whitman, Howells, and Emerson and running through the work of writers noted above such as John Macy, Van Wyck Brooks, and Vernon L. Parrington. Notable Marxist critics of the 1920s and 1930s included Floyd Dell, Max Eastman, V. F. Calverton, Philip Rahv, and Granville Hicks. Calverton and Hicks were perhaps the most prominent of the Marxist critics. In *The Liberation of American Literature* (1932) Calverton interprets the tradition of American literature through Marxist categories of class and economic infrastructure. Granville Hicks became a communist during the depression and his *The Great Tradition* (1933) assesses American writers in terms of their social and political awareness. This period saw the growth of a number of radical journals as well as the voicing of revolutionary views by non-Marxist critics such as Kenneth Burke and Edmund Wilson. The latter's most influential work, *Axel's Castle* (1931), traced the development of modern symbolist literature, identifying in this broad movement a "revolution of the word."

In Germany, a critique of modern capitalist culture was formulated by the Frankfurt School of Critical Theory, whose major figures included Theodor Adorno (1903–1969), Max Horkheimer (1895–1973), Herbert Marcuse, and Walter Benjamin. Some of these thinkers drew on Hegel, Marx, and Freud in attempting to revive the "negative dialectics" or negative, revolutionary potential of Hegelian Marxist thought. They insisted, following Hegel, that consciousness in all of its cultural modes is active in creating the world. In general, these theorists saw modern mass culture as regimented and reduced to a commercial dimension; and they saw art as embodying a unique critical distance from this social and political world. Walter Benjamin argued in his "The Work of Art in the Age of Mechanical Reproduction" that modern technology has transformed the work of art, stripping it of the "aura" of uniqueness it possessed in earlier eras. Modern works are reproduced for mass consumption, and are effectively copies which relate to no original form. However, this new status of art, thought Benjamin, also gave it a revived political and subversive potential. These thinkers had a large impact on the New Left and the radical movements of the 1960s.

The tradition of socialist criticism in Britain went back to William Morris, who first applied Marxist perspectives of labor and alienation to artistic production. In 1884 the Fabian Society was formed with the aim of substituting for Marxist revolutionary action a Fabian policy of gradually introducing socialism through influencing government policy and raising awareness of economic and class inequalities. The dramatist and critic

George Bernard Shaw (1856–1950) was a leader of this society and produced one of its first pamphlets, *A Manifesto* (1884). Shaw edited *Fabian Essays in Socialism* (1899), and advocated women's rights, economic equality, and the abolition of private property. George Orwell (1903–1950) in his later career saw himself as a political writer and a democratic socialist, who, however, became disillusioned with communism, as expressed in his political satire *Animal Farm* (1945).

A group of Marxist thinkers was centered around *The Left Review* (1934–1938). The poets W. H. Auden, Stephen Spender, and C. Day Lewis at various times espoused and propagated left-wing views. The most significant Marxist theorist of this generation was Christopher Caudwell, whose *Illusion and Reality: A Study of the Sources of Poetry* (1937) offered a Marxist analysis, correlating the development of English poetry with economic phases such as primitive accumulation, the Industrial Revolution, and the decline of capitalism.

The Fundamental Principles of Marxism

It may be useful to provide here a brief account of the principles of Marxist thought and literary criticism. The tradition of Marxism has provided a powerful and sustained critique of capitalist institutions and ethics. Its founder, Karl Heinrich Marx (1818–1883), was a German political, economic, and philosophical theorist and revolutionist. The influence of Marx's ideas on modern world history has been vast. Until the collapse in 1991 of the communist systems of the USSR and Eastern Europe, one-third of the world's population had been living under political administrations claiming descent from Marx's ideas. His impact on the world of thought has been equally extensive, embracing sociology, philosophy, economics, and cultural theory. Marxism has also generated a rich tradition of literary and cultural criticism. Many branches of modern criticism – including historicism, feminism, deconstruction, postcolonial and cultural criticism – are indebted to the insights of Marxism, which often originated in the philosophy of Hegel. What distinguishes Marxism is that it is not only a political, economic, and social theory but also a form of practice in all of these domains.

Marx attempted to understand the structural causes behind what he saw as a system of capitalist exploitation, and to offer solutions in the spheres of economics and politics. As with all socialists, Marx's main objection to capitalism was that one particular class owned the means of economic production: "The bourgeoisie ... has centralized means of production, and has concentrated property in a few hands." The correlative of this is the oppression and exploitation of the working classes: "In proportion as the bourgeosie, i.e., capital, is developed, in the same proportion is the proletariat, the modern working class, developed; a class of laborers, who live only so long as they find work, and who find work only so long as their labor increases capital. These laborers, who must sell themselves piecemeal, are a commodity." Marx's third objection is the imperialistic nature of the bourgeois enterprise: in order to perpetuate itself, capitalism must spread its tentacles all over the world: "The bourgeoisie cannot exist without constantly revolutionizing the instruments of production ... The need of a constantly expanding market ... chases the bourgeoisie over the whole surface of the globe." Marx explains that the bourgeoisie must necessarily give a cosmopolitan character to production and consumption in every country; that raw material is drawn from the remotest zones; that demand for new products ever increases; that the bourgeoisie "compels all nations, on pain of extinction, to adopt the bourgeois mode of production." In short, the bourgeoisie "creates a world after its own image." Finally, capitalism reduces all human relationships to a "cash" nexus, self-interest, and egotistical calculation.[2]

Influenced by Hegel but in contrast with his scheme of history as motivated by a divine or absolute spirit, Marx and Engels developed what they called a "materialist conception of history," as driven by class struggle, from the ancient slave mode of production through feudalism and capitalism to communism where classes and private property are abolished. In this conception, consciousness itself is viewed as a "social product." The realms of ideology, politics, law, morality, religion, and art are not independent but are an efflux of a people's material behavior: "Life is not determined by consciousness, but consciousness by life."[3] Hence an ideological superstructure arises out of a given economic "base" or infrastructure.

Also important is Marx's concept of ideology. He states that the class which is the ruling material force in society is also the ruling intellectual force. Having at its disposal the means of production, it is empowered to disseminate its ideas in the realms of law, morality, religion, and art, as possessing universal verity. Thus, the dominant ideas of the feudal aristocracy such as honor and loyalty were replaced after bourgeois ascendancy by ideas of freedom and equality, whose infrastructure is class economic imperatives (*GI*, 64–65). According to Marx's notion of ideology, the ruling class represents its own interests as the interests of the people as a whole. The modern state, as Marx says, "is but a committee for managing the common affairs of the whole bourgeoisie" (*MCP*, 45–47).

Marx acknowledged that capitalist society was an unprecedented historical advance over centuries of benighted feudalism. The bourgeois emphasis on reason, practicality, its technological enterprise in mastering the world, its ideals of rational law and justice, individual freedom and democracy were all hailed by Marx as historical progress. His point was not that communism would somehow displace capitalism in its entirety but that it would *realize* these ideals. Sadly, most of what has passed for "communism" has had but remote connections with the doctrines of Marx, Engels, or their followers. As an internal critique of the tendencies of capitalism and its crises, Marxism is uniquely coherent and incisive. The influence of Marxism has been fundamental in challenging the claims of the law to be eternal, of the bourgeoisie to represent the interests of the entire nation, of individuality and freedom to be universal. It has also been important in the analysis of women's oppression as structurally integral to capitalism. And its insights into language as a social practice with a material dimension, its awareness that truth is an interpretation based on certain kinds of consensus, its view of the world as created through human physical, intellectual, and ideological labor, its acknowledgment of the dialectical nature of all thinking, and its insistence that analysis of all phenomena must be informed by historical context were articulated long before such ideas made their way into modern literary theory.

Marxist Literary Criticism: A Historical Overview

Marx and Engels produced no systematic theory of literature or art. But Marxist aesthetics has been characterized by a persistent core of predispositions about literature and art deriving from Marx and Engels themselves. These predispositions include:

(1) The rejection, following Hegel, of the notion of "identity" and a consequent denial of the view that any object, including literature, can somehow exist independently. The aesthetic corollary of this is that literature can only be understood in the fullness of its *relations* with ideology, class, and economic substructure.
(2) The view that the so-called "objective" world is actually a progressive construction out of collective human subjectivity.
(3) The understanding of art itself as a commodity, sharing with other commodities an entry into material aspects of production.
(4) A focus on the connections between class struggle as the inner dynamic of history and literature as the ideologically refracted site of such struggle. This has sometimes gone hand in hand with prescriptions for literature as an ideological ancillary to the aims and results of political revolution.
(5) An insistence that language is not a self-enclosed system of relations but must be understood as social practice, as deeply rooted in material conditions as any other practice (*GI*, 51).

To these predispositions could be added, for example, Engels' comments on "typicality," recommending that art should express what is typical about a class or a peculiar intersection of ideological circumstances. We might also include the problem raised by Engels' granting a "relative autonomy" to art, and his acknowledgment that art and culture are determined only in the "last instance" by economic relations.

After Marx's death in 1883, Europe witnessed a widespread nascence of socialist political parties, together with the impact of Marxism in sociology, anthropology, history, and political science. The first generation of Marxist intellectuals included the Italian Antonio Labriola (1843–1904), who viewed the connection between economic and literary-cultural spheres as highly mediated; and George Plekhanov (1856–1918), the "father of Russian Marxism," who argued in his *Art and Social Life* (1912) that the idea of art for art's sake arises when the individual finds himself in hopeless disaccord with his society; when there exists a concrete possibility of social change, art tends to be more utilitarian, promoting the process of political transformation.

Vladimir Ilyich Lenin (1870–1924) occupied a central role not only in the Russian Revolution of 1917 but also in the unfolding of Marxist aesthetics. His controversial piece "Party Organization and Party Literature" (1905) was later misleadingly claimed to authorize "socialist realism," adopted in 1934 as the official party aesthetic. But he is not here prescribing partisanship (*partinost*) for *all* literature, only literature which claims to be party literature. He grants that there should be complete freedom of speech and the press. Hence the early debates on art during and after the revolutionary period in Russia focused on questions such as the degree of party control over the arts, the stance toward the bourgeois cultural legacy, and the imperative to clarify the connections between the political and the aesthetic. A related question was the possibility of creating a proletarian or working-class culture. The other major protagonist in the Russian Revolution, Leon Trotsky (1879–1940), played a crucial role in these debates. His *Literature and Revolution* (1923) stressed that the "domain of art is not one in which the Party is called upon to command. It can and must protect and help it, but can only lead it indirectly."[4] Trotsky also urges that the party should give "its confidence" to what he calls "literary fellow-travelers," those non-party writers sympathetic to the revolution (*LR*, 226). In a 1938 manifesto, *Towards a Free Revolutionary Art*, drawn up in collaboration with André Breton, Trotsky urges a "*complete freedom for art*" while acknowledging that all true art is revolutionary in nature. Throughout his comments on aesthetics, Trotsky seems to travel a fine line between granting art a certain autonomy and viewing it as serving, in a highly mediated fashion, an important social function.

The Communist Party, initially more flexible, officially adopted the aesthetic of socialist realism in 1934. This aesthetic was defined by A. A. Zhdanov as the depiction of "reality in its revolutionary development. The truthfulness ... of the artistic image must be linked with the task of ideological transformation."[5] Socialist realism received its most articulate theoretical expression in the work of the Hungarian philosopher György Lukács (1885–1971), the foremost Marxist aesthetician of modern times. Lukács' notion of realism collided with that of Bertolt Brecht (1898–1956). According to Lukács, modern capitalist society is riven by contradictions, by chasms between universal and particular, intelligible and sensible, part and whole. The realist artist expresses a vision of the possible totality embracing these contradictions, a totality achieved by embodying what is "typical" about various historical stages. Brecht, in his notebooks, also equates realism with the ability to capture the "typical" or "historically significant." Brecht holds that realist art battles false views of reality, thereby facilitating correct views.[6] Perhaps the conflict between the two thinkers is rooted in Lukács' (arguably Stalinist-inspired) aversion to modernist and experimental art on the grounds that the ontological image of humanity it portrayed was fragmented, decadent, and politically impotent. In contrast, Brecht's experimentalism was crucial to his attempts to combine theory and practice in a Marxist aesthetic. Contrasting dramatic theater (which follows Aristotle's guidelines) with his own "epic" theater, Brecht avers that the audience's capacity for action must be roused and, far from undergoing catharsis, it must be forced to take decisions, partly by its standard expectations being disappointed (a procedure Brecht called "the alienation effect").

Mention should also be made of the notion of "hegemony," formulated by the Italian Marxist Antonio Gramsci (1891–1937). The revolutionary potential of the proletariat could only be realized, argued Gramsci, through political *and* intellectual hegemony: any economic and political transformation must be facilitated by the working class, through its own "organic" intellectuals, projecting its own intellectual and ideological vision, thereby achieving an alternative hegemony to the prevailing bourgeois hegemony. Gramsci thus affirms the dialectical connection between economic and superstructural spheres, stressing the transformative role of human agency rather than relying on the "inevitability" of economic determinism. The foregoing represents the development of Marxist aesthetics during the earlier half of the twentieth century. A subsequent generation of Marxist critics such as Fredric Jameson and Terry Eagleton will be considered in a later chapter.

Early Feminist Criticism: Simone de Beauvoir and Virginia Woolf

Apart from Marxism, the other major modern critical outlook grounded in political practice is feminism, in all of its many currents. Feminism has antecedents going all the way back to ancient Greece, in the work of Sappho and arguably in Aristophanes' play *Lysistrata*, which depicts women taking over the treasury in the Acropolis, a female chorus as physically and intellectually superior to the male chorus, and the use of sexuality as a weapon in an endeavor to end the distinctly masculine project of the Peloponnesian War. Feminism also surfaces in Chaucer's Wife of Bath, who blatantly values "experience" over authority and was more than a match for each of her five husbands. In the Middle Ages, Christine de Pisan had the courage to enter into a debate with the predominant male critics of her day. During the Renaissance a number of women poets such as Catherine Des Roches emerged in France and England. In the seventeenth century, poets such as Aphra Behn and Anne Bradstreet were pioneers in gaining access to the literary profession. After the French Revolution, Mary Woll-stonecraft argued that the ideals of the Revolution and Enlightenment should be extended to women, primarily through access to education. And the nineteenth century witnessed a flowering of numerous major female literary figures in both Europe and America, ranging from Mme. de Staël, the Brontës, Jane Austen, George Eliot, and Elizabeth Barrett Browning to Margaret Fuller and Emily Dickinson. Modernist female writers included Hilda Doolittle, Gertrude Stein, Katherine Mansfield, and Virginia Woolf.

For most of this long history women were not only deprived of education and financial independence, but had to struggle against a male ideology condemning them to virtual silence and obedience, as well as a male literary establishment that poured scorn on their literary endeavors. Indeed, the depiction of women in male literature – as angels, goddesses, whores, obedient wives, and mother figures – was an integral means of perpetuating these ideologies of gender. It was only with women's struggles in the twentieth century for political rights that feminist criticism arose in any systematic way. Since the early twentieth century, feminist criticism has grown to encompass a vast series of concerns: a rewriting of literary history so as to include the contributions of women; the tracing of a female literary tradition; theories of sexuality and sexual difference, drawing on psychoanalysis, Marxism, and the social sciences; the representation of women in male literature; the role of gender in both literary creation and literary criticism (as studied in so-called "gynocriticism"); and the connection between gender and various aspects of literary form, such as genre and meter. Above all, feminist critics have displayed a persistent concern with both experience and language: is there a specifically female experience that has been communicated by women writers? And how do women confront the task of being historically coerced into using a language dominated by male concepts and values? Some feminists have urged the need for a female language, while others have advocated appropriating and modifying the inherited language of the male oppressor.

The significance of language rests ultimately on its expression of male ways of thinking that go all the way back to Aristotle: the laws of logic, beginning with the law of identity, as well as the Aristotelian categories divide up the world into strictly demarcated entities. These binary oppositions, as many modern theorists have argued, are coercive: according to Aristotle's laws, *either* one is a man *or* one is a woman, *either* black *or* white, *either* master *or* slave. Feminists have often rejected these divisive ways of viewing the world, stressing instead the various shades between female and male, between black and white, and indeed urging a vision of unity rather than opposition. In this process, such categories are recognized to be founded on no essence or natural distinctions, but are viewed as cultural and ideological constructions and performances. Hence, another fundamental feminist concern has been the rejection of "theory" as such, since in its very nature it houses these masculine presuppositions.

Indeed, one of the invaluable accomplishments of feminism has been utterly to reject the notions of objectivity and neutrality; feminists have pioneered a new honesty in acknowledging that they write from subjective positions informed by specific circumstances. This position rests largely on feminists' acknowledgment that thought is not somehow a disembodied and abstract process, but is intimately governed by the nature and situation of the body in place and time. The "body" has become a powerful metaphor of such specificity and concreteness, which rejects the male Cartesian tradition that thinking can somehow occur on a plane of disembodied universality. The body that I inhabit will shape my thinking at the profoundest levels: if my body happened to be born into a rich family with political ties, my political, religious, and social affiliations will inevitably reflect this. Whether my body is male or female will initially determine my thought and experience at a far deeper level than which books I read. Notwithstanding these insights of feminism, the days are still not past in which high-school students are forbidden to use the word "I" in their compositions, effectively perpetuating the pretense and self-delusion of objectivity.

It should be remembered that feminism has been broadly international in scope and its disposition is dictated by many local as well as general factors. For example, writers from Arab traditions such as Fatima Mernissi and Leila Ahmed have attempted to articulate a feminist vision distinctly marked by their specific cultural concerns; the same is true of African-American feminists such as Alice Walker and feminists of Asian heritage such as Gayatri Spivak. Feminism as it developed in French, American, and British traditions will be considered in a later chapter. The section below will briefly consider two of the landmark works of the early twentieth century, whose influence was disseminated through all three of these traditions, Virginia Woolf's *A Room of One's Own* (1929) and Simone de Beauvoir's *The Second Sex* (1949).

Virginia Woolf (1882–1941)

Virginia Woolf was in many ways a pioneer of feminist literary criticism, raising issues – such as the social and economic context of women's writing, the gendered nature of language, the need to go back through literary history and establish a female literary tradition, and the societal construction of gender – that remain of central importance to feminist studies. Woolf's most significant statements impinging on feminism are contained in two lectures presented at women's colleges at Cambridge University in 1928, subsequently published as *A Room of One's Own* (1929), and in *Three Guineas* (1938), an important statement concerning women's alienation from the related ethics of war and patriarchy. Woolf is also known as one of the foremost modernist writers of the English-speaking world. The most famous of her many novels include *Mrs. Dalloway* (1925), *To the Lighthouse* (1927), and *Orlando* (1928).

As the daughter of the Victorian agnostic philosopher Leslie Stephen, Woolf had access to his substantial library, and it was here that she received her education. After her parents' deaths, she settled, with her brothers and sisters, in Bloomsbury, a fashionable area of London which later gave its name to the intellectual circle in which Virginia and her sister Vanessa moved. The "Bloomsbury Group" included John Maynard Keynes, Lytton Strachey, Clive Bell, and the writer Leonard Woolf, whom Virginia was to marry in 1912. This group was unconventional in its outlooks and often in its sexuality. Woolf's own views of femininity and gender relations must have been rooted partly in her own sexuality; she was engaged in a relationship with the writer Vita Sackville-West, on whom Woolf's novel *Orlando* was based. Woolf suffered from nervous breakdowns and was acutely and sometimes debilitatingly conscious of her status as a female writer in an intellectual milieu dominated by males and masculine values. In 1941 she walked into a river, her pockets loaded with stones, and drowned herself, suffering the same fate as her imaginary character Shakespeare's sister who was driven to suicide on account of the overwhelming forces and institutions thwarting her female genius.

Woolf's literary criticism, like her fiction, can be approached from at least two perspectives – those of modernism and feminism. Perhaps the most fundamental point on which these overlap is their common rejection of the mainstream legacy of the bourgeois Enlightenment. Woolf reacted against the Enlightenment presumption that reason could master the world and reduce it to total intelligibility. At various points in her fiction and essays, Woolf expresses what has come to be seen as a characteristically feminist distrust of theorizing, which is seen as imbued with centuries of male values and strategies. Like most modernists, Woolf questioned the idea of an external reality that somehow existed independently of our minds. And her emphasis on time and change, inspired by Bergson and Proust, is profoundly symptomatic of a modernist perspective.

In *A Room of One's Own* Woolf raised a number of issues that would remain of central concern to feminists. The "room" of the book's title is a skillfully used metaphor around which the entire text is woven: Woolf's central claim is that "a woman must have money and a room of her own if she is to write fiction."[7] The most obvious meaning of this claim is that women need financial and psychological independence in order to exercise their creative potential. But Woolf's claim also situates literature within a material (economic, social, political) context. She compares fiction to a spider's web: this web is not spun in midair (literature does not arise in a vacuum) but is "attached to life at all four corners." Indeed, it is "attached to grossly material things" (*Room*, 43–44). Hence, intellectual freedom, the "power to think for oneself," rests on financial freedom (*Room*, 106). Until the beginning of the nineteenth century, Woolf notes, women were debarred from any "separate lodging" which might shelter them "from the claims and tyrannies of their families" (*Room*, 52).

But the "room" also represents psychological space. Woolf relates her famous anecdote of "Shakespeare's sister" Judith, who, being "wonderfully gifted," attempts to seek her fortune in the theater like her brother. The opposition to her endeavors ranges from her father's violent anger to the laughter and exploitation of men in the theater company; such is her frustration and fragility that she kills herself (*Room*, 46–48). The room may also signify resistance to the appropriation of language, history, and tradition by men. Woolf notes that "women have burnt like beacons in all the works of all the poets" but in reality they were "locked up, beaten and flung about the room" (*Room*, 43). An important task for women, as they look back through history, is to seek out the hitherto neglected and blurred outlines of a female literary tradition. "Poetry," affirms Woolf, "ought to have a mother as well as a father" (*Room*, 103). In this broader sense, the "room" might encompass a female tradition and female perspectives toward history.

A room of one's own might also represent the ideal of a female language or at least of appropriating language for female use. The "male" language women have inherited cannot express their female experience; this language, habituated to showing women exclusively in their relationship to men, could not express, for example, the liking of one woman for another (*Room*, 82). Woolf notes how woman has been at the "centre of some different order and system of life," contrasting sharply with the world inhabited by men (*Room*, 86). Not only must women craft a sentence, a language that will grasp the rhythms of their own experience, but also a literary form that is "adapted to the body" (*Room*, 78). Woolf's general point – that language and thought are ultimately and irreversibly grounded in the rhythms of the body, of one's particular situation in place and time – is one that has been richly pursued by a variety of feminisms. Importantly, however, the mental state that Woolf sees as most creative is what she calls "unity of the mind," a unity in which the sexes are not viewed as distinct (*Room*, 97). She characterizes such "androgyny" (a Greek term, taken over from Coleridge and, ultimately, from Plato) as follows: "in each of us two powers preside, one male, one female ... The normal and comfortable state of being is that when the two live in harmony together, spiritually co-operating ... Coleridge perhaps meant this when he said that a great mind is androgynous" (*Room*, 98).

Simone de Beauvoir (1908–1986)

Another classic feminist statement, *Le Deuxième Sexe* (1949; translated as *The Second Sex*, 1952), was produced by Simone de Beauvoir, a leading intellectual of her time, whose existentialist vision was forged partly in her relationship, as companion and colleague, with the existentialist philosopher Jean-Paul Sartre. De Beauvoir's text laid the foundations for much of the feminist theory and political activism that emerged during the 1960s in Western Europe and America. Since then, its impact, if anything, has broadened and deepened. The book's central argument is that, throughout history, woman has always occupied a secondary role in relation to man, being relegated to the position of the "other," i.e., that which is adjectival upon the substantial subjectivity and existential activity of man. Whereas man has been enabled to transcend and control his environment, always furthering the domain of his physical and intellectual conquests, woman has remained imprisoned within "immanence," remaining a slave within the circle of duties imposed by her maternal and reproductive functions. In highlighting this subordination, the book explains in characteristic existentialist fashion how the so-called "essence" of woman was in fact created – at many levels, economic, political, religious – by historical developments representing the interests of men.

In her renowned introduction to *The Second Sex*, de Beauvoir points out the fundamental asymmetry of the terms "masculine" and "feminine." Masculinity is considered to be the "absolute human type," the norm or standard of humanity. A man does not typically preface his opinions with the statement "I am a man," whereas a woman's views are often held to be grounded in her femininity rather than in any objective perception of things. Woman "has ovaries, a uterus; these peculiarities imprison her in her subjectivity, circumscribe her within the limits of her own nature."[8] De Beauvoir quotes Aristotle as saying that the "female is a female by virtue of a certain *lack* of qualities," and St. Thomas as stating that the female nature is "afflicted with a natural defectiveness" (*SS*, xvi). Summarizing these long traditions of thought, de Beauvoir states: "Thus humanity is male and man defines woman not in herself but as relative to him; she is not regarded as an autonomous being . . . she is the incidental, the inessential as opposed to the essential. He is the Subject, he is the Absolute – she is the Other" (*SS*, xvi). Indeed, a long line of thinkers, stretching from Plato and Aristotle through Augustine and Aquinas to modern bourgeois philosophers, has insisted on stabilizing woman as an object, on dooming her to immanence, to a life of subjection to given conditions, on barring her from property rights, education, and the professions (*SS*, xviii). Men have also consistently promoted certain myths about women – goddess, whore, mother, the mysterious "eternal feminine" – all of which have substituted a rigid and unchangeable idea of woman for actual women (*SS*, 239).

According to de Beauvoir, two essential factors paved the way for women's prospective equality: one was her ability (conferred by technology, which abrogated any innate male advantages of strength) to share in productive labor; and the second was her recently acquired freedom from the slavery of reproduction through contraception, adopted by many of the middle and then the working classes from the eighteenth century onward (*SS*, 109). In the conclusion to her book, de Beauvoir argues that woman's situation will be transformed primarily by a change in her economic condition; but this change must also generate moral, social, cultural, and psychological transformations. Eventually, both man and woman will exist *both* for self and for the other: "mutually recognizing each other as subject, each will yet remain for the other an *other.*" In this recognition, in this reciprocity, will "the slavery of half of humanity" be abolished (*SS*, 688).

Notes

1. F. R. Leavis, *The Common Pursuit* (1952; rpt. Harmondsworth: Penguin, 1966), p. 193. Hereafter cited as *CP*.
2. Karl Marx and Friedrich Engels, *Manifesto of the Communist Party* (1952; rpt. Moscow: Progress Publishers, 1973), pp. 11–16. Hereafter cited as *MCP*.
3. Karl Marx, *The German Ideology: Part One*, ed. C. J. Arthur (London: Lawrence and Wishart, 1982), pp. 47–51. Hereafter cited as *GI*.
4. Leon Trotsky, *Literature and Revolution* (New York: Russell and Russell, 1957), p. 218. Hereafter cited as *LR*.
5. A. A. Zhdanov, *Essays on Literature, Philosophy, and Music* (New York: International Publishers, 1950), p. 15.
6. Berel Lang and Forrest Williams, eds., *Marxism and Art: Writings in Aesthetics and Criticism* (New York: McKay, 1972), pp. 226–227.
7. Virginia Woolf, *A Room of One's Own* (1929; rpt. San Diego, New York, London: Harvest/Harcourt Brace Jovanovich, 1989), p. 4. Hereafter cited as *Room*.
8. Simone de Beauvoir, *The Second Sex*, trans. H. M. Parshley (New York: Bantam/Alfred A. Knopf, 1961), p. xv. Hereafter cited as *SS*.

Chapter 15

Phenomenology, Existentialism, Structuralism

The conclusion of World War II formalized the opposition between the Western powers and the Soviet bloc of nations. While some literature participated in this ideological conflict, much writing retreated in dismay from the political sphere. This retreat from an "objective" reality reached a climax in philosophies such as phenomenology (which parenthesized the objective world, viewing it as a function of perception) and existentialism (which called into question all forms of authority and belief). The flight from reality found voice also in literary developments such as the Theater of the Absurd, whose major proponents Samuel Beckett and Eugene Ionesco dramatized the existential absurdity, anguish, and ultimate isolation of human existence. The Italian thinker Benedetto Croce formulated an aesthetic which revived Hegelian idealist principles as against the tradition of bourgeois positivism and scientism. The German existentialist philosopher Martin Heidegger (1889–1976) increasingly saw poetry as transcending the discursive and rational limitations of philosophy. In France, the philosopher Gaston Bachelard (1884–1962) formulated a phenomenological and surrealist account of poetry, while the existentialist Jean-Paul Sartre (1905–1980) advocated a literature of political engagement. The phenomenological emphasis was further elaborated by Georges Poulet (1902–1991), Jean-Pierre Richard (b. 1922), and Georges Bataille (1897–1962); it was given a linguistic orientation in the work of Maurice Blanchot (1907–2003). It was in the 1950s that structuralism – another tendency which parenthesized the agency of the human subject by situating it within a broad linguistic and semiological structure – began to thrive through figures such as the anthropologist Claude Lévi-Strauss and the narratologist A. J. Greimas. Roland Barthes analyzed the new myths of Western culture and later proclaimed the "death of the author." The following sections will briefly consider phenomenology as formulated by Husserl, existentialism as expounded by Heidegger, the heterology of Georges Bataille, and structuralism as expressed in its foundations by Saussure and in its later phases by Barthes.

Literary Criticism from Plato to the Present: An Introduction   M. A. R. Habib
© 2011 M. A. R. Habib

Phenomenology

Edmund Husserl (1859–1938)

One of the foremost philosophies of this period, in which much reader-response theory had its philosophical origins, was the doctrine known as phenomenology, whose foundations were laid by the German philosopher Edmund Husserl. The Greek word *phainomenon* means "appearance." Hence, as a philosophical attitude, phenomenology shifts our emphasis of study away from the "external" world of objects toward examining the ways in which these objects *appear* to the human subject, and the subjective contribution to this process of appearing. Husserl gives the name "phenomenological reduction" to this "bracketing" of the external world, which underlies his attempt to achieve certainty in philosophy. He argues that we cannot be sure of the nature of the outside world; but we *can* have certainty about the nature of our own perception and about the ways in which we construct the world or the ways in which that world appears to our subjective apparatus. This emphasis on subjectivity proved to be enormously influential; it provided the foundations of the Geneva School of phenomenological criticism (including figures such as Georges Poulet and Jean Starobinski) which read literature as embodying the consciousness of its author; it exerted a considerable impact on the reception theories of Wolfgang Iser and Hans Robert Jauss; and it provided a starting point against which Martin Heidegger's thought reacted.

Existentialism

Martin Heidegger (1889–1976)

Husserl's student Martin Heidegger proved to be the major modern exponent of existentialism. His impact extends not only to existentialist philosophers such as Merleau-Ponty, Sartre, and Simone de Beauvoir but also to psychiatrists such as Ludwig Binswanger and to theologians such as Rudolph Bultmann, Paul Tillich, Martin Buber, and Karl Barth, as well to poststructuralist thinkers such as Jacques Derrida. Heiddegger's central project in his major work *Sein und Zeit* (*Being and Time*) (1927) consisted in a radical reexamination of the notion of "being," in its intrinsic relationship with time. He developed his own hermeneutic or method of interpretation of texts; his later work focuses increasingly on the analysis of poetry and language.

Heidegger was appointed Professor of Philosophy at the University of Marburg in 1923; he was subsequently, in 1929, elected Husserl's successor to the Chair of Philosophy at Freiburg and then elected rector in 1933 under

Hitler's recently inaugurated regime. It was in this year that Heidegger joined the Nationalist Socialist Party; in his inaugural address at the university, "The Role of the University in the New Reich," he decried freedom of speech in the interests of national unity, and lauded the advent of a glorious new Germany. He resigned his position as rector in early 1934. Did these events represent merely a brief flirtation on Heidegger's part with Nazism or an enduring collaboration and commitment? The controversy continues.

In *Being and Time* Heidegger states that what characterizes *dasein* or *human* being is its "throwness" into the world or "facticity": a human being is already cast into a series of relationships and surroundings that constitute his or her "world."[1] A second feature of being is "existentiality" or "transcendence," whereby a human being appropriates her world, impressing on it the unique image of her own existence and potential. In other words, she uses the various elements of her world as given to realize herself (*BT*, 235–236). Yet this positive feature is accompanied by a third characteristic, that of "fallenness": in attempting to create herself, the human being falls from true Being, becoming immersed instead in the distractions of day-to-day living, becoming entangled in particular beings (*BT*, 220). The authentic being, the authentic self is thus buried beneath the cares and distractions of life (*BT*, 166–168).

How does a human being overcome such inauthentic existence, such loss of true being? Heidegger's response comprises one of the classic statements of existentialism. He suggests that there is one particular state of mind which is unique: "dread" or *angst* (*BT*, 227–235). This refers to a sense of nothingness, of loss, of the emptiness, when we look at life or existence in its totality, as essentially orientated toward death. In such a mood, the human self attains knowledge of itself as a whole, as "being-to-death." In other words, death is the fundamental fact that shapes our existence and the course of our life. And the mental state of "dread" enables us to rise above our immanence, our dispersion in the immediate and transitory affairs of the world, to reflect upon our life as a whole, in the fullest glare of its finitude and its potential to lack meaning (*BT*, 293–299). The vehicle through which we acknowledge this responsibility to ourselves is "conscience," which acknowledges both our facticity, our being placed within a world, and our obligation actively to fashion our selves in relation to this very world. Conscience makes us aware of this guilt or obligation (*BT*, 313, 317–319).

In his later works, such as *Introduction to Metaphysics* (1953), Heidegger aims to guide Western man away from his inauthentic immersion in worldly aims, as well as in technology and gadgetry. In works such as "The Origin of the Work of Art" (1935), "Hölderlin and the Essence of Poetry" (1936), and "Language" (1950), he appeals, in this salvific enterprise, to the power of poetry to express the truths of authentic being. In his essay "Language," Heidegger's explication of a poem entitled *Ein Winterabend* ("A Winter

Evening") by Georg Trakl anticipates poststructuralist views of language as well as much reception and reader-response theory. The language of Trakl's poem, says Heidegger, does not merely name familiar objects such as "snow," "bell," "window," "falling," and "ringing." Rather, it "calls into the word ... The calling calls into itself," into a "presence sheltered in absence."[2] Inasmuch as we can "explain" this statement, we might take it to indicate that language does not name things which are somehow already there, waiting to be named. They achieve their very status as "things" only by being called into the word, only by being given a status, a position, a situation, in language.

Anticipating Derrida's notion of difference, Heidegger states that between "world" and "thing" prevails a condition of "betweenness," or what Heidegger calls *dif-ference* where the latter part of this noun may refer to the "bearing" or "carrying" of *world* by *thing*. The intimacy of world and thing, says Heidegger, "is present in the separation of the between; it is present in the dif-ference. The word dif-ference is now removed from its usual and customary usage. What it now names is not a generic concept for various kinds of differences. It exists only as this single difference" (*PLT*, 202). This formulation anticipates Derrida's hypostatization of difference – his treating of it as a primordial essence, a linguistic primum mobile, an aseitic first cause prescinded from the very relationality into which it plunges all else. Heidegger tells us that it is language which speaks, language which brings together world and things *in their intimacy which is a relation of absolute difference* (*PLT*, 202). Hence, Heidegger draws attention to the world not as a thing but as an *act*. It is language, language that speaks, which brings the processes of world-composition and thing-composition into the mutuality in which alone either can be realized.

Heidegger proceeds to explain that the "dif-ference does not mediate after the fact by connecting world and things through a middle added on to them. Being in the middle, it first determines world and things in their presence, i.e. in their being toward one another, whose unity it carries out" (*PLT*, 202). In other words, dif-ference is not an external relation that connects two entities (world and thing) that are already there: rather, dif-ference is internal to their relation, shaping the very entities themselves. If dif-ference primordially pre-exists identity, if dif-ference is prior to the constitution of world and thing, then language is the vehicle by which world and thing are called into being, through mutual relation, from this "primordial" dif-ference into the dif-ference which is language itself (*PLT*, 207). What ultimately takes place in the speaking of language is the creation of what is human: "mortals live in the speaking of language" (*PLT*, 210).

While much of what Heidegger says in these later works leans toward mysticism, his insights into language overlap with those of many modern theorists such as Barthes and even Lacan. Heidegger indicates that not only is the human being "thrown" into the world (his or her particular world) but that the human is characterized by a thrownness into language. It is the language that we are born into (not this or that particular language but language in general) that speaks through us and that speaks to us. At the core of language is dif-ference, the irreducible relation between world and thing, the irreducible self-transcendence of all of the elements of our world in a larger unity toward which they point; it is language which constitutes the human; all of our attempts to understand and act upon the world and thereby to create ourselves are mediated by the speaking of language, a speaking in which we must enter to find our own voice. It is when we arrive at a dialogue with language that we truly speak.

Heterology

Georges Bataille (1897–1962)

Loosely associated with the surrealist movement in the earlier twentieth century, Bataille was a radical thinker whose works spanned philosophy, poetry, economics, and pornography. His major works include *La Part maudite* (1949; *The Accursed Share*) and *La Littérature et le Mal* (1975; *Literature and Evil*). Sometimes called the "metaphysician of evil," and condemned as an "excremental philosopher" by the leading surrealist André Breton,[3] Bataille engaged in what he himself called "intellectual violence" to produce writings which were often designed to shock and appall, advancing his endeavor to write a "heterology," a science of the other, of the heterogeneous, of all that had been excreted and rejected as waste matter or undesirable by conventional thought: sacrifice, excrement, violence, blood, incest, all of this comprising the "accursed share," pertaining to the bodily and material part of us that has been suppressed and subordinated. All of these are constituents of forbidden and tabooed realms whose repudiation and expulsion are integral to the formation of the tradition of rationalism (as superordinate to the body), and the structures of transcendence (religious, social, political) through which order and meaning are imposed and created. Bataille's work, revived in the 1960s, heavily influenced poststructuralist thinkers such as Derrida and Kristeva, as well as theorists of postmodernism such as Lyotard and Baudrillard.

Bataille drew inspiration from "deviant" figures such as the Marquis de Sade, who saw the very notion of reason as coercive and violent. The concept of reason, since at least the time of Plato, has been used to control and suppress the desires and appetites of the body in the interests of political order and communal benefit. In the era of capitalism, desires must be subordinated to the principle of utility and the requirements of the market such as economy and efficiency. It should be remembered, however, that Bataille's project of heterology was hardly altogether new; he was continuing, with perhaps a more scatological emphasis, a heterological tradition stretching from Schopenhauer and Nietzsche through Bergson, Freud, Heidegger to feminist thinkers, which had stressed the role of the body, survival instincts, and ideology in the very processes of perception and cognition. Bataille's call is in some sense fundamental: to overturn the homogenizing project of philosophy, religion, and art. A skeptic might argue that the scatological tendencies that Bataille wishes to unleash already permeate the capitalist world and are in fact one of the important directions in which it has extended its markets and deepened its conditioning of human subjectivity.

Structuralism

Structuralism was to some extent anticipated in the work of the Canadian Northrop Frye, who was the most influential theorist in America of what is called Myth Criticism, which was in vogue from the 1940s to the mid-1960s and whose practitioners included Richard Chase, Leslie Fiedler, Daniel Hoffman, and Philip Wheelwright. Drawing on the findings of anthropology and psychology regarding universal myths, rituals, and folktales, these critics were intent on restoring spiritual content to a world they saw as alienated, fragmented, and ruled by scientism, empiricism, positivism, and technology. They wished to redeem the role of myth, which might comprehend magic, imagination, dreams, intuition, and the unconscious. They viewed the creation of myth as integral to human thought, and believed that literature emerges out of a core of myth, where "myth" is understood as a collective attempt on the part of various cultures and groups to establish a meaningful context for human existence. Frye's *Anatomy of Criticism* (1957) continued the formalist emphasis of the New Criticism but insisted even more strongly that criticism should be a scientific, objective, and systematic discipline. Frye held that such literary criticism views literature itself as a system. For example, the mythoi of Spring, Summer, Autumn, and Winter gave rise to fundamental literary modes such as comedy, tragedy, irony, and romance. Given the recurrence of basic symbolic motifs, literary history is a repetitive and self-contained cycle. Hence the historical element ostensibly informing Frye's formalism is effectively abrogated, literature being viewed as a timeless, static and autonomous construct.

Frye's static model, exhibiting recurrent patterns, is a feature shared by structuralist views of language and literature. The foundations of structuralism were laid by the Swiss linguist Ferdinand de Saussure, whose insights were developed by the French anthropologist Claude Lévi-Strauss, Roland Barthes, and others. Saussure saw language as a system of signs, constructed by convention, which lent itself to synchronic structural analysis. Also entailed in structuralist analyses was the anti-humanist view that, since language is an institution, individual human agency is unprivileged, neither human beings nor social phenomena having essences. Hence, structuralism diverges sharply from the Romantic notion of the author as the source of meaning, and shifts emphasis away from authorial intention toward the broader and impersonal linguistic structure in which the author's text participates, and which indeed enables that text. Structuralism was imported into America from France during the 1960s and its leading exponents included Roman Jakobson, Jonathan Culler, Michael Riffaterre, Claudio Guillen, Gerald Prince, and Robert Scholes. Other American thinkers working in the field of semiotics have included C. S. Peirce, Charles Morris, and Noam Chomsky. The major principles of structuralism can now be examined briefly in the work of Saussure and Roland Barthes.

Ferdinand de Saussure (1857–1913)

Saussure was effectively the founder of modern linguistics, as well as of structuralism; and, while much poststructuralism arose in partial reaction against his thought, it nonetheless presupposed his theoretical advances in linguistics. His lectures in linguistics, posthumously compiled by his colleagues as *Course in General Linguistics* (1916), proved to be of seminal influence in a broad range of fields, including anthropology, as in the work of Lévi-Strauss; the semiological work of Roland Barthes; the literary-philosophical notions of Derrida; the analyses of ideology by structuralist Marxists such as Louis Althusser; the psychoanalytic theories of Jacques Lacan; and the analyses of language conducted by feminists such as Julia Kristeva.

Prior to Saussure, the predominant modes of analyzing language were historical and philological. As opposed to a diachronic approach which studies changes in language over a period of time, Saussure undertook a synchronic approach which saw language as a structure that could be studied in its entirety at a given point in time. He pioneered a number of further influential and radical insights. Firstly, he denied that there is somehow a natural connection between words and things, urging that this connection is conventional. This view of language also challenges the view of reality as somehow independent and existing outside of language, a view which reduces language to merely a "name-giving system." Saussure's view implies that we acquire an understanding of our world by means of language and view the world *through* language. Secondly, Saussure argued that language is a system of signs in relation: no sign has meaning in isolation; rather its signification depends on its difference from other signs and generally on its situation within the entire network of signs. For example, in order to understand the word "black," we need to understand not only the other colors such as "white" and "red" but the word "color" itself. Finally, Saussure made a distinction between two dimensions of language: *langue*, which refers to language as a structured system, grounded on certain rules; and *parole*, the specific acts of speech or utterance which are based on those rules.

Saussure's exposition of the "Nature of the Linguistic Sign" provides a reference point for much subsequent literary and cultural theory. He attacks the conventional correspondence theory of meaning whereby language is viewed as a naming process, each word corresponding to the thing it names.[4] As against this view, Saussure urges that *both* terms of the linguistic sign (signifier and signified) are psychological in nature; the sign unites not a thing with a name but a *concept* with a *sound-image*. The latter is not the material sound but the "psychological imprint of the sound," the impression it makes on our senses; hence it too is psychological (*CGL*, 66). He suggests a new terminology: *signified* designates the *concept*, *signifier* designates the *sound-image*, and *sign* designates the combination of these or the entire construct. As Saussure states, the linguistic sign in its totality is "a two-sided psychological entity," consisting of both signifier and signified. The sign as a whole refers to the actual object in the world, as displayed in the following diagram:

Signifier (the word or sound-image "table")

Sign > Actual object: table

Signified (the concept of "table")

The sign has two primordial characteristics: firstly, the bond between signifier and signified is *arbitrary*: by this, Saussure means that the concept (e. g., "sister") is not linked by any inner relationship to the succession of sounds which serves as its signifier (in French, s-o-r). Saussure offers another clarification: the bond is not *natural* but unmotivated, based on collective behavior or convention, fixed by rules. Signifiers and gestures do not have any intrinsic value. Saussure is careful to suggest that "arbitrary" does not imply that the choice of the signifier is left entirely to the speaker: the individual has no power to change a sign in any way once it has become established in the linguistic community (*CGL*, 69).

Roland Barthes (1915–1980)

Roland Barthes' theoretical development is often seen as embodying a transition from structuralist to poststructuralist perspectives, though certain of his works are characterized by a Marxian outlook. Barthes effectively extended structural analysis and semiology (the study of signs) to broad cultural phenomena, and it was he also who confronted the limits of structuralism, pointing the way to freer and more relativistic assessments of texts and their role in culture. It was Barthes who made famous the notion of the "death of the author," the idea of the text as a site of free play or pleasure, and differences such as those between "work" and "text," and "writerly" and "readerly" works of art. As such, he anticipates many facets of poststructuralism, including certain elements of deconstruction, cultural studies, and queer studies.

Notwithstanding his suffering from tuberculosis, his homosexuality, and his esoteric and eclectic world view, Barthes was at times affiliated with mainstream French institutions, such as the National Center for Scientific Research and the Collège de France. His early works, *Writing Degree Zero* (1953) and *Mythologies* (1957), derived inspiration from Saussure, Sartre, and Marxism. His structuralist works include *Elements of Semiology* (1964) and "Introduction to the Structural Analysis of Narrative" (1966). His poststructuralist disposition is marked in his polysemic analysis of Balzac's novella *Sarrasine* in his *S/Z* (1970) and *The Pleasure of the Text* (1973).

In *Mythologies* Barthes undertook an ideological critique of various products of mass bourgeois culture (ranging from soap through advertising to images of Rome), attempting to account for this mystification of culture or history into a "universal nature."[5] Barthes suggests that myth is not an object, a concept or an idea but a *language*, a type of speech. It is a mode of signification (*Myth.*, 109). Barthes saw bourgeois ideology as a process of myth-making, whereby the bourgeoisie, instead of identifying itself as a class, merges into the concept of "nation," thereby presenting bourgeois values as being in the national interest. Through this depoliticizing and "universalistic effort" of its vocabulary, the bourgeoisie was able to postulate its own definitions of justice, truth, and law as universal; it was able to postulate its own definition of humanity as comprising "human nature"; and "bourgeois norms are experienced as the evident laws of a natural order" (*Myth.*, 138–140). According to Barthes, myth can be opposed or under-mined either by producing an artificial myth, highlighting its own mythical status, or by using speech in an explicitly political manner (*Myth.*, 135–136, 145–146).

Barthes challenged classical views of the human subject, and viewed an author or persona as a grammatical function rather than a psychological subject. In "The Death of the Author" (1968), he argues that as soon as narration occurs without any practical purpose, as an end in itself, "this disconnection occurs, the voice loses its origin, the author enters into his own death, writing begins."[6] The modern, individual, author, says Barthes, was "a product of our society insofar as, emerging from the Middle Ages with English empiricism, French rationalism and the personal faith of the Reformation, it discovered the prestige of the individual ... the epitome and culmination of capitalist ideology." Even in the present, says Barthes, our studies of literature are "tyrannically centred on the author" (*IMT*, 143). According to Barthes, we can no longer think of writing in the classical ways, as recording, representing, or depicting. Rather, it is a "performative" act (*IMT*, 145–146). What is more, a text can no longer be viewed as releasing in a linear fashion a single "theological" meaning, as the message of the "Author-God." Rather, it is "a multi-dimensional space in which a variety of writings, none of them original, blend and clash. The text is a tissue of quotations drawn from the innumerable centres of culture" (*IMT*, 146). The writer has only the power to mix writings. Hence literature, by refusing to assign an "ultimate meaning . . . to the text (and to the world as text)" facilitates an "anti-theological" activity which is revolutionary since "to refuse to fix meaning is, in the end, to refuse God and his hypostases – reason, science, law" (*IMT*, 147). A text's unity, says Barthes, "lies not in its origin but in its destination," in the reader. Yet Barthes cautions that the humanism we have rejected via removal of the author should not be reinstated through any conception of the reader as a personal and complete entity. The reader of which Barthes speaks is a reader "without history, biography, psychology; he is simply that *someone* who holds together in a single field all the traces by which the written text is constituted." In other words, the reader, like the author, is a function of the text. In this sense "the birth of the reader must be at the cost of the death of the Author" (*IMT*, 148).

In a subsequent essay, "From Work to Text" (1971), Barthes provides a succinct statement of a poststructuralist perspective. He distinguishes between a "work" and a "text." Whereas a "work" offers up to analysis a closed signified or definite meaning, a "text" can never allow investigation to halt at some signified, some concept which represents its ultimate meaning. Like language, the text "is structured but off-centred, without closure" (*IMT*, 159). Barthes states an important feature of poststructuralist analysis when he says that the text is held in "intertextuality," in a network of signifiers (*IMT*, 160–161). And, whereas the work is consumed more or less passively, the text asks of the reader a "practical collaboration" in the production of the work (*IMT*, 162–163). The implication here is that the text invites participation in its own play, its subversion of hierarchies, and its endless deferment of the definite (*IMT*, 164).

Notes

1. Martin Heidegger, *Being and Time*, trans. John Macquarrie and Edward Robinson (New York: Harper and Row, 1962), pp. 19, 21–23, 82–83. Hereafter cited as *BT*.
2. Martin Heidegger, *Poetry, Language, Thought*, trans. Albert Hofstadter (New York and London: Harper and Row, 1975), p. 199. Hereafter cited as *PLT*.
3. Quoted in Georges Bataille, "Introduction," in *Visions of Excess: Selected Writings 1927–1939*, ed. Allan Stoekl (Minneapolis: University of Minnesota Press, 1985), pp. x–xi.

4. Ferdinand de Saussure, *Course in General Linguistics*, ed. Charles Bally, Albert Sechehaye, and Albert Reidlinger, trans. Wade Baskin (New York: Philosophical Library, 1959), p. 65. Hereafter cited as *CGL*.

5. Roland Barthes, *Mythologies*, trans. Annette Lavers (London: Collins, 1973), p. 9. Hereafter cited as *Myth*.

6. Roland Barthes, *Image: Music: Text*, trans. Stephen Heath (Glasgow: Fontana, 1982), p. 142. Hereafter cited as *IMT*.

Chapter 16

The Era of Poststructuralism (I): Later Marxism, Psychoanalysis, Deconstruction

The broad term "poststructuralism" denotes a range of critical approaches emerging after the 1960s, which took from structuralism its insights into language as a system of signs, and the construction of identity, subjects, and objects through language. They rejected, however, the concept of structure, the use of binary oppositions, and structuralism's ahistorical approach, emphasizing instead the indeterminate and polysemic nature of semiotic codes and the arbitrary and constructed nature of the foundations of knowledge. These movements, born in a politically more volatile climate, laid greater emphasis on the operations of ideology and power in the construction of human subjectivity, which they described in gendered, racial, and economic terms. While Marxism itself cannot be classified as poststructuralist, Marxist thinking in this era interacted richly with other approaches and registered the impact of certain poststructuralist insights.

It was, ironically, the period of relative economic prosperity after the World War II that eventually gave impetus to the civil rights movement and the women's movement. The revolutionary fervor of the 1960s gave Marxist criticism a revived impetus. A group of Marxist critics was centered around the *New Left Review*, founded in 1960 and edited first by Stuart Hall and then by Perry Anderson. Its contributors included E. P. Thompson, Raymond Williams, and Terry Eagleton. This was also the period in which the radical journal *Tel Quel*, established in 1960 in France, fostered an intellectual milieu in which the writings of Derrida, Lacan, and feminist thinkers such as Julia Kristeva were fomented, eventually displacing the prominence of French existentialism. Many of the thinkers associated with the journal challenged the categories and binary oppositions which had acted as the foundation of much Western thought since Plato and Aristotle. Some feminists, notably Luce Irigaray and Hélène Cixous, indicted both Freud and Lacan's own discourse, which they saw as privileging the male and even as misogynistic.

Literary Criticism from Plato to the Present: An Introduction   M. A. R. Habib
© 2011 M. A. R. Habib

Feminists such as Monique Wittig and Kristeva reflected on the possibility of an *écriture féminine*.

Writers such as Gilles Deleuze, Félix Guattari, and Jean Baudrillard have variously offered powerful analyses of capitalist society in terms of psychological categories and drives, as well as of the symbolic processes that structure consciousness, and the lack of foundations for arriving at intellectual or moral judgment. More recent thinkers such as Clement Rosset, Jacques Bouveresse, and Richard Rorty have turned away from the tenets of poststructuralism, such as its reductive view of reality as ultimately linguistic. Feminists such as Nancy Chodorow and Jessica Benjamin have reacted against the predominant Freudian–Lacanian accounts of sexuality, seeking instead to trace the formation of gender to the infant's pre-Oedipal connections with the mother. Vincent Descombes has returned to the principles of early twentieth-century analytical philosophers such as Wittgenstein, and whereas many poststructuralists drew heavily on Hegelian notions, thinkers such as Jean-François Lyotard have turned instead to Kant. Lyotard has theorized influentially about the "postmodern condition," seeing it as marked by an absence of totalizing schemes of explanation, and the dissolution of human subjectivity.

Later Marxist Criticism

From the 1960s, Marxist critics continued to reinterpret and develop the insights of Marx and Engels. Louis Althusser, Lucien Goldmann, and Pierre Macherey turned away from Hegel and were heavily influenced by the structuralist movements of the earlier twentieth century, which stressed the role of larger signifying systems and institutional structures over individual agency and intention. Louis Althusser, in his *Pour Marx* (*For Marx*, 1965) and his often cited "Ideology and Ideological State Apparatuses," emphasized the later Marx's scientificity and his "epistemological break" from his own earlier humanism and Hegelianism. He rejected literary critical emphases on authorial intention and subjective agency. Goldmann also rejected the Romantic–humanist notion of individual creativity and held that texts are productions of larger structures representing the mentality of particular social classes. He developed the notion of "homology" to register the parallels between artistic and social forms. Pierre Macherey's *A Theory of Literary Production* (1966) saw the literary text as the product of the artist's reworking of linguistic and ideological raw material, unwittingly exposing, through its lacunae and contradictions, ideological elements which the author had attempted to suppress into a false coherence. In this way, a critique of ideology could emerge through the literary text.

In the Anglo-American world a "cultural materialist" criticism was first revived by Raymond Williams (1921–1988), notably in *Culture and Society*

1780–1950, which analyzed the cultural critique of capitalism in English literary tradition. Williams rejected a simplistic explanation of culture as the efflux of material conditions, and stressed the contribution of cultural forms to economic and political development. *The Long Revolution* (1961) continued and refined this project using categories such as dominant, residual, and emergent cultures, mediated by what Williams called "structures of feeling." Williams' work became overtly Marxist with the publication in 1977 of *Marxism and Literature*, where he attempts to integrate Marxist conceptions of language and literature. In general, Williams' work analyzed the history of language, the role of the media, mass communications, and the cultural connections between the country and the city.

The major American Marxist critic Fredric Jameson (b. 1934) outlined a dialectical theory of literary criticism in his *Marxism and Form* (1971), drawing on Hegelian categories such as the notion of totality and the connection of abstract and concrete. Such criticism recognizes the need to see its objects of analysis within a broad historical context, acknowledges its own history and perspective, and seeks the profound inner form of a literary text. Jameson's *The Political Unconscious* (1981) attempts to integrate this dialectical thinking with insights from structuralism and Freud, using the Freudian notion of repression to analyze the function of ideology, the status of literary texts, and the epistemological function of literary form. In subsequent work such as *Postmodernism, or the Cultural Logic of Late Capitalism* (1991), Jameson performed the valuable task of extending Marx's insights into the central role of postmodernism in determining the very form of our artistic and intellectual experience.

Terry Eagleton (b. 1943)

In Britain, the most prominent Marxist critic has been Terry Eagleton, who has outlined the categories of a Marxist analysis of literature, and has persistently rearticulated the terms of communication, as well as the differences, between Marxism and modern literary theory. Eagleton insists that there are at least two fundamental premises in Marx from which any Marxist criticism must begin. In the first place, all forms of consciousness – religious, moral, philosophical, legal, as well as language itself – have no independent history and arise from the material activity of men. Secondly, class struggle is viewed as the central dynamic of historical development. Eagleton adds a third, Marxist–Leninist, imperative, namely a commitment to the theory and practice of political revolution.[1] According to Eagleton, the "primary task" of Marxist criticism is "to actively participate in and help direct the cultural emancipation of the masses."[2] He repeatedly stresses that the starting point of theory must be a practical, political purpose.[3] He emphasizes that the "means of production" includes the means of production of human subjectivity, which embraces a range of institutions such as "literature." Eagleton regards the most difficult emancipation as that of the "space of subjectivity," colonized as it is by the dominant political order. The humanities as a whole serve an ideological function that helps to perpetuate certain forms of subjectivity. Eagleton's views here imply that for Marxist criticism, "ideology" is a crucial focus of the link between material and mental means of production.

Eagleton affirms that, in contrast with Marxist criticism, the allegedly radical movements of structuralism and deconstruction fail to articulate their connections with the material infrastructure. As such, they lapse into an effective, if sometimes unintended, complicity with ruling ideologies (*LT*, 141). In a later work, *After Theory*, he suggests that we need to return in some respects to a "plain realism." He cautions that

> If cultural theory is to engage with an ambitious global history, it must have answerable resources of its own, equal in depth and scope to the situation it confronts. It cannot afford simply to keep on recounting the same narratives of class, race and gender, indispensable as these topics are.[4]

Psychoanalysis

Like Marxist criticism, psychoanalysis has its roots in the nineteenth century, and has interacted richly with many streams of poststructuralist thought. The psychology of literature is hardly a new concern: ever since Aristotle, critics, rhetoricians, and philosophers have examined the psychological dimensions of literature, ranging from an author's motivation and intentions to the effect of texts and performances on an audience. The application of psychoanalytic principles to the study of literature, however, is a relatively recent phenomenon, initiated primarily by Freud and, in other directions, by Alfred Adler and Carl Jung. The notion of the "unconscious" can be found in many thinkers prior to Freud, notably in some of the Romantics such as Schlegel, in Schopenhauer, and in Nietzsche. Freud's fundamental contribution was to open up the entire realm of the unconscious to systematic study, and to provide a language and terminology in which the operations of the unconscious could be expressed.

To view the unconscious as the ultimate source and explanation of human thought and behavior represents a radical disruption of the main streams of Western thought which, since Aristotle, had held that man was essentially a rational being, capable of making free choices in the spheres of intellection and morality. To say that the unconscious governs our behavior is to problematize all of the notions on which philosophy, theology, and even literary criticism have conventionally rested: the ideal of self-knowledge, the ability to know others, the capacity to make moral judgments, the belief that we can act according to reason, that we can overcome our passions and instincts, the ideas of moral and political agency, intentionality, and the notion – held for centuries – that literary creation can be a rational process. In a sense, Freud postulated that we bear a form of "otherness" within ourselves: we cannot claim fully to comprehend even ourselves, why we act as we do, why we make certain moral and political decisions, why we harbor given religious dispositions and intellectual orientations. Even when we think we are acting from a given motive, we may be deluding ourselves; and much of our thought and action is not freely determined by us but driven by unconscious forces which we can barely fathom. Far from being based on reason, our thinking is intimately dependent upon the body, upon its instincts of survival and aggression, as well as obstinate features that cannot be dismissed (as they are in the Cartesian tradition where the mind is treated as a disembodied phenomenon) such as its size, color, gender, and social situation. This unbalancing of conventional notions extends to literature: we cannot presume that our conscious purposes represent our true aim, nor that language is a transparent medium of communication, of either thought or emotion.

Freud was aware of the problematic nature of language itself, its opaqueness and materiality, its resistance to clarity and its refusal to be reduced to any one-dimensional "literal" meaning. Some of his major concepts, such the Oedipus complex, were founded on literary models such as *Oedipus Rex* and *Hamlet*. Freud's own literary analyses tend to apply his models of dream interpretation to literary texts. Subsequent psychologists and literary critics have extended the field of psychoanalytic criticism to encompass: analysis of the motives of an author, of readers, and of fictional characters; relating a text to features of the author's biography such as childhood memories and relationship to parents; the nature of the creative process; the psychology of readers' responses to literary texts; interpretation of symbols in a text, to unearth latent meanings; analysis of the connections between various authors in a literary tradition; examination of gender roles and stereotypes; and the functioning of language in the constitution of the conscious and unconscious. What underlies nearly all of these endeavors is the perception of a broad analogy, fostered by Freud himself, between the psychoanalytic process and the production of a narrative. In a sense, the psychoanalyst himself creates a fiction: triggered by a patient's neurosis and recollection of traumatic events, the psychoanalyst creates a coherent narrative about the patient within which the traumatic event can take its place and be understood.

After Freud, psychoanalytic criticism was continued by his biographer Ernest Jones, whose book *Hamlet and Oedipus* (1948) interpreted Hamlet's indecisive behavior in killing his uncle Claudius in terms of his ambivalent feelings toward his mother. Another of Freud's disciples, Otto Rank, produced *The Myth of the Birth of the Hero* (1909), which reaffirmed Freud's notions of the artist producing fantasies of wish fulfillment, and which compiled numerous myths on subjects such as incest, and on the notion of the hero. Ella Freeman Sharpe (1875–1947) treated language and metaphor from a psychoanalytic perspective. Marie Bonaparte (1882–1962) wrote a large study of Edgar Allen Poe, attributing much of his creative disposition to the loss of his mother when he was a child. Melanie Klein (1882–1960) modified the Freudian theory of sexuality, rejecting the primacy of the Oedipus complex and elaborating a theory of the drives.

The influence of psychoanalysis has extended into nearly all dimensions of modern literary theory. I. A. Richards, William Empson, Lionel Trilling, Kenneth Burke, and Edmund Wilson all in various ways searched texts for latent content. Harold Bloom's influential theory of literary influence as mediated through "anxiety" drew upon Freud's account of the Oedipus complex. Simon O. Lesser (1909–1979) furnished a psychoanalytic account of the reading process. Influenced by Lesser, Norman Holland (b. 1927) used ego psychology and the notion of the literary text as fantasy to elaborate his version of reader-response criticism, studying the manner in which texts appeal to the repressed fantasies of readers. Feminist critics such as Juliet Mitchell have used Freud's ideas in their explanations of the operations of patriarchy; others, such as Kristeva, have modified his notions in their analyses of language and gender. Members of the Frankfurt School of Marxist thinkers, such as Herbert Marcuse, have enlisted Freudian concepts in their analyses of mass culture and ideology. Other significant theorists include Norman O. Brown (b. 1913), D. W. Winnicott, Gilles Deleuze, and Félix Guattari, who have explored the ideological bases of psychoanalysis, and Jacques Lacan. The following account of Freud's own literary analyses places them in the context of his theories as a whole.

Sigmund Freud (1856–1939)

Sigmund Freud was born to Jewish parents in Moravia, in a small town in what is now called the Czech Republic.[5] His father was somewhat aloof and authoritarian while his mother was a warmer and more accessible figure. When Freud first began his medical studies at the University of Vienna in 1873 he found himself somewhat excluded from the academic community and looked down upon, on account of his Jewish origins. He saw this period, where he was forced into the role of outsider, as furnishing the foundation for his independence of thought. We can briefly look at some of the important themes in Freud's work. Among these are *repression*, whereby thoughts and impulses which are viewed as alarming, painful, or shameful are expunged or repressed from the conscious memory. Freud also pioneered the notion of *infantile sexuality*: contravening conventional notions of childhood innocence, he viewed normal adult sexual life as the result of a long development of the sexual function in an individual since infancy. Perhaps the most important of Freud's notions was the *Oedipus complex*: after the first stage of auto-eroticism, the first love-object for both sexes is the mother, who is not yet perceived as distinct from the child's own body. As infancy progresses, sexual development undergoes the Oedipus complex: the boy focuses his sexual wishes upon his mother and develops hostile impulses toward his father. At this stage, Freud thought that girls underwent an analogous development but his views on this changed drastically. Under the threat of castration, the male child represses its desire for the mother and accepts the rules laid down by the father. Again in the face of established beliefs, Freud saw the constitution of the human being as "innately bisexual." Only later was sexuality differentiated in terms of gender, children being initially unclear as to the differences between the sexes. Freud's continuing observations led him to believe that the Oedipus complex was both the climax of infantile sexual life and the foundation of all the later developments of sexuality.

Freud extended the meaning of sexuality to encompass not merely genital satisfaction but a broader bodily function, having pleasure as its goal and only subsequently serving a reproductive function. Sexuality now encompassed all of the emotions of affection and friendliness traditionally subsumed under the word "love" (*Freud*, 23). Freud hoped thereby to foster a greater understanding of sexuality, since it was so restricted in Western civilization, where object-choice is narrowed to allow only the opposite sex and where there is basically one standard of sexual life for all (*Freud*, 746).

Also central to Freud's work is his interpretation of dreams, which he claimed psychoanalysis could analyze scientifically. From the associations produced by the dreamer, the analyst could infer a thought-structure, composed of *latent dream-thoughts*. These were expressed not directly but only as translated and distorted into the *manifest* dream, which was composed largely of visual images. In *The Interpretation of Dreams* (1900), Freud argued that the latent dream thoughts are obliged to undergo alteration, a process he called *dream-distortion*, so that the forbidden meaning of the dream is unrecognizable. Freud defined a dream as the disguised fulfillment of a repressed wish (*Freud*, 28). The *dream-work*, or process by which the latent thoughts are converted into the manifest or explicit content of the dream, occurs through a number of functions: *condensation* of the component parts of the preconscious material of the dream; *displacement* of the psychical emphasis of the dream; and *dramatization* of the entire dream by translation into visual images.

Freud's literary analyses   Around 1907 Freud's interests in the implications of psychoanalysis began to extend over the entire domain of culture. He sought to apply psychoanalytic principles to the study of art, religion, and primitive cultures. Even in his earlier work, he had already viewed Sophocles' play *Oedipus Rex* as expressing a "universal law of mental life." He also saw the Oedipus complex as governing the tragedy of *Hamlet*, though he later altered his views on this play. In analyzing Leonardo da Vinci's picture of "The Madonna and Child with St. Anne" (1910), Freud's examination of Leonardo da Vinci's character generated a prototype for psychoanalytic biography. In 1914 he published (anonymously) an acute reading of the "meaning" of Michelangelo's statue of Moses in Rome. Freud never claimed, however, that psychoanalysis could adequately explain the process of artistic creation. In his paper "Dostoevsky and Parricide" (1928), he stated: "Before the problem of the creative artist analysis must, alas, lay down its arms."[6]

We can obtain a sense of Freud's psychoanalytic "literary-critical" procedure by looking at his paper "Creative Writers and Day-Dreaming" (1907). Freud suggests that, like the child who fantasizes, the creative writer engages in a kind of play: "He creates a world of phantasy which he takes very seriously – that is, which he invests with large amounts of emotion – while separating it sharply from reality" (*Freud*, 437). Freud observes that popular stories typically have "a hero who is the centre of interest," a hero who is invulnerable. Through "this revealing characteristic of invulnerability," says Freud, "we can immediately recognize His Majesty the Ego, the hero alike of every day-dream and of every story" (*Freud*, 441). Freud's point here is that the fiction is not a "portrayal of reality" but has all the constituents of a phantasy or daydream: the hero is invulnerable, women invariably fall in love with him, and the other characters in the story are "sharply divided into good and bad" in a manner that contravenes the more subtle variations found in real life (*Freud*, 441). Hence the story expresses a phantasy on the part of the creative writer, who can indulge in this parading and projection of his ego.

Freud surmises that a creative work is "a continuation of, and a substitute for, what was once the play of childhood" (*Freud*, 442). His understanding of play implies a self-created world of language, a language that reconfigures the conventional idioms that are held to express reality; it implies a kind of "return" to a Lacanian imaginary realm of infantile security and satisfying wholeness, where everything is ordered just as we might *wish* it. In this brief paper, Freud opens up a number of literary-critical avenues: the linking of a creative work to an in-depth study of an author's psychology, using a vastly altered conception of human subjectivity; the tracing in art of primal psychological tendencies and conflicts; and the understanding of art and literature as integrally related to deeper, unconscious, impulses that lie hidden in recurring human obsessions, fears and anxieties. Such paths will be further explored by Carl Jung, Northrop Frye, Lacan, and others.

Freud on history and civilization In his later work *Civilization and its Discontents* (1930) Freud situates creative art within the broader contexts of culture and religion. Essentially, the human psyche, frustrated in its attempts to mold the world in a self-comforting image, resorts to art to create its world in phantasy. Art – in a broad sense that includes science, philosophy, and religion – is the embodiment of civilization itself, which is erected on the graveyard of repressed instincts. Freud views religion as a form of mass delusion, which regards "reality as the sole enemy," and encourages a turning away from the world (*Freud*, 732). Indeed, the evolution of civilization is a struggle between *eros* (the life instinct, embodied in sexuality) and *thanatos* (the death instinct, expressed in aggression) (*Freud*, 755–756). Civilization checks both aggression and sexuality by the superego, which internalizes communal moral standards. The authority of the father or of both parents, says Freud, is assumed by the larger human community, hence the demands of an individual's superego will "coincide with the precepts of the prevailing cultural super-ego" (*Freud*, 756–757, 769). The resulting tension between the superego and the ego is characterized by Freud as the sense of guilt (*Freud*, 759).

What Freud gives to, and shares with, much cultural and literary theory is a view of the human self as constructed to a large extent by its environment, as a product of familial and larger social forces; a profound sense of the limitations of reason and of language itself; an intense awareness of the closure effected by conventional systems of thought and behavior, of the severe constraints imposed upon human sexuality; a view of art and religion as issuing from broader patterns of human need; and an acknowledgment that truth-value and moral value are not somehow absolute or universal but are motivated by the economic and ideological demands of civilization. Like Schopenhauer and Nietzsche, Freud has no illusions about where our ideas ultimately derive from: "man's judgments of value follow directly his wishes for happiness – that, accordingly, they are an attempt to support his illusions with arguments" (*Freud*, 771).

Jacques Lacan (1901–1981)

The French psychoanalyst Jacques Lacan used insights furnished by linguistics and structuralism to reformulate Freud's account of the unconscious and his own account of human subjectivity. Lacan's reputation was established by his publication of *Écrits* (1966). His influence has not only extended over the field of psychoanalysis but also reaches into the work of Marxists such as Louis Althusser (whose theories were influenced by Lacan and who, ironically, became Lacan's patient, after which he killed his wife) and feminists such as Julia Kristeva and Jane Gallop, as well as deconstructive thinkers such as Barbara Johnson. Other feminists have reacted strongly against the phallocentric thrust (a not altogether inapt expression) of Lacan's own work.

It may be useful to outline some of Lacan's pivotal views. He posits three orders or states of human mental disposition: the *imaginary* order, the *symbolic* order, and the *real*. The imaginary order is a pre-Oedipal phase where an infant is as yet unable to distinguish itself from its mother's body or to recognize the lines of demarcation between itself and objects in the world; indeed, it does not as yet know itself as a coherent entity or self. Hence, the imaginary phase is one of unity (between the child and its surroundings), as well as of immediate possession (of the mother and objects), a condition of reassuring plenitude, a world consisting wholly of images (hence "imaginary") that is not fragmented or mediated by difference, by categories, in a word, by language and signs. The mirror phase – the point at which the child can recognize itself and its environment in the mirror – marks the point at which this comforting imaginary condition breaks down, pushing the child into the symbolic order which is the world of predefined social roles and gender differences, the world of subjects and objects, the world of language.

In this way, Lacan effectively reformulates in linguistic terms Freud's account of the Oedipus complex. Freud had posited that the infant's desire for its mother is prohibited by the father, who threatens it with castration. Faced with this threat, the infant represses his desire, thereby opening up the dimension of the unconscious, which is for Lacan (and Freud as seen through Lacan) not a "place" but a relation to the social world of law, morality, religion, and conscience. According to Freud, the child internalizes through the father's commands (what Lacan calls the Law of the Father) the appropriate standards of socially acceptable thought and behavior. Freud calls these standards internalized as conscience the child's "superego." The child now identifies with the father, sliding into his own gendered role, in the knowledge that he too is destined for fatherhood. Of course, the repressed desire continues to exert its influence on conscious life.

As Lacan rewrites this process, the child, in passing from the imaginary to the symbolic order, continues to long for the security and wholeness it previously felt: it is now no longer in full possession of its mother and of entities in the world; rather, it is distinguished from them in and through a network of signification. The child's desire, as Lacan explains it, passes in an unceasing movement along an infinite chain of signifiers, in search of unity, security, of ultimate meaning, in an ever elusive signified, and immaturely clings to the fictive notion of unitary selfhood that began in the imaginary phase. The child exists in an alienated condition, its relationships with objects always highly mediated and controlled by social structures at the heart of whose operations is language. For Lacan, the phallus is a privileged signifier, signifying both sexual distinction and its arbitrariness. Lacan never accurately describes the "real": he seems to think of it as what lies beyond the world of signification, perhaps a primordial immediacy of experience prior to language or a chaotic condition of mere thinghood prior to objectivity. For Lacan, the real is the impossible: that which occurs beyond the entire framework of signification. The real is a sign of its own absence, pointing to itself as mere signifier.

Lacan rejects any notion that the mind of either child or adult has any intrinsic psychical unity; it is merely a "subject" rather than a self or ego, merely the occupant of an always moving position in the networks of signification; hence, for Lacan, as he indicates in a famous statement, even "the Unconscious is structured like a language." The unconscious is as much a product of signifying systems, and indeed is itself as much a signifying system, as the conscious mind: both are like language in their openness, their constant deferral of meaning, their susceptibility to changing definition and their constitution as a system of relations (rather than existing as entities in their own right). In Lacan's view, the subject is empty, fluid, and without an axis or center, and is always recreated in his encounter with the other, with what exceeds his own nature and grasp. Influenced by Hegel's master–slave dialectic, as well as by his account of objectivity, Lacan sees the individual's relation to objects as mediated by desire and by struggle. Lacan's extrapolation of what he considered to be the genuine implications of Freud's theories was furthered by the structuralist Marxist Louis Althusser, who adapted Lacan's insights in his account of the workings of the ideological apparatus of the political state, thereby exploring the connections – which are merely latent in Freud – between the unconscious and social structures.

Deconstruction

Jacques Derrida (1930–2004)

The term "poststructuralism" is often identified with "deconstruction," a pervasive phenomenon in modern literary and cultural theory originated by the French thinker Jacques Derrida. While Derrida himself has insisted that deconstruction is not a theory unified by any set of consistent rules or procedures, it has been variously regarded as a way of reading, a mode of writing, and, above all, a way of challenging interpretations of texts based upon conventional notions of the stability of the human self, the external world, and of language and meaning.

Derrida was born in Algeria to a Jewish family and suffered intensely the experience of being an outsider. He studied in France, and then taught in Paris and at various American universities. Derrida's transatlantic influence can be traced to a seminar held at Johns Hopkins University in 1966, where he presented a paper entitled "Structure, Sign, and Play in the Discourse of the Human Sciences." The following year, 1967, marked Derrida's explosive entry onto the international stage of literary and cultural theory, with the publication of his first three books, which included *De la grammatologie* (*Of Grammatology*), whose subject was the "science" of writing, and

L'Écriture et la différence (*Writing and Difference*), which contained important essays on Hegel, Freud, and Michel Foucault. Later works included *La Dissémination* (*Dissemination*) (1972) which included a lengthy engagement with Plato's views of writing and sophistry; *Marges de la philosophie* (*Margins of Philosophy*) (1982), which included essays on Hegel's semiology and the use of metaphor in philosophy; and *Spectres de Marx* (*Specters of Marx*) (1994) which looks at the various legacies of Marx.

The most fundamental project of deconstruction is to display the operations of "logocentrism" in any "text." What is logocentrism? Etymologically and historically, this term refers to any system of thought which is founded on the stability and authority of the *Logos*, the divine Word. The scholar C. H. Dodd explains that in its ancient Greek philosophical and Judeo-Christian meaning, the *Logos* referred both to the Word of God which created the universe and to the rational order of creation itself.[7] In other words, it is in the spoken *Logos* that language and reality ultimately coincide, in an identity that is invested with absolute authority, absolute origin, and absolute purpose or teleology. If we think of the orders of language and reality as follows, it is clear that one of the functions of the *Logos* is to preserve the stability and closure of the entire system:

LOGOS

Language		*Reality*
Signifier 1 -*a*- Signified 1	—————**b**—————	Object 1
Signifier 2 – Signified 2	—————————————	Object 2
Signifier 3 – Signified 3	—————————————	Object 3
Signifier 4 – Signified 4	—————————————	Object 4
	Ad Infinitum	

It is because the *Logos* holds together the orders of language and reality that the relation between signifier (word) and signified (concept), i.e., relation *a*, is stable and fixed; so too is relation *b*, the connection between the sign as a whole and the object to which it refers in the world. For example, in a Christian scheme, the signifier "love" might refer to the concept of "self-sacrifice" in relation to God. And this sign as a whole, the word "love" as meaning "self-sacrifice," would refer to object 1 which might be a system of social or ecclesiastical relationships institutionally embodied in a given society, enshrining the ideal of self-sacrifice. In other words, the meaning of "love" is sanctioned by a hierarchy of authority, stretching back through institutional Church practice, theology, philosophy, as well as political and economic theory, to the authority of the scriptures and the Word of God Himself. In the same way, all of the other signifiers and signifieds in language would be constrained in their significance, making for a stable and closed system. The *Logos* thereby authorizes an entire world view, sanctioned by a theological and philosophical system and by an entire political, religious, and social order.

If, now, the *Logos* is *removed* from this picture, what happens? The entire order will become destabilized; historically, of course, this disintegration does not happen all at once but takes centuries, as indeed does the undermining of the *Logos*. Once the *Logos* vanishes from the picture, there is nothing to hold together the orders of language and reality, which now threaten to fly apart from each other. The relations *a* and *b* both become destabilized: if we are not constrained by a Christian perspective, we might attribute *other* meanings to the word "love," meanings which may even conflict with the previously given Christian signification. Moreover, various groups might give different meanings to the word so that a general consensus is lost. In this way, signifier 1 may be defined by a meaning attributed to signified 1. But since there is no authoritative closure to this process, it could go on ad infinitum: signified 1 will itself need to be defined, and so this signified will itself become a signifier of something else; this process might regress indefinitely so that we never arrive at a conclusive signified but are always moving along an endless chain of signifiers. Derrida attributes the name of "metaphor" to this endless substitution of one signifier for another: in describing or attempting to understand our world, we can no longer use "literal" language, i.e., language that actually describes the object or reality. We can only use metaphor, hence language in its very nature is metaphorical. Hence there cannot be a sharp distinction between, say, the spheres of philosophy and science, on the one hand, which are often presumed to use a "literal" language based on reason, and literature and the arts, on the other hand, which are characterized as using metaphorical and figurative language in a manner inaccessible to reason.

Logocentrism takes a variety of guises: for example, the stabilizing function of the *Logos* might be replaced by Plato's Forms, the Aristotelian notion of "substance," or Hegel's "absolute idea." Modern equivalents in Western society might be concepts such as freedom or democracy. All of these terms function as what Derrida calls "transcendental signifieds," or concepts invested with absolute authority, which places them beyond questioning or examination. An important endeavor of deconstruction, then, is to bring back these various transcendental signifieds within the province of language and textuality, within the province of their relatability to other concepts.

Hence, in one sense, the most fundamental project of deconstruction is to reinstate *language* within the dualisms that have conventionally dominated Western thought: the connections between thought and reality, self and world, subject and object. In deconstructive thought, these connections are not viewed as already existing prior to language, with language merely being the instrument of their expression or representation. Rather, all of these terms are linguistic to begin with: they are enabled by language. We do not simply have thought which is then expressed by language; thought takes place in, and is made possible by, language. This deconstructive view of language is partly influenced by Saussure's notion of language as a system of relations; the terms which are related have no independent meaning; they *depend* on their relations with other terms for their significance. Also implicit in this view of language is the arbitrary and conventional nature of the sign: there is no natural connection between the sign "table" and an actual table in the world. Moreover, there is no "truth" or "reality" which somehow stands outside or behind language: truth is a relation of linguistic terms, and reality is a construct, ultimately religious, social, political, and economic, but always of language, of various linguistic registers. Even the human self, in this view, has no pregiven essence but is a linguistic construct or narrative. Derrida's much-quoted statement that "il n'y a pas de hors-texte," often translated as "there is no outside of the text," means precisely this: that the aforementioned features of language, which together comprise "textuality," are all-embracing; textuality governs all interpretative operations. For example, there is no history outside of language or textuality: history itself is a linguistic and textual construct. At its deepest level, the insistence on viewing language (as a system of relations and differences) as lying at the core of any world view issues a challenge to the notion of *identity*, installed at the heart of Western metaphysics since Aristotle.

An important deconstructive strategy is the undermining of certain oppositions which have enjoyed a privileged place in Western metaphysics. Derrida points out that oppositions, such as those between intellect and sense, soul and body, master and slave, male and female, inside and outside, center and margin, do not represent a state of equivalence between two terms. Rather, each of these oppositions is a "violent hierarchy" in which one term has been conventionally subordinated. Intellect, for example, has usually been superordinated over sense; soul has been exalted above body; male has been defined as superior in numerous respects to female. Perhaps the most significant opposition for Derrida is that between speech and writing. According to Derrida, Western philosophy has privileged speech over writing, viewing speech as embodying an immediate presence of meaning, and writing as a mere substitute or secondary representation of the spoken word.

For Derrida, "writing" designates all of the differences by which language is constituted. Writing refers to the diffusion of identity (of self, object, signifier, signified) through a vast network of relations and differences. Writing expresses the movement of difference itself. In an attempt to subvert the conventional priority of speech over writing, Derrida coins the term *différance*, which embodies an ambivalence in the French word *différer* which can mean both "to differ" and "to defer" in time. Hence Derrida adds a temporal dimension to the notion of difference. Moreover, the substitution of *a* for *e* in the word différance cannot be *heard* in French: it is a silent displacement that can only be discerned in writing, as if to counter the superior value previously accorded to speech. The terms that recur in Derrida's texts – their meanings often changing according to contexts – are usually related to the extended significance that Derrida accords to "writing." Such terms include "trace," "supplement," "text," "presence," "absence," and "play."

The privileging of speech over writing has perpetuated what Derrida calls a "metaphysics of presence," an assumption that meaning is always stable and immediately present, effecting a closure and disabling any "free play" of thought which might threaten or question this structure of meaning. Another way of explaining the term "metaphysics of presence" might be as follows: an entity's content is viewed as coinciding completely with its existence. For example, an isolated entity such as a piece of chalk would be regarded as having its meaning completely within itself, completely in its immediate "presence." Even if the rest of the world did not exist, we could say what the piece of chalk was, what its function and constitution were. Such absolute self-containment of meaning must be sanctioned by a higher authority, a *Logos* or transcendental signified, which ensured that all things in the world had specific and designated meanings. If, however, we were to challenge such a "metaphysics of presence," we might argue that in fact the meaning of the chalk does *not* coincide with, and is not confinable within, its immediate existence; that its meaning and purpose actually lie in relations that extend far beyond its immediate existence; its meaning would depend, for example, upon the concept of a "blackboard" on which it was designed to write; in turn, the relationship of chalk and blackboard derives its meaning from increasingly broader contexts, such as a classroom, an institution of learning, associated industries and technologies, as well as political and educational programs. Hence the meaning of "chalk" would extend through a vast network of relations far beyond the actual isolated existence of that item. In this sense, the chalk is *not* self-identical since its identity is *dispersed* through its relations with numerous other objects and concepts. Viewed in this light, "chalk" is not a name for a self-subsistent, self-enclosed entity; rather it names the provisional focal point of a complex set of relations. It can be seen, then, that a metaphysics of "presence" refers to the *self-presence*, the immediate presence, of meaning, as resting on a complete self-identity that is sanctioned and preserved by the "presence" of a *Logos*.

A deconstructive reading of a text, as practiced by Derrida, will be a multifaceted project: in general, it will attempt to display logocentric operations in the text, by focusing on a close reading of the text's language, its use of presuppositions or transcendental signifieds, its reliance on binary oppositions, its self-contradictions, its *aporiai* or points of conceptual impasse, and the ways in which it effects closure and resists free play. Derrida's engagement with the history of Western thought is not one of mere critique but also one of inevitable complicity (where he is obliged to use the very terms he impugns). This dual gesture must necessarily entail play on words, convolution of language that accommodates its fluid nature, and divergence from conventional norms of essayistic writing. It might also be argued that the very form of his texts, not merely their content, is integral to his overall project.

Derrida's American disciples included the Yale critics Paul de Man, J. Hillis Miller, and Geoffrey Hartman, as well as Barbara Johnson, who applied and richly extended deconstructive techniques. Derrida's own thought is nonetheless open to a number of substantive criticisms. His notion of "difference" – a concept treated far more articulately by Hegel – effectively abolishes all historical specificity. It simply abstracts into its own self-identical structure all the endless variety of true historical relation; it dissolves actual relations into a principle of abstract relationality. For Derrida, *différance* is effectively elevated to the status of a transcendental signified. Given that this notion underlies Derrida's critiques of philosophical systems which vary widely from one another, it is evident that he coerces all of these systems into a uniform assailability: they all suffer from the same defects, the same kinds of *aporiai* or impasses. And it is only against a simplistic and positivistic understanding of truth, meaning, presence, and subjectivity that his notions of trace, difference, and writing can articulate themselves.

Finally, there has been a tendency to overestimate Derrida's originality. The relational and arbitrary nature of language has been perceived by many thinkers, ranging from Hellenistic philosophers and rhetoricians through Locke and Hume to Hegel, Marx, the French symbolists, and Saussure. The notions that "reality" is a construction, that "truth" is an interpretation, that human subjectivity is not essentially fixed, and that there are no ultimate transcendent foundations of our thought and practice are as old as the Sophists of Athens in the fifth century BC. Many of the *aporiai* "revealed" by Derrida were encountered as such long ago by the neo-Hegelian philosophers. We can indeed benefit from a detailed reading of Derrida's texts, one which situates them in a balanced manner within the history of thought rather than merely using them as a privileged lens to view that history.

Notes

1. Terry Eagleton, *Against the Grain: Essays 1975–1985* (London: New Left Books, 1986), pp. 81–82.
2. Terry Eagleton, *Walter Benjamin or Towards a Revolutionary Criticism* (London: New Left Books, 1981), p. 97.
3. Terry Eagleton, *Literary Theory: An Introduction* (Oxford and Minnesota: Blackwell/University of Minnesota Press, 1983), p. 211. Hereafter cited as *LT*.

4. Terry Eagleton, *After Theory* (Harmondsworth: Allen Lane and Penguin, 2003), pp. 221–222.
5. This treatment of Freud's life is based on his own account, "An Autobiographical Study" (1925), in *The Freud Reader*, ed. Peter Gay (New York and London: W. W. Norton, 1989). Hereafter cited as *Freud*.
6. Quoted by Peter Gay in *Freud*, p. 444.
7. C. H. Dodd, *The Interpretation of the Fourth Gospel* (Cambridge: Cambridge University Press, 1953), pp. 284–285.

Chapter 17

The Era of Poststructuralism (II): Postmodernism, Modern Feminism, Gender Studies

The term "postmodernism" resonates in at least three registers: firstly, in the context of historical development, it appears as "postmodernity," designating the latest phase in the broad evolution of capitalist economics and culture, especially since the later part of the twentieth century. This historical phenomenon has generated two further registers: that of postmodern theory, which has attempted to account for and explain it; and that of literature and art, which has variously attempted to express it. In the sphere of literary and cultural theory, the terms "postmodern" and "postmodernism" have been applied to the works of numerous writers, such as Jacques Derrida, Julia Kristeva, and Michel Foucault, who have also been labeled "poststructuralist." Postmodernism might be viewed as a broader phenomenon, one of whose manifestations is poststructuralism. Alternatively, the two terms might be viewed as two perspectives from which to view the history of modern literary and cultural criticism. The major theorists of postmodernism have included Jean-François Lyotard, Jean Baudrillard, and Georges Bataille, whose work enjoyed a revival in the 1960s. Left-wing perspectives on postmodernism have been offered by Jürgen Habermas, Fredric Jameson, and Terry Eagleton. Finally, in the register of literature and art, "postmodernism" has been used by critics such as Ihab Hassan to distinguish the experimental literature produced after World War II from the high modernism of the period roughly between 1910 and 1930. We can now briefly look at each of these three senses of the postmodern.

In the register of historical development, postmodernity designates a society and culture that has evolved beyond the phases of industrial and finance capitalism. This society is often called consumer capitalism, a phase characterized by the global extension of capitalist markets, mass migration of labor, the predominating role of mass media and images, unprecedented economic and cultural interaction between various parts of the world, and an unprecedented pluralism and diversity at all levels of culture. According to

Literary Criticism from Plato to the Present: An Introduction   M. A. R. Habib
© 2011 M. A. R. Habib

many of the theorists of postmodernism, this contemporary social order is no longer based on, or even attempts to pursue, the Enlightenment ideals of progress and justice based on universal reason, a notion of human subjectivity as autonomous, and of the world as knowable (and conquerable) by scientific and technological advance. Rather, the external world is viewed as an ideological construction, refracted through an endlessly circulating world of signs, through media images and the various technologies and institutional codes (of school, workplace, religious centers) that hold us in their sway. Even subjectivity itself is regarded as a product of power structures; power is no longer viewed as an isolable and centralized agency that dominates or coerces subjects that are already there: rather, it is intimately involved in the very production of subjectivities which are then conditioned to regulate themselves. Just as the worlds of objective reality and unified autonomous subjectivity have been dissolved, dissipated through the linguistic and social structures and semiotic codes that ultimately form and define them, so too the conventional worlds of morality and culture are viewed as without absolute foundations and grounded in human desire, material need, a libidinal economy, and self-projection. Reason itself is viewed as integral to capitalism, as coercive and exclusive, a faculty used to label alternative visions as mad or irrational; even the category of "experience" as used by the bourgeois philosophers has become suspect, as well as their understanding of fundamental notions such as space and time. Many radical critics entering the debates over postmodernism no longer hold the conventional Marxist view of the economic infrastructure and class struggle as the ultimate determinants of social development: instead, language, images, and the entire cultural sphere are all viewed as crucial to the social and political order, with economics reduced to one of several determinative elements in a complex of causes. In this scenario, literature and art are given a high role in impugning the existing orders of capitalism. Culture itself becomes viewed as a site of ideological struggle. Some Marxists, however, would argue that Marxism itself comprehends the interaction of cultural and economic elements, and that the subsumption of economics into the cultural sphere or superstructure – a kind of "superstructuralism" which collapses the terms of conventional Marxist analysis – is itself an ideological strategy of late capitalism.

In general, postmodern and postmodernism denote a contemporary economic and cultural situation, and a series of perspectives, where the major grand narratives of the recent past – such as the progress of humanity toward knowledge and freedom – no longer command credibility, and lie in ruins. The universal has given way to the local, identity has yielded to difference, depth (the notion of an underlying reality) has given way to a world of surfaces or mere appearances, and reality is submerged in, and indeed defined by, a world of signs. What has been called the "crisis of representation" – the inability of language to represent reality – reverberates through all of these positions. And all of these positions are shared by postmodernism and poststructuralism. We might add that this so-called crisis – like most of the "crises" identified by poststructuralism – is hardly new; it was recognized by Locke and the bourgeois philosophers, including Hegel and the neo-Hegelian philosophers such Bradley and Bosanquet. The reaffirmation of such crises highlights the roots (*radices*) of these "radical" modes of thought in the liberal humanist tradition, in the very mode of their reaction against which they reveal themselves as variants, at once gesturally subversive and substantively complicit.

The third register of postmodernism, that of literature and the arts, can be dealt with briefly here. The work of the high modernists, such as Proust, Joyce, T. S. Eliot, Pound, Virginia Woolf, Kafka, and Brecht, was characterized by a number of underlying assumptions: a recognition of the complex nature of reality and experience, of the role of time and memory in human perception, of the self and world as historical constructions, and, underlying all of these, the problematic nature of language. In terms of style, the modernists engaged in a breakdown of narrative structures and conventional poetic forms, the use of allusion, parody, hyperbole, collage, and pastiche. Postmodernism, as expressed in the writings of Beckett, Robbe-Grillet, Borges, Marquez, Naguib Mahfouz, and Angela Carter, also rests on the same assumptions and exhibits the same characteristics.

What, then, is the difference between modernism and postmodernism? We can perhaps identify three salient features which differentiate them. Firstly, postmodernism – in both subject matter and style – is marked by a recognition of ethnic, sexual, and cultural diversity. Whereas modernist texts like Conrad's *Heart of Darkness* could only describe the other (in this case, Africans) from the outside, postmodernist works tend to give the other a voice, to analyze cultural difference from within (as in the work of Mahfouz). Secondly, whereas high modernism (with exceptions such as Brecht) prided itself on its highbrow status and learned allusions, postmodernism – with equal self-consciousness – deliberately extends into the domain of popular culture, abrogating distinctions between high and low art, and indeed often attempting to expose the structures of cultural coercion and domination. T. S. Eliot's "The Love Song of J. Alfred Prufrock" may subvert the form and content of a love song and exhibit the painful, unidealized nature of love in the modern world; but some later poets from the Indian subcontinent such as N. M. Rashed and Kishwar Naheed express a colonial condition where the very possibility of love is withered.

Finally, postmodernist writing unabashedly exhibits difference, diversity, incoherence, and a world of surfaces, with no attempt to subsume these under identity, a framework of coherence or depth, or any vision of implied unity. Heterogeneity is presented as irreducible, recalcitrant to any form of redintegration. With modernism, difference is still rooted in identity, experimentation in tradition, and relativism in the memory of various absolutes. Even stylistic innovations such as free verse or disruptions of narrative were haunted by the ghosts of the forms that lurked behind them. T. S. Eliot's *The Waste Land*, supposedly an expression of a fragmented world marooned from the past, relies heavily on allusions which point to a retrospective unity in traditional forms of life; Joyce's *Ulysses* insinuates a coherence in its use of the *Odyssey* as an implied background. But a postmodernist work such as Beckett's *Waiting for Godot* exhibits no structure in its allusions, which are random and repetitive, and where the "action" of the play defies the very category of action (and of the dramatic unities) and its location is entirely abstract and unnameable. The only possible modes of coherence are those that the reader or audience might impose, bringing to bear their own assumptions and effectively writing or rewriting the play themselves. Where modernism is nostalgic and retrospective toward vanished schemes of unity and order, postmodernism insists on the heterogeneity of the present. We can now look briefly at some of the major theorists of postmodernism, beginning with a thinker whose opposition to postmodernism inspired much debate.

Jürgen Habermas (b. 1929)

The work of the German philosopher and sociologist Jürgen Habermas has spanned social theory, the genesis of capitalism, and the meanings of democracy, rationality, and law. He is best known for his account of the "public sphere" or the elements of the public world not directly under state control but open to the exchange of private opinion, as in the various levels of media, religious organizations, and social gatherings. Though he was for some time associated with the Frankfurt School of Marxist social and cultural theory, the main impetus of Habermas' work has been a defense of modern liberal democracy and its theorization in the Enlightenment ideals of reason, justice, progress, and freedom. Against poststructuralist opponents who claim that reason is relative, coercive, and exclusive, he formulates a notion of "communicative reason," of a rationality grounded in the very process of communication, on the basis of which "communicative action" will be possible.

In a lecture of 1980 entitled "Modernity – An Incomplete Project" (later published as "Modernity Versus Postmodernity"), Habermas observes that the Enlightenment philosophers saw the arts and sciences as promoting understanding of the world, the self, moral progress, and justice.[1] But since the mid-nineteenth century, art has become regarded as increasingly autonomous and devoid of reference to any real world, immersed rather in self-reference. This tendency reaches new intensity in poststructuralism

(*MP*, 133). We can remedy this situation, says Habermas, only by redintegrating the aesthetic with the cognitive and the moral-practical (*MP*, 134). We should reject the exclusive focus on aesthetic concerns which excludes consideration of truth and justice, and which tempts us, mistakenly, to denounce the surviving Enlightenment tradition as rooted in a "terroristic reason" (*MP*, 135).

Jean Baudrillard (1929–2007)

The sociologist Jean Baudrillard has sometimes been called the high priest or prophet of postmodernism. Baudrillard was teaching at the University of Paris at Nanterre in 1968, and so was at the heart of the student unrest and revolt of that era, a phenomenon which (largely through its failure) deeply influenced his outlook. His early work, such as *The System of Objects* (1968) and *The Consumer Society* (1970), was broadly Marxist in orientation. But a further study, *The Mirror of Production* (1973), was highly critical of Marx, viewing his analysis of capital as insufficiently radical and trapped within the very categories of capitalism (such as "production"). This criticism was continued in Baudrillard's own assessment of capitalist economics in *Symbolic Exchange and Death* (1976), and subsequent collections such as *Simulations* (1983).

The underlying theme running through Baudrillard's analyses of modern culture and society is that "reality" has in the late capitalist era been replaced by codes of signification. What we are witnessing now is a "precession of simulacra," a series of images which do not even claim to represent reality but offer themselves in its place: "Simulation . . . is the generation by models of a real without origin or reality: a hyperreal." What we have inherited is the "desert of the real itself."[2] And with this has also disappeared the entire subject matter of metaphysics, its quest to define reality (*S.*, 3). There is no longer a question of imitating or even parodying reality: "it is rather a question of substituting signs of the real for the real itself" (*S.*, 4). A perfect model of such simulation is Disneyland, which exists to conceal the fact that it is the real, infantilized, America which is Disneyland: America itself is "no longer real, but of the order of the hyperreal and of simulation" (*S.*, 23–25). The tendencies Baudrillard describes are even more pronounced today: the infantilism has deepened its grip to all kinds of game shows, cartoon movies whose audience is just as much adults as children, and, indeed, the manufacture of entire political and social visions through the news media, in their coverage of war, other nations, education, and a host of social and ethical issues.

In *The System of Objects* Baudrillard argues that the ideology of competition has shifted from the sphere of production to the sphere of consumption.[3] The "philosophers of consumption," such as Dichter and Martineau, claim that this "new humanism" of consumption offers individuals an opportunity for fulfillment and liberation, and the ability to feel moral even as they indulge in a hedonistic morality, even as they regress to childlike and irrational behavior, thereby releasing drives that were blocked by guilt, superego, or taboo (*SO*, 185). In industrial society, it is the system of objects (not human relations or needs) that imposes its own coherence on and structures an entire society (*SO*, 188).

Jean-François Lyotard (1924–1998)

Like Baudrillard, Jean-François Lyotard was at the University of Nanterre during the student revolt of 1968, and he was also an activist against French imperialism in Algeria. He deeply opposed Jürgen Habermas' sanction of the project of Enlightenment, universal reason, and modernity. Lyotard's reaction against Marxism in *Starting from Marx and Freud* (1973) expressed the misgivings of much poststructuralist thought toward Marxist categories of analysis. For example, Lyotard saw the function of social class as displaced by modern technocratic and bureaucratic regimes. He saw capitalism and totalitarianism as suppressing what he called the "libidinal economy" of desire, and saw the task of experimental art as revolutionary in releasing desire. Lyotard is perhaps best known for his work *The Postmodern Condition* (1979). In the preface to this, he suggests that the term "postmodern" designates the state of our culture after the transformation of the sciences, literature, and the arts since the end of the nineteenth century.[4] Modern science, he says, needs to legitimate its own rules by a discourse of legitimation, a metadiscourse which appeals to some "grand narrative," such as the emancipation of the human subject in terms of reason or economics, or the creation of wealth (he sees the two modern grand narratives as liberal humanism and Marxism). These came out of the Enlightenment narrative of rationality which Lyotard views as coercive. Indeed, he defines postmodern as "incredulity toward metanarratives." Postmodern knowledge, Lyotard suggests, "is not simply a tool of the authorities; it refines our sensitivity to differences and reinforces our ability to tolerate the incommensurable" (*PC*, xxv). Lyotard suggests that the postmodern artist is like a philosopher, seeking new foundations. In fact, a work can become modern only by first being postmodern: it must break the rules and seek a new grounding (*PC*, 77–81).

In another article called "Defining the Postmodern," Lyotard characterizes modernity in general as a principle of breaking with the past and beginning "a new way of living and thinking." He cites three attributes of postmodernity. Firstly, it no longer appeals to "the idea of progress," and in terms of style it employs bricolage or collections of quotations from previous styles and periods.[5] A second feature is loss of belief in the idea that the arts, technology, and liberty can be profitable to mankind as a whole ("DP," 2). Finally, it is expressed in literature and art by an investigation of the foundations and presuppositions of modernity itself ("DP," 3).

bell hooks (Gloria Jean Watkins; b. 1952)

Another important critique of postmodern theory has issued from African-American critics such as Cornel West and bell hooks, who have observed that, for all its emphasis on difference, postmodern theory has ignored the work of black writers and intellectuals. hooks (who writes her name in lower case to direct emphasis to the substance of her books rather than her self) is a feminist scholar and activist who has produced much work on the intersections of gender, race, and class. In her essay "Postmodern Blackness," hooks argues that postmodernist discourses have been exclusionary and are dominated by white male voices.[6] A radical postmodernist practice should incorporate the voices of oppressed blacks, and the politics of difference should be integrated with the politics of racism (*RGCP*, 25). Postmodernism's critique of identity politics comes at a time when black people are just coming to consciousness of their identity, and are in the process of forming a radical black subjectivity (*RGCP*, 28).

hooks stresses that postmodernity is a social and economic condition. She observes that even in the era of postmodernity the collective African-American condition is one of "continued displacement, profound alienation, and despair" (*RGCP*, 26). This hopelessness creates a "yearning" which, at its profoundest, is a "longing for critical voice," intensified by postmodern deconstruction of master narratives (*RGCP*, 27). Hence, postmodernism's critique of essentialism can be useful to black studies in a number of ways: by promoting the notion of multiple black identities and experiences, by resisting colonial paradigms of a monolithic black identity, and by seeing the connections of race with issues such as class mobility. In general, the critique of essentialism needs to be harmonized with an emphasis on the "authority of experience" (*RGCP*, 29).

Modern Feminism

Like most critical tendencies since the 1960s, modern feminism is distinguished from its precursors by having been forged in the same fire as much poststructuralist thought, questioning fixed and stable notions of gender, sexuality, and even the category of "woman." It has, moreover, moved into further areas of inquiry such as the connections of gender with class and race, power structures, the semiotic codes through which ideology operates, and the construction of subjectivity itself. The rich flowering of feminist thinking in America, Britain, and France, each with its specific areas of emphasis, can be considered in the following sections.

American feminism

Feminist criticism in America received a major stimulus from the civil rights movement of the 1960s, and has differed somewhat in its concerns from its counterparts in France and Britain. A seminal work, *The Feminine Mystique* (1963), was authored by Betty Friedan, who subsequently founded the National Organization of Women in 1966. This book expressed the fundamental grievance of middle-class American women, their entrapment within private, domestic life and their inability to pursue public careers. A number of other important feminist texts were produced around this time: Mary Ellman's *Thinking About Women* (1968), Kate Millett's *Sexual Politics* (1969), Germaine Greer's *The Female Eunuch* (1970), and Shulamith Firestone's *The Dialectic of Sex* (1970), which used gender rather than class as the prime category of historical analysis. Millett's influential book concerned female sexuality and the representation of women in literature. It argued that patriarchy was a political institution; it also distinguished between the concept of "sex," which was rooted in biology, and that of "gender," which was culturally acquired. Other critics examining masculine portrayals of women included Carolyn Heilbrun and Judith Fetterly.

A number of feminist texts have attempted to identify alternative and neglected traditions of female writing. These have included Patricia Meyer Spacks' *The Female Imagination* (1975), Ellen Moers' *Literary Women* (1976), and Sandra Gilbert and Susan Gubar's *The Madwoman in the Attic* (1979). The most influential work of this kind was Elaine Showalter's *A Literature of their Own* (1977), which traced three phases of women's writing, a "feminine" phase (1840–1880) where women writers imitated male models, a "feminist" phase (1880–1920) during which women challenged those models and their values, and a "female" phase (from 1920) which saw women advocating their own perspectives. Recent debates within American feminism, conducted by figures such as Showalter, Lillian Robinson, Annette Kolodny, and Jane Marcus, have concerned the relationship of female writers to male theories, the need for feminist theory and a female language, the relation of feminism to poststructuralist perspectives, as well as continuing problems of political and educational activism.

A notable recent development has been the attempt to think through feminism from black and minority perspectives, as in Alice Walker's

In Search of Our Mothers' Gardens (1983) and Barbara Smith's *Toward a Black Feminist Criticism* (1977).

British feminism

Much British feminist criticism has had a political orientation, situating both feminist concerns and literary texts within a material and ideological context. In her landmark work *Women: The Longest Revolution* (1966), later expanded into *Women's Estate* (1971), Juliet Mitchell examined patriarchy in terms of Marxist categories of production and private property as well as psychoanalytic theories of gender. Her later works, such as *Psychoanalysis and Feminism* (1974), continue to refine her attempt to integrate the insights of Marxism and psychoanalysis. Another seminal text was Michèle Barrett's *Women's Oppression Today: Problems in Marxist Feminist Analysis* (1980), which attempted to formulate a materialist aesthetics and integrated Marxist class analysis with feminism in analyzing and influencing gender representation.[7] She focuses on three concepts that have been central to the Marxist–feminist dialogue: patriarchy, reproduction, and ideology. According to Barrett, the most significant elements of the oppression of women under capitalism are "the economic organization of households and its accompanying familial ideology, the division of labor and relations of production, the educational system and the operations of the state," as well as the processes of creation and recreation of gendered subjects (*WT*, 40–41). Other works in this vein include Judith Newton and Deborah Rosenfelt's *Feminist Criticism and Social Change* (1985), which also argues for feminist analysis that takes account of social and economic contexts. Other important critics have included Jacqueline Rose and Rosalind Coward, who has formulated a materialist feminism, Catherine Belsey, who has assessed Renaissance drama from a materialist feminist perspective, and Toril Moi, who has engaged in a critique of the humanism and implicit essentialism of some American feminists. Finally, a number of critics such as Cora Kaplan, Mary Jacobus, and Penny Boumelha have comprised the UK Marxist-Feminist Collective, formed in 1976.

French feminism

The impetus for much modern French feminism was drawn from the revolutionary atmosphere of May 1968 which saw massive unrest on the part of students and workers. In that atmosphere, an integral component of political revolution was seen as the transformation of signifying practices and conceptions of subjectivity, based on a radical understanding of the power of language. Drawing somewhat on the ideas of Jacques Lacan and Jacques Derrida, feminists such as Annie Leclerc, Marguerite Duras, Julia Kristeva,

Luce Irigaray, and Hélène Cixous variously advanced a notion of *l'écriture féminine*, a feminine writing that would issue from the unconscious, the body, from a radically reconceived subjectivity, in an endeavor to circumvent what they held to be phallocentric discourse. For Kristeva, such language came from a pre-Oedipal state, from the realm of the "semiotic," prior to the process of cultural gender formation. Luce Irigaray advocated undermining patriarchal discourse from within, a strategy she pursues in her readings of several discourses from Plato through Freud and Marx to Lacan. She indicates that a feminine language would be more diffuse, like women's sexuality, and less rigidly categorizing than male discourse. Hélène Cixous also sees a "solidarity" between logocentrism and phallocentrism (where the phallus is a signifier, a metaphor of male power and dominance), an alliance that must be questioned and undermined. Women, she urged, must write their bodies, to unfold the resources of the unconscious. All of these writers revaluate the significance of the maternal, viewing this as empowering rather than as oppressed. Other feminists, however, such as Christine Fauré, Catherine Clément, and Monique Wittig, have challenged this emphasis on the body as biologically reductive, fetishistic, and politically impotent. Monique Wittig wishes to do away with the linguistic categories of sex and gender. The following section will consider briefly the work of two of the more difficult but influential feminist thinkers, Julia Kristeva and Hélène Cixous.

Julia Kristeva (b. 1941)   Kristeva's most influential work is *Revolution in Poetic Language* (1974), where she distinguishes between two orders whose interaction makes up the human subject: the "semiotic," and the "symbolic."[8] The "semiotic" consists of the pre-Oedipal drives and immediate surroundings of the body. Kristeva sees this as challenging the "ego of conventional Western thought (*RPL*, 30). The "symbolic" encompasses the emergence of subject and object as well as the constitution of meaning structured according to social categories (*RPL*, 86).

Kristeva sees the arts as engaging a *jouissance* that threatens to disrupt the symbolic order. She sees this potential especially in poetry and literature. This "revolutionary" poetic language has a subversive potential inasmuch as it threatens to reach back into the semiotic realm, to release energies and drives that have been thwarted by the conventional structure of the symbolic, disrupting the symbolic from within and reconceiving its notions of subject, object, and their connections. In the signifying practices of late capitalism, according to Kristeva, only certain avant-garde literary texts, such as those of Mallarmé and Joyce, have the ability to transgress the boundaries between semiotic and symbolic; such texts can open up new possibilities of meaning, new modes of signification. The text, therefore, is instrumental in social and political change: it is the site where the explosive force of the semiotic realm expresses itself (*RPL*, 103). She thus draws attention to the "social function of texts: the production of a different kind of subject, one capable of bringing about new social relations, and thus joining in the process of capitalism's subversion" (*RPL*, 105).

Hélène Cixous (b. 1937)   Hélène Cixous' peculiar contribution to feminism was to promote *écriture féminine* or feminine writing, as expressed in her powerful manifesto "Le Rire de la Méduse" ("The Laugh of the Medusa") (1975). This text might be seen as structured like a poem in its implicit refusal to engage with conventional rhetorical formats of argumentation and expository prose. While its themes – the need for a female writing, the nature of such writing, and its momentous implications at both personal and societal levels – are clear, these themes surface into prominence in Cixous' text through an almost poetic refrain, through patterns of recurrence, employing the materiality of language, wordplay, and the metaphor of the Medusa.

This metaphor is not taken up until the middle of Cixous' text, where, addressing women (as she does throughout the text), she charges that men have "riveted us between two horrifying myths: between the Medusa and the abyss."[9] The "abyss" refers to Freud's "myth," his designation of woman as a "dark continent," pregnant with mystery and signifying lack, castration, negativity, and dependence. And, countering the other myth, that of woman as Medusa, she affirms: "You only have to look at the Medusa straight on to see her. And she's not deadly. She's beautiful and she's laughing" ("LM," 289). Why beautiful? And why laughing? For Cixous, laughter is a way of *exceeding* the very notion of truth as defined by masculine traditions. Cixous states that a "feminine text" is designed to "smash everything, to shatter the framework of institutions, to blow up the law, to break up the 'truth' with laughter" ("LM," 292).

Cixous exhorts women to bring to birth a female language, which acknowledges its rootedness in the body: "Write your self. Your body must be heard" ("LM," 284). The significance of "body" is far-reaching, since it is the body, especially the female body, that has been repressed historically by male theology and philosophy, social systems, and even psychoanalysis. Male visions of the world have achieved the status of "theory" precisely by abstracting from the data of actual experience, by withdrawing from the world of the senses and the unconscious into an ideal world, whether of pure forms, substance, the absolute idea, the transcendental ego, or the soul. To write *with* the body implies facilitating a return of the repressed, a resurrection of that which has been subordinated and treated and secondary, as dirty, as weighing us down and preventing us from rising to the perception of higher truths. Cixous suggests that, more "than men who are coaxed toward social success, toward sublimation, women are body" ("LM," 290). Whereas Simone de Beauvoir had viewed the rootedness of woman's experience in bodily functions as a kind of imprisonment within immanence,

Cixous regards woman's greater attunement to bodily needs and drives as potentially liberating.

Feminism has shown that individuality cannot be wholly abrogated; its richness and uniqueness cannot be wholly left behind, in the process of thinking through general concepts. As Cixous insists, "there is ... no general woman" and no "female sexuality" that might be "uniform, homogeneous, classifiable into codes" ("LM," 280). Hence the implications of a "new," feminine, writing will be momentous: "writing is precisely *the very possibility of change*, the space that can serve as a springboard for subversive thought, the precursory movement of a transformation of social and cultural structures" ("LM," 283).

Gender Studies

In general, gender studies includes feminist studies of gender, gay and lesbian criticism, and queer theory. These fields often overlap considerably. Gender studies is interdisciplinary in both its roots and its methods, having arisen in literary and cultural theory, sociology, anthropology, and psychoanalysis. It examines the oppressive history of gays, lesbians, and other erotic groups, the formation and representation of gender, as well as gender as a category of analysis of literature and culture, and the intersection of gender with divisions of race, class, and color.

The birth of the gay rights movement in America is often traced to the "Stonewall Riots" of 1969 in New York City, a prolonged conflict over several days in which gays, transvestites, and other oppressed groups (of various color and nationality) offered resistance against police raiding the Stonewall Inn. Prior to this, especially just after World War II (a time when young men were experimenting sexually), a number of gay and other erotic communities had taken root in the margins of big cities such as New York, San Francisco, and Los Angeles. This led to a series of repressions in the 1950s. But during the 1960s, even before Stonewall, policies toward gays had relaxed somewhat, and as gays assumed a certain solidarity and political identity, further liberalization followed during the early 1970s, after which further backlashes erupted, in terms of both legal enactments and popular feeling. The effect of such repression was partly to solidify the alternative erotic communities, who self-consciously struggled in the political sphere to achieve a voice, and to achieve self-definition in theoretical terms. Even prior to the Stonewall Riots, gay self-consciousness emerged in many aspects of culture: in the history of literature, where figures such as Walt Whitman, Walter Pater, Oscar Wilde, members of the Bloomsbury Group with its ethic of androgyny, and the 1930s poets W. H. Auden, Christopher Isherwood, and Stephen Spender had variously articulated their sexuality; in the novels of

James Baldwin and Gore Vidal, which portrayed homosexual relations and encounters; in leading personalities of pop art such as Andy Warhol and Jasper Johns; and in pornography.

By the early 1970s, gay studies were beginning to proliferate and to achieve a theoretical self-consciousness. In 1974 an issue of *College English* was devoted to the questions of gay identity and formulating a gay literary tradition. Just as women's studies established the importance of gender as a fundamental category of analysis, so lesbian/gay studies aims to establish the analytic centrality of sex and sexuality in several fields. The overlap between gay/lesbian studies and women's studies is a matter of continuing debate. Like women's studies, lesbian/gay studies are informed by the "social struggle for ... sexual liberation" and personal freedom, as well as by resistance to homophobia and heterosexism or the "ideological and institutional practices of heterosexual privilege."[10] Some of the important early gay and lesbian scholars include: Guy Hocquenghem, who analyzed the psychological motivations of homophobia; the gay historian Jeffrey Weeks, who has analyzed the history of homosexuality in Britain in relation to nineteenth-century sexual ideologies; the scholar K. J. Dover, who published his celebrated study *Greek Homosexuality* in 1978; Lillian Faderman, who studied lesbianism in the Renaissance; and Terry Castle, who conducted wide-ranging studies of the lesbian presence in Western literary history.

Gender studies has its roots partly in feminist theory, and, indeed, was until the 1980s associated with the feminist enterprise, until lesbian critics such as Bonnie Zimmerman attacked the implicit feminist assumption that there was some essential female identity underlying differences of race, class, and sexuality. Some critics, such as those associated with the Radicalesbian collective, whose manifesto was "The Woman-Identified Woman" (1970), urged the need for a field of inquiry distinct from mainstream feminism, which had marginalized lesbianism. They saw lesbianism as the purest feminism since it asserted female autonomy and refused complicity with all forms of masculinist exploitation. Jill Johnston's *Lesbian Nation* (1973) saw lesbianism as the "solution" for feminism. The lesbian feminist poet and theorist Adrienne Rich also affirmed lesbianism as a kind of archetypal image of the broad feminist endeavor, and also urged a dissociation of lesbian from male gay allegiances. In an influential and controversial essay entitled "Compulsory heterosexuality and lesbian existence" (1980), she introduced the idea of a "lesbian continuum" to denote a range of experiences between women, including mutual practical and political support, bonding against male tyranny, and sharing a rich inner life. Separatist lesbianism was also advocated by the Chicana lesbian poet and critic Gloria Anzaldua in *Borderlands – La Frontera: The New Mestiza* (1987) and by Monique Wittig in her essay "The Straight Mind" (1980), as well as by Luce Irigaray's *This Sex Which Is Not One* (1977), which urged the autonomous existence of lesbians. During the 1970s the separatist modes of lesbian theory grew, helped by the development of women's studies programs. This era saw the beginnings of an attempt to integrate issues of sexuality, gender, and race. In her powerful essay "Toward a Black Feminist Criticism" (1977), Barbara Smith offered a controversial lesbian interpretation of Toni Morrison's *Sula*. Much of this earlier work aimed to deconstruct stereotypes of lesbians as unnatural or sexless, and to redeem a hitherto neglected tradition of lesbian thought and writing, as well as reinterpreting "conventional" figures such as Emily Dickinson and Virginia Woolf. It was underlain by certain assumptions: that there was a definable lesbian identity, and that there was an analyzable category of lesbian experience.

A more radical kind of approach, known as queer theory (a derisive term subversively adopted as a positive designation), emerged in the 1990s, grounded in a Conference on Queer Theory at the University of California, Santa Cruz. Queer theory was imbued with many of the anti-essentialist assumptions of poststructuralism, especially the undermining of any fixed sexual identity, viewing identity as a subject position created by cultural and ideological codes. It more clearly emphasized sexuality rather than gender in the formation of identity. Indeed, the lines of allegiance were also shifted from gender to sexual orientation: lesbian theorists now identified with the theorizing of gay men rather than with straight women. But much of this theory, as in work by Diana Fuss, Judith Butler, and Eve Sedgwick, attempts to deconstruct any absolute distinction between hetero- and homo-sexuality. Lee Edelman's *Homographesis* (1994) deconstructed the notion of gay identity. Much queer theory, such as Simon Watney's *Policing Desire* (1987) and Donna Haraway's "The Biopolitics of Postmodern Bodies" (1989), attempted to analyze the AIDS epidemic in the late 1980s and its presentation in the media. Other queer theorists such as Michael Moon drew attention to the "queer" attributes of what presumed to be sexual normality. The American photographer Robert Mapplethorpe stirred public controversy, related to government funding for art, with his homoerotic, sadistic, and masochistic photographs which aimed to exhibit gay sexuality. Later gay and lesbian theory also attempted to cast attention on writers from other cultural backgrounds such as Garcia Lorca and Yukio Mishima.[11] Gender theory continues to debate issues of sexuality and its relation to power structures. The following section will briefly consider the work of three of the pioneers in this field: Gayle Rubin, Eve Kosofsky Sedgwick, and Judith Butler.

Gayle Rubin (b. 1949)

A feminist anthropologist, Gayle Rubin has produced influential studies of gender, her work embracing anthropological theory, lesbian literature, sadomasochism, and feminism. In her early essay "The Traffic in Women"

(1975), she originated the expression "sex/gender system" whereby she saw sex – spanning gender identity, fantasy, and notions of childhood – as itself a social product. In a later essay, "Thinking Sex: Notes for a Radical Theory of the Politics of Sexuality" (1984), she made an influential new distinction between gender and sexuality. She acknowledged that feminism was a potent theory of gender oppression. But this must be incorporated into a radical theory of sex which explains sexual oppression (she points out that lesbians are persecuted on account not just of their gender but also of their sexual orientation).[12] In general, she argues in this essay that, like gender, sexuality is political, and that the modern sexual system has been the object of political struggle. Industrialization and urbanization have led to a reorganization of family relations and gender roles, enabling the formation of new identities and new erotic communities such as gays, transsexuals, and transvestites (*LGR*, 16, 34).

Rubin urges that a radical theory of sex must explain and denounce erotic injustice and oppression. Some of the obstacles to its formation include: sexual essentialism, the idea – fostered by medicine and psychoanalysis – that sexuality is somehow natural, standing above time, context, and history; sexual negativity, the idea that sexuality is a dangerous and destructive force; and the notion of a sexual hierarchy which ranges from acts which are permissible, through questionable acts to those considered with extreme contempt. Underlying this hierarchy is the notion of a single, ideal sexuality (*LGR*, 35).

Eve Kosofsky Sedgwick (b. 1950)

An American critic and poet, Eve Kosofsky Sedgwick has produced pioneering work in the field of gender studies, especially in queer theory. Her major works include *Between Men: English Literature and Male Homosocial Desire* (1985), *Epistemology of the Closet* (1990), *Tendencies* (1993), *A Dialogue on Love* (1999), and *Touching Feeling* (2003). In general, Sedgwick aims to show that the discourses of gender and sexuality, usually confined to a narrow ghettoized mode of analysis, are not marginal but integral to Western culture, and to the operations of power, race, and class. Indeed, in *Between Men*, she argues that all human culture is structured by the "drama of gender difference."[13] She defines the term "homosocial" as denoting "social bonds between persons of the same sex" (*BM*, 1). Sedgwick's basic purpose is to analyze male homosocial bonds "through the heterosexual European erotic ethos," and to reconcile historicist Marxist approaches, using ideology as an analytic category, with structuralist feminist perspectives in the analysis of sexuality (*BM*, 16). In general, Sedgwick's work shows the sheer fluidity of the distinctions between homosexuality and heterosexuality, as well as the contextual and indeterminate and contingent nature of both gender and sexuality. What counts as "sexual" or "homosexual" can vary.

Judith Butler (b. 1956)

Judith Butler's *Gender Trouble: Feminism and the Subversion of Identity* (1990) is arguably the most important book in the field of gender studies. Her central argument is that what we call gender is not an inherent fact or attribute of human nature but a *performance*, a cultural performance composed of signifying gestures.[14] The effect of Butler's work, in deconstructing the category of woman, has been to distinguish lesbian studies from feminism. She argues that the very concept of woman, the starting point of much feminism, is not stable but produced by power structures and intersects intimately with race, class, politics, and culture (*GT*, 1–3, 128).

In the most brilliant section of her book, Butler argues that the body itself is shaped by political forces. Both the distinction between sex and gender and the category of sex itself presuppose that there exists a somehow neutral body prior to its sexual signification. Indeed the tradition of Christianity saw the body as a non-entity, as a "profane void," signifying a fallen state. Equally, Cartesian dualism (between mind and matter) saw the body as so much inert matter, attached to the thinking essence of the human. Even the existentialism of Sartre and de Beauvoir viewed the body as "mute facticity." Nietzsche and Foucault, too, saw the body as a surface or blank page on which cultural values were inscribed. In all these cases, materiality and the body are assumed to exist prior to signification: not only is the body indifferent to signification, but signification (as in Descartes' dualism) is the act of a disembodied consciousness. The body is simply regarded as external to the signifying process, which is the province of the thinking mind (*GT*, 129–130).

It is cultural norms, urges Butler, that maintain the boundaries of the body, which is not a being but a surface, a signifying practice within a field of gender hierarchy and compulsory heterosexuality (*GT*, 139). There is no essence of gender: it is generated by repeated acts. This performative character of gender opens up performative possibilities for gender configurations "outside the restricting frames of masculinist domination and compulsory heterosexuality" (*GT*, 140–141). Butler's powerful critique of the notions of identity and body on which gender is constructed is an important step toward reconfiguring the performative potential of gender.

Notes

1. This lecture is reprinted in *Modernism/Postmodernism*, ed. Peter Brooker (London and New York: Longman, 1992), p. 132. Hereafter cited as *MP*.

2. Jean Baudrillard, *Simulations*, trans. Paul Foss, Paul Patton, and Philip Beitchman (New York: Semiotext[e], 1983), p. 2. Hereafter cited as *S*.

3. Jean Baudrillard, *The System of Objects*, trans. James Benedict (London and New York: Verso, 1996), p. 183. Hereafter cited as *SO*.

4. Jean-François Lyotard, *The Postmodern Condition: A Report on Knowledge*, trans. Geoff Bennington and Brian Massumi (Minneapolis: University of Minnesota Press, 1989), p. xxxiii. Hereafter cited as *PC*.

5. Jean-François Lyotard, "Defining the Postmodern," p. 1. This article can easily be accessed online at: http://qcpages.qc.edu/ENGLISH/Staff/richter/Lyotard.htm. Hereafter cited as "DP."

6. This essay is contained in bell hooks, *Yearning: race, gender, and cultural politics* (Boston: South End Press, 1990), p. 23. Hereafter cited as *RGCP*.

7. Michèle Barrett, *Women's Oppression Today: The Marxist/Feminist Encounter* (London and New York: Verso, 1980), p. 8. Hereafter cited as *WT*.

8. Julia Kristeva, *Revolution in Poetic Language*, trans. Margaret Waller (New York: Columbia University Press, 1984), p. 24. Hereafter cited as *RPL*.

9. Hélène Cixous, "The Laugh of the Medusa," trans. Keith Cohen and Paula Cohen, in *The Signs Reader: Women, Gender, and Scholarship*, ed. Elizabeth Abel and Emily K. Abel (Chicago and London: University of Chicago Press, 1983), p. 289. Hereafter cited as "LM."

10. Henry Abelove, Michele Aina Barale, and David M. Halperin, eds., "Introduction," in *The Lesbian and Gay Studies Reader* (London and New York: Routledge, 1993), p. xvi. Hereafter cited as *LGR*.

11. This account is indebted to an excellent article on "Gay Theory and Criticism" by Richard Dellamora and Bonnie Zimmerman in *The Johns Hopkins Guide to Theory and Criticism*, ed. Michael Groden and Martin Kreiswirth (Baltimore and London: Johns Hopkins University Press, 1994), pp. 324–331.

12. Gayle Rubin, "Thinking Sex," in *LGR*, pp. 32–34. This article was first published in *Pleasure and Danger*, ed. Carole Vance (London and New York: Routledge, 1984).

13. Eve Kosofsky Sedgwick, *Between Men: English Literature and Male Homosocial Desire* (New York: Columbia University Press, 1985), p. 11. Hereafter cited as *BM*.

14. Judith Butler, *Gender Trouble* (New York and London: Routledge, 1990), p. x. Hereafter cited as *GT*.

Chapter 18

The Later Twentieth Century: New Historicism, Reader-Response Theory, Postcolonial Criticism, Cultural Studies

In the 1980s, the political mood in both Europe and America swung to the right. The increasingly unchallenged predominance of capitalism in the 1980s and 1990s oversaw the emergence of New Historicism, which called for the literary text to be situated not, as in Marxist criticism, within the context of an economic infrastructure, but within a superstructural fabric of political and cultural discourses, with the economic dimension itself given no priority. One of the prime influences on New Historicism was Michel Foucault, who saw knowledge as a form of power and analyzed power as highly diffused and as not distinctly assignable to a given set of political or ideological agencies. Another approach that attained prominence during these decades was reader-response theory, whose roots went back to the reception theories of the German writers Hans Robert Jauss and Wolfgang Iser, as well as to Wayne Booth's *The Rhetoric of Fiction* (1961). This perspective recognized the dialogical nature of textual production, redefining the meaning of the "text" as the product of an interaction between text and an appropriately qualified community of readers. It could be argued that both the New Historicism and reader-response theory represented a return of the literary and cultural critic to political non-commitment in a newer and more fashionable guise – laden with all the trimmings of poststructuralist terminology – in which liberal humanist notions of pluralism, tolerance, and claims to political neutrality could stride once more on the academic stage.

The 1990s saw the concerted growth of two critical tendencies that were inextricably political. One was postcolonial studies, whose roots can be traced back through Edward Said's landmark work *Orientalism* (1978) to writers such as Frantz Fanon and Aimé Césaire, who were directly engaged in struggles against colonialism. The other was ethnic studies, inspired largely by critics such as Henry Louis Gates. In general, both postcolonial and ethnic

Literary Criticism from Plato to the Present: An Introduction   M. A. R. Habib
© 2011 M. A. R. Habib

studies engage in a broad redefinition of terms – such as identity, gender, sexuality, and power – that had already undergone a radical critique in the works of feminist and, more generally, poststructuralist, thinkers. These studies insisted on examining such terms in the altered contexts of colonial and racial oppression. For example, it was held that the insights of white, middle-class feminism did not apply universally over diverse races and cultures. Each of these approaches can now be considered briefly.

The New Historicism

Historicism began toward the end of the eighteenth century with German writers such as Herder, and continued through the nineteenth-century historians Von Ranke and Meinecke to twentieth-century thinkers such as Wilhelm Dilthey, R. G. Collingwood, Hans Georg Gadamer, Ernst Cassirer, and Karl Mannheim. Powerful historical modes of analysis were formulated by Hegel and Marx, who themselves had a profound impact on historicist thinking; and literary historians such as Sainte-Beuve and Hippolyte Taine also insisted on viewing literary texts as integrally informed by their historical milieux. Much of what passes under the rubric of the "New" Historicism is not new, but represents a return to certain foci of analysis as developed by previous traditions of historicism.

Historicism has been characterized by a number of features. Most fundamentally, there is an insistence that all systems of thought, all phenomena, all institutions, all works of art, and all literary texts must be situated within a historical perspective. They cannot be somehow torn from history and analyzed in isolation since they are determined in both their form and content by their specific historical circumstances, their specific situation in time and place. Hence, we cannot bring to our analyses of Shakespeare the same assumptions and methods that we bring to Plato. A second feature of historicism is that history is sometimes held (as by Hegel and Marx) to operate according to certain identifiable laws, yielding a certain predictability and explanatory power. A third concern arises from the recognition that societies and cultures separated in time have differing values and beliefs: how can the historian "know" the past? The historian operates within the horizon of her own world view, a certain broad set of assumptions and beliefs; how can she overcome these to achieve an empathetic understanding of a distant culture? Thinkers such as Dilthey, Gadamer, and E. D. Hirsch have offered various answers to this dilemma. Hirsch's position aspires to be "objectivist," effectively denying the historical and context-bound nature of knowledge, and proposing a distinction between "meaning," which embraces what the author meant or intended by his particular use of language, and "significance," which comprehends the subjective evaluation of the text according to the values and beliefs of the critic. Gadamer proposed a notion of "horizonfusion" whereby we acknowledge both that the "text" is in fact a product of a tradition of interpretation (with no "original" meaning) and that our own perspective is informed by the very past we are seeking to analyze. Recognizing both of these limitations, we can begin to effect an empathetic "fusion" of our own cultural horizon with that of the text.

The "New" Historicism, a term coined by Stephen Greenblatt in 1982, became popular in the 1980s, reacting against both the formalist view of the literary text as somehow autonomous and Marxist views which ultimately related texts to the economic infrastructure. It saw the literary text as a kind of discourse situated within a complex of cultural discourses – religious, political, economic, aesthetic – which both shaped it, and in their turn, were shaped by it. Perhaps what was new about this procedure was its insistence, drawn from Foucault and poststructuralism, that "history" itself is a text, an interpretation, and that there is no single history. It also rejected any notion of historical progress or teleology, and broke away from any literary histori-ography based on the study of genres and figures. In the same way, the "culture" in which New Historicism situated literary texts was itself regarded as a textual construct. Hence, New Historicism refused to accord any kind of unity or homogeneity to history or culture, viewing both as harboring networks of contradictory, competing, and unreconciled forces and interests. The language of Marxist economics gave way before Foucault's terminology of "power," viewed as operating in diffuse ways without any definable agency. The New Historicists tended, then, to view literature as one discourse among many cultural discourses, insisting on engaging with this entire complex in a localized manner, refusing to engage in categorical general-izations or to commit to any definite political stance. But some New Historicists have seen literary texts as crucially participating in conflicts of power.

In Britain, the New Historicist critics have identified themselves in Raymond Williams' terminology as "cultural materialists," and have often brought out the subversive potential of literature, especially in relation to the Renaissance. Greenblatt's own work has focused on this period, and critics such as Jonathan Dollimore have produced groundbreaking studies, such as *Radical Tragedy* (1984), which have reassessed the work of Shakespeare and his contemporaries, recognizing the increasingly historical and ideological functions of drama.[1] The book *Political Shakespeare*, edited by Jonathan Dollimore and Alan Sinfield, also challenged the liberal-humanist notion of Shakespeare as a timeless and universal genius, emphasizing instead Shakespeare's subversion of authority, sexuality, and colonialism.[2] Another powerful reinterpretation was formulated in *Alternative Shakespeares* (1985), in which a range of writers, including Catherine Belsey, Terence Hawkes, Jacqueline Rose, John Drakakis, and Francis Barker challenged the liberal-humanist language of character analysis, artistic coherence, and harmony. Instead, they drew attention to the manner in which Shakespeare's texts produce meaning, construct the human subject, and engage in larger structural and ideological issues.[3] Other critics such as Jerome McGann have extended New Historical concerns into other historical periods such as Romanticism. We can now look briefly at the work of Michel Foucault, the primary influence on this critical tendency.

Michel Foucault (1926–1984)

Along with figures such as Derrida, Foucault has exerted an enormous influence on many branches of thought in the later twentieth century, including what is broadly known as "cultural studies." He had a seminal impact on queer theory. Born in France, the son of a physician, Foucault criticized the institutions of medical practice in his first two publications, *Madness and Civilization* (1961) and *The Birth of the Clinic* (1963). Indeed, the central theme of most of Foucault's works was the methods by which modern civilization creates and controls human subjects, through institutions such as hospitals, prisons, education, and knowledge; corollary to these investigations was Foucault's examination of power, its execution and distribution. Foucault's next works, *The Order of Things* (1966) and *The Archaeology of Knowledge* (1969), offered a characterization of the growth of knowledge in the modern Western world, as manifested in the emergence of disciplines such as linguistics, economics, and biology. He elaborated a historical scheme of three "epistemes" (outlooks underlying the institutional organization of knowledge) that characterized the Middle Ages, the Enlightenment, and the modern world. Foucault's essay "What is an Author?" (1969) questions and examines the concept of authorship and, in insights that were taken up by the New Historicism, argued that analysis of literary texts could not be restricted to these texts themselves or to their author's psychology and background; rather, the larger contexts and cultural conventions in which texts were produced needed to be considered. Subsequently, Foucault offered extended critiques respectively of the institutions of the prison and of sexuality in *Discipline and Punish: The Birth of the Prison* (1975) and *The History of Sexuality* (1976).

In *The History of Sexuality*, Foucault's investigation of the discourse on sexuality is equally an investigation into the workings of power, which is seen as more complex and subtle than a procedure of mere repression.[4] New methods of power, Foucault maintains, operate not "by right but by technique, not by law but by normalization, not by punishment but by control" (*HS*, 87, 89). Foucault states that power is not "a group of institutions and mechanisms that ensure the subservience of the citizens of a given state." Nor is it a "mode of subjugation" or a "general system of domination exerted by one group over another ... these are only the terminal forms that power takes" (*HS*, 92). Nor must power be sought "in the primary existence of a central point, in a unique source of sovereignty" (*HS*, 93). Moreover, "there is no binary and all-encompassing opposition between rulers and ruled at the root of power relations." Nor is power something that is "acquired, seized, or shared" (*HS*, 94).

What *is* it, then? According to Foucault, power must be understood as a "multiplicity of force relations" (*HS*, 92). Foucault insists that power "is everywhere; not because it embraces everything, but because it comes from everywhere." It is "simply the over-all effect that emerges from all these mobilities" (*HS*, 93). A conventional Marxist critique of Foucault would impugn his apparent removal of political agency from the operations of power. Yet he characterizes power relations as "both intentional and non-subjective." He acknowledges that "there is no power that is exercised without a series of aims and objectives. But this does not mean that it results from the choice or decision of an individual subject" (*HS*, 94–95). He also concedes that where "there is power, there is resistance, and yet . . . this resistance is never in a position of exteriority in relation to power." Foucault stresses that there is "no single locus of great Refusal, no soul of revolt, source of all rebellions, or pure law of the revolutionary. Instead there is a plurality of resistances, each of them a special case" (*HS*, 95–96). What makes revolution possible, he claims, is a "strategic codification of these points of resistance" (*HS*, 96).

Reader-Response and Reception Theory

Another critical approach that has proved widely congenial since the 1980s is reader-response theory, with roots in earlier thinkers such as Husserl. The role of the reader or audience of a literary work or performance has been recognized since classical times. Many classical and medieval writers viewed literature as a branch of rhetoric, the art of persuasive speaking or writing. As such, literature had to be highly aware of the composition and expectations of its audience. Subsequently, several Romantic theories stressed the powerful emotional impact of poetry on the audience, and various later nineteenth-century theories such as symbolism and impressionism stressed the reader's subjective response to literature and art. Marxism and feminism have long acknowledged that literature, necessarily operating within social structures of class and gender, is always orientated toward certain kinds of audiences, in both aesthetic and economic terms. The hermeneutic theories developed by Friedrich Schleiermacher, Martin Heidegger, Hans Georg Gadamer, as well as the phenomenological theories inspired by Edmund Husserl, such as that of Roman Ingarden, examined the ways in which readers engaged cognitively and historically with literary texts.

Hence, reader-response theory was not only a reaction against the formalism and objectivism of the earlier twentieth century, but also a renewal of a long tradition that had acknowledged the important role of the reader or audience in any given literary or rhetorical situation. There are elements of a reader-response outlook in the theoretical writings of Virginia Woolf and Louise Rosenblatt. Wayne Booth was the author of an influential work, *The Rhetoric of Fiction* (1961). His distinctions between real author and the "implied author" who tells the story, between actual reader and the "postulated reader" created by the text itself, and his critical expressions such as "unreliable narrator," became standard terms in analyzing fiction. All of these figures recognized that the author of a literary text uses certain strategies to produce given effects in their readers or to guide their responses. But it was not until the 1970s that a number of critics at the University of Constance in Germany (the "Constance School") began to formulate a systematic reader-response or "reception" theory. The leading members of this school were Wolfgang Iser (b. 1926) and Hans Robert Jauss, whose aesthetics had their roots not only in the hermeneutic and phenomenological traditions mentioned above but also in the earlier thought of Alexander Baumgarten, Kant, and Friedrich von Schiller. One of Jauss' most important texts was "Literary History as a Challenge to Literary Theory" (1969, 1970), where he urged that the history of a work's reception by readers played an integral role in the work's aesthetic status and significance. The American reader-response critic Stanley Fish has argued in works such as "Is There a Text in this Class?" that what constrains interpretation is not fixed meanings in a linguistic system but the practices and assumptions of an institution. The following section will briefly consider the seminal work of Wolfgang Iser.

Wolfgang Iser (b. 1926)

Iser's theories of reader response were presented in two major works, *The Implied Reader* (1972) and *The Act of Reading* (1976). In the first of these, Iser suggests that we might think of the literary work as having two poles: the "artistic" pole is the text created by the author, and the "aesthetic" pole refers to "the realization accomplished by the reader."[5] We cannot identify the literary work with either the text or the realization of the text; it must lie "halfway between the two," and in fact it comes into being only through the convergence of text and reader (*IR*, 275). His point here is that reading is an active and creative process. It is reading which brings the text to life, which unfolds "its inherently dynamic character" (*IR*, 275). It is because the text has unwritten implications or "gaps" that the reader can be active and creative, working things out for himself. This does not mean that *any* reading will be appropriate. The text uses various strategies and devices to limit its own unwritten implications, but the latter are nonetheless worked out by the reader's own imagination (*IR*, 276).

In *The Act of Reading*, Iser further elaborates his important concept of the "implied reader." In analyzing responses to a literary work, he says, "we must allow for the reader's presence without in any way predetermining his character or his historical situation." It is this reader, who is somehow lifted above any particular context, whom Iser designates the implied reader.[6] The implied reader is a function not of "an empirical outside reality" but of the text itself. Iser points out that the concept of the implied reader has "his roots firmly planted in the structure of the text; he is a construct and in no way to be identified with any real reader." What the implied reader designates is "a network of response-inviting structures," which prestructure the role of the reader in the latter's attempt to grasp the text (*AR*, 34). In a novel, there are four main perspectives: those of the narrator, characters, plot, and the fictitious reader. The meaning of the text is generated by the convergence of these perspectives, a convergence that is not itself set out in words but occurs during the reading process (*AR*, 35). Iser also sees the notion of the "implied reader" as explaining the tension that occurs within the reader during the reading process, a tension between the reader's own subjectivity and the author's subjectivity which overtakes the reader's mentality, a tension between two selves that directs the reader's ability to make sense of the text.

Postcolonial Criticism

Another, more overtly political, approach to interpretation gathered intensity in the 1980s, concerned with the economic, cultural, and psychological effects of imperialism and emancipation from colonial rule. Since postcolonial theory is rooted in the history of imperialism, it is worth briefly looking at this history. In modern times, there have been at least three major phases of imperialism. Between 1492 and the mid-eighteenth century, Spain and Portugal, England, France, and the Netherlands established colonies and empires in the Americas, the East Indies, and India. Then, between the mid-nineteenth century and World War I, there was an immense scramble for imperialistic power between Britain, France, Germany, Italy, and other nations. By the end of the nineteenth century, more than one-fifth of the land area of the world and a quarter of its population had been brought under the British Empire: India, Canada, Australia, New Zealand, South Africa, Burma, and the Sudan. The next largest colonial power was France, whose possessions included Algeria, French West Africa, Equatorial Africa, and Indochina. Germany, Italy, and Japan also entered the race for colonies. In 1855 Belgium established the Belgian Congo in the heart of Africa, a colonization whose horrors were expressed in Conrad's *Heart of Darkness*

(1899). Finally, the periods during and after World War II saw a struggle involving both the countries just mentioned as well as a conflict between America and the Communist Soviet Union for extended control, power, and influence. Needless to say, these imperialistic endeavors have survived into the present day in altered forms and with new antagonists.

The motives behind imperialism have usually been economic. A second and related motive has been (and still is) the security of the home state. A third motive is related to various versions of Social Darwinism. Figures such as Machiavelli, Bacon, Karl Pearson, Hitler, and Mussolini saw imperialism as part of the natural struggle for survival. The final motive, propounded by figures such as Rudyard Kipling (in poems such as "The White Man's Burden") and questioned by writers such as Conrad, rests on moral grounds: imperialism is a means of bringing to a subject people the blessings of a superior civilization, and liberating them from their benighted ignorance. Clearly, much of this rationale rests on Western Enlightenment notions of civilization and progress.

After the end of World War II in 1945 there occurred a large-scale process of decolonization of the territories subjugated by most of the imperial powers (Britain, France, Netherlands, Belgium), beginning with the independence of India in 1947. Colonial struggle is hardly dead: it has continued until very recently in East Timor, and still persists bitterly in many parts of the world, including Tibet, Taiwan, Kashmir, and the Middle East.[7] Postcolonial literature and criticism arose both during and after the struggles of many nations in Africa, Asia, Latin America (now referred to as the "tricontinent" rather than the "third world"), and elsewhere for independence from colonial rule. The year 1950 saw the publication of seminal texts of postcolonialism: Aimé Césaire's *Discours sur le colonialisme*, and Frantz Fanon's *Black Skin, White Masks*. And in 1958 Chinua Achebe published his novel *Things Fall Apart*. George Lamming's *The Pleasures of Exile* appeared in 1960 and Frantz Fanon's *The Wretched of the Earth* followed in 1961. Fanon's now classic text analyzed the conditions for effective anti-colonial revolution from a Marxist perspective, modified somewhat to accommodate conditions specific to colonized nations. It also articulated the connections between class and race. Indeed, Fanon pointed out the utter difference in historical situation between the European bourgeois class, a once revolutionary class which overturned feudalism, and the African bourgeoisie emerging as successor to colonial rule.

According to Robert Young, the "founding moment" of postcolonial theory was the journal the *Tricontinental*, launched by the Havan Tricontinental of 1966, which "initiated the first global alliance of the peoples of the three continents against imperialism" (Young, 5). Edward Said's *Orientalism* appeared in 1978. More recent work includes *The Empire Writes Back* (1989) by Ashcroft, Griffiths, and Tiffin, Gayatri Spivak's *The Post-Colonial*

Critic (1990), as well as work by Abdul JanMohamed, Homi Bhabha, Benita Parry, and Kwame Anthony Appiah. Robert Young sees postcolonialism as continuing to derive its inspiration from the anti-colonial struggles of the colonial era, both having certain common characteristics such as "diaspora, transnational migration and internationalism" (Young, 2). Bill Ashcroft, Gareth Griffiths, and Helen Tiffin also use the term postcolonial in a comprehensive sense, "to cover all the culture affected by the imperial process from the moment of colonization to the present day," on account of the "continuity of preoccupations" between the colonial and postcolonial periods.[8]

Postcolonial criticism has embraced a number of aims: most fundamentally, to reexamine the history of colonialism from the perspective of the colonized; to determine the economic, political, and cultural impact of colonialism on both the colonized peoples and the colonizing powers; to analyze the process of decolonization; and, above all, to participate in the goals of political liberation, which includes equal access to material resources, the contestation of forms of domination and the articulation of political and cultural identities (Young, 11). Early voices of anti-imperialism stressed the need to develop or return to indigenous literary traditions so as to exorcise their cultural heritage of the specters of imperial domination. Other voices advocated an adaptation of Western ideals toward their own political and cultural ends. The fundamental framework of postcolonial thought has been furnished by the Marxist critique of colonialism and imperialism, which has been adapted to their localized contexts by thinkers from Frantz Fanon to Gayatri Spivak.

This struggle of postcolonial discourse extends over the domains of gender, race, ethnicity, and class. Class divisions and gender oppression operate both in the West and in colonized nations. Many commentators have observed that exploitation of workers occurred as much in Western countries as in the areas that they subjugated. Hence, postcolonial discourse potentially embraces, and is intimately linked with, a broad range of dialogues within the colonizing powers, addressing various forms of "internal colonization" as treated by minority studies of various kinds, such as African-American, Native American, Latin American, and women's studies. All of these discourses have challenged the main streams of Western philosophy, literature and ideology. In this sense, the work of African-American critics, such as Henry Louis Gates Jr., of African-American female novelists and poets, of commentators on Islam such as Fatima Mernissi and Aziz al-Azmeh, and even of theorists such as Fredric Jameson, is vitally linked to the multifarious projects of postcolonialism.

One of these projects was "multiculturalism." Many critics held that oppressive ideas were embodied and reproduced in the conventional canons of literature and philosophy which we offer to our students: the literary tradition from Homer to T. S. Eliot and the philosophical spectrum from Plato to logical positivism. In these canons, the voices of minorities, women, and the working classes were suppressed. The growth of English literature was from the beginning imbued with ideological motives. Arnold and subsequent professors at Oxford saw poetry as the sole salvation for a mechanical civilization. The "timeless truths" of literature were intended to "promote sympathy and fellow feeling among all classes," to educate citizens as to their duties, to inculcate national pride and moral values. And English was a pivotal part of the imperialist effort. In 1834 Macaulay argued the merits of English as the medium of instruction in India, stating: "I have never found one ... who could deny that a single shelf of a good European library was worth the whole native literature of India and Arabia." We can refrain from commenting on this except to add Macaulay's own subsequent statement that "I have no knowledge of either Sanscrit or Arabic." Such statements reveal the depth to which constructions of Europe's self-image, resting on the Enlightenment project of rationality, progress, civilization, and moral agency, were premised on the positing of various forms of alterity or "otherness," founded on polarized images such as superstitiousness, backwardness, barbarism, moral incapacity, and intellectual impoverishment.

It is in profound recognition of this integral relationship between the literary canon and cultural values that writers such as the Kenyan Ngugi Wa Thiong'o have written essays with such titles as "On the Abolition of the English Department" (1968), and important texts such as *Decolonizing the Mind* (1986). Indian-born Gayatri Spivak's work focuses on the structures of colonialism, the postcolonial subject, and the possibility of postcolonial discourse. In her essay "Can the Subaltern Speak?" (1983), later expanded in her book *Critique of Postcolonial Reason* (1999), she addresses the issue of whether peoples in subordinate, colonized positions are able to achieve a voice. Like Spivak, Homi Bhabha extends certain tenets of poststructuralism into discourses about colonialism, nationality, and culture. The notion of "hybridity" – a state of "in betweenness" with respect to two cultures – is central to Bhabha's work in challenging notions of identity, culture, and nation as coherent and unified entities. Many writers, notably Chinua Achebe, have struggled with the dilemma of expressing themselves in their own dialect, to achieve an authentic rendering of their cultural situation and experience, or in English, to reach a far wider audience. It should be noted also that what conventionally passes as "English" is Southern Standard English, spoken by the middle classes around London and the south of England. This model of English has effectively peripheralized the English spoken not only in other parts of England but also in other areas of the world. Today, there are innumerable varieties of English spoken in many countries, and only recently has their expression in literature been institutionally acknowledged. These various debates can now be considered briefly in some of the major figures who have made contributions to postcolonial criticism and theory.

Edward Said (1935–2004)

Known as a literary and cultural theorist, Edward Said was a Palestinian who taught at various institutions in the United States. His thinking has embraced three broad imperatives: (1) to articulate the cultural position and task of the intellectual and literary critic; (2) to examine the historical production and motivations of Western discourses about the Orient in general and Islam in particular; (3) to attempt to bring to light and clarify the Palestinian struggle to regain a homeland.

In *Orientalism* (1978) Said examines the vast tradition of Western "constructions" of the Orient. This tradition of Orientalism has been a "corporate institution" for coming to terms with the Orient, for authorizing views about it and ruling over it. Central to Said's analysis is that the Orient is actually a production of Western discourse, a means of self-definition of Western culture as well as of justifying imperial domination of oriental peoples.[9] Said's aim is not to show that this politically motivated edifice of language somehow distorts a "real" Orient, but rather to show that it is indeed a language, with an internal consistency, motivation, and capacity for representation resting on a relationship of power and hegemony over the Orient.

The book is also an attempt to display Orientalism as but one complex example of the politically and ideologically rooted nature of all discourse. Thus, "liberal cultural heroes" such as Mill, Arnold, and Carlyle all had views, usually overlooked, on race and imperialism (*Orientalism*, 14). Using a vast range of examples, from Aeschylus' play *The Persians* through Macaulay, Renan, and Marx, to Gustave von Grunbaum and the *Cambridge History of Islam*, Said attempts to examine the stereotypes and distortions through which Islam and the East have been consumed. These stereotypes include: Islam as a heretical imitation of Christianity (*Orientalism*, 65–66), the exotic sexuality of the Oriental woman (*Orientalism*, 187), and Islam as a culture incapable of innovation (*Orientalism*, 296–298). Said suggests that the electronic postmodern world reinforces dehumanized portrayals of the Arabs, a tendency aggravated by the Arab–Israeli conflict and intensely felt by Said himself as a Palestinian.

Henry Louis Gates Jr. (b. 1950)

The most prominent contemporary scholar of African-American literature, Henry Louis Gates Jr., has sought to map out an African-American heritage of both literature and criticism. Central to this project has been his endeavor to integrate approaches from modern literary theory with modes of interpretation derived from African literary traditions. Gates has edited a number of pioneering anthologies such as *Black Literature and Literary Theory* (1984), *"Race," Writing, and Difference* (1986), and *The Norton Anthology of African American Literature* (1997), as well as helping to found African-American journals. The important works authored by Gates include *Figures in Black: Words, Signs, and the "Racial" Self* (1987) and *The Signifying Monkey: A Theory of African-American Literary Criticism* (1988). One of his goals in these texts is to redefine the notions of race and blackness in the terms of poststructuralist theory, as effects of networks of signification and cultural difference rather than as essences. Gates' work has influenced, and displays analogies with, the output of critics such as Houston A. Baker Jr. and Wahneema Lubiano.

In the introduction to his *Figures in Black*, which is perhaps the most succinct statement of his overall endeavor as a black critic, Gates suggests that the connection between the development of African-American criticism and contemporary literary theory can be charted in four stages, corresponding broadly to his own development: the first was the phase of the "Black Aesthetic"; the second was a phase of "Repetition and Imitation"; the third, "Repetition and Difference"; and, finally, "Synthesis."[10] The Black Aesthetic theorists of the first stage attempted both to resurrect "lost" black texts and to formulate a "genuinely black" aesthetic, and were persistently concerned with the "nature and function of black literature vis-à-vis the larger political struggle for Black Power"(*FB*, xxvi). Gates identifies his own radical innovation as lying in the emphasis he accorded to the "language of the text," a hitherto repressed concern in African-American criticism. His engagement with formalism and structuralism led to the second phase of his development, that of "Repetition and Imitation." Realizing that a more critical approach to theory was called for, Gates' work moved into the stage of "Repetition and Difference," using theory to read black texts but thereby also implicitly offering a critique of the theory itself. The final stage of Gates' work, that of "Synthesis," involved a "sustained interest in the black vernacular tradition as a source field in which to ground a theory of Afro-American criticism, a theory at once self-contained and related by analogy to other contemporary theories" (*FB*, xxix). Drawing on poststructuralist theories, Gates argues that, charged with lack of intellectual capacity and correlative lack of humanity, black authors have literally attempted to write themselves into existence, to achieve an identity through the narratives of their own lives, an identity that subsists primarily in language: the very language in which they had been designated as absences was itself appropriated as the sign of presence (*FB*, xxxi). Gates valuably articulates the problems surrounding any black critical use of so-called "theory." And his own project is indeed informed by recourse to native African idioms and traditions.

Cultural Studies

It is worth making brief mention of another, related, field which developed rapidly over the last decades of the twentieth century: cultural studies. In the nineteenth century, Coleridge, Burke, Arnold, Carlyle, Ruskin, and William Morris all wrote extensively on the larger cultural issues surrounding the study of literature. Earlier twentieth-century writers on the subject have included D. H. Lawrence, Virginia Woolf, T. S. Eliot, many Marxist thinkers, F. R. Leavis, and Raymond Williams. As it is practiced now, cultural studies has a wide designation, encompassing sociology, anthropology, history, literature, and the arts. As applied to the study of literature, cultural criticism is marked foremost by its broad definition of "literature": this includes not only the conventional genres of poetry, drama, and fiction but also popular fiction such as thrillers and romances, television and mass media, cinema, magazines, and music. Indeed, the conventionally entitled "Department of English" might nowadays more accurately be termed a "Department of Cultural Studies," since it sees literature as situated within a larger fabric of cultural discourses.

Cultural criticism grounds literature in a larger framework which can include the economic institutions of literary production, ideology, and broad political issues of class, race, gender, and power. Hence cultural analysis tends to stress what is specific or unique – in terms of time, place, and ideology – to a given cultural and literary moment. Typically, cultural studies has extended its methodology beyond conventional reading and research to encompass field study, empirical observation, interviewing, and interdisciplinary collaboration.

Marxist thinking has given the term "culture" a political valency, viewing it as a part of the ideological process. The Frankfurt School saw modern mass culture as reduced to a bland commercialism. Leading figures of the school included Max Horkheimer, Theodor Adorno, Herbert Marcuse, and Walter Benjamin, who all produced analyses of modern culture, drawing on Marxist and sometimes on Freudian theory. In collaboration, Adorno and Horkheimer produced an incisive critique of modern culture that was to prove seminal for cultural studies: *Dialectic of Enlightenment* (1944). They argued that culture under the monopoly of capitalism imposes a sterile uniformity on everything: "Films, radio and magazines make up a system which is uniform as a whole and in every part."[11] In general, the culture industry serves to control people's consciousness, impressing upon them their own powerlessness, stubbornly refusing to engage their ability to think independently, equating pleasure with complete capitulation to the system of power, reducing individuals to mere expendable copies of the identities manufactured by the media and film, presenting the world as essentially meaningless and governed by blind chance (rather than on such virtues as merit and hard work) (*DE*, 147). In this system, even art is a commodity, its value defined by market forces (*DE*, 158).

In contrast with the Frankfurt School, Marxists such as Antonio Gramsci have seen culture – as in the development of a working-class counterculture – as an instrument of possible resistance to the prevailing ideologies. The view of culture as oppositional or potentially subversive was developed in England by figures such as Raymond Williams, one of the founders of the New Left movement, the historian E. P. Thompson, and the socialist Richard Hoggart who in 1964 founded the Centre for Contemporary Cultural Studies at Birmingham University. Leading figures in the Centre included Stuart Hall, author of an important essay, "Cultural Studies and its Theoretical Legacies," and Dick Hebdige, known for his book *Subculture: The Meaning of Style*. As well as analyzing the subversive nature of youth cultures, critics at the Centre examined the ideological function of the media and issues in education. In America, the Marxist critic Fredric Jameson saw modern mass culture as essentially postmodernistic in its form; Janice Radway wrote on the popular form of the romance novel in her widely selling *Reading the Romance* (1984), and examined the institutional workings of middle-brow fiction in her subsequent *A Feeling for Books* (1997). Whereas Radway locates in the reading of popular fiction a space of resistance to patriarchal norms, other critics such as Susan Bordo, in her *Unbearable weight: Feminism, Western Culture, and the Body* (1993), emphasize the profound and imposing impact of popular culture on women's self-image and cosmetic practices, showing how much of their alleged freedom to form themselves is illusory.

Many cultural critics have drawn on semiotics to analyze popular culture. In his *Television Culture* (1987) John Fiske argues that the techniques and codes employed by television mold our perceptions but he rejects the idea that audiences are wholly passive consumers of ideological meanings, arguing instead that a text "is the site of struggles for meaning that reproduce the conflicts of interest between the producers and consumers of the cultural commodity. A program is produced by the industry, a text by its readers."[12] The French sociologist Pierre Bourdieu saw his work as politically motivated, opposing globalization and cultural forms of oppression. His work in general attempted to understand how the human subject was positioned in larger social structures, and he saw aesthetic judgment as integrally located within such structures.

In summary, cultural studies might be characterized by its broad definition of literature as including all aspects of popular culture, its situation of literature as a set of semiotic codes among broader social codes, its view of culture as an instrument of subordination or subversion, as a site of ideological struggle, its commitment to broadly left-wing political aims, and its generally empirical, interdisciplinary, and collaborative methodology.

Notes

1. Jonathan Dollimore, *Radical Tragedy: Religion, Ideology and Power in the Drama of Shakespeare and his Contemporaries* (New York and London: Harvester Wheatsheaf, 1984), pp. 8, 18, 54, 59, 63, 78.
2. Jonathan Dollimore and Alan Sinfield, *Political Shakespeare: New Essays in Cultural Materialism* (New York and London: Cornell University Press, 1985).
3. John Drakakis, ed. *Alternative Shakespeares* (New York and London: Routledge, 1985).
4. Michel Foucault, *The History of Sexuality: An Introduction*, trans. Robert Hurley (Harmondsworth: Penguin, 1978), p. 69. Hereafter cited as *HS*.
5. Wolfgang Iser, *The Implied Reader: Patterns of Communication in Prose from Bunyan to Beckett* (Baltimore and London: Johns Hopkins University Press, 1974), p. 274. Hereafter cited as *IR*.
6. Wolfgang Iser, *The Act of Reading: A Theory of Aesthetic Response* (Baltimore and London: Johns Hopkins University Press, 1978), p. 34. Hereafter cited as *AR*.
7. Several points in this account are taken from the excellent chapter "Colonialism and the Politics of Postcolonial Critique," in Robert Young's *Postcolonialism: An Historical Introduction* (Oxford: Blackwell, 2001). Hereafter cited as Young.
8. Bill Ashcroft, Gareth Griffiths, and Helen Tiffin, *The Empire Writes Back: Theory and Practice in Post-Colonial Literatures* (London and New York: Routledge, 1989), p. 2. Hereafter cited as *EWB*.
9. Edward Said, *Orientalism* (New York: Vintage, 1978), p. 3. Hereafter cited as *Orientalism*.
10. Henry Louis Gates, Jr., *Figures in Black: Words, Signs, and the "Racial" Self* (New York and Oxford: Oxford University Press, 1987), p. xxv. Hereafter cited as *FB*.
11. Max Horkheimer and Theodor W. Adorno, *Dialectic of Enlightenment*, trans. John Cumming (New York: Continuum, 2001), pp. 120, 147. Hereafter cited as *DE*.
12. John Fiske, *Television Culture* (London: Methuen, 1987), p. 14.

Epilogue
New Directions: Looking Back, Looking Forward

New Directions: The New Liberalism, Aestheticism, and Revolutionism

Our own era has witnessed a decline of "theory" in the sense of a grand narrative of historical development, or a series of archetypes with claims to universal explanatory power. By the early twenty-first century, even deconstruction and New Historicism were viewed as excessively comprehensive. Critiques of "metaphysics" or generalizations about "history" or indeed "theory" were seen in many quarters as impossibly general. These larger visions gave way to more empirical modes of inquiry, based on more narrowly defined fields and interests. Cases in point are ecocriticism, which examines the manifold significance of nature and the environment in literature; and narratology, or the study of narrative, which engages in detailed, factual study of specific historical periods, localities, and authors.

Recent political events – the attacks of September 11, 2001, the consequent wars in Afghanistan and Iraq, and the "war on terror" – have somewhat shifted the parameters of literary and cultural thinking. Some critics have attempted to restore what they see as the neglected ethical dimension of literature, and its potential to impinge upon larger debates concerning morality, classical questions regarding the good life, and more pressing political and even economic issues. Others have reaffirmed a commitment to the aesthetic. Among the most prominent recent critics are: Slavoj Žižek, who has reformulated, in Lacanian categories, some Marxist imperatives in the light of present political dilemmas, such as the Palestinian–Israeli conflict; Antonio Negri and Michael Hardt, who have formulated a new conception of "Empire"; Marxists such as Terry Eagleton and poststructuralists such as Jean Baudrillard, who have analyzed the meanings of "terror";

Literary Criticism from Plato to the Present: An Introduction M. A. R. Habib
© 2011 M. A. R. Habib

the newer liberal humanists, including Elaine Scarry, Martha Nussbaum, and John Carey, who have analyzed the public status of the arts, the notions of beauty and justice, as well as the meanings of democracy and good citizenship; the new formalistic critics, who include figures such as Michael Berube and Geoffrey Harpham, who wish to reserve a space for the aesthetic, for the study of literature *as* literature. With the exception of formalism, most of these approaches effect a broadening of "literary" study into the public sphere, into the cultural and political "texts" that commonly surround us. We can now briefly look at these contemporary developments.

A New Liberalism

Martha Nussbaum (b. 1947)

The very public range of Martha Nussbaum's concerns is indicated by the titles of some of her major works: *The Fragility of Goodness* (1986), *Cultivating Humanity: A Classical Defense of Reform in Liberal Education* (1997), *Sex and Social Justice* (1998), and *Frontiers of Justice* (2005). Nussbaum's thought can be characterized as universalist and focused on ethical and political concerns, in particular on issues of social justice, especially regarding women and other disadvantaged groups. Perhaps her work could be viewed as united by a central humanistic endeavor to ask the Aristotelian questions "What is the good life?" and "How should one live?" Her objective is to contribute to, and articulate the ideals of, universal peace, tolerance, and justice, enlisting the ethical and cognitive power of emotions in their complex connection with reason. In this endeavor, she stresses the importance of a genuinely liberal education and in particular of the potential of literature and philosophy to help us understand and overcome many of the ethical and political dilemmas we commonly face.

Elaine Scarry (b. 1946)

Elaine Scarry first achieved prominence through her book *The Body in Pain: The Making and Unmaking of the World* (1985). She exemplifies well the recent venturing by academics into public discussion, engaging a wide spectrum of issues, ranging from the attacks of September 11, war, torture, citizenship, and the Patriot Act, through beauty and the body to law and the social contract. Her books include *Literature and the Body* (1988), *On Beauty and Being Just* (1999), and *Who Defended the Country?* (2003). As Scarry has said in an interview: "There is nothing about being an English professor that exempts you from the normal obligations of citizenship . . . In fact, you have an increased obligation, because you know how to do research."[1] Accordingly,

Scarry has controversially discussed the defense of America after 9/11, she has argued that the Patriot Act actually represents an abuse of the notion of patriotism, and has suggested that what comprises the gravest threat of terror is the American government itself which has undermined the American constitution and fundamental principles of democracy. She has also urged in various articles that nuclear war and current military arrangements are (like torture), in their refusal to be based on consent, profoundly undemocratic.

John Carey (b. 1934)

Former Merton Professor of English at Oxford, John Carey is known for his anti-elitism and sometimes unorthodox views on literature and the arts, as expressed in his acerbic wit and his Orwellian commitment to plain language. As such, he has been one of the few to broaden the function of scholar to public intellectual, combining academic duties with decades of discussion in newspapers, on the radio, and on television, and serving as member, then chair, of the Booker Prize committee. Carey co-edited with Alastair Fowler the complete poetry of John Milton (1968), still regarded as the most scholarly single-volume edition of Milton's complete poems. His monographs include a study of Dickens, *The Violent Effigy* (1973), the highly praised *Thackeray: Prodigal Genius* (1977), and *John Donne: Life, Mind, and Art* (1981), a historical and psychological analysis which, through its investigation of the traumatic influence of Catholicism on Donne's literary imagination, has effectively transformed critical perception of Donne as both poet and preacher. In a recent book, *What Good Are the Arts?* (2006), Carey attempts to dethrone extravagant claims about the spiritual or moral benefits of the arts.[2] He suggests that art should not be the province of a privileged elite, and that there is no absolute standard or value of art (*WG*, 167). But, drawing on research which exhibits the redemptive potential of art and literature, Carey argues that literature is superior to the other arts on two accounts: it is uniquely critical, and self-critical; and it can moralize, often in diverse and contradictory ways. Literature is the only art capable of reasoning (*WG*, 159–166, 173–181).

The New Aestheticism

Something is wrong, terribly wrong, in the department of English. Full professors and graduate students alike are failing – in some cases refusing – to read literature as literature. The integrity of the discipline of literary study, perhaps the integrity of literature itself, is being undermined by the very people who are supposed to guard the flame of literacy and watch over our cultural treasures. Ideologues swarm the halls.[3]

This is how Michael Berube (accurately) characterizes the perspective of conservatives such as Lynne Cheney (head of the NEH in the Reagan era), Roger Kimball, author of *Tenured Radicals* (1990), and Jonathan Yardley, an art critic for the *Washington Post*. Critic Geoffrey Galt Harpham talks of "*the* project of theory" (my emphasis) which, by proclaiming the death of the author, killed the interest of literature, and bequeathed a climate of "professional occultation" in which literature lost its "aesthetic specificity" and "became enfolded within a generalized textuality."[4] Harpham himself appears to revert to Aristotelian notions of subjectivity, character (as expressed in criticism), and criticism "as a mimetic practice whose primary purpose is to produce an accurate representation of its object," whereby the critic realizes "his own true and essential nature" (CC, 9, 11). This gesture is symptomatic of a common desire – perhaps a desperation – among certain critics to repress the entire history of critical interpretation and return to a primordial condition or time when literature was viewed simply *as* literature. There is, however, nothing in Aristotle's philosophy or literary criticism or rhetoric which sanctions such a narrow aestheticism or such a narrow vision of literary-critical practice. And there is a danger that, if we isolate the "purely" literary, leaving out all of the human interest – psychological, social, moral, political – we will end up with little more than a series of empty techniques and exercises.

In fairness to Harpham, it could be argued that his project is one of reaffirmation of the aesthetic rather than origination of ideas of critical practice. This project has also been advanced by scholars such as Helen Vendler, who urge that our love of literature – rooted in a response to it which suspends scholarship, criticism, and theory – should focus on its unique uses of language. But the call for such a return has also surfaced in the work of more culturally minded critics such as George Levine. Like Arnold, Levine urges an endeavor to reclaim the aesthetic, as a province relatively free of the infringements of ideology and politics, as one of the few remaining spaces of free play. He notes that over the last decade the real subject of literary study has become ideology, and its purpose is political transformation. Instead, the aesthetic should be a realm which enables the exercise of disinterest and impersonality, allowing a sympathy for, and understanding of, people and events, furnishing us with a "vital sense of the other." Finally, as against much theory which sees literature as co-opted into the exercise of state power, Levine suggests that much literature is genuinely subversive. Indeed, the aesthetic has a function in the exercise of academic freedom.[5] While there may be some merit to Levine's project, its vision of the aesthetic somewhat rehearses what was already articulated long ago by Kant, Arnold, and many others.

The New Theorists of Revolution

Slavoj Žižek (b. 1949)

Slavoj Žižek has been called "the most vital interdisciplinary thinker to emerge in recent years." He contends essentially that Lacan is heir of the Enlightenment but he radicalizes the quest of European metaphysics from Plato to Kant and Hegel to understand "the nature of being." Born in former Yugoslavia, Žižek worked with other Lacanians at the Institute of Philosophy in Ljubljana. The interests of this group included European philosophy, popular culture, and the operations of ideology. Žižek's major works include *The Sublime Object of Ideology* (1989), *Tarrying with the Negative* (1993), and the *Ticklish Subject* (1999). He published a self-interview entitled *The Metastases of Enjoyment* in 1994. According to Sarah Kay, one of Žižek's primary projects is an anti-totalitarian critique of ideology, and an "impassioned attack on capitalism," as well as a plea for a return to universality.[6]

Some of Žižek's arguments concerning ideology are expressed in *The Sublime Object of Ideology*. His use of Lacanian categories is directed toward the ideological and political spheres, and has a broadly Hegelian disposition. Žižek points out that traditional Marxism sees a basic social antagonism – premised on economics and class – which underlies other antagonisms of race, gender, and political systems; and that a revolution in the economic sphere would resolve all of these antagonisms.[7] The basic feature of so-called post-Marxism, he says, is a break with this logic: for example, feminists argue that gender is more fundamental than class and that inequalities in this sphere must be addressed first. But it is Lacanian psychoanalysis, insists Žižek, that advances decisively beyond the usual post-Marxist anti-essentialism in "affirming the irreducible particularity of particular struggles" (*SOI*, 4). Žižek sees the first post-Marxist in this respect as none other than Hegel, whose dialectic comprehends the inherent contradictions of capitalism, such as the fact that a radical or pure democracy is impossible. For Žižek, Hegelian dialectics embody an acknowledgment of antagonism: far from being a "story of its progressive overcoming," Hegel's dialectic expresses the failure of all radical attempts at revolution, and his notion of absolute knowledge accepts contradiction "as an internal condition of every identity" (*SOI*, 5–6).

Žižek's aim in this book is threefold: to introduce the basic concepts of Lacan free of the distortions that interpret him as a post-structuralist. Indeed, Lacanian theory is "perhaps the most radical contemporary version of the Enlightenment" (*SOI*, 7). The second aim is to effect a return to Hegel, by reading Hegelian dialectics on the basis of Lacanian psychoanalysis: what we find in Hegel is "the strongest affirmation yet of difference and contingency."

Finally, Žižek wishes to contribute to the theory of ideology via a new reading of classical motifs such as commodity fetishism and of Lacanian concepts such as sublime object. This Hegelian heritage, as "salvaged" by Lacan, will allow a new approach to ideology, one that resists post-modernist traps such as the illusion that we live in a "post-ideological" age (*SOI*, 7). Žižek rejects the conventional Marxist notion of ideology as a false consciousness or illusory representation of reality. Rather, reality *itself* is already conceived of in ideological terms: ideology "*is a social reality whose very existence implies the non-knowledge of its participants as to its essence*" (*SOI*, 21). Clearly, Lacan's salvaging powers – encompassing not only Freud, but Hegel and Marx – have hitherto been overlooked.

Michael Hardt and Antonio Negri: the Concept of Empire

In the year 2000, the left-wing American philosopher Michael Hardt and the Italian Marxist dissident and philosopher Antonio Negri published their collaborative book *Empire*. This was hailed by Žižek as a new communist manifesto for our age, though others derided it as fashionable, vague, and speculative. Hardt and Negri argued that, following the collapse of various colonial regimes throughout the world, and then of communism with its barriers to the expansion of capitalism, a new phenomenon – which they call "Empire" – is materializing in our postmodern world. Along with the globalization of economic and cultural markets, there "has emerged a global order, a new logic and structure of rule – in short, a new form of sovereignty. Empire is the political subject that effectively regulates these global exchanges, the sovereign power that governs the world." The power of the nation-state, they observe, while still effective, has progressively declined, having less and less power to regulate the flow of money, technology, people, and goods across national boundaries.[8] Sovereignty, in fact, has taken a new form, composed "of a series of national and supranational organisms united under a single logic of rule." Empire is the name for this new global form of sovereignty.

Empire, however, is distinct from imperialism, which was "an extension of the sovereignty of the European nation-states beyond their own boundaries." These states policed the purity of their own identities and excluded all that was other. In contrast, Empire has no center of power and does not rely on fixed boundaries: it is a decentered and deterritorializing "apparatus of rule that progressively incorporates the entire global realm ... The distinct national colors of the imperialist map of the world have merged and blended in the imperial global rainbow" (*E.*, xii–xiii). The old divisions of the globe into first world (the capitalist West), second world (Communism), and third world have dissolved into a "smooth" world. The dominant productive processes have been transformed: industrial factory labor has largely given way to communicative, cooperative, and affective labor. In this postmodern global economy, the creation of wealth comprehends "biopolitical" production, the production of the entire realm of social life, in which the economic, political, and cultural spheres increasingly overlap (*E.*, xiii).

Looking Back, Looking Forward

Looking back over the history of literary criticism (or at least one version of that history), we can see that, since Plato, there has been a series of complex tendencies moving toward totalizing and unifying schemes, reaching a climax in the intellectual hierarchies of the Middle Ages in which theology stood at the apex of knowledge, where all dimensions of humanity – bodily, emotional, intellectual, and spiritual – had their appointed place, and where humanity itself had a defined location both within the universe and within the historical scheme of providence. Since the Renaissance or early modern period, there has been a dissolution of these coherent and totalizing visions, spurred by economic and political development, the Protestant Reformation, the Enlightenment, the French Revolution, the Industrial Revolutions, and the rise to hegemony of the middle classes throughout Europe. This movement from general to particular has been underlain by a deepening vision of the intellect as rooted in sense-perception, of rationality as tied to our physical and emotional apparatus of survival, and of an increasing awareness that the world is not an objective datum but a human historical and social construct. Certain totalizing philosophies such as that of Hegel attempted to reconfigure a unified vision of the fragmented modern world, situating it as the latest phase of historical development. But Hegel's system collapsed, leaving in its aftermath various more localized approaches (many of which reacted against it) including Marxism, positivism, Anglo-American idealism, and existentialism. Hence, the preoccupation with the particular and the local which we now witness, in literary theory and criticism as well as in mass culture – in realism, in the veneration of science, in our empirical, piecemeal, "common sense" approach to life – is not new (though it has reached new intensities), but is the product of a long historical development.

Notwithstanding this historical movement from the general to the particular, much of the literary theory covered in this book has shown us that literature and criticism cannot be insulated from their political, social, and economic frameworks. The acts of reading, writing, and interpretation are not somehow value-free and do not subsist in some atemporal, academic vacuum; they are informed by a much broader cultural and political fabric. As such, literary criticism furnishes the tools for analyzing not only Shakespeare and Milton, Toni Morrison, and Naguib Mahfouz, but also the "texts" of a soccer game, television programs, advertisements, political speeches, press conferences, rock concerts, and news presentations. We can draw on the insights furnished by a host of thinkers – ranging from Plato and Aristotle through Emerson and Whitman to Alexis de Tocqueville and contemporary politicians – to analyze the nature of democracy in an array of uniquely modern contexts. We can probe the various readings of the connection between "literal" and figurative language – from Augustine through Aquinas and Ibn Rushd to Locke, Schleiermacher and Derrida – to facilitate analyses of the Qur'an and the various texts of Islam, as well as the texts of democracy and liberalism on all its levels. These are among the most urgent tasks confronting the twenty-first century.

In the context of the history of literary criticism, we can see more clearly the deficiencies of some of the literary theory of the last half century: it has claimed an excessive originality, it has often been infected with a tiresome and pretentious jargon; its departures from the ideal of clarity are not sufficiently controlled or informed; it has insulated itself in discussions of issues which are of little interest to the larger society, and, correspondingly, it has ignored some of the crucial issues which pulse at the heart of the contemporary world: morality, religion, fundamentalism, family, the nature of the state, and the public and educational roles of both literature and criticism. But the best theoretical work has indeed addressed these issues in a dazzling variety of contexts, deepening and enriching the study of both literature and culture.

Looking forward, we can struggle to ensure that the skills fostered by our diverse and rich critical heritage are not insulated within academia: by showing the continuity between our critical languages and the languages of the public sphere, by practicing in an exemplary fashion the skills of close and critical reading, by articulating the political implications of our work, by confronting the crucial moral and religious dimensions of our lives, by extending our inquiries over the fields of popular culture, by refashioning our departments in the humanities to accommodate prevailing cultural concerns, and by support-ing the participation of our institutions in the larger community. We can draw on the richness of our literary, philosophical, and literary-critical heritage in realizing the potential of the humanities to help shape the political, educational, and economic discourses that will determine our future, and to foster an increased understanding of our world, ourselves, and others.

Notes

1. Interview with Emily Eakin, *New York Times Magazine*, November 19, 2000, online version: http://partners.nytimes.com/library/magazine/home/20001119mag -scarry.html.
2. John Carey, *What Good are the Arts?* (Oxford: Oxford University Press, 2006), pp. ix–xii. Hereafter cited as *WG*.

3. Michael Berube, "Aesthetics and the Literal Imagination," in David Richter, ed., *Falling into Theory* (Boston and New York: Bedford/St. Martin's, 2000), p. 391.
4. Geoffrey Galt Harpham, *The Character of Criticism* (London and New York: Routledge, 2006), pp. 5–6. Hereafter cited as *CC*.
5. George Levine, "Reclaiming the Aesthetic," in Richter, ed., *Falling into Theory*, pp. 378, 386–389.
6. Sarah Kay, *Žižek: A Critical Introduction* (Cambridge: Polity Press, 2003), pp. 1, 3–6, 7–14.
7. Slavoj Žižek, *The Sublime Object of Ideology* (London and New York: Verso, 1989), p. 3. Hereafter cited as *SOI*.
8. Michael Hardt and Antonio Negri, *Empire* (Cambridge, MA and London: Harvard University Press, 2000), p. xi. Hereafter cited as *E*.

Index

Académie Française (French Academy), 100

Achebe, Chinua: and language choice, 273

Addison, Joseph, 121–2

Adorno, Theodor: *Dialectic of Enlightenment*, 276–7

aestheticism, 174, 175, 176; new, 281–2

d'Alembert, Jean, 117

allegory, 27; Christian, 39, 53, 55–6, 61–2, 69, 70–1; Coleridge on, 157

Alternative Shakespeares, 266–7

Althusser, Louis, 231

"ancients" vs. "moderns" debate, 87, 99

Anzaldua, Gloria, 259

Aquinas, *see* Thomas Aquinas, St.

Ariosto, Ludovico: *Orlando Furioso*, 81, 87

Aristophanes: *Clouds*, 25; *Frogs*, 10

Aristotle, 15–22; legacy of, 21–2; and logic, 16–17; in Middle Ages, 58, 59–60, 64, 65, 66, 67; *Nicomachean Ethics*, 18; *Poetics*, 18–21, 31, 63, 85, 86; and poetry, 17–19, 21; *Rhetoric*, 25–6; and tragedy, 19–21

Arnold, Matthew, 185–8; on criticism, 186; *Culture and Anarchy*, 187; "Dover Beach," reading of, 2–5; and humanist tradition, 193; "The Study of Poetry," 187–8

"art for art's sake," 129, 152, 176, 177

associationism, 119

Auden, W. H., 208

Augustine of Hippo, St., 53–6; and classical heritage, 53, 54; *Confessions*, 53, 54; *De doctrina christiana*, 30; on drama, 52; on signs, 54–5

Averroës, *see* Ibn Rushd

Avicenna, *see* Ibn Sina

Bacon, Sir Francis, 82, 115

Bakhtin, Mikhail, 199–201; on dialogism, 199, 200; "Discourse on the Novel," 199–200; on language, 199, 200–1; on the novel, 199–200, 201

Barrett, Michèle, 255

Barthes, Roland, 226–8; "death of the author," 219, 227; and poststructuralism, 227, 228

Bataille, Georges, 223–4; influence of 223; and phenomenology, 219

Baudelaire, Charles, 175, 176–7; *Les Fleurs du Mal*, 176; and Poe, 177; and symbolism, 176

Baudrillard, Jean, 251–2, 279; on consumption, 252; *System of Objects*, 251–2

Beardsley, Monroe C., 204; "Affective Fallacy," 204–5; "Intentional Fallacy," 204

Literary Criticism from Plato to the Present: An Introduction   M. A. R. Habib
© 2011 M. A. R. Habib